DUKE · UNIVERSITY · PUBLICATIONS

HAITI
AND
THE UNITED STATES
1714-1938

HAITI
AND
THE UNITED STATES
1714-1938

BY

LUDWELL LEE MONTAGUE

WITH A FOREWORD BY

J. FRED RIPPY

NEW YORK / RUSSELL & RUSSELL

1966

PRINTED IN THE UNITED STATES OF AMERICA

FOREWORD

THE POLICY of the United States in respect to the region of the Gulf of Mexico and the Caribbean Sea can be defined with greater precision than its policy with reference to any other region. This is possible because the Gulf-Caribbean area is the most vital zone in the defense strategy of the United States.

In that area the policy of the United States accords with a maxim almost as unchanging as a law of mathematics or physics. That maxim is the domination of the area at least to the extent deemed necessary to prevent its domination by any other first-rate power.

If the control exercised in the region has occasionally been less than required by the maxim, this has usually been due to the temporary imprudence of enforcing it. If the domination has ever been greater than that maxim demanded, this has been caused by nervous apprehension, by temporary attacks of land hunger in rare instances, by the pressure of economic interests, or by zeal to improve the inhabitants of the region and their environment.

No statesman has ever baldly formulated the maxim. Perhaps that would have been undiplomatic. But one may assert with confidence that the policy which the maxim describes began to take form before 1800. At first it embraced the lands bordering on the Gulf, but gradually it was extended to the whole of the Gulf-Caribbean area.

In this region the policy of the United States has departed from ideal standards of international morality more widely than elsewhere. A nation's code of honor is subjected to the severest strain at the point where its most vital interests are thought to be involved. The United States has endeavored to attain its objectives in the region by diplomacy—straightforward or devious —but when diplomacy failed or patience, sometimes too meager, was exhausted, force and the menace of force occasionally were employed as instruments of national policy.

[v]

In the execution of the policy of dominating the region against control from the outside, four major devices have been employed separately or conjointly or in immediate succession: (1) the invocation of the Monroe Doctrine, (2) the control of the interoceanic routes of transportation, (3) the control of the sites for naval bases and coaling stations, and (4) the establishment of semiprotectorates.

In respect to Isthmian routes and naval bases the purpose of the United States, in general, has been to acquire those it desired to utilize and to control the rest in order to prevent their utilization by aggressive rivals. The protectorates were established in part because of a desire to mingle appeasement with Monrovian defiance of Europe. In a measure they were the result of a disposition to placate the European governments by taking care of their nationals in an area where those governments were not free to redress grievances because of an expanding Monroe Doctrine. In order more graciously to regulate the conduct of European states in the Gulf and the Caribbean, the United States undertook also to regulate the conduct of certain nations of the region in reference to Europeans.

In securing possession or control of interoceanic routes and naval bases as well as in setting up protectorates, the United States usually adopted the procedure of giving financial and military aid to some eager political group or individual with the definite understanding or the full expectation that such a group or individual would make the concessions desired. The procedure was likely to be effective sooner or later because the Gulf-Caribbean region has not lacked leaders or dictators who were willing to gamble with fortune. In this manner were acquired Guantánamo Bay and a measure of control over Cuba, the Panama Canal Zone and a protectorate over Panama, the initial management of the finances of the Dominican Republic, and the Nicaraguan canal option together with the potential naval bases related thereto as well as control over the finances of Nicaragua.

The Haitian protectorate and fuller control over the Dominican Republic were effected through military operations and almost completely without the voluntary co-operation of any leader or group in either nation. These two Caribbean countries bore the brunt of the most drastic procedure the United States ever followed in the region. And the United States was most aggressive during the administration of an executive who most frequently denounced aggression on general principles—a fact which may be explained by the reformer zeal of Woodrow Wilson, demands or supposed demands of defense strategy during the critical period of the World War, and perhaps a little economic pressure covertly applied by American speculators upon subordinates of the diplomatic service.

But the protectorates have now been relinquished. The Republicans, who were the first after the Civil War in the United States to initiate a vigorous Caribbean policy, were also the first to begin the recession. For a time the threat of domination from the outside had vanished, and with it disappeared the strategic justification for the protectorates. From the economic and moral viewpoint likewise the advisability of retaining them seemed doubtful. The Republicans had therefore begun the withdrawal before the Democrats took charge of the national government of the United States early in 1933. By President Franklin Delano Roosevelt, the champion of the policy of the Good Neighbor, the recession was continued with increased speed. All the protectorates have been abandoned.

These withdrawals are undoubtedly important, but their significance should be viewed in the proper perspective. The abandonment of the protectorates does not signify the abandonment of the maxim. Only one of the devices of control against potential intrusion or domination from the outside has been discarded.

The extent and firmness of the Gulf-Caribbean controls of the United States are likely to be commensurate with American conceptions of the magnitude and proximity of the outside menace. If the danger appears near and gigantic, the controls may be tightened and broadened. The Monroe Doctrine will be invoked more frequently, and the demand will be heard for more naval bases, more canals, and perhaps even for the resumption of the protectorates, although it is to be hoped that these will never again become necessary. And because of the multiplicity, speed, and effectiveness of the technological instruments in command of aggressors the maxim may be applied in regions beyond the Gulf and the Caribbean area.

Into this broad frame of reference many of the facts presented by Dr. Montague may be fitted. Although he also treats of an earlier period when commercial interests and race prejudice determined American attitudes toward Haiti, his work is in the main a study of one phase of the strategic diplomacy of the United States. It deals with invocations of the Monroe Doctrine, the search for naval bases or for negative control over strategic sites, and the establishment of Caribbean protectorates, in so far as these policies relate to Haiti, with consideration of "dollar diplomacy" and reforming zeal as incidental to those themes. Nor has Dr. Montague failed to consider the people, the politics, and the physical geography of Haiti itself. Indeed, he has carefully examined every profitable ramification of his subject. He has searched diligently for the facts and presented them with sound judgment and in superior literary style. In my opinion he has produced an attractive and useful volume.

J. FRED RIPPY

University of Chicago
November 1, 1939

PREFACE

The Declaration of Lima has emphasized American determination to resist the extension into this hemisphere of the ideology and political influence of a new "Holy Alliance." The passage of the United States fleet into the Atlantic and the creation of a new military command in the West Indies have dramatized the significance of the Caribbean in American naval strategy. The popularity of George Fielding Eliot's *The Ramparts We Watch* has indicated the extent of a reawakened interest in these matters, while in his pages may be found a thorough demonstration of the vital importance of the Caribbean to the defense of all America from Newfoundland to Cape Horn and back again to Alaska. Eliot concurs with Mahan in declaring the Windward Passage to be the most important gateway in our Antillean ramparts.

The historical accident of Haiti's location on the Windward Passage has given that country a significance for the United States out of proportion to its size and resources. The republic's unique character as an independent negro state has made the association a peculiar one.

Relations between Haiti and the United States have existed for more than two hundred years, antedating the independence of either. In the eighteenth century the trade of Cap François and Leogane was second to that with Great Britain alone in value to Yankee merchants, and its influence upon American history was considerable. During the first half of the nineteenth century the slavery controversy then dominating American domestic politics also determined American attitudes toward the "Black Republic." Since that time considerations of naval strategy, centered about the defense of interoceanic communication at the isthmus, have played the leading role. Reinforced by conviction of a *mission civilisatrice*, they resulted in a military occupation of Haiti for nineteen years, from 1915 to 1934, a state of affairs happily brought to an end as a manifestation of a new "good neighbor" policy.

Such attention as Haiti has received from American writers has been limited almost entirely to the period of the revolution —the heroic age of Toussaint Louverture, Dessalines, Christophe, and Pétion—or to the intervention. Even the single work essaying to survey the entire history of the republic conforms to this rule, bridging the gap between 1818 and 1908 in twenty-four pages. As for a general account of the relations of the United States with Haiti before 1908, none exists.[1] Except for perhaps a cursory glance, the innumerable discussions of the intervention never look back more than half a dozen years in introducing the subject. Most of them are plainly controversial, and the best of them are written by men who were personally connected, in one way or another, with the events under consideration. The situation in the Caribbean may be quiescent at the moment, but if, as some earnestly believe, the Monroe Doctrine may soon be subjected to new tests in that region, an examination of the whole course of American relations with the most strategically important of Antillean states may not be amiss.

[1] The principal works touching on earlier American relations with Haiti are Mary Treudley's *United States and Santo Domingo, 1789-1866*, and Charles C. Tansill's *United States and Santo Domingo, 1798-1873* (the latter published after the present study was substantially complete). Both authors have followed without discrimination the shifting meaning of "San Domingo" in American usage. Before 1844 the term suggested *La partie française de Saint Domingue*, or Haiti, with which the United States had important relations, rather than *La partie espagnole*, in which there was little American interest; thereafter it came to apply more particularly to the Dominican Republic, to the exclusion of Haiti. This shift is detrimental to the integrity of their works, in that they treat of American relations with two distinct communities, ignoring one in the earlier period and the other in the later. Thus the opening chapters of both deal with Haitian-American relations, principally those with Toussaint Louverture, but both, and especially the latter, are concerned more particularly with the Dominican Republic, having little to say of Haiti beyond 1806 and still less of Haitian-American relations in the period following the establishment of Dominican independence, apart from the tripartite intervention in behalf of the Dominicans in 1851. It is impossible to suppose, for instance, that Professor Tansill intends the ambiguous term, Santo Domingo, to include independent Haiti when only fifty-three of his 464 pages have any bearing on Haitian-American relations after 1806, thirty-four of them being devoted to the tripartite intervention, with his five scattered allusions to Haiti after 1851 likewise only incidental to Dominican affairs. The eventual recognition of Haiti by the United States is not even mentioned.

It has not been possible to treat of every interesting episode in Haitian-American relations, but an effort has been made to present all that was necessary to indicate the basic problems and the spirit in which they have been met. The chapter on claims, for instance, is only a sample, taken from a period when little else engaged the attention of the American legation, since claims, like the poor, are always with us. The same may be said of the chapter on neutrality. Lest it be argued that disproportionate space has been allotted to the events of 1888-1891, it should be explained that the Mole affair, the most striking incident of Haitian-American relations between recognition and intervention, has been the subject of more misunderstanding and misrepresentation by authors, Haitian and American, than any other. The chapters on the occupation are not intended to present that episode in the detail possible in works devoted exclusively to it, but rather to consider it in the light of the whole course of Haitian history and of Haitian-American relations and in a way that writers limited to those years have been unable to do.

Without wishing to ignore Haitian sensibilities, I am compelled to use "Hispaniola" rather than "Haiti" when referring to the island as a whole in order to make a distinction between it and the republic which occupies only a third of its area. The origins of those terms and the difficulties involved in their employment are discussed in a footnote on page 4. A Haitian critic might accuse me of inconsistency in using "American" with reference to both America and the United States, but I know of no alternative, since it is impossible to make an English adjective out of "United States." "Yankee" may be deemed satisfactory beyond our borders, but in origin and domestic usage the term applies more properly to the inhabitants of New England and the Northeast generally. With reference to them, or when seeking to express a Latin-American attitude, I have employed it. "American" developed as an intra-empire distinction before independence, the title "United States of America" was adopted as a matter of course at a time when these states were the only sovereigns in the Western Hemisphere, and it now seems too late to do anything about it.

I regret that I have been unable to supplement information gleaned from American manuscript sources and from the British Public Records Office with citations from Haitian diplomatic archives. The Haitian foreign office, with all its papers, was destroyed by fire in 1883, and other adverse circumstances have operated against the survival of any considerable body of material of this character. I have endeavored to supply the deficiency in part by seeking the Haitian point of view in an extensive examination of the works of Haitian publicists, and Dr. Jean Price-Mars has generously assisted me by local investigation of specific points.

To Mrs. Natalia Summers and her assistants in the State Department Archives and to Miss Margaret Hall, I owe thanks for many kindnesses. I am obligated to Dr. William R. Manning for the use of the manuscript of the sixth volume of his *Diplomatic Correspondence of the United States: Inter-American Affairs, 1831-1860,* since published. The late Professor William K. Boyd and Professor William T. Laprade, of Duke University, made helpful suggestions at an early stage of the work, and Professor Laprade has kindly read the manuscript. Conversations with Major General John A. Lejeune, former Commandant of the Marine Corps, and Dr. Robert R. Moton, former President of Tuskegee Institute, both of whom have conducted investigations in Haiti, and a lengthy correspondence with Dr. Price-Mars, President of the Société d'histoire et de géographie d'Haiti, have given me invaluable "background," but I would not have them held responsible for views which are entirely my own and with some of which one or another of them might wish to take exception. Above all, I am indebted to Professor J. Fred Rippy, whose friendly counsel and encouragement have sustained me since the inception of the work.

L. L. M.

Lexington, Virginia
May 15, 1939

CONTENTS

[xiii]

MAPS

CHAPTER I

TERRA INCOGNITA

The essential qualities of a true Pan Americanism must be the same as those which constitute a good neighbor, namely, mutual understanding, and, through such understanding, a sympathetic appreciation of the other's point of view.—FRANKLIN D. ROOSEVELT, April 12, 1933

On ne peut pas sympathiser avec un peuple que l'on ne connait pas ou que l'on méprise.—DANTÈS BELLEGARDE, 1934

HAITI LIES only six hundred miles from Florida. Its coast forms the eastern shore of the Windward Passage, the only direct route from the Atlantic seaboard of the United States to the Panama Canal and therefore a channel of immense significance in American naval strategy.[1] Considering its neighborhood, its strategic location, and its unique character as the only self-constituted negro republic in the world, it is remarkable that the land and its people should be little known to Americans. Although Haitian history has been closely related to that of the United States for more than two centuries, to the American mind Haiti remains a land of foreboding and mystery—*terra incognita.*

This lack of understanding, which has been mutual, has been the inevitable consequence of lack of contact. Haitians have rarely visited the United States, where they would be subjected to numberless inconveniences on account of color, and relatively few Americans have ever resided in Haiti long enough to acquire a sympathetic appreciation of conditions there. The American impression of Haiti was the creation of terrified *émigrés,* supplemented by the gossip of the ports as brought home by mariners, merchants, missionaries, and occasional

[1] The passage is fourteen hundred miles due south of New York, nine hundred northeast of Colon. There the sea lane to the Panama Canal is crossed by the Antillean air lane to South America.

travelers, none of whom were free from prejudice.[2] Thus it has been that Americans, if they thought of Haiti at all, were apt to conceive of it either as a land where savage blacks, having exterminated the whites, had reverted to African barbarism, or else as a place where comic opera generals scuffled for the possession of a bankrupt treasury. A glance at Haitian history will reveal the factual basis for these ideas and at the same time their inadequacy.

Hispaniola,[3] discovered by Columbus on his first voyage, became the site of the first European colony in the New World. For a brief period it flourished as the center of all Spanish colonial activity, but the rush to the mainland after the discovery of Aztec and Inca treasures relegated the island settlements to secondary importance, the few remaining Spaniards applying themselves with little energy or enthusiasm to stock raising and the cultivation of the sugar cane. Under the rigors of conquest and the *encomienda* system the large native population all but disappeared in the course of forty years,[4] and to procure laborers for the cane fields the Spaniards resorted to the importation of negro slaves, thus inaugurating a practice of tremendous significance to the future of Brazil and the United States as well as that of the Antilles. In Santo Domingo the result was a

[2] Even the missionaries, who might be expected to show the most good will, had gone out on the assumption that the Haitians dwelt in outer darkness.

[3] *Haiti* (mountainous land) was an aboriginal name for the island. Columbus called it Española (little Spain), of which the latinized form, *Hispaniola*, was frequently employed, especially in English. Eventually the island became known to the Spaniards as *Santo Domingo*, after their chief city, and, consequently, the French called their colony *La partie française de Saint Domingue.* Yankee traders evolved San Domingo, an illegitimate form which still persists in American usage. On achieving independence the blacks of Saint Domingue revived the name of Haiti to mark the obliteration of white influence, and, through their annexation of the Spanish colony, re-established its application to the entire island. However, when the Dominicans regained their freedom, great confusion ensued between the names of the two republics and the designation for the island as a whole. The United States Hydrographic Office has recently sought to overcome this difficulty by reviving "Hispaniola" in American usage as a term for the island, the respective divisions of which are properly called the Republic of Haiti and the Dominican Republic.

[4] Herbert M. Kreiger, "The Aborigines of the Ancient Island of Hispaniola," *Annual Report of the Smithsonian Institution* (1929), p. 478. Some six hundred were surviving in 1533, but no trace of them can be found in the island today.

population predominantly mulatto, consisting, in 1790, of some 40,000 whites and 85,000 persons of color, only 15,000 of whom were slaves.[5]

The weak Spanish colony was unable to defend itself against the intrusion of French buccaneers, who gained a lodgment on the northwest shore in 1630. Seventy years later Spain recognized the title of France to the western coasts of the island, although the limits of *La partie française* were not definitely fixed until 1777. They included only the land between the outer mountain ranges and the sea, never reaching more than twenty-five miles inland. The French had acquired some impressive scenery, with here and there a small alluvial plain, but they possessed nothing to be compared with the Vega Real of Santo Domingo.

Given this narrow stage and an interval of peace, French enterprise and ingenuity worked something like a miracle. The hunting grounds of the buccaneers were transformed into well-ordered plantations producing coffee, cotton, cacao, tobacco, indigo, and, above all, sugar. Highways, sugar mills, and elaborate irrigation systems were constructed to serve the plantations, while distilleries, lime kilns, brickyards, potteries, and tanneries were operated as subsidiary industries. By 1742 the sugar production of Saint Domingue alone exceeded that of all the British West Indies combined;[6] by 1783 the colony contributed substantially two thirds of all French-grown tropical produce,[7] its commerce constituting more than a third of the foreign trade of France.[8]

Needless to say, the labor of the plantations was not performed by Frenchmen; the remarkable prosperity of Saint Domingue was founded on an immense concentration of negroes. In 1790 the population included 32,000 resident whites,

[5] T. Lothrop Stoddard, *The French Revolution in San Domingo,* p. 6; C. L. Jones, *Caribbean Backgrounds and Prospects,* p. 19.

[6] Lawrence Henry Gipson, *The British Empire before the American Revolution,* II, 294 n.

[7] Lowell Joseph Ragatz, *The Fall of the Planter Class in the British Caribbean, 1763-1833,* p. 126.   [8] H. P. Davis, *Black Democracy,* p. 25.

24,000 freedmen, and 480,000 slaves.[9] The freedmen were
for the most part, though not exclusively, mulattoes, while
some 40,000 mulattoes remained in slavery. A majority of
the slaves were African born. As might have been expected
in such a situation, a rigid caste system prevailed. The *grands
blancs*, least numerous element in the population, dominated
the community as masters of the plantations and, under the
royal officials, the ruling class. The *petits blancs* served as their
overseers and skilled workmen or followed minor independent
occupations in the towns. Between these two classes of whites
there existed that antagonism that comes of marked distinctions
in wealth and social prestige. Some few *affranchis* lived like
grands blancs, not scrupling to hold less fortunate colored men
in slavery, but racial discrimination forced on them an inferior
social status and denied them the political privileges of even a
petit blanc. The slaves, who constituted 90 per cent of the
population, had no rights or standing whatever, yet the color
line was known even among them, the mulattoes holding themselves superior to their fellow bondsmen.[10] Each stratum of
society in Saint Domingue regarded every other with either
jealous hatred or contempt.

Such a social structure could not withstand the shock of the
French Revolution. The *grands blancs*, long restive under
royal control, demanded local autonomy, but they were indignant when the *petits blancs* insisted on equality—for whites
only. When the *affranchis* likewise demanded equality—for
freemen only—the situation became complex, but when, in
August, 1791, the hitherto inert black masses began to stir,
Saint Domingue fell into indescribable confusion in which all
parties displayed inhuman ferocity. The progressively more
radical agents of successive governments at Paris were unable
to control the chaotic situation. A tragic climax was reached
at Cap Français on June 19, 1793, when a water-front riot

[9] In 1790 the population of the United States (four million) included 60,000
free persons of color and 700,000 slaves. In no state were negroes as much as half
the number of inhabitants.

[10] Stoddard, *The French Revolution in San Domingo*, pp. 8 f., 37-47.

ended in a pitched battle between the republican governor, supported by the white inhabitants, the regular garrison, and the sailors of the fleet, and the Jacobin commissioners, backed by the colored population, the mulatto militia, and National Guards from France. Defeated, the Jacobins called in the insurgent slaves of the Plaine du Nord, promised them freedom, and loosed them on the town. The wretched whites fled with the fleet, and the chief city of Saint Domingue was given over to arson and pillage.

The Spanish in Santo Domingo and the British in Jamaica could not view with indifference such occurrences in their neighborhood. Aided, curiously, by the insurgent slaves themselves, the Spaniards overran the North. Even a proclamation of general emancipation failed to win back the negroes in the service of Spain, but it did alienate the mulattoes, hitherto the Jacobins' chief support. In response to the appeals of the whites and mulattoes still dominant in the West, a British expedition occupied most of that department. The Jacobins decamped, leaving a French governor at Port-de-Paix and a loyal mulatto general, André Rigaud, at Les Cayes as the only representatives of the authority of France remaining in the island.

Late in 1794 the tide took a sudden and dramatic turn. Toussaint Louverture, a former slave, commander of four thousand negroes in the Spanish service, changed sides, and with his defection the Spanish invasion collapsed. The British were not so readily overcome. They held their ground for four more years, but then, weakened by fever,[11] they withdrew in return for Louverture's pledge of neutrality in the Anglo-French war. The wily Toussaint had maneuvered with finesse, using Spain and Britain to destroy French authority without allowing either to take the place of France, which he reserved for himself. Only the loyal Rigaud was in a position to challenge him, but that defect was remedied by a life and death struggle which immediately ensued between the negro and

---

[11] The British sent 18,000 reinforcements to Saint Domingue in 1795-1796, of whom 12,300 had died of yellow fever by the end of the latter year (Ragatz, *The Fall of the Planter Class*, p. 228).

mulatto chieftains.   In August, 1800, Toussaint Louverture entered Les Cayes in triumph.   Six months later Santo Domingo fearfully yielded to his summons, and the "First of the Blacks" was supreme throughout the island.

In due course Toussaint Louverture promulgated a constitution, which while it acknowledged the nominal sovereignty of France, named him governor general for life with the power of appointing his successor.   Meanwhile his efforts were devoted to restoring the plantations, the source of former prosperity.   White *émigrés* were encouraged to return and resume the management of their estates.   Although slavery was officially abolished, the vagrant "cultivators," who had assumed that emancipation meant freedom from labor, found themselves at work in the fields again under the compulsion of regulations not unlike the "Black Codes" to which Southern legislatures resorted in 1865 in the hope of solving a similar problem— regulations strictly enforced, "not without severity in some places."[12]   This plan of reconstruction, conceived by an ex-slave, was effective in restoring order and a certain degree of prosperity, but, for the time being at least, it relegated the freedmen to something akin to their former status.   A cultivator might have been excused for considering that the sacrifices of the revolution had been of profit only to the negro generals and their picked troops.

What Toussaint Louverture might have accomplished had he been left unmolested, remains a subject for speculation.   His assumption of authority was viewed with alarm at Paris, and, as soon as peace with Great Britain had reopened the sea lanes, Napoleon dispatched his brother-in-law, Leclerc, with twenty thousand veterans, to bring the self-made governor general to book.   Toussaint resisted, but whites and mulattoes hailed the pro-consul as their deliverer, and even the trusted negro generals, Jean Jacques Dessalines and Henri Christophe, deserted when assured that they might retain their rank in the French service.   In May, 1802, Toussaint himself submitted, and appar-

---

[12] Tobias Lear to James Madison, July 20, 1801, Consular Letters (hereinafter abbreviated Cons. Let.), Cape Haytien, III.

ently French authority had been fully restored. However, although Toussaint was deported, his regiments remained intact, under their own officers; the natives were subdued, but not broken. The summer brought yellow fever, inflicting terrible losses among the European troops. Indications that the old regime would be restored, with slavery for blacks and subordination for mulattoes, united the natives in a general insurrection. On November 29, 1803, the eight thousand survivors of the forty-three thousand men whom Napoleon had sent overseas, surrendered to a British fleet, regarding their captivity as a rescue from a worse fate.

The chiefs of the revolutionary army recognized Jean Jacques Dessalines as "governor general" of independent Haiti. He, remembering that Toussaint Louverture's policy of conciliation toward the whites had not prevented their desertion to Leclerc, desiring vengeance, and fearing a new invasion, demanded the extermination of those French inhabitants who yet dared to remain in their homes. A new constitution forbade that any white man should own Haitian real estate and designated as "blacks" all Haitians of whatever complexion. French Saint Domingue had been obliterated, and Haiti prepared to seek her destiny as the first experiment in negro self-government within the pale of civilization.[13] The experiment was to be conducted under distinctly unfavorable conditions and without hope of aid from a uniformly hostile world.

The physical factors in the situation have had considerable bearing on the result. Haiti is 183 miles long and 114 miles wide, yet, because of its irregular coastline, it contains only 10,700 square miles, which means an unusual degree of dispersion in proportion to the area involved. This characteristic is further accentuated by the nature of the terrain, for Haiti is a land of rugged mountains, small isolated valleys, and narrow coastal plains.[14] Steep ranges, rising abruptly to a usual alti-

[13] This was twenty-two years after Yorktown and twenty-one before Spanish-American independence was finally established at Ayacucho.

[14] Alluvial plains constitute only 30 per cent of the total area (*Geological Survey of the Republic of Haiti*, p. 69).

tude of three thousand feet, but with some peaks above eight thousand, make roadbuilding difficult and expensive, constituting a serious obstacle to internal communication and restricting urban centers to the seaboard. These conditions intensify distinctions between town and country, foster sectionalism and individualism, and weaken the control of the government over the provinces.

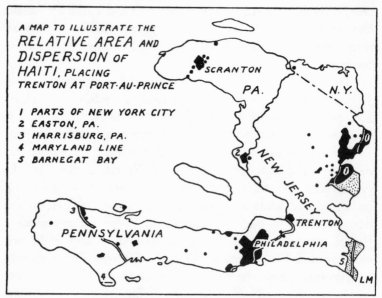

A MAP TO ILLUSTRATE THE
RELATIVE AREA AND
DISPERSION OF
HAITI, PLACING
TRENTON AT PORT-AU-PRINCE

1 PARTS OF NEW YORK CITY
2 EASTON, PA.
3 HARRISBURG, PA.
4 MARYLAND LINE
5 BARNEGAT BAY

SCRANTON
PA.
N.Y.
NEW JERSEY
TRENTON
PHILADELPHIA
PENNSYLVANIA

With no mineral deposits of importance, Haiti's chief resource has been the fertility of the soil, but, except in the well-watered Plaine du Nord, this could be fully exploited only through extensive irrigation.[15] Twelve years of war and neglect had ruined the elaborate works constructed by the French, and the skill and energy required to rebuild them were not available. Even where water was plentiful the plantation system could not be maintained. Labor could be had only under compulsion, and, although the regulations of Toussaint

[15] The trade winds blow across Haiti from the northeast, depositing their moisture on the near slopes of the northernmost range, the rest of the country remaining arid or semiarid (*Report on Irrigation Possibilities in the Republic of Haiti*, pp. 13-17).

Louverture were re-enacted time and again, they became a dead letter. The more spirited cultivators drifted away to the mountains, where nature supplied the necessities of a simple life and coffee could be gathered for sale with a minimum of effort. The planters themselves abandoned the land and drifted into town, where they could live at ease and in style upon the proceeds of a public treasury sustained by an export tax on coffee. The remaining sharecroppers in the plains, left to their own devices, were soon producing little more than garden truck for themselves and the local market. Thus master and man alike attained the manner of life each desired, yet the master continued to live on the labor of the peasant. This development meant more than the substitution of coffee for sugar as the Haitian staple; it meant the abandonment of the intensive agriculture upon which rested the commercial greatness of Saint Domingue.

As indicated in the disappearance of the plantations, the character of Haitian society presented problems as difficult as those inherent in the nature of the country. Instead of the united Haitian family of the patriotic orations, there existed two Haitis, the one consisting of a small exploiting class, the other of the mass of ex-slaves—a situation differing from the colonial regime only in externals.

To realize the difficulty of the problems, it is only necessary to recall that in 1804 more than half the population had been born in Africa, that some 90 per cent of it had had no experience save that to be found in Africa, in slavery, or in one of the most atrocious wars in history. To them the culture of the old country had more meaning than the civilization of France, which they had been able to observe only in the person of the slave driver and the invading soldier. Nearly all of these people were peasants and fully half of them mountaineers, fugitives from civilization as they knew it,[16] dwelling in isolation by preference and following the ways of their ancestors little affected by their European contacts. Their language was not

---

[16] The first settlers in the mountains were runaway slaves, who were followed by war refugees and finally by fugitives from compulsory labor for their "liberators."

French but a *patois*, they were entirely illiterate, and their political conceptions had not advanced beyond the point of loyalty
to a local chief.

In contrast to the African Haiti of the hills there existed an
urban Haiti, composed of the new ruling class and its attend-
ants, which consciously modeled its life upon European forms.
The *élite*, never as much as one per cent of the population,[17]
had as its nucleus the remnant of the more fortunate *affranchis*,
the only group available with pre-revolutionary experience in
the management of affairs, to whom were added rude men of
action whom the troubled times had brought forward. The *élite*
represented authority, since it filled all the offices; it represented
wealth;[18] it represented education, such as there was of it.[19]   It
was intensely proud of its European style, the visible evidence
of these advantages and the badge of its social superiority, and
it was fiercely patriotic to the extent that it was determined
never to surrender its control of Haiti to any outside authority,
but, as a class, it lacked any sense of social responsibility, in this
differing little from the *grands blancs*, its only model of what
a ruling class should be.   Reared in the colonial hierarchy,
Haitians regarded with disdain not only unskilled labor but
even those tasks once performed by the *petits blancs* and lesser
affranchis.   The education of the *élite* provided for its sons—
and it cared little for the education of other men's sons—was
literary rather than technical, with a government post as the
end in view.   In consequence, it produced some creditable men

[17] In 1921 it was estimated that they numbered less than five thousand in a population of about two million (Arthur C. Millspaugh, *Haiti Under American Control*,
pp. 13 f.).   In the same period it was estimated that 50 per cent of the Haitians
were mountaineers, 35 per cent peasants in the plains, and only 15 per cent inhabitants of towns of more than one thousand (*Geological Survey*, pp. 67-69).   In 1804
the proportion of townsmen must have been much less.

[18] The *affranchis* retained title to their pre-revolutionary property, while the
estates of the *grands blancs* were distributed among the revolutionary chiefs.   Ultimately, though the plantations were abandoned, access to the treasury amounted to
the same thing.

[19] The educational advantages of the *affranchis* have been greatly exaggerated.
There were no schools in Saint Domingue, even for *grands blancs*, and those
affranchis who returned from schooling in France, while individually influential,
were numerically insignificant (Rayford W. Logan, "Education in Haiti," *Journal
of Negro History*, XV, 1930, 405-410).

of letters,[20] an array of politicians, but no engineers, scientific farmers, or skilled artisans, although these would have been more serviceable in the reconstruction of Haiti.

Implicit in the Haitian social structure was the problem of color prejudice, too deeply rooted in colonial experience to be erased from the character of the revolutionary generation. Mulatto and negro had been able to co-operate in the final expulsion of the French because France had threatened both, but men had not forgotten the struggle between Rigaud and Louverture or the discriminations of colonial times. Because the *élite* were predominantly mulatto, this prejudice merged with the other distinctions between that class and the masses, enabling some Haitians to deny its very existence,[21] but, apart from the testimony of foreign observers, there is abundant evidence in Haitian political literature to show that Haitians have always been acutely color conscious. Thus, despite the extirpation of the whites, despite the pronouncements of constitutions and laws, the Black Republic continued to be divided by a color line.

The revolution deprived Haiti of every inhabitant experienced in civil government, since even the *affranchis* had been denied political rights under the old regime, but had there been any such class available, it could hardly have exerted much influence on the reorganization of the country. After twelve years of warfare the only authority recognized was that derived from military rank. Dessalines as governor general or emperor enjoyed no powers he had not already exercised as commander-in-chief. No civil administration existed and none was established. In anticipation of a new invasion the entire Haitian population was organized as an army ready for instant mobilization, all local officials being merely commanders of military districts. This extreme militarism was amply justified, since no power deigned to recognize Haitian independence till 1825 and a satis-

[20] Emerson Brewer Christie, "Haiti's Contribution to Literature," *Pan American Magazine*, XLIV (1931), 216-236; Jean Price-Mars, *Une étape de l'évolution haïtienne*, pp. 46-83. Price-Mars has likened the *élite* to the mandarins of old China (*La vocation de l'élite*, p. 66).

[21] Thus Dantès Bellegarde argues that the distinction was purely educational and tends to disappear as more negroes qualify in that regard (*Un haïtien parle*, p. 22).

factory settlement with France was not reached until 1838, during which time the country was in constant danger of attack, yet the tradition thus established never ceased to exert a baneful influence on Haitian politics. After a century of independence the president still appointed military commandants to rule the departments, arrondissements, and communes of the republic.

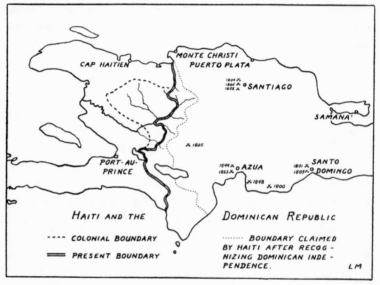

A sense of insecurity dominated the foreign policy of Haiti as well as its internal organization. For the very reason that they were sensitive to outside interference, the Haitians were themselves prone to interfere in the affairs of their eastern neighbors. Toussaint Louverture annexed the *partie espagnole* on the supposition that its possession was essential to the safety of his regime, and for three quarters of a century thereafter Haiti claimed the whole island, yet in all that time Haitians were in actual control of Santo Domingo for an aggregate of only twenty-three years.[22] During much of the remainder of that

[22] In 1801-1802 and 1822-1844. Repelling Dessalines in 1805, the French lost Santo Domingo to Spain in 1809. Twelve years later the Dominicans, breaking away from Spain, moved for incorporation in Simon Bolivar's Gran Colombia, but were reannexed by Haiti instead. They regained their independence in 1844, but Haiti retained a considerable area never included in French Saint Domingue, which became the subject of a boundary dispute not finally settled until 1935. A remark-

period a state of border warfare existed, punctuated by five unsuccessful invasions, and even after open hostilities had ceased, Haitian governments did not scruple to lend clandestine aid to Dominican rebels, an attention which the Dominican authorities were not slow to reciprocate. If the Haitians were reluctant to surrender their pretensions to sovereignty in the East, they were determined that no overseas power should gain lodgment there. Their attitude was akin to that embodied in the Monroe Doctrine—they were convinced that such a condition would imperil their national security.

Considering this heritage, physical, economic, social, and political, it is not remarkable that Haiti's national life has been marred by violence and instability. Whatever constitutions may have said about elections,[23] whatever steps may have been taken to regularize *faits accomplis*, political power in Haiti has always been acquired, exercised, and defended by force, overt or latent. Revolutions have been most often accomplished by coups d'état or campaigns of *pronunciamiento*—really destructive civil conflicts have been relatively few—but the effect has been to create an atmosphere of insecurity, to make the possession of power an end in itself, a prize to be enjoyed to the utmost while it yet might be.

Until 1820 Haitian history was but a continuation of the internal conflict that had accompanied the struggle for freedom. The elimination of the French had dissolved the bond between Dessalines, the heir of Louverture, and Pétion,[24] the heir of Rigaud, although two years elapsed before the renewal of the feud through the assassination of Dessalines by Pétion's adherents. Thereafter the country was divided during fourteen years of civil war between Pétion and Henri Christophe, Louverture's surviving lieutenant. The latter ruled the north as he

---

ably candid discussion of Haitian-Dominican relations, especially in 1821-1822, may be found in Dr. Price-Mars, "L'unité politique de l'île d'Haiti . . . ," *Revue d'histoire et de géographie d'Haiti*, No. 27 (1937), 1-27.

[23] The customary provision has been for the direct election of a chamber of deputies which in turn elects a senate, the two combining as a national assembly to elect a president.

[24] Alexandre Pétion, a free-born mulatto educated in France, had been Rigaud's principal lieutenant and had returned to Haiti with Leclerc.

would an army, adopting the forms of feudal monarchy and enforcing Louverture's compulsory labor system. In the south his milder and somewhat doctrinaire adversary essayed to found an oligarchic republic (pleasing to the *élite*) supported by a community of peasant proprietors (to placate the masses), but in practice even he exercised dictatorial powers. These two archetypes embodied the only principles ever of any significance in Haitian politics—in Christophe the dictatorship of an individual; in Pétion the dictatorship of a class, the *élite*.

By 1822 Pétion and Christophe were both dead, and Pétion's protégé, Jean-Pierre Boyer, ruled the whole island. Reunion, soon followed by recognition, gave promise of a new era. Boyer should have been able to establish a civil government at last, but, although he borrowed French legislative and judicial forms, the militarized executive continued to dominate. After twenty-five years in office he was overthrown by ardent youths who demanded that Pétion's earlier liberal policies be put into effect (and who also complained that Boyer had limited his patronage to old-timers), but their "new era" was even more sterile, producing three years of confusion ending in the twelve-year dictatorship of Faustin Soulouque, the imitator of Dessalines and Christophe.[25] The "liberals," led by Fabre Geffrard, again seized power in 1859, but when eight years of "regeneration" had failed to alter the hard fact of military dictatorship there was another upheaval—and so on, through the "presidencies" of Sylvain Salnave (1867-1869), Nissage-Saget (1870-1874), Michel Domingue (1874-1876), Boisrond-Canal (1876-1879), Lysius Salomon (1879-1888), Florvil Hyppolite (1889-1896), Tiresias Simon Sam (1896-1902), and Nord Alexis (1902-1908), until it seemed that the experiment in negro self-government had degenerated into a scramble for the spoils of office among a swarm of self-seeking *caciques*. However, although Haitian politics were opportunist and personal to a degree, there were several points with respect to which they showed some coherence.

---

[25] Soulouque, an ex-slave who had pursued an undistinguished military career under Boyer, was elected president in 1847, and made himself emperor in 1849.

For one, there was the issue of rotation in office. As monarchs Dessalines, Christophe, and Soulouque assumed life tenure. In opposition to that tendency, Pétion's constitution of 1806 and the abortive reform constitution of 1843 had embodied the principle of a limited term, but Pétion himself and Boyer had assumed a life presidency, and in restoring the republic Geffrard had been content to follow their example. Salnave was elected for four years only, but he too ventured to assume life tenure, as a result of which he faced a firing squad. Since then no Haitian has ever claimed the presidency for life. Neither has any Haitian ever retired voluntarily from office,[26] but none has been suffered to remain overlong. This represents some progress on the road from autocracy to responsible government, but, in a land where electoral procedure has been impotent against the military power of the executive, it has been accomplished only at the cost of periodic revolutions. Obviously, the cure could become worse than the disease, but at least there was no political apathy.

Another fruitful source of internal strife has been the issue of responsibility of the military to the civil authority, generally presented in the form of the responsibility of the executive (as represented by the cabinet) to the legislature. This idea was also embodied, but never effectively applied, in the constitutions of 1806 and 1843. The "regenerators" of 1859 made parliamentary government the keystone of their program, yet as soon as the legislature showed signs of independence Geffrard dissolved it. The parliamentarians at once conspired to overthrow the tyrant, their late hero, and in 1867 Salnave became president as the new champion of ministerial responsibility, but within four months of his inauguration he, too, had driven the legislature out of the capitol. Again a revolutionary party made the familiar promises and, after a bitter struggle, put Nissage-Saget in office. For some time the new president succeeded in

[26] Only three presidents (before 1915) ever reached the end of their terms. Nissage-Saget hoped to stay on, no successor having been elected, but found that Michel Domingue had gained control of the army, and retired in chagrin. Salomon had himself elected to a second term and was soon thrown out. Simon Sam argued that his term did not expire till 1903, but was persuaded that it ended in 1902.

avoiding a conflict with the legislature, but when the issue of ministerial responsibility was eventually raised he, like his predecessors, refused to give in. His successor, Michel Domingue, escaped such difficulties by never having a legislature elected.

The only president to adhere strictly to the constitution in his relations with the Corps Législatif was Boisrond-Canal. Elected as a Liberal after the scandalous administration of Domingue, he was sincere in subordinating himself to the law, believing that most of Haiti's ills sprang from the arbitrary character of her executives. He had a nominal legislative majority, but the unprecedented circumstance of having a president who really meant to put the parliamentary system into practice proved too much for it. The chambers never ceased to lecture him on his duties, remind him of his responsibility to them, and exult over the abolition of military dictatorship. They spent so much time asserting their supremacy in petty details of administration that they forgot to enact the promised reforms of the latest "new era."[27] It all ended in a tragedy of futility. The elections of 1879, to determine the composition of the assembly that would choose Canal's successor, were honestly conducted, with the result that the opposition won. This remarkable event was too good to be true—the victors were sure that they would be robbed of their triumph by a coup d'état, for although the Liberal party was supposed to advocate the supremacy of the ballot, its candidate, Boyer Bazelais, was not expected to permit the peaceful election of his hated and dreaded rival, Lysius Salomon. Bazelais did provoke a disturbance that might have resulted in a coup had not Canal stepped in to restore order by suppressing his own party. Then, convinced that the constitutional regime was a failure, Haiti's most scrupulous president resigned in disgust.

The Liberals squandered their opportunities in 1822, 1843, 1859, 1870, and 1876. They were never to have another. Boyer Bazelais gambled for power in 1883, only to meet a defeat

[27] Bassett to Evarts, No. 506, June 21; No. 509, June 24, 1877, Despatches, Haiti, X.

which cost him his own life and virtually liquidated his party. Thereafter no serious effort was ever made to establish responsible government, and the problem of subordinating the military to the civil power remained unsolved. Nevertheless, it must be admitted that a real issue had been involved in Haiti's internal struggles during the third quarter of the last century, even though it must also be noted that the advocates of the parliamentary system were not seeking to establish popular government, but only to curb military autocracy in the interest of an oligarchy.

Even as Haiti's inheritance of color prejudice was barely distinguishable from class prejudice, so its political manifestation merged with the division on the responsible government. The classic autocrats, Louverture, Dessalines, Christophe, and Soulouque, had been negroes and slaves, while Pétion, Boyer, the reformers of 1843, the regenerators of 1859, and the parliamentary party generally had been mulattoes. The mulatto *élite*, observing that negroes seemed invariably to rule with the simplicity of African tribal chiefs, naturally favored a system better suited to their own forensic talents. A government responsible to the Corps Législatif would be responsible to their class. They saw the issue as one between barbarism and civilization and so justified to themselves minority rule, by fair means or foul, in the name of republicanism. However, liberal management of affairs invariably enabled those of the *élite*, mulatto or black, who had been left out by the "Ins," to strike back by arousing the masses against oligarchy. Raised to power, this group, calling itself Nationalist, would proceed to rule autocratically, having reason to distrust the legislative body and sufficient popular support to disregard it. In turn, the arbitrary proceedings of an untrammeled Nationalist executive would enable Liberals to inspire a reaction in favor of parliamentary government as a guard against despotism—and so the vicious cycle ran, at least until the debacle of 1879. In the words of a disillusioned Liberal: "The mulattoes in office are impolitic or powerless, the blacks frankly criminal or incapable. . . . They occupy the presidential chair in turn, the machiavellism of the minority serving as a step to the vandalism of the majority."[28]

The political color line was frequently crossed, mulattoes not hesitating "to conspire, in connection with the blacks, against a ruler of their own color."[29] Moreover, sectional influences obscured it. As in the days of Louverture and Rigaud, of Christophe and Pétion, the North was the black stronghold, while the mulattoes predominated, morally if not numerically, in the West and South. A Northern mulatto or a Southern black with political aspirations would find it expedient to work with the local ring. Finally, to confuse the issue, mulatto politicians sometimes resorted to the device of putting up a black president as front. This trick, originated in 1844-1847—the election of Soulouque on this plan had been a mistake!—was again resorted to, especially after 1883 when no mulatto could hope for the presidency for himself.[30] These exceptions, however, do not destroy the point that Haitian politics were conducted on a basis of color, with Liberal and Nationalist meaning, roughly, mulatto and black.

These party distinctions obtained only among the literate, politically conscious, *élite*. A genuine conflict of black and mulatto could have had only one conclusion, but both parties, by rabble-rousing, obtained followings of credulous blacks. Earlier Haitian civil strife involved only the townsmen and the peasants of the more accessible countryside, but in the war of 1868-1869 the *cacos*, denizens of the Northern hinterland, and *piquets*, mountaineers of the South, were called forth by the contending factions. These names, *caco* and *piquet*, were soon associated with savagery and terror, yet had these primitive people been left alone, they would have remained quietly in their remote homes. Their deeds were done at the behest of men who, as the *élite*, prided themselves on their civilization

[28] Edmond Paul, *Questions politico-économiques*, p. 37.

[29] Benjamin S. Hunt, *Remarks on Hayti as a Place of Settlement for Afric-Americans*, p. 11. This observation by an American, made in the bright dawn of Geffrard's "regeneration," was a fair anticipation of Sylvain Salnave, mulatto leader of the blacks.

[30] Alcius Charmant, *Haïti, vivra-t-elle? Étude sur le préjugé des races* . . . , pp. 218-254, 287-310.

and culture. The *cacos* gained an appetite for the spoils of war and became the Swiss mercenaries of Haitian politics. There was an economic motive in revolutionary activity, more pressing than mere cupidity. The very livelihood of a considerable group had come to depend on government employment, and there were not enough places to go around. According to Frederick Douglass, "The fault is not with the ignorant many, but with the educated and ambitious few. Too proud to work, and not disposed to go into commerce, they make politics a profession and are forever plotting to get into their hands the large revenues of the country. . . . No president, however virtuous, wise, and patriotic, ever suits them when they themselves happen to be out of power."[31]

Haitian economic backwardness was both a cause and a result of political unrest. The Haitians could not restore the old plantations, nor would they allow anyone else to do so, the constitutional prohibition against alien ownership of real estate being among the most cherished of Haitian traditions. The peasants were constantly uprooted by military impressments, and most of them became mere squatters with no incentive to improve their holdings, while their very ignorance and poverty made them susceptible to political agitation. During a century of independence the population had quadrupled, yet it was debatable whether Haitian production equaled that of 1790. The exportation of sugar and indigo had ceased entirely, that of cotton had decreased 50 per cent, that of coffee, the new staple, had increased only 26 per cent, and the only compensatory gains had occurred in the exportation of cocoa, logwood, and miscellaneous articles not deemed worthy of consideration in colonial times.[32] Certainly there had been an immense decrease in production per capita. Moreover, even if the volume of exports were approximately the same, their value was less than a fifth of what it had been in 1791.[33] Although the peasant might

[31] *Lecture on Haiti*, p. 16.
[32] J. N. Léger, *Haiti: Her History and Her Detractors*, pp. 292 f.
[33] Davis (*Black Democracy*, p. 25) estimates the exports of 1791 to have been worth $50,000,000 at modern prices. Those for 1903 were valued at $8,585,687. According to Antenor Firmin (*M. Roosevelt . . . et la République d'Haiti*, pp.

enjoy freedom of a sort, his material condition had not been improved, nor could the government launch any program of social betterment on the basis of such an economy, had it the will to do so.

The complete absence of local capital and engineering experience meant that the government must depend upon foreign concessionaires for the construction of public works. Responsible capitalists hesitated to invest in such a turbulent community, with the result that most contracts fell to shoestring speculators, and Haitian experience with persons of that ilk sufficiently demonstrates why, as late as 1915, there existed in the entire republic only one wharf, two lighthouses, one electric plant, and one hundred and twelve miles of railroad. The practice was to grant a concession, without competitive bids, to some favored individual, native or foreign, who was to receive all the profits of the enterprise and a subsidy as well for a limited period, after which possession would revert to the state. The concessionaire would leave for Paris or New York to sell his rights or raise capital, or else he would remain at Port-au-Prince in the attitude of the dog in the manger, doing nothing, but refusing to surrender his unearned privileges except at an exorbitant price. Eventually the government would grant a second concession, whereupon the first adventurer would enter a claim for breach of contract. Under diplomatic pressure, the treasury would have to pay heavily out of the funds allotted to the enterprise, only to be confronted with a claim from the second concessionaire for nonpayment of the subsidy. Under new diplomatic pressure, the government would be fleeced again, while the desired utility stood unfinished and abandoned.[34]

The fault of the Haitian authorities is apparent, yet one can appreciate President Salomon's complaint that "they constrain us . . . to maintain a system of exclusion whose inconveniences we understand, but which we prefer . . . to the extortions, to

---

435 f.), the value of exports in 1789 was 461 million livres, of those for 1891, one hundred million francs.

[34] Thompson to Bayard, No. 101, Aug. 20, 1886, Despatches, Haiti, XXI; Powell to Hay, No. 677, Dec. 15, 1899, loc. cit., XXXV.

the humiliations of every minute . . ."[35] or the exclamations of *La Vérité* of Port-au-Prince: "Haiti must learn that she can count only on herself. . . . Ah! even if we be considered to have retrograded, we must be less hasty, less willing to make contracts with foreigners. Our desire for progress must not lead us like Egypt to shame, to servitude or death."[36]

Perhaps it was this fear of political vassalage through financial entanglement that was responsible for Haiti's remarkable record of debt payment, despite the poverty of her resources, the questionable character of some of her obligations, and the bad example of her neighbors. A foreign debt had been inescapable since the day when Boyer undertook to indemnify the former colonists as the price of French recognition. In 1875 Domingue floated a new loan in Paris, a transaction so obviously tainted that repudiation was threatened, although the matter was ultimately adjusted by Salomon. In 1896 Hyppolite's credit was good enough to enable him to secure a Paris loan on comparatively reasonable terms. Eight years later the balance due on the foreign debt, held entirely in France, was twelve million dollars. Haiti had never defaulted, but the French navy had made one or two dunning expeditions.

Thoughtful Haitians were not blind to the fact that all was not well with the *patrie*. They produced a considerable body of literature diagnosing the case and prescribing the remedy,[37] but the patient was set in her ways and declined to take the medicine. Perhaps she lacked the means to have the prescription filled. It called for honesty in public office, the divorce of the army from politics, an end to color prejudice and class discrimination, a new deal for the peasants, more efficient ex-

---

[35] Langston to Frelinghuysen, No. 656, Aug. 4, 1884, *loc. cit.*, XVIII.

[36] Thompson to Bayard, No. 132, April 29, 1887, *loc. cit.*, XXI.

[37] Among others, Alexandre Bonneau, *Haiti: ses progrès, son avenir;* Demesvar Delorme, *La misère au sein des richesses;* Edmond Paul, *Questions politico-économiques,* and *Les causes de nos malheurs;* Emmanuel Edouard, *Essai sur la politique intérieure d'Haiti;* L. J. Marcelin, *Haiti: ses guerres civiles;* Leonidas Laventure, *Haiti: le danger de la patrie;* Joseph Justin, *Étude sur les institutions haitiennes;* Frédéric Marcelin, *Une évolution nécessaire, L'haleine du centenaire,* and *Le passé;* Antenor Firmin, *M. Roosevelt . . . et la République d'Haiti;* Alcius Charmant, *Haiti, vivra-t-elle?;* and Auguste Magloire, *L'erreur révolutionnaire et notre état social.*

ploitation of natural resources, sounder and more general education—but no one explained how an adequate educational program could be put into effect in advance of a general change
of heart and an increase in national wealth, or how either of
these could be accomplished except through long years of educational effort. If this riddle, reminiscent of the chicken and the
egg, proved too much for Haitian publicists, it was to baffle
certain alien experts also later on.

Meanwhile Americans were forming horseback opinions on
the case, with little knowledge of or consideration for its com-
plexities. Their views were distorted not only by inadequate
information, but by color prejudices of their own, economic
influences, sentimental imperialism (and its converse), and considerations of naval strategy.

It is not difficult to perceive how the idea of an independent
negro nationality in America would affect the ante-bellum
planter, to whom public order and private fortune were alike
based on the premise that negroes were unfit for self-government. It would appear to him both ridiculous and terrifying,
according to whether he thought of his butler trapped in
Soulouque's robes of imperial majesty or imagined sudden rebellion in the quarters of his field hands. Yet his was not color
prejudice in its bitterest form—indeed, he, secure in his social
position, could in most cases achieve a relationship of mutual
affection with his dependents. "White supremacy" was more
really vital to the Southern *petit blanc,* whom even a slave could
regard as "po' white trash." These people, whose economic and
social standing had been so depressed by unequal competition
with the plantation system that only freedom and color distinguished them from the lowliest black, regarded the negroes
themselves as the cause of their undoing[38] and conceived a

[38] During the seventeenth century extremes of wealth and poverty had been
unknown in Virginia, a white yeomanry constituting the bulk of the population.
The introduction of negro slavery on a large scale at the close of the century
destroyed this class, compelling its members to become small slaveholders, to emigrate,
or to suffer degradation, of which the very presence of the negro was a continual
reminder (T. J. Wertenbaker, *The Planters of Colonial Virginia,* pp. 38-60, 134-
160). What happened in Virginia was repeated, successively, in other Southern
states. Color prejudice in the South owes more to the animosity thus engendered
than to the attitude of master toward servant.

prejudice so keen that they could take abolitionist propaganda as a personal affront and fight to preserve the very institution that had ruined them. Nor was color prejudice a Southern monopoly. It would be a mistake to assume that Northern magnates were free of class consciousness or that Northern *petits blancs* were incapable of negrophobia when they conceived their own interests to be affected.[39] Only the abolitionists, never more than a handful of zealots, were without this animus, but their vision was equally distorted by their negrophile ardor.

American commercial interest in Haiti, originally very considerable but later relatively unimportant, was confined almost exclusively to the northeastern seaboard. Merchants and bankers deplored the Revolution, which upset trade, then advocated recognition in hope of restoring it, but finally came to adopt the planters' views on negro self-government. After 1845 mercantile influence was never so considerable as that of naval strategy, based on Haiti's location with reference to the Panama route, or that of sentimental imperialism, appearing under the flattering alias of "Manifest Destiny" but latterly stirring up an anti-imperialism equally sentimental.

Creole *émigrés* may have been voluble in recounting their experiences to sympathetic Southern planters, ship captains and agents may have had much to tell Yankee merchants, but the information on Haiti that found general circulation in print was meager indeed. During the first three quarters of the nineteenth century the reader's fare consisted principally of horror tales of revolutionary atrocities,[40] exposure of military despotism concealed behind the republican façade, and criticism of economic backwardness and of the exploitation of the cultivators.[41] The most ambitious effort of the period was a two-volume presentation of *The History and Present Condition of*

---

[39] See below, pp. 82 f., 89 f.

[40] An extreme example was the Massachusetts Sabbath School Union's *Brief History of the Island of Hayti*, designed to solicit support for missionary activity among the savage and benighted Haitians.

[41] Archibald Alexander, *A History of Colonization on the Western Coast of Africa*, pp. 263 ff.; J. Dennis Harris, *A Summer on the Borders of the Caribbean Sea*; Benjamin S. Hunt, *Remarks on Hayti* . . . ; Mark Baker Bird, *The Black Man* . . . ; Victor Hugo, *The Slave King*—the last a Philadelphia "adaptation" of *Bug-Jargal* with a lengthy preface on Haitian history.

St. Domingo (1837), the moral of which was that, considering what had transpired in that unhappy isle, "we should not, by ignorant or unnecessary legislation [such as the abolitionists proposed], disturb the arrangement of the social order under which experience has assured us that our national prosperity is safe."[42]   However, it was not until this social order, cherished by Yankee textile manufacturer as well as Southern planter, had been dead eight years that an author went beyond this defensive attitude to argue that the United States should intervene to regenerate Haiti.[43]

In 1880 a former British minister at Port-au-Prince founded a new school in the reporting of the Haitian scene.   Sir Spencer St. John not only popularized, in its Haitian application, an old Southern thesis of negro reversion to African barbarism in the absence of white control,[44] but he also revealed to the world the journalistic virtues of voodoo.   His *Hayti, or the Black Republic* has had a numerous progeny, even to the present day, works of which the inspiration is obvious, with or without due acknowledgment.[45]   It may be supposed that some writers actually thought they saw what St. John had taught them to expect—one distinguished author naïvely confessed that he could find no trace of cannibalism, yet in doing so assumed the truth of St. John's reports of its prevalence[46]—but it is evident that what all of them saw was St. John's journalistic success. Not until 1937 did a work in English cut through this mass of "distortion, misrepresentation, and misplaced emphasis" to approach the subject in a truly scientific spirit.   It revealed that the Haitian hinterland was predominantly African, but by no means degenerate.[47]

[42] The author was one Jonathan Brown, apparently of New Hampshire.

[43] Samuel Hazard, *San Domingo, Past and Present*.

[44] See William Sumner Jenkins, *Pro-slavery Thought in the Old South*, pp. 244 ff.

[45] Frederick A. Ober, *In the Wake of Columbus* and *Our West Indian Neighbors;* Hesketh Prichard, *Where Black Rules White;* Blair Niles, *Black Haiti;* William B. Seabrook, *The Magic Island;* John H. Craige, *Black Bagdad* and *Cannibal Cousins;* and, finally, Richard A. Loederer, *Voodoo Fire in Haiti.*

[46] James Anthony Froude, *The English in the West Indies.*

[47] Melville J. Herskovitz, *Life in a Haitian Valley*, sponsored by the Social Science Research Councils of Columbia and Northwestern universities.   Some Haitian authors have endeavored to pass off *vaudaux* as a primitive dance, all in fun, but Herskovitz recognizes it as a genuine survival of African religious forms.

If, in the lurid light of semifictional voodoo fires, the belief could be established that the Haitians had relapsed into bloodthirsty barbarism, the idea that the United States must intervene in the name of civilization and for the sake of the poor wretches themselves (among others) might follow. This thesis fitted in too snugly with the *mission civilisatrice* implicit in "Manifest Destiny" to be neglected, and soon St. John had another group of disciples who, caring less for voodoo as a literary device, cherished it as a justification of imperialism.[48] Other imperialists, while specifically rejecting St. John's theory of retrogression, deemed political instability and economic backwardness sufficient warrant.[49] Moreover, ridicule had been discovered as a weapon no less formidable than horror.[50]

While these books were being written, Haiti also suffered from a bad press, metropolitan journals having discovered the relationship between sensationalism and circulation. The palm for virulence goes to a *Harper's Weekly* story on "Terror in Haiti . . . crimes . . . assassination . . . bloody outrage . . . slaughter . . . the ghastly acts of a madman,"[51] but the longtime championship of abuse was won by the New York *Herald,* whose lurid despatches were a constant subject of complaint from the American legation at Port-au-Prince as well as the Haitian legation at Washington.

It cannot be supposed that the occasional diatribes of a few Eastern newspapers, supplemented by a scattering of sensational travel books, could either create or reflect an active American public opinion such as would impel the government to adopt any specific policy. A vast majority of Americans had never

---

[48] Archibald R. Colquhoun, "The Future of the Negro," *North American Review,* CLXXVI (1903), 657-674, and *Greater America;* George W. Crichfield, *American Supremacy;* P. P. Wells, "Hayti and San Domingo, 1802-1906," *The History of Nations,* XXII, 491-504; W. A. MacCorkle, *The Monroe Doctrine in Its Relation to the Republic of Haiti.* Wells's work was notably unsound—he even imputed Marxian principles to the *cacos!*—but significant because done under the editorial supervision of Henry Cabot Lodge.

[49] Robert T. Hill, *Cuba and Porto Rico,* pp. 283-287, 403; Sir Harry Johnston, *The Negro in the New World,* pp. x, 205.

[50] Stephen Bonsal, *The American Mediterranean.* Under the heading, "Rotation in office as it works in Haiti," *Public Opinion* (XXXVIII, 1905, 42) depicted Haitian generals waiting in line at the door of the treasury.

[51] June 20, 1891.

heard of Haiti, or, at best, were only dimly aware of the existence of a Black Republic. The effect of these writings was that, even among those who considered themselves informed, there was no disposition to question whatever the government, in its wisdom, might decide to do under the pressure of national or special interests.

CHAPTER II

MOLASSES AND THE RIGHTS OF MAN

We are necessary to them, and they are to us; and there will be commerce between us. If the governments forbid it, it will be carried on clandestinely.—JOHN ADAMS, 1783

Independence is the worst and most dangerous condition they can be in, for the United States.—JOHN ADAMS, 1799

RELATIONS between the United States and Haiti antedate the independence of either, having their origin in commercial intercourse that had become of vital importance to both communities more than two centuries ago. Before 1700 the English sugar islands in the Caribbean served as the primary marketing area for the fish, meat, breadstuffs, lumber, and horses exported from Boston, Newport, New York, Philadelphia, and Baltimore, and in return they were able to supply the entire demand of the continental colonies for tropical products; but at the turn of the century the more rapid development of the northern region led to an overbalance on the temperate side of the exchange which compelled merchants to resort to foreign islands in search of a market for their surplus.[1] In the French West Indies a complementary condition existed. As much as the English sugar plantations, they depended on outside sources for provisions, lumber, and horses, needs which Canada, Louisiana, and even France could not satisfy. Moreover, the French planter had no market for his rum and molasses, since France forbade their importation in order to protect French brandies. With these products otherwise worthless, Saint Domingue could underbid Jamaica and Barbados for the North American trade. Yankee merchants were soon dealing exclusively with the French or else demanding specie in Jamaica and buying a

[1] Ragatz, *The West Indian Approach to the Study of American Colonial History,* p. 7.

French return cargo[2]—both crimes against mercantilism, but
not against the letter of the navigation acts. Saint Domingue
entered this commerce in 1714,[3] at the very beginning of the
stupendous development of the colony, which was undoubtedly
aided by the exchange. Seventy years later, when it had become the source of two thirds of French tropical production,[4]
it presumably commanded an even greater share in the trade
with British North America.

Cheap French molasses came to be regarded as the foundation of New England prosperity, "the great support of all their
trade and fishery." It was a profitable exchange for "refuse"
fish, a quarter to half the catch, otherwise of little value. Dis-
tillation became the chief industry of the towns, rum the basis
of their trade with the Southern continental colonies, the Indians, Newfoundland, and Guinea. Slaves bought with rum
could be sold in the British West Indies for cash, with which
to buy more French molasses to be made into rum.[5] By 1730
New England, New York, and Pennsylvania regarded Saint
Domingue, Guadeloupe, and Martinique as natural outlets and
met attempts to check such intercourse with declarations that
the population and living standards of North America depended upon free access to the French West Indies.

A cheaper labor supply, fresher soil, and less burdensome
navigation laws and customs duties enabled French sugar to
undersell the British in Europe. With that continent slipping
from their grasp, the English market saturated, and their own
production nevertheless increasing, British planters took thought
to recover the North American trade. Not only would this
be of direct benefit, but it might result in the reconquest of
Europe, since their rivals' margin of profit lay in the sale of
molasses, the loss of which would check their expansion. Unable to meet French competition under existing handicaps, they

[2] Frank W. Pitman, *The Development of the British West Indies, 1700-1763*,
pp. 188 ff., 415 f. Thus molasses from Leogane was cheaper in Philadelphia than
was the Jamaica product on the plantation (Gipson, *The British Empire Before the
American Revolution*, II, 299 n.).

[3] Treudley, *The United States and Santo Domingo, 1789-1866*, p. 86.

[4] Ragatz, *The Fall of the Planter Class in the British Caribbean, 1763-1833*, p. 126.

[5] Gipson, *The British Empire Before the American Revolution*, III, 15, 64-67.

called for the intervention of Parliament, and, over the protests of their northern brethren, they were answered, in 1733, with prohibitive duties on the importation of foreign sugar products. However, no serious effort was made to enforce the act, which was universally evaded.[6]

Not even war could check the commerce of New England with Saint Domingue. During the hostilities of 1743-1748 and 1755-1763 the British anticipated the easy capture of the French islands, cut off from essential North American supplies, but the trade continued through the Spanish (Dominican) port of Monte Cristi, or directly, under the pretext of exchanging prisoners. Colonial governors made a racket of granting flags of truce for that purpose. Admiral Knowles claimed that he could have taken Martinique had it not been provisioned by the Yankees.[7]

Thus provoked, the British undertook to break up the contraband traffic, finding in writs of assistance (general search warrants) an effective weapon. The "Molasses Act" of 1733 was supplanted, in 1764, by a new measure reducing the duty but providing for strenuous enforcement. From the colonial point of view a lower duty, enforced, was worse than a prohibitive one disregarded. So important was the trade attacked that a commercial depression resulted, the ensuing dissatisfaction opening the way to revolutionary ideas.[8] The arguments of James Otis against the constitutionality of the writs and of the act of 1764 were signs of the times; the burning of the revenue cutter *Gaspé* by citizens of Rhode Island revealed a more ominous reaction. Other more important issues were ultimately involved, but British interference with trade to Saint

---

[6] *Ibid.*, II, 289-292; III, 59, 291-294.

[7] Pitman, *British West Indies*, pp. 298, 314, 317, 417, 426 f. A typical case: the sloop *Endeavor* sailed from New York in Jan., 1747, as a "flag of truce" with twelve prisoners and a cargo of fish, flour, beef, bread, and beer. At Cap Français (Cap Haitien) she received in exchange nine prisoners and a quantity of molasses and sugar. Arrested on the return voyage, she was carried to Boston, where both vessel and cargo were acquitted. Governor Shirley of Massachusetts complained that the elected governor of Rhode Island made a regular business of trading with the enemy, over sixty "flags of truce" having sailed thence for Cap Français, Leogane, and Martinique during eighteen months, 1746-1748. H. M. S. *Viper* found twenty-nine Yankee vessels at Monte Cristi on Feb. 5, 1759.

[8] Pitman, *British West Indies*, p. 325.

Domingue[9] had a significant part in bringing on a controversy that ended in the independence of the United States.[10]

The Revolution freed the Americans from British trade restrictions and made them allies of France, but the result did not measure up to eager anticipations. Cut off from the British West Indies, except for limited concessions liable at any time to be revoked, they realized belatedly that those islands had been important to them too. France had never wholeheartedly welcomed Yankee intercourse with her West Indian possessions in time of peace, and, consequently, the commercial treaty of 1778 did not grant the complete freedom of trade in that quarter desired by the United States. Instead, American vessels of limited tonnage were allowed to enter specified ports to exchange enumerated articles for molasses and rum only.[11] Nevertheless, in 1790 Saint Domingue, with a population of little more than half a million, stood second to Great Britain alone in the foreign commerce of the United States.[12]

The cataclysm that engulfed the French colony in 1791 brought dismay to all parts of the United States. The North had a stake in the preservation of the *status quo* measurable in terms of commerce. Threatened was a plantation system that had operated to the profit of Boston merchants as well as

[9] This trade was of no direct consequence to the Southern continental colonies, of course. Commercially, they were closer kin to Jamaica than to Massachusetts, in that their exports consisted of plantation-raised staples enumerated under the navigation acts.

[10] There is a persistent Haitian tradition, traceable at least to Thomas Madiou (*Histoire d'Haiti*, 1847, I, 87) that eight hundred black and mulatto volunteers from Saint Domingue, including most of the Haitian revolutionary heroes, fought for American independence at Savannah in 1779 as part of the French force under the Comte d'Estaing. However, L. E. Moreau de St. Méry (*Description de la partie française de St. Domingue*, 1798, I, 321) described this force as "*grenadiers-volontaires-blancs.*" Two battalions of colored emigrants from Saint Domingue did fight under Jackson at New Orleans in 1815, but it is questionable whether these men, who had fled their country during its struggle for independence, could claim the name of Haitian.

[11] *American State Papers* (hereinafter abbreviated *A. S. P.*), *Foreign Relations*, I, 300 ff.

[12] *A. S. P., Commerce and Navigation*, I, 24. Exports to the French West Indies, of which Saint Domingue probably took two thirds or more, were valued at $3,285,000, 16 per cent of the total. Moreover, this trade showed a favorable balance in the ratio of nearly two to one (Emile Levasseur, *Histoire du commerce de la France*, p. 531).

creole masters. The South had no such direct interest involved, but Southern planters naturally took alarm at servile insurrection so close to home. The sympathies of these elements, predominant in the administration, were entirely with the old regime in Saint Domingue.

At the outbreak of the negro insurrection the colonial assembly appealed directly to the United States for aid, to the annoyance of Jean de Ternant, the French minister, and the embarrassment of Thomas Jefferson, secretary of state. Both were disturbed by this attitude of independence, Ternant because the planters had already shown a disposition to break away from the control of the National Assembly, Jefferson because he feared that an independent Saint Domingue would fall under British influence, to the ruin of American commerce.[13] Since there was no hope of aid from France, Ternant clothed the appeal in his own authority, requesting that the United States supply the colony out of sums due on the revolutionary debt, then seven years in arrears.[14] One thousand stand of arms and $40,000 were furnished him immediately,[15] and in 1792 an additional $760,000 was placed at his disposal for colonial relief and defense.[16] These credits went out to Saint Domingue in the form of munitions and foodstuffs, without which the French authorities could hardly have maintained themselves. The object of American policy was the preservation of a profitable commerce, which, it was felt at that time, could best be accomplished by keeping the colonies under French control. The problem was to give aid without arousing French jealousy; to give sufficient aid to enable the colonies to resist British and Spanish attack, but not enough to enable them to break away from France. In June, 1794, when the French appeared to be overwhelmed by Great Britain and Spain, Jefferson feared that the United States might

[13] F. J. Turner, "Correspondence of the French Ministers to the United States, 1791-1797," *American Historical Association Reports*, 1903, II, 74 f.
[14] *A. S. P., Foreign Relations*, II, 171.
[15] Jared Sparks, *The Writings of George Washington*, X, 194.
[16] S. F. Bemis, "Payment of the French Loans to the United States, 1777-1795," *Current History*, XXIII (1926), 829-831. By 1793 the whole amount in arrears had been paid off, and the request of Ternant's successor, Edmond Gênet, for an advance was refused. In 1795 the balance due on the debt was made available to the French purchasing agent in the United States by conversion into domestic bonds.

have to intervene directly.[17]   Toussaint Louverture soon relieved him of his anxiety.

As early as October, 1791, there were enough refugees from Saint Domingue in the United States to create a problem;[18] the sack of Cap Français in June, 1793, sent some ten thousand more at one time.[19]   The legislatures of the Carolinas, Virginia, Maryland, Pennsylvania, and Massachusetts made appropriations for their relief, as did the Federal Congress when it assembled.[20]   The personal safety of Jacobin consuls at Charleston and Baltimore who had attempted to interfere with them was threatened.[21]

It was to be assumed that the Federalists (all sane and reputable people) would be horrified at the excesses of Jacobins and rebellious slaves in Saint Domingue.   They had favored the preservation of French authority when that meant planter control and "business as usual."   After the holocaust of Cap Français, when French authority came to represent the destruction of the old order and the planters' only hope seemed to lie in British intervention, Federalist sentiment underwent a corresponding change.   More complex and interesting were the reactions of Thomas Jefferson, to whom the American Revolution had meant more than cheap molasses, even more than the right of the ruling class in America to rule without the interference of its English counterpart.

Jefferson had looked with misgivings upon an independent attitude on the part of colonial planters, but when the Jacobin revolution struck Saint Domingue he was well pleased.   In May, 1793, he exulted with Genêt that the "Patriots," in coalition with the mulattoes and negroes, controlled the situation in the colony, and suggested that if the four hundred "aristocrats" about to be deported to the United States could be distributed among the Indians, they might learn a lesson in liberty and

[17] Ford, The Writings of Thomas Jefferson, VI, 502.
[18] Turner, "Correspondence of the French Ministers," p. 63.
[19] Stoddard, The French Revolution in San Domingo, p. 220.
[20] Treudley, United States and Santo Domingo, p. 114.
[21] A. S. P., Foreign Relations, I, 187.

equality.[22] But two months later, after the sack of Cap Français, he wrote, "The situation of the St. Domingo fugitives (aristocrats as they are) calls aloud for pity and charity." As Jefferson pondered their wretched state, he evidently remembered that he, too, was a planter and that what had happened to Cap Français might happen in Virginia. He became convinced that the whites were about to be totally expelled from the West Indies and that it behooved the people of the South to take heed and remove the danger from their own midst before it was too late,[23] but his new-found sympathy for the creole *émigrés* did not entail hostility toward the Haitians, whom he still wished well in their struggle for liberty.

The South shared Jefferson's anxiety, but sought salvation in vigilance and repressive measures. Virginia, having already forbidden the further immigration of negroes (1778), acted at once "to restrain the practice of their going at large," while North Carolina in 1795 prohibited negro immigration from the West Indies and required free persons of color to give security for good behavior. South Carolina followed suit in 1803, and in 1806 Orleans Territory (Louisiana) acted specifically "to prevent the introduction of free people of color from Hispaniola and other French islands."[24] The planters denounced Jefferson as a *philosophe*, an intimate of the *Amis des Noirs*, and cited Saint Domingue as the horrible example of the effect of the application of French theories to a servile population.[25] Fear dominated the South, and hostility bred of fear would dictate policy toward presumptious blacks wherever it had influence.

But meanwhile the voice of the planter was growing faint in Federalist councils as John Adams and Alexander Hamilton

[22] Ford, *The Writings of Thomas Jefferson*, VI, 268.
[23] *Ibid.*, VI, 349.
[24] John Codman Hurd, *The Law of Freedom and Bondage in the United States*, II, 5, 84, 96, 157. The statute books soon bristled with acts "for the more effective prevention of insurrections, conspiracies, etc." The ultimate in this sort of thing were the Negro Seamen Acts of South Carolina (1823) and Georgia (1829) requiring that free negro sailors be lodged in jail while their vessels were in port.
[25] Jenkins, *Pro-slavery Thought in the Old South*, p. 62.

contended for possession of the mantle of Washington, and Jefferson, the *philosophe*, had retired from the government to head an opposition largely dependent on Southern votes. The Federalists, divided as they were, had several years of power yet before them. Commerce ruled—and in Saint Domingue the planters and their British allies were going down before the waxing power of Toussaint Louverture. Toussaint had molasses with which to bargain, the planters had none, and the Federalists had a change of heart. So did the British, who were also interested in commerce.

In August, 1798, General Thomas Maitland, commanding the British expedition in Saint Domingue, concluded that, if Louverture could not be overcome, Jamaica could best be protected from subversive influences by coming to amicable terms with him. Accordingly, without waiting to consult London,[26] he negotiated an "armistice" providing for British withdrawal and securing amnesty for their native partisans, who were to return to their homes and resume cultivation, Toussaint ensuring the planters a labor supply and enjoying the benefit of economic recovery in his dominions. The British would get the resulting trade, for Maitland had provided that ships might call, under flag of truce, ostensibly to supply the needs of his late protégés. Thus all parties gained by the deal, but it was clearly inconsistent with Toussaint's professed loyalty to France. It would be hard to say whether he had gone over to the British or the British had gone over to him, but certainly both parties adhered to their original aims.[27]

At this time war between France and the United States seemed imminent, and the Federalists had hopes that they too

---

[26] The British cabinet was rather dubious of the wisdom of Maitland's unanticipated action (Rufus King to Timothy Pickering, No. 11, Dec. 7, 1798, in Charles R. King, *The Life and Correspondence of Rufus King*, II, 476).

[27] Touissaint was evidently strengthening himself for a final reckoning with Rigaud and France. Maitland reported that he would declare independence if assured of British support. But the British general regarded the convention as no more than a temporary expedient for the security of Jamaica, in no sense a recognition of independence, since he did not "apprehend it could ever suit the character of the British Nation to enter into any further Agreement with a Person of Toussaint's Description" (Maitland to Grant, June 17, 1799, Cons. Let., Cape Haytien, I).

might make a deal with Toussaint Louverture.[28]   Since Franco-American relations had broken under the strain of French spoliation of American commerce and the notorious XYZ affair, in the early summer of 1798 Congress adopted such warlike measures as the alien and sedition laws, army and navy increases, authorization of the capture of French armed vessels, abrogation of the alliance of 1778 (which had guaranteed French possessions in America), and suspension of commerce with all places under the acknowledged power of France. The last provision was an invitation to rebellion. When the Secretary of State learned, in November, that the principal French agent had been expelled from Saint Domingue, he suggested that Louverture might claim exemption from the embargo.[29] His letter crossed with one from the black general asking if some arrangement could not be made.[30]   In March, 1799, Edward Stevens was sent to Saint Domingue as consul general with instructions to secure the total suppression of privateering, the exclusion of French armed vessels from Toussaint's ports, the free use of them by American warships, and the protection of American property from seizure as spoils of war.[31]   For Toussaint to agree to this policy would be treason, considering the existing hostilities, but Hamilton insisted that nothing be done to recognize or guarantee his independence, that nothing be put in writing. Toussaint could have in exchange only verbal assurances that trade would be reopened.[32]

As Franco-American tension had grown, Anglo-American relations had become cordial, under Hamilton's guiding hand. Now, when Rufus King, American minister at London, in ignorance of what was transpiring at Philadelphia, demanded that the United States be admitted to the benefits of Maitland's "armistice," the British cabinet, alarmed lest the United States

[28] Richard Yates to Timothy Pickering, April 30, 1798; Pickering to Jacob Mayer, June 27, 1798, Cons. Let., Cape Haytien, I.

[29] Pickering to Mayer, Pvt., Nov. 30, 1798, loc. cit.

[30] Toussaint Louverture to John Adams, Nov. 6, 1798, loc. cit.

[31] Pickering to Stevens, March 7, 1799, loc. cit.

[32] Hamilton to Pickering, Feb. 9, 1799, in John C. Hamilton, The Works of Alexander Hamilton, VI, 395.

endorse Toussaint Louverture's anticipated declaration of independence, readily agreed to joint action by the two powers to render such independence harmless.[33] On his return from London to Saint Domingue, Maitland stopped at the American capital to arrange for concerted action. It was agreed that Toussaint Louverture must be required not only to bar French cruisers from his ports, but to maintain no naval force of his own (lest he disseminate "dangerous principles" among the slaves of Jamaica and the South), and that entry must be limited to Cap Français (Cap Haitien) and Port Republicaine (Port-au-Prince), whence vessels might trade along the coast with consular permission (thus preventing trade with Rigaud). Stevens was instructed to act in perfect concert with Maitland, since an extension of his armistice on these terms would satisfy the requirements of the embargo act as recently modified,[34] while, if the British failed to get what they wanted, they would renew hostilities, to the ruin of the new trade (if the United States acted independently) and to the danger of an Anglo-American collision[35] (which the Hamilton faction were most anxious to avoid).

Timothy Pickering acted for the United States in these negotiations—and Pickering, though Adams's secretary of state, was Hamilton's henchman. To understand what was in the wind, it is necessary to consider that at this time Hamilton seriously contemplated a general attack on French and Spanish America with the aid of the British navy and of the revolutionary adherents of Francisco Miranda.[36] Lord Grenville had just proposed that the United States seize Louisiana and Florida and the British take Saint Domingue.[37] President Adams had no sympathy with these ideas—he agreed only reluctantly to the Pickering-Maitland plan—because he feared that, by becom-

---

[33] Henry Dundas to King, Dec. 9, 1798; King to Pickering, Nov. 17 and Jan. 10, 1799, in King, *Rufus King*, II, 485, 499.

[34] Pickering to Stevens, April 20, 1799, Cons. Let., Cape Haytien, I.

[35] Pickering to Adams, June 5, 1799, *loc. cit.*

[36] S. F. Bemis, *A Diplomatic History of the United States*, p. 119.

[37] J. A. James, "Louisiana as a Factor in American Diplomacy, 1795-1800," *Mississippi Valley Historical Review*, I (1914), 51.

ing involved with the British, the United States might raise a barrier to a settlement with France. Indeed, even while the business of Saint Domingue was under discussion, the President reduced his Hamiltonian secretary of state to frantic despair by announcing his intention to send a new mission to Paris.[38] His interest was the security of American commerce, better served by peace with France than by any deal with Toussaint, while Hamilton and Pickering were playing a deeper game. Moreover, Adams, with a keener appreciation of Southern sensibilities, feared that Hamilton's intrigues would result in the independence of the West Indies, "the most dangerous condition they [could] be in for the United States."[39]

How, indeed, had the Federalists hoped to hold the South in line while they negotiated with the "First of the Blacks"? They "discovered" that France had ordered an invasion of the Southern States from Saint Domingue, to carry thither the tide of black revolt, that Toussaint had refused to obey, and that Rigaud had undertaken the task. Considering the actual situation in Saint Domingue, the idea was fantastic. Even Stevens, who had it from a source probably inspired by Toussaint himself, could take it seriously only by supposing that the Directory planned to make South Carolina a second Egypt, to rid itself of Toussaint as it had rid itself of Bonaparte.[40] Nevertheless, the South was asked to believe that Louverture was a true ally, Rigaud a dangerous enemy.[41]

In June, 1799, Maitland concluded a secret extension of his secret armistice embodying substantially the same terms as those agreed upon in Philadelphia, although Toussaint was allowed

[38] Pickering to Hamilton, Feb. 25, 1799, in John C. Hamilton, *The Works of Hamilton*, III, 634.

[39] Adams to Pickering, April 17, 1799, in Adams, *The Works of John Adams*, VII, 686. Years later Adams described the Hamiltonian faction as "fools who were intriguing to plunge us into an alliance with England, an endless war with the rest of the world, and wild expeditions to South America and St. Domingo; and what was worse, a civil war which I knew would be the consequence of the measures the heads of that party wished to pursue" (*ibid.*, VIII, 155).

[40] Stevens to Maitland, May 23; Stevens to Pickering, Sept. 30, 1799, Cons. Let., Cape Haytien, I.

[41] Elizabeth Donnan, "Papers of James A. Bayard, 1796-1815," *American Historical Association Reports*, 1913, II, 90.

certain modifications designed to avoid the appearance of dis-
loyalty to France. Stevens urged that the agreement be kept
secret, since its publication would ruin Toussaint with the black
chiefs, and that the embargo be lifted without delay. Twelve
thousand men had been assembled for an attack on Rigaud (in
order to prevent him from attacking Jamaica and the United
States!), but they were entirely without bread or meat and
Toussaint was deeply worried.[42] Accordingly, on June 26, 1799,
Adams proclaimed that American vessels might once more clear
with munitions and provisions for Cap Français and Port Republicaine—but none for Les Cayes.[43]

Although outnumbered four to one, Rigaud was well
equipped and ready. Toussaint lacked everything. Therefore
Rigaud attacked, before supplies could reach his antagonist, at
the same time publishing the original Maitland armistice with
telling effect. Stevens became alarmed. Rigaud was gaining
ground in the south, his vessels commanded the Gulf of
Gonave, his partisans had risen in the northwest. If Toussaint
should fall, the trade agreement would fall with him. The
consul general called for American warships to blockade Rigaud's ports and cut off the supplies that he was receiving from
the United States, despite the embargo, and Toussaint Louverture addressed a personal appeal to President Adams.[44] Thus
the United States Navy came to take an important part in a struggle which might be considered a phase of the Franco-American
hostilities then in progress, but one which was fundamentally
a Haitian civil war. The decisive intervention was the blockade
and bombardment of Jacmel, compelling Pétion to evacuate that
post which Christophe had vainly besieged by land.[45] Aided
thus, and strengthened by the supplies and revenue obtained
through the reopening of commerce with the United States,

---

[42] Stevens to Pickering, June 23, 1799, Cons. Let., Cape Haytien, I.

[43] A. S. P., Foreign Relations, II, 240.

[44] Stevens to Pickering, June 24; Toussaint Louverture to John Adams, Aug.
14, 1799, Cons. Let., Cape Haytien, I.

[45] Stevens to Pickering, Oct. 26, 1799, loc. cit., I; idem to idem, Jan. 16, 1800,
loc. cit., II. Although empowered only to capture French armed vessels or American
ships violating the embargo, the navy actually barred Rigaud's ports to all commerce.

Toussaint Louverture was enabled to push his campaign against Rigaud to a successful conclusion.

Les Cayes fell on August 1, 1800. On September 30 Adams's mission to France signed the treaty of Mortfontaine ending the quasi-war and, with it, Toussaint's peculiar position in relation to the United States. Jefferson, entering the presidency in March, 1801, approved of Adams's reorientation of policy, not because he wished ill to Toussaint Louverture, but because he welcomed a restoration of friendship with France. Indeed, the treaty was as much his as Adams's. Not only were Jeffersonian votes required to overcome Hamiltonian opposition in the Senate, but, long before that, it had been Jefferson's indirect intimation that French policy was playing into the hand of Hamilton, injuring the Francophile Jeffersonian party, and forcing the United States into alliance with Great Britain that had persuaded Talleyrand to make the original overture to Adams for a *rapprochement*.[46]

Talleyrand had a special reason for seeking to draw the United States away from Great Britain. He was thinking of a revival of the French colonial empire on the Mississippi, and if Hamilton, prompted by the British, were to seize New Orleans before France was ready to act, his scheme would be ruined. Unknown to the American plenipotentiaries, the secret treaty of San Ildefonso was being negotiated concurrently with that of Mortfontaine.[47] Reconciliation with the United States was only incidental to a larger plan directed toward the recovery of both Louisiana and Saint Domingue.

Jefferson had hardly been inaugurated when he heard rumors of the retrocession of Louisiana to France.[48] In July he had direct information of French intentions to reduce Toussaint Louverture at the first opportunity.[49] He could not be indifferent to the establishment of Napoleonic power at New Or-

[46] J. A. James, "French Opinion as a Factor in Preventing War between France and the United States, 1795-1800," *American Historical Review*, XXX (1924), 53.

[47] Bemis, *Diplomatic History*, pp. 123 f.

[48] *A. S. P., Foreign Relations*, II, 509.

[49] Carl Ludwig Lokke, "Jefferson and the Leclerc Expedition," *American Historical Review*, XXXIII (1928), 324.

leans, but, pending confirmation of that report, he could pursue a wary neutrality with regard to Saint Domingue. He valued the *rapprochement* with France above any American interest in the island, and therefore he would do what he could to avoid friction with the French, even to give them the impression that their project enjoyed the favor of the United States; but he bore no ill-will toward Toussaint Louverture. He still believed that the West Indies were destined to belong to the negroes of America, and, by inference, he doubted the ability of the French to recover their lost colony.[50] Tobias Lear, who had succeeded Stevens as consul general, was warned that an attempt to subdue Toussaint, with the moral support of Great Britain, was expected, and that the United States awaited the event with great anxiety; but his instructions were simply to do nothing that might offend the French and, so far as might be compatible with that, to do nothing to offend the people of the island.[51]

In December, 1801, Leclerc sailed for Saint Domingue,

[50] Jefferson to Monroe, Nov. 24, 1801, in H. A. Washington, *The Writings of Thomas Jefferson*, IV, 419-422.

[51] Madison to Lear, in cipher, Jan. 8, 1802, Cons. Let., Cape Haytien, IV. Lokke, in "Jefferson and the Leclerc Expedition," an article based on despatches found in the French archives, concludes that Jefferson was "personally eager to see French authority restored" and had given his pledge to lend material aid to the French attack, which was certainly the impression the French minister meant to convey to his government. However, the language ascribed to Jefferson is so un-Jeffersonian (in particular is it at variance with the letter to Monroe, with whom he had more reason to be candid, and with Lear's instructions), and it is so exactly what the Frenchman wanted to hear, that the present writer is led to the conclusion that Pichon put his own arguments into Jefferson's mouth, transmuting a disposition to listen, with vague encouragement, into positive assurances of support. An astute French diplomat did not catch a naïve Jefferson off guard, as Pichon boasted and Lokke repeats, but rather the roles were reversed, with Jefferson leading Pichon on and learning all he knew of French hopes and intentions. Charles C. Tansill bases the third chapter of his *United States and Santo Domingo* on conclusions identical with those of Lokke, citing the same sources, and this is the more remarkable in that a goodly portion of the chapter goes on to show that Jefferson did not actually pursue such a policy during the period in question. Pichon, Lokke, and Tansill are evidently misled by a failure to appreciate that Jefferson's attitude on the negro question was not typically Southern (see above, pp. 34 f.; below, pp. 67, 69). Jefferson entertained no hostility toward Toussaint Louverture and never seriously considered active aid to the French. Indeed, Leclerc attributed Louverture's resistance to the moral and material aid of the United States (Thomas H. Lechaud, "Lettres du General Leclerc," *Revue d'histoire et de géographie d'Haiti*, No. 27 (1937), p. 28), but that was also a misconception.

and at the same time the American minister at Paris wrote, "I know that the armament destined in the first instance for Hispaniola is to proceed to Louisiana provided Toussaint makes no opposition."[52] This positive information ended Jefferson's neutrality regarding Saint Domingue—it made Toussaint Louverture his first line of defense—but Lear was again instructed: "It is particularly the wish of the President that no just grounds or specious pretext may be left for complaint or suspicion on the part of the French Republic of want of respect for its authority in the Government of the United States."[53] If Toussaint would only provide sufficient time, Jefferson still hoped to keep the French out of New Orleans, not by force but by persuasion, preserving American interests on the Mississippi and Franco-American friendship as well. Although a Napoleonic establishment in Louisiana would constitute a serious menace to the territorial integrity of the United States on the western waters, the President remained calm, contenting himself with another unofficial intimation that unwise French policy might drive the United States into the arms of Britain. Only when the Federalists seized the issue to threaten his position in domestic politics did he press vigorously for the purchase of New Orleans and the Floridas.[54] One reason for his composure was his expectation that the next European crisis would take Napoleon out of America—and that he would not yield till then.[55] Another was that he counted on Toussaint Louverture to "make opposition."

Lear soon obtained positive information that some of Leclerc's regiments were destined for Louisiana, but at the same time he was able to observe that no troops could be spared from Saint Domingue for an indefinite period.[56] Accepting his opinion, Jefferson wrote in June: "What has been called the surrender of Toussaint to Leclerc, I suspect was in reality the

[52] Livingston to King, Dec. 30, 1801, Despatches, France, VIII. This news could not have reached Washington before Lear's instructions of Jan. 8 were sent out.
[53] Madison to Lear, Feb. 28, 1802, Cons. Let., Cape Haytien, IV.
[54] Bemis, *Diplomatic History*, pp. 129 ff.
[55] Ford, *The Writings of Jefferson*, VIII, 295.
[56] Lear to Madison, March 22 and 29, 1802, Cons. Let., Cape Haytien, IV.

surrender of Leclerc to Toussaint."[57] It was so in effect, for, although Toussaint might be removed, the negro regiments were still intact, under their own officers—and Tobias Lear had observed that the unsanitary condition of twice-devastated Cap Français boded ill for the French during the approaching sickly season.[58]

On November 28, 1802, Leclerc succumbed to yellow fever, leaving but a remnant of his army to face a population once more risen in arms, the occupation of New Orleans indefinitely postponed. Undaunted, Napoleon assembled reinforcements in Holland, only to see his transports caught fast in early ice. A new European crisis came before the thaw. On March 8 Monroe sailed for France to try to buy New Orleans. On April 11 Talleyrand astonished Livingston by offering to sell the whole of Louisiana to the United States.[59]

American commerce returned to Haitian ports as they were successively evacuated by the French, the vessels sailing in armed convoys for protection from privateers, the government giving no sign either to encourage or restrain them. The British, at war with France and therefore not bound to be so circumspect, approached Dessalines with an offer of protection in exchange for exclusive commercial privileges. As in 1798, their real object was to obtain a degree of political ascendancy that would render Jamaica secure, as the alternative threat to destroy any Haitian vessel found more than five leagues from the coast showed.[60] At the moment Haiti needed no protection from France, but the British used the word in the gangster sense. The Haitian chiefs feared the British accordingly and would have liked to invoke the United States as a counterpoise, but they were afraid that France would be able to compel the American government to side against them. American merchants begged Jefferson to give Dessalines some sign of friendship in order that the British might be forestalled.[61]

[57] Jefferson to McKean, June 14, 1802, in Henry Adams, *History of the United States*, I, 414.

[58] Lear to Madison, April 8, 1802, Cons. Let., Cape Haytien, IV.

[59] Bemis, *Diplomatic History*, pp. 134 f.

[60] A. N. Léger, *Histoire diplomatique d'Haiti*, pp. 7 ff.

[61] J. Lewis to Madison, Oct. 1, 1804, Cons. Let., Cape Haytien, IV.

Haitian anxiety concerning American policy was well justified, for Napoleon had been demanding, in most peremptory tones, that all trade with the rebels be stopped forthwith.[62]   It happened that at that juncture Jefferson was involved in a serious dispute with Spain over the undefined boundaries of Louisiana and could not afford to offend imperial France, on whose diplomatic support he relied.   Consequently, an administration bill was introduced in Congress prohibiting trade with any portion of "St. Domingo" that did not acknowledge the authority of France[63]—exactly the reverse of the embargo of 1798.   It was opposed by the Federalists, on party grounds and in the interest of commerce, and was defeated in 1805, but when the newly elected Congress assembled, the Jeffersonian steam-roller was found to be in better order and the bill was duly enacted in February, 1806.[64]

The new embargo had its *raison d'être* in the diplomatic situation of 1804-1806 and did not spring from any antipathy toward Haiti.   The bill was introduced by a senator from Pennsylvania and was supported by administration members from all sections of the country.   A Federalist senator from North Carolina voted with his New England colleagues against it.   Yet the debates revealed a cleavage more fundamental than that between the administration and the opposition.   The representatives of the mercantile interest of the Northeast were ready to recognize Haitian independence for the furtherance of trade; the spokesmen of the plantation interest were eager to establish a quarantine against the contagion of servile revolt.

Before 1790 the only section of the United States particularly concerned with Saint Domingue had been New England, and its sole concern had been with trade—low-grade fish for cheap molasses.   In 1793 both the mercantile and the plantation interests had been shocked by the consequences of the introduction of the Declaration of the Rights of Man to the servile population of the French colony.   But such was the nature of the

---

[62] *A. S. P., Foreign Relations*, II, 725.

[63] The French still held two thirds of the island, the former *partie espagnole*.

[64] *Annals of Congress*, 8th Cong., 2d Sess., p. 65; 9th Cong., 1st Sess., pp. 26, 138, 515.

mercantile interest that it must adapt itself to changing conditions in order to survive, so that, by 1806, it was ready to
accept the results of measures it had deplored. The planters
were under no such immediate compulsion—indeed, their survival seemed to them to depend on holding their ground. In
1799 commerce had ruled, but in 1806 the planters were in
power, and, such are the paradoxes of politics, they were there
under the captaincy of Thomas Jefferson, champion of the obnoxious Rights of Man.

CHAPTER III

RECOGNITION REFUSED

*Our policy with regard to Hayti is plain. We never can acknowl-
edge her independence . . . which the peace and safety of a large portion of our Union forbids us to even discuss.*—ROBERT Y. HAYNE, 1825

THE SPECIAL embargo against Haiti, re-enacted in 1807 and
again in 1808, was allowed to lapse in 1809, none daring to
propose its renewal in the midst of the uproar attendant upon
the repeal of Jefferson's unfortunate general embargo of 1807.
Merchants were then free to salvage what they could from the
ruin of their former commerce, but it was clear that planters
stood ready to pounce on any suggestion of recognition.

In 1809 there was no rush of traders to Haiti such as there
had been when commerce was reopened in 1799.[1] Exports to
the French West Indies (including Haiti) in the fiscal year 1810
amounted to only $109,000, a paltry 2 per cent of the value of
goods sold to Toussaint Louverture alone in 1800, and for the
duration of the world war then in progress the annual average
was no more than $237,000. This average increased tenfold
for the peace years, 1815-1819, and in 1821, when Haiti was
listed separately for the first time, exports thither were valued
at $2,270,000, but, even though somewhat better than the figure
for 1790, this was at best only 44 per cent of the business done
with Louverture. Moreover, during the interval the total
value of American export trade had trebled, so that Haiti, having taken some 11 per cent of it in 1790 and 7 per cent in 1800,
drew only 3 per cent in 1821. Similarly, although the value
of American imports from Haiti was $2,246,000 in 1821, as
compared to some $1,663,000 in 1789, it constituted little more

---

[1] American exports to Haiti in the fiscal year 1800 were valued at $5,123,000,
more than double the estimated figure for 1790, about the same as that for 1797
(*A. S. P., Commerce and Navigation,* I).

than 3 per cent of the total.[2] Thus, even if independent Haiti should be able to maintain the production and consumption standards set during the colonial regime, the relative importance of its commerce to the United States had declined to such a degree that its political influence was no longer comparable to that of the trade with Saint Domingue.

When Yankee merchants returned to Haiti, they discovered that their British competitors had not been idle during their absence. The Haitians had rejected Great Britain's more extreme demands for commercial monopoly and a quasi-protectorate, but, abandoned by the United States, they had been obliged to grant British ships and British goods a 50 per cent reduction in duties.[3] Even so, American merchants could undersell all others in the provisions trade (and they were unprepared to compete in any other), but in 1811 Henri Christophe dealt them another blow that reduced their commerce with his dominions to naught. The Anglophile king of the North, finding himself unable to recover certain sums which he had entrusted to the firm of Von Kapff & Brune, of Baltimore, seized the property of other American merchants to the amount of $124,955.19, informing his innocent victims that they might obtain redress from his debtors, if they could.[4] The failure of the United States to present spoliation claims at once is explained by the fact that there had been no American agent at Cap Haitien since Leclerc expelled Tobias Lear, and no special emissary could find an American vessel that dared visit the realm of King Henri.[5]

Three special agents did succeed in reaching the Cape during Christophe's reign, all arriving on board warships for lack of any other means of conveyance rather than in hope of overawing the black chief. All met with the same frigid reception.

[2] A. S. P., Commerce and Navigation, I-II; Emile Levasseur, Histoire du commerce de la France, p. 531.

[3] William Taylor to James Monroe, March 22, 1816 (Cons. Let., Cape Haytien, V).

[4] House Document No. 36, 27th Cong., 3d Sess., p. 36.

[5] Septimus Tyler to Pleasanton, March 20, 1817 (Cons. Let., Cape Haytien, V); Jacob Lewis to Rush, May 1, 1817 (Special Agents, hereinafter abbreviated Spec. Agts., II).

Monsieur le Comte de Limonade,[6] secretary of state for foreign
affairs, declined to recognize the official character of a stranger
appearing with an informal certificate to the effect that he was
to act as agent of the United States at "Cape François in the
Island of St. Domingo." These were declared to be "unusual
and inadmissable terms . . . both improper and injurious to
the government of His Majesty."[7] It being well known that
"Cap Français" and "Saint Domingue" had been suppressed
locally for more than a dozen years, as being too suggestive
of French sovereignty, their use did indicate that the United
States was studiously avoiding even an implied recognition of
Haitian independence, but lack of formal recognition was not
the real difficulty. No bother about credentials marred the welcome of British agents at Christophe's court, although it still
suited "the character of the British Nation" to deal informally
"with a Person of Toussaint's Description." Even the agents
of the governor of Louisiana could get a hearing there, denied
to the agents of the President of the United States.[8] In fact,
King Henri was anxious to avoid, on any pretext, a discussion of
his impulsive sequestration.

Pétion at Port-au-Prince was glad to maintain friendly relations with the United States, however informal they might be,
perhaps because he sought a counterpoise for British intimacy
with Christophe. In 1813 he received a commercial agent whose
real mission was to secure leave for American cruisers to bring
their prizes into his ports. The Haitian president dared not
go so far, lest Great Britain take the occasion to intervene in
behalf of Christophe, but he did allow American vessels to
refit and provision in his harbors.[9] In 1814, when, except for
an occasional raider, the American navy had been driven from

---

[6] American writers invariably exploit this title and that of the Count of Mar-
melade. Both are pre-revolutionary place-names in northern Haiti.

[7] *House Document No. 36* (27.3), p. 117.

[8] The question concerned the release of a young gentleman of New Orleans,
held as a French spy. While a Federal agent spent two years in fruitless search for
a merchant vessel that would take him to the Cape, the governor hired a boat, sent
a demand for his man, and got him. No pecuniary claim was involved (Monroe to
Lewis, June 8, 1816; Lewis to J. Q. Adams, Jan. 25, 1819, Spec. Agts., II).

[9] Taylor to Monroe, Dec. 10, 1813, Cons. Let., Cape Haytien, V.

the seas, the agent complained that Pétion had become "barely
friendly,"[10] but, considering his precarious position between
Great Britain, Christophe, and the restored Bourbons—and the
impotence of the United States—it is remarkable that he ventured to be friendly at all. At the end of the war Pétion indicated that he would gladly terminate the tariff favors accorded
to Great Britain if he could have some assurance of American
friendship,[11] but Madison ignored his overture.

Early in 1821 an agent was sent to see whether anything
could be collected from Jean-Pierre Boyer for Christophe's
great sequestration of 1811. He was well received, but there
were pointed remarks about credentials. As head of a reunited
country Boyer could adopt a firmer tone than Pétion had ever
used. Although he had come into possession of Christophe's
well-stocked treasury (including the ill-gotten gains of 1811),
he denied responsibility for the acts of that "rebel." If the
United States would cite international law on the question, let
the United States first recognize Haiti as a nation. When the
agent suggested that the tariff discriminations in favor of Great
Britain constituted an obstacle to good relations, Boyer seized
the opening, saying that he did not insist on formal recognition,
that he would deprive the British of their special privileges
the moment the United States showed him the same consideration as that accorded the unrecognized revolutionary governments of Spanish America. He was proud, the agent reported,
but pathetically eager to win the friendship of the United
States.[12]

The overture having passed unnoticed, on July 6, 1822,
Joseph Balthazar Inginac, Boyer's secretary general, addressed
himself directly to Secretary of State John Quincy Adams,
pointing to the commercial ties between the two countries,
Haiti's eighteen years of independence, and the recent reunion
of the whole island. Inviting the United States to be the first
power to recognize the second republic of the New World, he

[10] *Idem* to *idem*, Aug. 30, 1814, *loc. cit.*
[11] Pétion to Taylor, May 9, 1815; Taylor to Monroe, March 22, 1816, *loc. cit.*
[12] Edward Wyer to J. Q. Adams, April 10, 1821, Spec. Agts., IX.

requested the courtesy of a reply.[13] The letter was transmitted by an American merchant, who added that Haitian imports from the United States, worth some two million dollars, were a fifth of Haiti's total, and that this trade would be immensely stimulated by recognition, which would mean the destruction of the privileged position of Great Britain.[14] Simultaneously the northeastern press began to plug for recognition. *Niles' Register*, in an article condemning Christophe but praising Boyer, acknowledged that the independence of Haiti was an undeniable fact, even though the editor regarded its recognition as inexpedient in the existing organization of society.[15] In December the Senate called for information. President Monroe replied, admitting that the island had been united and that its government was not molested in the exercise of sovereignty by any European power, but arguing that France had withheld recognition, that the Haitian constitution betrayed an anti-white, not merely anti-French, animus, and that American commerce was discriminated against. The policy of the government, he declared, was to promote commerce while guarding against anything likely to disturb the tranquility of any portion of the Union[16]—that is, while refusing recognition on account of the fears of the South.

By 1824 Boyer was willing to forego recognition until American opinion was ready for it, but he wanted assurances of American neutrality in the event of a Franco-Haitian war, which then seemed imminent. The Monroe Doctrine was of no comfort to him; he anticipated a Franco-American alliance for his subjugation.[17] With no assurances forthcoming, in 1825 he pressed for recognition once more, offering to forbid Haitians to travel in the United States south of the Potomac and to send

<hr>

[13] Cons. Let., Cape Haytien, V. It was endorsed, "Not to be answered—(By direction of the President)—."

[14] William Dawson to J. Q. Adams, Aug. 8, 1822, *loc. cit.* American exports to Haiti in the fiscal year 1822 were actually valued at $2,119,811 (*A. S. P., Commerce and Navigation*, II, 738).

[15] *Niles' Register*, XXV (1823), 50-53.   [16] *A. S. P., Foreign Relations*, V, 240.

[17] Andrew Armstrong to J. Q. Adams, Oct. 8, 1824, Cons. Let., Cape Haytien, V. As in 1801, the British, still nervous about Jamaica, had given the French their blessing.

a diplomatic agent "such in color as not to offend the prejudices of the country."[18]   Moreover, without further bargaining he acted to place British commerce on the same footing as that of the United States.[19]   All in vain.   Although Christophe's victims were still clamoring for recognition as their only hope, the Cabinet decided against it.[20]

In April, 1825, the King of France decreed that the ports of "Saint Domingue" should be open to the commerce of all nations, that French vessels should enjoy a 50 per cent reduction in duties there, that the present inhabitants should pay a huge indemnity to the former colonists, and that, on these conditions, they might establish an independent government.[21]   In this peculiar fashion France acknowledged the loss of a colony that had been actually independent for a generation by inviting her former slaves to buy the freedom that they already possessed.   Boyer submitted to the decree as an unpleasant alternative to war, which, even if successful, would have been ruinous, and thus the way was opened to recognition by other powers. Great Britain, the Netherlands, Sweden, and Denmark acted promptly, and it appeared that the United States, having hitherto officially regarded Haiti as an errant French dependency, might have occasion to reconsider.

At the same time President John Quincy Adams proposed to accept the invitation of Colombia to send a delegation to a congress of American states at Panama.   In Congress the adherents of Andrew Jackson opposed the plan, for purely partisan reasons, but one group among them was in bitter earnest. Colombia, having herself refused recognition to Haiti[22] and denied her an invitation to the congress, had suggested that the assembled American nations might consider a uniform rule of

[18] *Idem* to *idem*, Jan. 25, 1825, *loc. cit.*
[19] *Idem* to *idem*, April 8, 1825, *loc. cit.* This was partly to satisfy American demands, partly to punish the British for having ignored Haiti when recognizing the Spanish American republics.
[20] C. F. Adams, *Memoirs of John Quincy Adams*, VI, 233.
[21] J. N. Léger, *Recueil des traités et conventions de la République de Haiti*, p. 1.
[22] This despite the fact that Pétion had materially aided Bolívar to achieve Colombia's own independence, and because of Colombian umbrage at Boyer's annexation of Santo Domingo.

conduct toward their negro neighbor.[23] The capitol rang with Southern cries of indignation.

> With nothing connected with slavery [exclaimed Senator Robert Y. Hayne of South Carolina] can we treat with other nations. . . . Our policy with regard to Hayti is plain. We never can acknowledge her independence. . . .[24]

Senator Thomas Hart Benton of Missouri voiced an argument long the favorite among the opponents of recognition:

> Our policy towards Hayti . . . has been fixed . . . for three and thirty years. We trade with her, but no diplomatic relations have been established between us. . . . We receive no mulatto consuls, or black ambassadors from her. And why? Because the peace of eleven states will not permit the fruits of a successful negro insurrection to be exhibited among them. It will not permit black ambassadors and consuls to . . . give their fellow blacks in the United States proof in hand of the honors that await them for a like successful effort on their part. It will not permit the fact to be seen, and told, that for the murder of their masters and mistresses, they are to find friends among the white people of these United States.[25]

Senator McPherson Berrien of Georgia compared the mercantile and plantation interest in this question:

> These merely *commercial* considerations sink into insignificance —they are swallowed up in the magnitude of the danger with which we are menaced. . . . Do our brethren differ from us as to the danger of this intercourse? . . . *Ours* is the *post of danger. They* are in comparative *safety*. Who, then, should decide the question?[26]

The planters had spoken, and the question had already been decided. President Adams, anxious to save his cherished Panama mission from the assaults of his enemies, sought to quiet the storm by demonstrating his orthodoxy. In a message to the House of Representatives he pointed out that it had long been the deliberate policy of the government (in which he had

---

[23] *A. S. P., Foreign Relations*, V, 836.
[24] *Register of Debates in Congress*, II, Pt. I, pp. 165-166.
[25] *Ibid.*, p. 330. [26] *Ibid.*, p. 291.

been secretary of state before succeeding to the presidency) to deny recognition to Haiti, and continued:

> Additional reasons for withholding that acknowledgment have recently been seen in their acceptance of a nominal sovereign[ty] by the *grant* of a foreign prince under conditions equivalent to the concession by them of exclusive commercial advantages to one nation, adapted altogether to a state of colonial vassalage, and retaining little of independence but the name.   Our plenipotentiaries will be instructed to present these views to the assembly at Panama and, should they not be concurred in, to decline acceding to any arrangements which may be proposed upon different principles.[27]

The American commercial agent wrote despairingly that trade must suffer if the United States insisted on being the only maritime power refusing recognition to Haiti,[28] but to no avail. In January, 1827, an angry Haitian government informed him that he could no longer be received officially.[29] In March, 1829, a discriminatory 10 per cent increase in customs and tonnage duties was levied against American vessels in Haitian ports.[30] This action was ostensibly in retaliation against a similar imposition on alien vessels in American ports, but, since there was no Haitian merchant marine and since the law objected to had been on the books for forty years, the pretense was transparent, as it was intended to be.   Alien vessels could obtain exemption from the American imposition by treaty only.   Thus Haiti gave subtle notice that American vessels could obtain relief from discrimination in Haitian ports only at the price of recognition and a commercial treaty.

From 1821 through 1825 American exports to Haiti averaged $2,237,793 a year, with imports about evenly balanced, but in 1826 there was a sharp break followed by a dizzy plunge to $823,178 in 1830.   A rebound from this low figure was inevitable, since, despite extra duties, no competitor could supply

---

[27] *A. S. P., Foreign Relations*, V, 885. Thus the curious ordinance of Charles X was made a reason for denying recognition to Haiti rather than for granting it.

[28] Armstrong to Henry Clay, June 8, 1826, Cons. Let., Cape Haytien, V.

[29] Inginac to Armstrong, Jan. 31, 1827, *loc. cit.*, VI.

[30] Samuel Israel to Clay, March 20, 1829, *loc. cit.*

Haiti with essential provisions so cheaply and conveniently as could the Americans and no indignation could hold out against low prices. American exports to Haiti did level off at an annual average value of $1,177,000 during the next twenty years, reaching a peak of $1,815,812 in 1835 and striking new lows at $653,370 in 1843 and $602,592 in 1849, but the United States had definitely fallen from first or second to third or fourth place in the Haitian market, where fourth place was customarily reserved for "All Others." Moreover, after 1825 the balance of trade was regularly in Haiti's favor, sometimes by wide margins, although the decline of American exports pulled American imports of Haitian products down with it.[31] Merchants at home and commercial agents in Haiti agreed that these deplorable conditions could be remedied only by the recognition of Boyer's long-established government.[32]

It had been demonstrated that on the issue of Haitian recognition the mercantile interest could not prevail, unaided, against the fierce determination of the planters, but in the eighteen-thirties the merchants found welcome allies in the growing abolitionist movement. During the fight on the "Gag Rule," which caused petitions on the subject of slavery to be automatically tabled when presented in the House, John Quincy Adams substituted petitions for the recognition of Haiti for those thus thrust aside. Consequently, the occasional memorials of merchants and claimants in behalf of recognition were suddenly increased to 203 during the session of 1838-1839 and 159 during that of 1839-1840.[33] Southern members perceived the significance of the development. Hugh S. Legaré, of South Carolina, declaimed: "It is not for the paltry commerce of a horde of barbarians that agitation is beginning on this subject. . . . It

---

[31] *Report on the Commercial Relations of the United States,* 1856, I, 778-781.

[32] Petition of certain merchants of New York, Philadelphia, and Baltimore to President Jackson, March 15, 1830; Samuel Israel to Louis McLane, July 23, 1833, Cons. Let., Cape Haytien, VI.

[33] Adelaide R. Hasse, *Index to United States Documents Relating to Foreign Affairs, 1828-1861,* I, 720 f. They came principally from New England, New York, and Ohio, where abolitionists were most numerous. The number dwindled to six in 1840-1841 and remained low thereafter.

aims at *abolition*—is *not* for the benefit of commerce but for the ruin of the South."[34]   Waddy Thompson, of South Carolina, rose, "not to discuss the question, but, if possible, to arrest the discussion." It was dishonorable and degrading for a Southern man to discuss it. Nevertheless, he did, depicting anew the effect of the appearance of a black ambassador upon the security of the South.[35] The agitation did not result in the recognition of Haiti, but a militant combination of Northern merchants and abolitionists for that purpose was definitely established.

When, in 1844, the disorders accompanying the fall of Boyer enabled the Dominicans to assert their independence, they hastened to represent themselves to the United States as a white population struggling to escape from negro domination.[36]   This idea was uncritically received by Southern statesmen and enlisted their sympathy on the side of the insurgents. In sending an agent to investigate, Secretary of State John C. Calhoun made it plain that he favored recognition of the Dominicans if their claims were sustained.[37]   The agent brought back the sort of report that he thought was wanted,[38] but the Tyler administration had meanwhile retired from office and nothing was done, although Calhoun urged his successor, James Buchanan, to take favorable action.[39]   Renewed appeals from Santo Domingo induced President Polk to send another investigator, but the outbreak of the Mexican War shelved the question.[40]   Nevertheless, the Dominicans were not forgotten; the Whigs, in power from 1849 to 1853, held the "white" republic in as tender regard as had their Democratic predecessors. Secretary

[34] *Congressional Globe*, 25th Cong., 3d Sess., p. 48.

[35] Waddy Thompson, *Remarks on the Proposition to Recognize the Republic of Hayti*.

[36] José María Caminero to John C. Calhoun, Jan. 8, 1845, Notes from the Dominican Republic, I.

[37] Calhoun to John Hogan, Feb. 22, 1845, Special Mission, hereinafter abbreviated Spec. Miss., I.

[38] Hogan to James Buchanan, Oct. 4, 1845, Spec. Agts., XIII.

[39] Calhoun to Buchanan, Aug. 30, 1845, in John Bassett Moore, *The Works of James Buchanan*, VI, 230.

[40] David D. Porter, Journal of a Mission to Santo Domingo, 1846, Duke University MSS; "Secret Missions to San Domingo," *North American Review*, CXXVIII (1879), 616.

of State Daniel Webster, the antagonist of Hayne in the great debate of 1830, outdid Calhoun himself in his solicitude for Dominican liberties. This was a period of angry contention over slavery, the period of the Nashville Convention and the Compromise of 1850, and the Whig administration was evidently leaning over backward to avoid antagonizing, on one of its touchiest points, a section in which there had been so much rash talk of secession.

Secretary Clayton, in 1849, dispatched Benjamin C. Green as special agent to counteract European influence at Santo Domingo. Green saw that his mission could not be accomplished unless he could assure the Dominicans of American protection. He repeatedly urged the intervention of the United States, not on account of the Monroe Doctrine, but because the ambitions of the Haitian emperor, Faustin Soulouque, menaced the domestic security of the Southern States.[41] Clayton was unwilling to go so far, perhaps because he realized that it might lead to a collision with France and Britain, jeopardizing the Clayton-Bulwer Treaty, then in process of negotiation, and defeating its own purpose by causing those powers to throw their support to Haiti. In February, 1850, he was willing to leave the Dominicans to European protection.[42] They, however, afraid of Haiti and unable to persuade Great Britain, France, or the United States to intervene singly in their behalf, proposed a joint intervention of those powers, and Green urged American participation because he feared the Europeans would betray their clients to Soulouque.[43] Clayton no doubt understood that to oppose a probable Anglo-French intervention would be in

---

[41] Green to Clayton, No. 2, Sept. 27; No. 3, Oct. 24, 1849; No. 8, Feb. 19, 1850, Spec. Agts., XV.

[42] Clayton to Green, Feb. 16, 1850, Spec. Miss., I. The European powers had hitherto given the Dominicans their moral support, but their jealousy of each other as well as of the United States had prevented either from gaining an ascendancy at Santo Domingo. Their local agents had been active and ambitious, but the governments at Paris and London had been more conservative (Elliott to Clayton, May 2, 1849, Cons. Let., Santo Domingo, 1; Green to Clayton, No. 2, Sept. 27, 1849, Spec. Agts., XV; Schomburgk to Palmerston, May 22, 1849, P. R. O., F. O. 23/3; Palmerston to Schomburgk, June 8, 1849, F. O. 23/2).

[43] Delmonte to Green, Feb. 22, 1850; Green to Clayton, No. 8, Feb. 19; idem to idem, June 15, 1850, Spec. Agts., XV.

effect to support Haiti, the very opposite of his intention. However, he now had an opportunity, by participation, to keep check
on them, in the interest of the Dominicans, American ambitions
in Santo Domingo, and the Monroe Doctrine, without giving
offense. Casting off the spirit of resignation which had dictated
his instruction of February 16, he took an initiative in promoting
the plan by indicating to the British minister his readiness to
enter into a tripartite intervention. He also planned to recognize the Dominican Republic forthwith (another change of
front since February 16), but the death of President Taylor
caused his retirement before that had been accomplished.

Daniel Webster, Fillmore's secretary of state, appointed
another special agent, Robert M. Walsh, to act jointly with
the French and British consuls at Port-au-Prince in requiring
Soulouque to conclude a permanent peace or at least a ten-year
truce. "If," said Webster, "the remonstrance should prove to
be unavailing, you will signify to the Emperor that you shall
give immediate notice to your government that the President,
with the concurrence of Congress, may adopt such measures
. . . as may cause the intervention of the three powers to be
respected."[44] Walsh did not limit himself to this threat of war,
couched in the customary American diplomatic formula. He
told Soulouque that a filibustering expedition was being organized at Norfolk to go to the aid of the Dominicans, according
to his colleagues "the most effective shape of terror that could
be brought before the Imperial eyes."[45] Yet neither attempt at
intimidation had the desired effect. The emperor avoided an
answer for three months and then proposed to transfer the
negotiations to Paris, London, and Washington in an effort to

---

[44] Webster to Walsh, Jan. 18, 1851, Spec. Miss., I.
[45] Walsh to Webster, No. 3, March 3, 1851, Spec. Agts., XVIII. A. N.
Léger, in his *Histoire diplomatique d'Haiti*, p. 275, quotes the *Weekly Herald*
(N. Y.?) of April 17, 1850, as saying that it would not be surprised to see an
expedition leave some Southern port with the sanction of Washington to aid the
Dominicans, in the end annexing the whole island to the United States and reducing
Faustin I "to the condition for which nature has fitted him"—i.e., slavery. At the
time filibustering expeditions were sailing from Southern ports for Cuba, but with-
out the sanction of Washington (R. B. Caldwell, *The López Expeditions to Cuba*).

break up the combination of powers. His commission expiring at the end of April, 1851, Walsh left matters as they stood on his arrival. The European consuls eventually wrung a two-year truce from Soulouque by threatening a blockade, but the United States had no part in that accomplishment except to give its blessing.[46] If their tripartite intervention was a fiasco, the Whigs did at least succeed in restoring American commerce with Haiti to a most-favored-nation basis. In addition to his mission to Santo Domingo, Green had been instructed to touch at Port-au-Prince and negotiate to that end. Soulouque agreed to receive commercial agents and to remove the discriminatory customs and tonnage duties,[47] perhaps hoping to drive a wedge between the United States and the European powers, perhaps seeking to propitiate one American interest while preparing to offend another by attacking the Dominicans. Clayton's system of "partial recognition" resulted in some embarrassment, however, when Soulouque proceeded to appoint an American citizen to be Haitian consul at Boston. Webster was obliged to say that the appointee could not be accorded that title, implying recognition, although any person "not of African extraction" would be welcomed as a commercial agent."[48]

Although political relations might remain awkward and embittered because of nonrecognition, commerce, freed of its shackles, quickly returned to normal. American exports to Haiti were valued at $602,592 in 1849, $1,350,188 in 1850,

[46] This brief account of the tripartite intervention is based on voluminous correspondence in Spec. Agts., XV and XVIII, and in F. O. 35/40-41 and 23/7-11. Anyone wishing to follow these fruitless exchanges in detail can find the American documents printed in the sixth volume of W. R. Manning, *Diplomatic Correspondence of the United States: Inter-American Affairs, 1831-1860*, Vol. VI. The principal secondary accounts are H. M. Wriston, *Executive Agents in American Foreign Relations*, pp. 444-452; Dexter Perkins, *The Monroe Doctrine, 1826-1867*, pp. 262-266; and Tansill, *The United States and Santo Domingo, 1798-1873*, pp. 137-171.

[47] Usher to Clayton, May 13, June 20, 1850, Cons. Let., Port-au-Prince, III. Green was unable to obtain a settlement of the sequestration claims, but Clayton had regarded that as hopeless "so long as this government may deem it expedient to adhere to the punctilio in regard to recognizing that of Haiti, which has hitherto been paramount in our councils" (Clayton to Green, June 13, 1849, Spec. Miss., I).

[48] Webster to Walsh, Jan. 18, 1851, Spec. Miss., I.

$1,847,290 in 1851, and $2,245,052 in 1855. In addition to the natural monopoly of the provisions trade, American textiles and other manufactured goods began to enter competition with those of Europe. By 1856 Haiti had become a more valuable customer than Mexico, although her population was hardly an eighth of that of the continental republic.[49] However, instead of bringing recognition nearer, this development militated against it. The commercial agent at Port-au-Prince was enabled to argue that the United States no longer had anything to gain by such a measure, which might result in harm, and that citizens should therefore cease to agitate so "excitable" a question.[50] Indeed, there was not the least likelihood that the powers-that-were in Washington in the eighteen-fifties would even remotely consider recognizing Haiti.

The Pierce administration entered office in 1853 with the declaration that its policy would not be controlled "by any timid forebodings of evil from expansion." In November, William L. Cazneau was sent to make the fourth American investigation of the Dominican situation in ten years. His real mission was to secure the lease of a coaling station at Samaná Bay, but the indiscretions of Captain George B. McClellan, sent by Secretary of War Jefferson Davis to survey the site, gave his game away.[51] Anglo-French propaganda to the effect that the United States would seize the country, thrust the native whites aside, and enslave the blacks, created an uproar among the Dominicans; direct Anglo-French menaces persuaded their congress to reject not only the lease, but also a commercial treaty that would have embodied recognition.[52] When Faustin Soulouque launched his second invasion of the East, to combat the already defunct Yankee peril, the Dominicans, denied hope of American support, turned once more to

[49] *Commercial Relations*, 1856, I, 570, 778-781.
[50] Usher to Marcy, July 15, 1853, Cons. Let., Port-au-Prince, III.
[51] Marcy to Cazneau, June 17, 1854, Spec. Miss., III; Cazneau to Marcy, Aug. 8, 1854, Spec. Agts., XIX.
[52] Cazneau to Marcy, July 24, Aug. 8 and 19, Sept. 23, Nov. 23, 1854, Spec. Agts., XIX; Schomburgk to Clarendon, Aug. 22 and 28, Sept. 20, Oct. 5 and 7, Nov. 6 and 22, Dec. 7 and 21, 1854, F. O. 23/19; Clarendon to Schomburgk, Sept. 29, 1854, F. O. 23/19.

Europe for protection.[53] Soulouque was repelled, but the rout of the Americans was no less complete.

The Haitians had good reason to fear and resist American encroachment. Behind the face of the Dominican treaty they had to consider the frankly expansionist attitude of Pierce and the confirmed hostility of interests dominant in an administration in which Jefferson Davis was the power behind the throne. Moreover, Americans, both private individuals and official agents such as Green and Cazneau, had been speculating in Dominican concessions and colonization schemes which might, indeed, have made of that republic a second Texas.[54]

In 1858 the United States and Haiti came into direct conflict over a bit of territory claimed to be a part of Haiti proper. It was the island of Navassa, a barren, waterless square mile of limestone thrust above the sea some thirty miles west of Cape Tiburon, the nearest point on the Haitian coast, and about seventy-five miles east-north-east of Jamaica.[55] Until 1857 it had remained uninhabited and apparently derelict. It would never have been known except as a menace to navigation had its desolate shores not been the resort of countless generations of sea birds.

In September, 1857, Peter Duncan, a Baltimore shipmaster, took possession of Navassa under the Guano Islands Act of 1856, which provided that "whenever a citizen of the United States discovers a deposit of guano on any island . . . not within the lawful jurisdiction of any other Government, and not occupied by the citizens of any other Government, and takes peaceable possession thereof, and occupies the same, such island . . . may . . . be considered as appertaining to the United States." Duncan gave the required notice of his discovery, meanwhile assigning his rights to his employer, E. O. Cooper, who was extensively engaged in the Caribbean guano trade with his base at Kingston, Jamaica. E. K. Cooper, manager of the Baltimore

---

[53] Schomburgk to Clarendon, Jan. 6, 1855, F. O. 23/22.
[54] Schomburgk to Palmerston, June 8, 1850, F. O. 23/7; *idem* to Malmesbury, Aug. 23, 1852, F. O. 23/14; idem to Clarendon, Feb. 24, 1854, F. O. 23/18. Sumner Welles, *Naboth's Vineyard*, I, 154.
[55] U. S. Hydrographic Office, *Charts No. 1487* and *3500*.

branch of the business, dispatched an expedition to Navassa, and digging was started early in 1858.[56]

Cooper excluded his Jamaican partner, one Ramos, from a share in the Navassa venture.[57]   Ramos, harboring a grudge, knew how to get even.   He offered Her Britannic Majesty's consul general at Port-au-Prince a share in the venture if he would secure for him an exclusive Haitian concession for the exploitation of guano at Navassa.[58]   In this he merely copied a maneuver by means of which a Philadelphia firm had employed Venezuela to oust Boston and New York rivals from a derelict guano island in 1854, a story which must have been familiar to all guano traders in the Caribbean.[59]   When Henry Byron, the consul, inquired at the foreign office concerning Haiti's title to Navassa, he found the minister unaware of the existence of such a place and "evidently in complete ignorance as to whether Navassa was Haytian territory or not."   After Ramos had explained his scheme and depicted the handsome revenue which Haiti would enjoy as royalty, all doubt vanished from Haitian minds.[60]

Early in March, Byron learned for the first time that Americans had been in possession of Navassa since September and were already digging guano there.   Greatly excited by this blow to Haitian sovereignty (and to Ramos's prospects), he rushed to the foreign office with the news.   The Haitians, who for some time had been haggling with Ramos over their proper share in the anticipated profits of his enterprise, were equally shocked.   They had not become aware of this Yankee "invasion"

[56] *Senate Executive Document No. 37*, 36th Cong., 1st Sess., pp. 2-6.   See also Roy F. Nichols, "Navassa: A Forgotten Acquisition," *American Historical Review*, XXXVIII (1933), 505-510.

[57] Cooper said the breach resulted from losses attributed to Ramos's mismanagement *(ibid.)*.   Ramos later explained self-righteously that it was because he wished to take no guano from Navassa without Haiti's consent (Byron to Malmesbury, No. 30, June 26, 1858, F. O. 35/51), a pretension which may be regarded skeptically in the circumstances.

[58] Byron to Malmesbury, No. 30, June 26, 1858, F. O. 35/51.

[59] *Senate Executive Document No. 25*, 34th Cong., 3d Sess., pp. 4-7.   It was expressly to forestall similar occurrences that the Guano Islands Act had been passed in 1856.

[60] Byron to Clarendon, No. 12, March 10, 1858, F. O. 35/51.

until six months after the event, and had learned of it then only by way of Jamaica,[61] but it wounded them none the less deeply, for, Ramos having taught them that the unheard-of rock had value, they were sure that it had always been theirs indeed.[62] They would defend their title—and their golden dreams.

Six weeks later, on April 20, the Haitian navy put to sea,[63] and on May 21 it appeared off Navassa. Haitian officials landed, declared the island to be a dependency of the empire, and invited the American manager to apply for Haitian permission to operate there. He witnessed their declaration, but refused either to abandon the place or to acknowledge himself to be a trespasser. No attempt was made to expel him by force. In July the Haitians returned with Ramos, they ordering the Americans to withdraw and he suggesting that they might remain if they would turn the place over to him and enter his employ. This expedition also was a complete failure.[64]

Meanwhile, on June 24, the Coopers had appealed to President Buchanan for protection and declared that the Haitians had blockaded the island, imperiling the lives of eighty-odd Americans on that barren and waterless rock, and on July 7 the navy had been ordered to the rescue. When the U. S. S. *Saratoga* reached Navassa in August, no Haitians were in sight, but her commander decided to proceed to Port-au-Prince to warn

[61] Commodore Kellett to Byron, Feb. 26, 1858, in Byron's No. 12. Prompted by the inquiries of Ramos, Byron had written to Kellett at Port Royal to ask if Navassa might be a dependency of Jamaica. The commodore replied that he did not know to whom Navassa belonged, but that Americans had been in possession since September.

[62] Byron to Clarendon, No. 12, March 10, 1858, F. O. 35/51.

[63] Byron and his French colleague, Mellinet, had suggested that a Haitian vessel be sent to reconnoitre Navassa. On learning that gunboats had sailed they protested vigorously, demanding precise explanations of the strength and true destination of the force. Their language suggests that they were less afraid of a Haitian-American collision, which the United States might use as a pretext for forceful intervention in Haitian affairs, than suddenly reminded of their probable instructions to discourage all Haitian naval activity. An expedition, ostensibly to Navassa, might cloak a subversive attempt on Jamaica or a raid on the Dominican Republic (Mellinet and Byron to Dufrene, April 24 and 28, 1858, in Léger, *Histoire diplomatique*, pp. 305 f.).

[64] Léger, *Histoire diplomatique*, pp. 307 f.; *Senate Executive Document No. 37*, 36.1, p. 12; Appendix A, Preston to Fish, July 19, 1872, Notes from Haiti, II.

Soulouque against molesting the guano diggers. He found that Haiti still claimed the island, but that Ramos had been repudiated, Byron having refused to support him. Commander Turner was convinced that Soulouque had acted in anticipation of British support, which had failed to materialize.[65] Since Cooper could not be dislodged, the emperor could hope for guano revenue only if he could induce him to accept a Haitian concession, eliminating Ramos,[66] or if he could persuade the United States to withdraw its protection.

In November the Haitian commercial agent at Boston addressed a protest to the Secretary of State, essaying to trace the Haitian title from Navassa's first discovery by a Spaniard through the Treaty of Ryswick to the recognition of Haiti by France. A sufficient demonstration of Haitian sovereignty on the mainland, this failed to show that the island had ever been included definitely in Haitian jurisdiction. The Secretary's reply, accompanied by a copy of the Guano Islands Act, was a simple statement that Navassa was considered to have been derelict. The Haitian agent attempted to argue the question, but he could never get more than that assertion from the department, which soon ceased to answer his letters.[67]

Fourteen years later a Haitian minister reopened the case and debated it at length (136 pages of foolscap, accompanied by numerous charts), without being able to do more than embellish the argument submitted in 1858.[68] After combing the archives of Paris as well as those of Port-au-Prince, he was able

[65] *Senate Executive Document No. 37, 36.1*, pp. 7-10, 16-18. Byron had certainly encouraged the Haitians to claim Navassa. On March 9, while noting the peculiar ignorance of the island at the Haitian foreign office, he had assumed that the Haitian title was good, perhaps for the sake of the success of the Ramos project. However, on June 26, while still expressing confidence in Ramos, he had described the Haitian claim as open to "considerable doubt" (Byron to Clarendon, No. 12, March 10; to Malmesbury, No. 30, June 26, 1858, F. O. 35/51). Turner believed that Byron's eventual repudiation of Ramos had followed his discovery of the latter's true character and motive.

[66] The Guano Islands Act fixed a maximum price, but under a Haitian concession the law of diminishing returns would be the only restraint. Thus Cooper could afford to cut Soulouque in on the deal without loss to himself, perhaps even with gain—if he dared forego the protection of the United States.

[67] Appendix B, Preston to Fish, July 19, 1872, Notes from Haiti, II.

[68] *Idem* to *idem*, July 19, 1872, March 19, 1873, *loc. cit.*

to prove conclusively that the existence of Navassa had been known for centuries, but not that it had ever been occupied, ever inhabited, ever specifically incorporated in the jurisdiction of Haiti or of any other power. In the imposing array of his citations there was one notable omission, the *Géographie de l'île d'Haïti* of Beaubrun Ardouin, foremost Haitian authority on the subject. According to Ardouin, "the adjacent islands belonging to Haiti, were la Gonave, Ile-a-Vaches, la Beate, Altavela, la Saone, Ste. Catherine, la Mona, Monica, and la Tortue." He did not mention Navassa.[69] His work was published in 1856, the year of the passage of the Guano Islands Act, before Peter Duncan had revealed the value of Navassa, before Ramos had visited Port-au-Prince.[70]

In the discussions of 1872-1873 the Haitian minister did score one point. He was able to show that in 1858 the United States had not acted toward Haiti with the consideration shown other powers in similar cases. No Navassa affair was needed to demonstrate that discrimination. The policy of the United States toward Haiti since 1806—particularly since 1825—had been controlled by a deliberate determination to deny her the consideration to which her actual independence and generally acknowledged sovereignty entitled her. Such a policy was inevitable as long as the South could exert decisive influence in the councils of the Union.

[69] Ardouin, *La géographie de l'île d'Haïti*, p. 23.

[70] The American guano diggers remained in unvexed possession of Navassa until 1898, when the place was evacuated in panic to escape capture by the Spaniards. It had been regularly supplied with vegetables by boatmen from Jamaica, Haiti, and Inagua, and when these simple folk found no one there they helped themselves to all that they could carry away. The Spaniards, who never came, could hardly have wrought more havoc. The guano company did not survive the blow. It sold all that was left of its movable property to the admiral of the Haitian navy for $500 and went out of business (Powell to Hay, No. 511, Feb. 13, 1899, Despatches, Haiti, XXXIV; New York *Times*, May 31, 1901). In 1917 the United States erected a lighthouse there, the island lying, a serious menace, directly in the track of vessels sailing between Panama and the Atlantic seaboard. The present population of Navassa consists of a lighthouse keeper and radio operators (U. S. Hydrographic Office, Jan. 30, 1935).

CHAPTER IV

NEGRO COLONIZATION

Nothing is more certainly written in the book of fate than that these people are to be free; nor is it less certain that the two races equally free cannot live under the same government.
—THOMAS JEFFERSON, 1821

Listen, then, all ye negroes and mulattoes who, in the vast continent of America, suffer from prejudice of caste: the Republic calls you.
—FABRE GEFFRARD, 1860

FROM 1806 to 1862 the Haitian policy of the United States, determined by Southern influences, was founded upon anxiety concerning the security of the institution of slavery and of the social order based upon it. That institution, inherited from a less enlightened age, was easier to condemn in theory than to discard in practice. Any considered program to that end must reckon with the necessity for profound social and economic readjustments involving the interests of the freedmen as well as those of the masters, and so face a problem more fundamental than slavery itself, a problem that emancipation would intensify rather than solve—prejudice of color. Would freedmen be admitted to a plane of social and political equality? Public sentiment, in the North as well as in the South, was not prepared to give an affirmative answer. Should they then be discriminated against, though technically free? That was the fate of the free negro, but obviously, while it disposed of slavery, it left the basic problem of the mixed community still unsolved. The unpleasant fact was that, according to the prejudice of the times, negroes were not regarded as desirable members of the community and their presence in large numbers could be tolerated only if most of them were held in bondage and all of them in subordination.

The only attempt to deal with slavery which reckoned also with race prejudice was the negro colonization movement, itself a surrender to prejudice since it sought to avoid that difficulty by separating the two elements of the mixed community. A Jefferson, *ami des noirs*, could look upon the creation of purely negro states as the only practicable means of procuring for the negroes an opportunity for untrammeled development—and also as the only means of freeing the white community of an awkward, perhaps dangerous, incubus. Logically, this conception of a separate negro nationality was favorable to the interests of Haiti, the original embodiment of the idea, yet actually the history of the colonization movement illuminates the passions and prejudices which prevented the recognition of Haitian independence.

In 1776 slavery existed in all the states, for colonial efforts to arrest its growth had been frustrated by royal tenderness for the slave trade of England and New England. During the next thirty years the institution was summarily abolished in New Hampshire and Massachusetts, and its gradual extinction was provided for in Pennsylvania, Connecticut, Rhode Island, New York, and New Jersey. In all those states negroes were relatively few in number, so that their liberation would not disturb the established social order, but thence southward a different situation existed.[1] The progress of emancipation was checked at the northern border of Maryland because the best minds of the South, while detesting slavery, could devise no solution for the problems which the abolition of slavery must inevitably raise. This failure is no reflection on them, since those problems remain largely unsolved today.

While Southern leaders pondered the question, the revolutionary opportunity was lost and a reaction set in, as illustrated by the trend of thought in Virginia during the first thirty years of independence. The several attempts of the colonial legislature to prevent or curtail the introduction of negroes having been defeated by royal prerogative, the subject was taken up by the revolutionary assembly, to which Thomas Jefferson pro-

---

[1] In 1790 the ratio of white to negro population in the free states was ninety-nine to one, that in the states which eventually adopted gradual emancipation was twenty to one, and that in the South less than two to one.

posed gradual emancipation coupled with deportation of the freedmen.[2] His scheme was dismissed as impracticable, but in 1778 the further importation of slaves was prohibited, with provision that those brought in illegally should be set free, and in 1782 manumission was authorized.[3] Thus, although there was an evident desire to limit the colored population, there was no objection to an increase in the proportion of free negroes among those already in the community. However, in 1806, after events in Haiti and at home had bred a fear of race conflict, it was enacted that negroes illegally imported should be confiscated and sold (not set free), and that freedmen must emigrate within one year of their manumission or forfeit their freedom and be sold.[4] In this way the idea of making emigration an essential condition of emancipation finally reached the statute book, but the law, applying only to individual cases, fell far short of Jefferson's proposal. Not only was hope of ridding the commonwealth of slavery growing dim, but there was evident a feeling that if negroes must remain in a white community they had better be bond than free.[5]

In 1800 the detection of a servile conspiracy at Richmond had resulted in the execution of thirty negroes in compliance with the laws for the preservation of the peace,[6] but public opinion had been more profoundly shocked by the necessity for this harsh action than by the fact of the conspiracy itself. In their hearts Virginians were inclined to admit that a bondsman might be justified in plotting to secure his freedom, even by violence against society. Consequently, the assembly requested Governor Monroe to correspond with President Jefferson regarding the purchase of land in the West "whither persons obnoxious to the laws or dangerous to the peace . . . might be removed," and Monroe raised the question of whether all the

---

[2] Washington, *The Writings of Thomas Jefferson*, I, 48 f.

[3] W. W. Hening, *The Statutes at Large, 1619-1792*, IX, 471 f.; XI, 39.

[4] Samuel Shepherd, *The Statutes at Large of Virginia, 1792-1806*, III, 251 ff.

[5] The act of 1806 did not apply to persons set free before that date, and in 1816 provision was made to enable those subsequently liberated to obtain special permission to remain. Despite the harsh tone of the statutes, in 1860 Virginia had a larger free negro population than had any other state save Maryland.

[6] Washington, *The Writings of Jefferson*, IV, 442.

unwanted freedmen, as well as the more spirited slaves, might not be disposed of in that way.[7] Jefferson naturally approved the idea, but he objected to planting a negro colony in the path of American expansion, since it was inconceivable that a purely negro state would ever be admitted to the Union (and, of course, in 1801 no enlightened person would deliberately plan another mixed community). Instead, he pointed to the West Indies:

Nature seems to have formed these islands to become the receptacles of the blacks transplanted to this hemisphere. . . . The most promising . . . is the island of St. Domingo, where the blacks are established into a sovereignty de facto, and have organized themselves under regular laws and government. I should conjecture that their present ruler [Toussaint Louverture] might be willing . . . to receive even that description which would be exiled for acts deemed criminal by us, but meritorious perhaps by him.[8]

Jefferson ridiculed the argument that Haiti, strengthened by immigration from the Southern States, might in turn menace their security, but such was that country's reputation as a center of subversive influence that the Virginia Assembly rejected the President's offer to communicate with Toussaint Louverture in its behalf. In 1802 the Sierra Leone Company was approached instead, unsuccessfully.[9] By 1811 Jefferson had concluded that an African colony under the protection of the United States would be the proper means of drawing off the negro population. In compensation for the wrong of slavery, it would carry back to the negro motherland the arts of civilization.

In 1817 the American Colonization Society was founded to execute this design for the relief of the free people of color, of whom it was said:

[7] Monroe to Jefferson, June 15, 1801, in S. M. Hamilton, *The Writings of James Monroe*, III, 292-295.

[8] Washington, *The Writings of Jefferson*, IV, 419-422. At this time Jefferson was supposed to be eager for Louverture's destruction and engaged to support a French campaign against him. See above, p. 42 n.

[9] Archibald Alexander, *A History of Colonization on the Western Coast of Africa*, pp. 73 ff., 81. Sierra Leone, founded to isolate wild blacks deported from Jamaica, had undergone an unpleasant experience with negroes carried from Southern states to Nova Scotia during the revolution and thence to Africa.

Of all descriptions of our population [they] are, by far, as a class, the most corrupt, depraved, and abandoned. . . . It is not so much their fault as the consequence of their anomalous condition. . . . They are not slaves, and yet they are not free. The laws, it is true, proclaim them free; but prejudices, more powerful than any laws, deny them the privileges of freemen.[10]

The Society, formed by the fusion of movements originating in New Jersey and in Virginia, flourished in the North, where the outcaste freedmen constituted a serious police problem, as well as in the South, where their presence was a constant embarrassment to slaveholders. It took no stand on the issue of slavery itself, with the consequence that opponents of the institution could endorse it as a system of attrition that would ultimately result in universal emancipation, while "slavocrats" could argue that by removing the free negro it strengthened the existing order. During the eighteen-twenties the Society transported 1,420 emigrants to Liberia, of whom 1,180 came from North Carolina, Virginia, Maryland, and the District of Columbia.[11]

It occurred to President Boyer that if some of this emigration could be diverted to Haiti it would serve to recruit a population decimated by thirty years of strife and to introduce the skilled artisans sorely needed there. He argued that to banish to barbarous Africa colored people reared in civilized society was cruel when they might find both civilization and freedom in the Black Republic. As inducements he offered to pay part of the expense of passage and to support the immigrants until they could be settled on the fertile lands to be granted to them. In May, 1824, a Haitian agent was sent to New York with funds for putting the project into execution. Boyer hoped to procure six thousand agricultural workers the first year, considering that there were five times six thousand free negroes in the state of New York alone.[12]

---

[10] Henry Clay before the Colonization Society of Kentucky, 1829 (Alexander, *Colonization*, p. 315).   [11] *African Repository*, X (1834), 292.

[12] Loring D. Dewey, *Correspondence Relative to the Emigration to Hayti of the Free People of Colour.* In 1820 there were 29,279 free negroes and 10,088 slaves in New York.

The Colonization Society, jealous for Liberia, refused to co-operate, yet even so in four years Boyer succeeded in persuading some thirteen thousand freedmen to seek their fortunes in Haiti. However, eight years later few could be found on the lands assigned to them. Many had returned to the United States; others had drifted to the towns; only a score could be said to have made a success of the venture.[13] What was the trouble?

The immigrants had just begun to arrive when the American commercial agent at Port-au-Prince reported that, while there was room enough in Haiti for every freedman in the United States, the

religion, laws, language, manners, habits, customs, and in fact everything is so totally different from what they have been accustomed to, that they cannot feel so happy or so comfortable as in a country where the difference of soil or climate was the only change they had to encounter [Liberia]. Here too, they come with the impression that where there is no prejudice against color there is no difference in the ranks of society, but they have the mortification to find that they are as distinctly marked here as elsewhere, and that if they had chosen to be laborious where they came from they would have been much better off.[14]

In 1826 the British consul general found sixty North Carolina negroes on the estate of the commandant of Les Cayes. They praised their master, but complained that Haitian peasants stole their goods, let cattle into their gardens, and persecuted them generally.[15] Three years later, when they were visited by one of the Quakers who had procured their emancipation and emigration, they said that they had rather be slaves in North Carolina than sharecroppers in Haiti.[16] Exploited by the *élite* (who dealt with their own people in the same way) and per-

[13] Benjamin S. Hunt, *Remarks on Hayti as a Place of Settlement for Afric-Americans*, pp. 11, 14. Hunt declared that except for two lawyers, seven merchants, two tailors, four mechanics, one baker, two carters, and four peasant proprietors, all the settlers had sunk to the level of day laborers.

[14] Armstrong to Adams, Nov. 25, 1824, Cons. Let., Cape Haytien, V.

[15] Charles MacKenzie, *Notes on Haiti*, I, 89.

[16] Alexander, *Colonization*, p. 263.

secuted by peasants (resentful toward any upstart alien who tried to improve his holding and be superior to his neighbors), the industrious lost heart. The indolent were disillusioned when manna failed to fall from heaven. Boyer, disgusted with American freedmen, sought no more immigrants.

Meanwhile, in the United States colonization was losing favor with the extremists of both sides as lines were more tightly drawn on the issue of slavery. The invention of the cotton gin had granted the moribund system a new lease on life, greatly increasing the financial sacrifice required for its abolition. The new generation in the South lacked revolutionary enthusiasm for the "natural rights of man," maintaining, on the contrary, that inequality was evident in nature. Slavery, once held to be an evil difficult to remove, then accepted as an irrevocable fact, was finally exalted as a positive good, the foundation of Southern prosperity, a boon to the slave himself, and the only guarantee of order in a mixed society. A turning point was reached in 1832, when a last effort was made to pass gradual emancipation, coupled with colonization, in the Virginia Assembly. Although the decision was close, it became apparent that the majority would accept colonization only as a means of disposing of surplus free negroes, strengthening rather than reducing slavery. Colonization eliminated, the only alternatives were complete abolition, with the freedmen remaining in the community, or the maintenance of the *status quo*. The choice was predetermined. The South closed ranks to defend its "peculiar institution," and, in this mood, condemned wholesale colonization as a plot to break down slavery.[17]

In the North a similar hardening was taking place, in part the cause, in part the result, of that in the South. The earlier antislavery movement had been supported by "peaceable and reflecting people, who took consequences into account," appreciated the dilemma of the slaveholders, and hoped in time to gain their end through persuasion. They accepted colonization as a means of wearing down slavery. By 1829 it was becoming

---

[17] Jenkins, *Pro-slavery Thought in the Old South*, pp. 74-76, 85-88.

apparent that persuasion had failed and that colonization was unable to keep pace with the natural increase of the negro population. In that year William Lloyd Garrison first spoke out to show the inadequacy of these measures and to demand the immediate, unconditional abolition of slavery, as a crime against man and a sin against God. That this agitation ignored serious problems, antagonized the planters, provoked further repression of the slaves, and aroused passions that made a reasoned solution impossible, did not deter the abolitionists, who made up in energy and conviction what they lacked in discretion. Garrison at first tolerated colonization as a palliative, preferring Haiti to Liberia,[18] but in time his followers denounced the idea as a surrender to race prejudice, while condemning the Society as a device for the perpetuation of slavery.

In 1832 a convention of free negroes, under abolitionist inspiration, rejected all plans for colonization, but twenty years later (after the passage of the Fugitive Slave Law, imperiling the liberty of freedmen), there was a revival of sentiment in favor of emigration. In 1853 a convention of persons interested in colonization anywhere save in Liberia sent James Theodore Holly[19] to investigate the possibilities in Haiti. After negotiations with Soulouque, he returned to make a favorable report to a similar convention in 1856[20] and to campaign in favor of the project, arguing that it was better to build up a negro nationality than to remain in the United States "asking for political rights, which, if granted, a social prescription stronger than conventional legislation [would] ever render nugatory."[21]

The Holly-Soulouque colonization project was not a great success, but it paved the way for a similar enterprise sponsored

[18] Wendell Philips Garrison and Francis Jackson Garrison, *William Lloyd Garrison, 1805-1879*, I, 141-143.

[19] Holly had been born in Washington in 1829, of Catholic negro parents, natives of Maryland, and he had become an Anglican priest in Canada. He became bishop of Haiti in 1874 and died there in 1911 (John W. Cromwell, *The Negro in American History*, p. 241).

[20] Louis R. Mehlinger, "The Attitude of the Free Negro toward African Colonization," *Journal of Negro History*, I (1916), 290-300.

[21] J. T. Holly, *A Vindication of the Capacity of the Negro Race . . .*, p. 46.

by Geffrard. The "regenerators" of 1859, undismayed by Boyer's experience, told themselves:

Slavery will soon be abolished in North America, and a host of negroes, becoming masters of their fate, will hasten to leave the United States, where color prejudices will long survive slavery, to enjoy in Haiti all the rights of free men and citizens. . . . [Haiti] will be enriched by a population familiar with all the industries and arts which are practiced in America.[22]

While the plan was still no more than an idea inspired by Holly, there arrived at Port-au-Prince the very man to put it into execution, James Redpath, militant abolitionist, promoter of emigration from New England to Kansas, and partner in the bloody enterprises of John Brown. Geffrard wanted to build up Haiti; Redpath wanted to strike a blow at the South by calling into existence a formidable competitor in the production of cotton, sugar, rice, and tobacco.[23] Geffrard appointed Redpath to be "general agent of emigration to Hayti from the states and provinces of North America."

By the spring of 1861 Redpath had published a guidebook, established a newspaper, and organized a bureau at Boston with eight local employees and ten traveling agents. He was then ready to offer the free negroes of the United States and Canada (and fugitive slaves, too, though the Haitian government officially frowned on that) free passage to St. Marc and support there until they were settled on allotments in the public domain, which were to become theirs in fee simple when they had become naturalized (after one year) and had raised a crop. They were guaranteed religious freedom, equal protection of the laws, and exemption from military service.[24]

The census of 1860 provided Redpath with a convenient directory of the free negro population of the United States. There were 226,000 in the free states, 118,000 in accessible slave states, and 133,000 in the Confederacy. (Of these last nearly half resided in Virginia, which was to be speedily overrun

[22] Alexandre Bonneau, *Haiti: ses progrès, son avenir*, p. 107.
[23] James Redpath, *A Guide to Hayti*, p. 9.   [24] *Ibid.*, p. 94.

by the Federal armies.[25]) Reports from the field indicated an emigration of at least five thousand in 1861, if means could be found to get those in the interior down to the coast.[26] Actually, twelve hundred had been embarked for Haiti by mid-November.[27] During the summer more people were seeking passage than Redpath could accommodate,[28] but letters from St. Marc had begun to circulate in Boston complaining that no land allotments had been made, after weeks of delay, and warning that emigrants should bring furniture, utensils, and bedding, such things being unknown and unobtainable in the Artibonite.[29] Next, emigrants themselves began to straggle home, reporting high mortality in Haiti and attributing it to insanitary conditions at the receiving station. Critics arose who charged that all Haitians were so morally corrupt that no Christian dare take his family among them, that the land was a prey to revolutionary disorder, despotism, and idolatry.[30] There were new reports that settlers, after waiting for months, had received waterless land, while promised irrigation ditches were abandoned incomplete; that Haitian officials appropriated their goods, peasants plundered them with impunity, and preventable diseases carried them away. By November public meetings were being held in Boston to denounce Haiti and emigration, and prospective colonists were refusing to sail. Redpath, at last convinced that something was terribly wrong at St. Marc, wrote bitterly to his Haitian chief:

It has been no easy work to rouse up the enthusiasm of a people scattered, suspicious . . . , indifferent to the idea of a colored nationality—some of them even hostile to it; to contend against the vast influence of a selfish priesthood, who oppose emigration because they

[25] Redpath to Plésance, May 27, 1861, Haytian Bureau of Emigration, Official Correspondence, II (Library of Congress MSS).

[26] *Idem* to Elie, July 15, 1861, *loc. cit.*

[27] *Idem* to Plésance, Nov. 11, 1861, *loc. cit.* Bonneau (*Haiti*, p. 105) states that twelve hundred had arrived by March, 1861 (before Redpath's first ship sailed) and that "more than two thousand" had reached Haiti by January, 1862.

[28] *Idem* to *idem*, June 24, Aug. 24, 1861, *loc. cit.*

[29] *Idem* to *idem*, Aug. 20, 1861, *loc. cit.*

[30] Redpath to Elie, Aug. 22; to Plésance, Sept. 7, 1861, Official Correspondence, II.

fear to lose their congregations (who now support them in indolence) . . . to have also no sympathy to expect from the old tried friends (among the whites) of the colored race, whose policy is expressed in the phrase, "stay here and fight it (prejudice) out". . . . Shall I fail now? It lies in your power, Honorable Secretary, and yours only, to defeat me.[31]

Thus Geffrard's project ended in a disaster which must be attributed to the shortcomings of the Haitian administration.[32] Of the sixteen hundred emigrants sent out by Redpath, only some two hundred were still in Haiti two years later.[33] Just as this failure became evident, the government of the United States decided to try its hand at the colonization of American freedmen there.

In the spring of 1862 the Federal authorities were confronted with the problem of what to do with large numbers of negroes made dependent on the government by the fortunes of war. President Lincoln and some of his cabinet were convinced colonizationists. An appropriation was obtained and a site for a colony was sought, Haiti being rejected because of its "Roman Catholicism, low grade of civilization, and the fear of annexation by Spain."[34] Central America was favored, but when all the states in that region refused to entertain such a proposal,[35] attention was once more directed to the Black Republic. On December 31, 1862, Lincoln signed a contract engaging the United States to pay one Bernard Kock $250,000 for settling five thousand freedmen at Ile-a-Vache.

Kock had appeared at Washington in September with a Haitian concession for the exploitation of the forests of that island, including the right to cultivate cleared land for pro-

---

[31] *Idem* to Plésance, Nov. 22, 1861, *loc. cit.*

[32] Mark Baker Bird, *The Black Man, or Haytien Independence*, p. 389. In 1862 Plésance was dismissed on account of his maladministration of the departments of commerce and finance (Byron to Russell, July 9, 1862, P. R. O., London, F. O., 35/56).

[33] Donnohue to Usher, March 26, 1864, Department of the Interior, Letters Received, Slave Trade (Library of Congress MSS).

[34] Smith to Lincoln, May 9, 1862, Department of the Interior, Letters Sent, Slave Trade.

[35] Seward to Smith, Oct. 1 and 30, 1862, Domestic Letters.

visions. The laborers brought in to do the work were to be negroes, who would be naturalized immediately and would receive title to their gardens at the expiration of the concession, which could not be transferred without the consent of the Haitian government.[36] Kock depended for success, not on the hardwood forests of his domain, but on the unauthorized cultivation of cotton, then commanding top prices because of the blockade of the South. He promised to feed his people well, to erect comfortable quarters, a church, a hospital, a school, and a nursery, and "to enforce wise and paternal regulations for the physical and moral good of his charges."[37] Lincoln's contract also required him to pay cash wages at specified rates.

The contract was signed against the advice of the Attorney General, who for over a month had been denouncing Kock as an impostor.[38] A few days later Lincoln himself became sufficiently suspicious to direct the Secretary of State not to countersign and seal it, while the American representative at Port-au-Prince was belatedly called upon for a report on the concessionaire's character and title.[39] Before Port-au-Prince could be heard from, the Federal marshal at New York accused Kock, who happened to be from New Orleans, of being a rebel who planned to take the government's money and then have his five thousand negroes captured by the *Alabama* and sold into slavery.[40] Investigation failed to substantiate the charge, but it did reveal that Kock had left New Orleans to avoid the sheriff. Finally, word came from Haiti that he had no visible resources and was rated there as an adventurer. The concession was genuine, but had already lapsed for nonfulfillment.[41]

In March, 1863, the New York firm of Forbes & Tuckerman bought Kock's rights for one dollar and applied to the government for the colonization contract. This arrangement was

[36] Whidden to Seward, No. 20, March 4, 1863, Despatches, Haiti, I.
[37] Philadelphia *Press*, Sept. 26, 1862.
[38] H. K. Beale, *The Diary of Edward Bates, 1859-1866*, p. 268.
[39] Lincoln to Seward, Jan. 6, 1863, Miscellaneous Letters, hereinafter abbreviated Misc. Let.; Seward to Whidden, No. 14, Jan. 5, 1863, Instructions, Haiti, I.
[40] Whiting to Usher, Jan. 15, 1863, Misc. Let.
[41] Whidden to Seward, No. 20, March 4, 1863, Despatches, Haiti, I.

readily agreed to, the Secretary of the Interior being delighted to be rid of Kock, but the number of emigrants was reduced to five hundred and the new contractors were required to obtain the written consent of Haiti in terms embodying an assumption of responsibility for the protection of the colonists after their arrival.[42]   On April 14 Forbes & Tuckerman announced that the five hundred had sailed from Fortress Monroe, and on April 17 they presented Kock's old concession, invalid on two counts, as evidence of Haiti's consent.[43]   On June 1 the acting consul at Les Cayes reported the arrival of 453 colonists, and stated that the establishment was flourishing under "the able, wise and humane direction of its Projector, Bernard Kock"![44]

In July, Forbes & Tuckerman presented their claim for payment under the contract, only to receive the censure of the Secretary for having dispatched the emigrants before obtaining the consent of Haiti, as specifically required.   The Secretary did not disguise his feelings, for he had just read in a Confederate newspaper that half of his wards were dead and the rest dying.[45]

The first official report on the "Avache" colony came from James De Long, consul at Les Cayes, who declared that, although local authorities had furnished Kock with an armed guard, they considered him responsible for the trouble.   Having collected the colonists' money on the pretext of converting their greenbacks into specie and Haitian currency, he now owed them a month's wages as well, but refused to pay in anything save his own private scrip.   No houses had been erected except Kock's, and the settlers had nothing to eat but salt pork and

[42] Usher to Forbes & Tuckerman, April 13, 1863, Letters Sent, Slave Trade.

[43] Forbes & Tuckerman, April 13, 1863, Letters Received, Slave Trade. Usher to Forbes & Tuckerman, April 17, 1863, Letters Sent, Slave Trade.

[44] Usher to Donnohue, Oct. 17, 1863, Letters Sent, Slave Trade. This officer was Kock's creditor. There is nothing to indicate the exact nature of Kock's relationship to Forbes & Tuckerman, but they evidently gave him the good name and financial backing he lacked, on speculation, leaving the actual management of affairs to him. The chagrin of the Secretary of the Interior on learning that Kock, rejected as unfit to conduct the venture, had retained control of it under the cloak of Forbes & Tuckerman, may be imagined.

[45] Usher to Forbes & Tuckerman, July 7 and 8, 1863, Letters Sent, Slave Trade.

musty corn meal. Forty had died of exposure while ill with smallpox.[46]

Eventually Forbes & Tuckerman produced countercharges against De Long. He had made an unsuccessful effort to obtain freedmen for a project of his own,[47] and they accused him of deliberately wrecking their colony in order to secure control of the negroes for his own purposes.[48] De Long's reports indicate that he did indeed incite the settlers to repudiate Kock's authority and that, as consul, he did assume charge and have some of them plant twenty acres of cotton for him. Nevertheless, his intervention did not occur until Kock had brought the colony to the brink of disaster, and he cannot be made primarily responsible for its failure, as Forbes & Tuckerman endeavored to do.

When D. C. Donnohue, special agent for the Secretary of the Interior, reached Ile-a-Vache, he found only 378 of the 431 freedmen whom Forbes & Tuckerman had actually transported thither. Of the missing fifty-three, eight had deserted and forty-five were dead; of the remainder, thirty-one were sick, of whom four died later. The company had done nothing for any of them for six weeks. It had never furnished quarters or decent rations, although it had provided six stocks, three dozen leg chains, and five dozen handcuffs. Donnohue attributed the failure to Kock's mismanagement alone and thought that the settlers might yet succeed at Ile-a-Vache, but they wanted to go home. Although De Long tried to keep some to pick his cotton, the Haitian government settled the question by ordering that none be left behind. On March 5, 1864, a transport bore away Donnohue, De Long, thirty-nine of Redpath's emigrants who had begged to be rescued, and all of the surviving colonists save three lodged in the Les Cayes jail and several who had fled to the mountains and could not be found.[49]

Forbes & Tuckerman continued to press their claim, but all they got was a scorching refusal.[50] To add to their woe, the

[46] Whidden to Seward, No. 31, July 30, 1863, Despatches, Haiti, I.
[47] Seward to Usher, Feb. 9, 1863, Letters Received, Slave Trade.
[48] Forbes & Tuckerman, *Papers Relating to the Colonization Experiment at A'Vache.*
[49] Donnohue to Usher, March 26, 1864, Letters Received, Slave Trade.
[50] Usher to Tuckerman, Oct. 19, 1863, Letters Sent, Slave Trade.

Haitian government seized all the immovable property at Ile-a-Vache, while their agents in Les Cayes sold the movables and kept the proceeds to satisfy Kock's indebtedness to them.[51] Their losses were undoubtedly heavy, but they had only them-selves (and Kock) to blame. Their criticism of De Long and the poor freedmen[52] begged the question. The Federal authorities, for all their good intentions, were not above criticism in their care for their wards, who, innocent and inarticulate, were the real victims of the fiasco.

By 1864 the Haitian government had permanently lost interest in large-scale immigration, and at the same time the American government's attitude on the racial problem had changed. The War Department had forbidden the emigration of able-bodied negro men, whose services were needed on the battlefield, and in the opinion of the Secretary of the Interior, the movement would not be resumed.[53] The idea of the gradual deportation of the colored population had been abandoned, and, in disregard of Jefferson's dictum, an attempt was to be made to prove that two races could live in equal freedom under one government. The ill-fated colony of Ile-a-Vache was the last venture of its kind.

[51] Whidden to Seward, Nos. 65 and 66, May 7, 1864, Despatches, Haiti, I.

[52] Charles K. Tuckerman, "President Lincoln and Colonization," *Magazine of American History,* XVI (1887), 329-332.

[53] Usher to Lincoln, May 18, 1863, Letters Sent, Slave Trade.

CHAPTER V

RECOGNITION GRANTED

If any good reason exists why we should persevere longer in with-holding our recognition of the independence and sovereignty of Hayti and Liberia, I am unable to discern it.
—ABRAHAM LINCOLN, December 3, 1861

THE REVOLUTION of 1859 cleared away one obstacle to the recognition of Haiti. The forms of monarchy were peculiarly distasteful to the liberty-loving democrats of the United States (dictatorship in republican trappings was somehow less objectionable), and the tinsel court of Faustin Soulouque had been especially open to ridicule. In contrast, Geffrard's regime, in its early years, had all the appearance of the dawn of a new day in Haiti. But could Geffrard hope to secure recognition where Boyer had failed?

Significant developments were also taking place in the United States. In June, 1860, the long-dominant Democratic party split asunder on the issue of slavery, and at the polls in November the "Black Republicans," with a minority of the popular vote, gained control of the executive branch of the Federal government. In the four months between the election and the inauguration seven Southern states withdrew from the Union, to be followed shortly by four more, leaving the Republicans with a majority in Congress that they could not otherwise have obtained. However, the rout of the forces that had blocked recognition did not mean the triumph of its ancient advocates. The Republican party was a fusion of heterogeneous elements hostile to planter power in Federal councils, but there was cold comfort for merchant or abolitionist in its platform, which was based on a protective tariff for industry (at the expense of foreign commerce), free land for settlers in the West, and the exclusion of slavery from Federal territories (in order to prevent extension of the political influence of the "slavocracy" and to protect white farmers from negro competition). It expressly recognized the right of the states to judge of their own domestic institutions.

The abolitionist was prepared to attack slavery wherever he found it, because he considered it sinful and its continued existence, even in another state, a charge upon his own conscience. His attitude was based upon a sentiment of universal brotherhood that included the independent negroes of a Caribbean isle as well as those held in bondage south of the Ohio. On the contrary, the free-soiler,[1] whatever his private opinion of the "peculiar institution" of the South, denied any intention to interfere with its existence in the states where it was already established and concerned himself solely with the prevention of its westward expansion. Such a policy would not free a single slave. Indeed, it was an attitude that betrayed a certain negrophobia—a determination to escape the paralyzing effect which competition with slave labor had had upon Southern "po' white trash," a desire to exclude the negro from his own neighborhood, to keep the West open to white homesteaders. States subject to free-soil influence not only prohibited slavery but also discriminated against negroes, discouraging their immigration and denying them political privileges.[2] Nothing in a free-soil policy gave promise of a cordial attitude toward Haiti.

Abraham Lincoln, the newly elected President, was a man of broad sympathies, but a free-soiler rather than an abolitionist. In 1837, as a member of the Illinois legislature, he had showed his disapproval of both slavery and abolitionist agitation. His first highly publicized declaration of faith, made on October 4, 1854, expressed his hatred of the "monstrous injustice of slavery," but he confessed:

[1] Using the term in the general sense. The Free-Soil party of 1848-1852 adopted a distinctly abolitionist tone. Incidentally, it advocated the recognition of Haiti (Edward Stanwood, *History of the Presidency*, pp. 253-256).

[2] Until after the Civil War negroes were disfranchised in every state except New York (where a discriminatory property qualification amounted to virtual disfranchisement), Rhode Island, Massachusetts, Vermont, New Hampshire, and Maine. Western states, such as Ohio and Indiana, enacted black codes similar to those of the South (W. E. Burghardt Du Bois, *Black Reconstruction*, p. 8).

If all earthly power were given me, I should not know what to do as to the existing institution. My first impulse would be to free all the slaves, and send them to Liberia. . . . [This not being immediately practicable], what next? Free them and make them politically and socially our equals? My own feelings will not admit of this, and if mine would, we well know that those of the great mass of whites will not. Whether this feeling accords with justice and sound judgment is not the sole question, if indeed it is any part of it. A universal feeling, whether well or ill founded, cannot be safely ignored.

He rejected the third alternative—to free them and "keep them among us as underlings"—and concluded that gradual emancipation and colonization offered the only hope. In any event, he wanted the territories reserved "for homes of free white people." His sentiments had not changed when he came to the presidency in March, 1861.[3] He would not oppose recognition of Haiti on principle, but neither would he insist upon it.

Moreover, secession itself at first hindered rather than facilitated recognition. Of the fifteen slave states, eight had shown a disinclination to leave the Union, and any unnecessary action offensive to them would have been exceedingly impolitic. When the call to arms added four of them to the Confederacy, it was all the more important to deal tactfully with the four that remained uncertainly loyal. Of necessity, as well as by inclination, Lincoln's policy in the crisis was to emphasize preservation of the Union and to tread softly on the issue of slavery. Any other course would have added Missouri, Kentucky, and Maryland, at least, to the number of his enemies.

A month after the inauguration James Redpath came to Washington to sound the new administration on recognition, bearing favorable resolutions of the Ohio and Massachusetts legislatures. Secretary of State William H. Seward was noncommittal, but Redpath left his office feeling that he had been encouraged to continue his efforts to create a favorable public

[3] Albert J. Beveridge, *Abraham Lincoln, 1809-1858*, I, 194; II, 244-258. These ideas were distinctly Jeffersonian. In a purely negro community, such as Liberia, the very practical consideration of race prejudice would be no barrier to ideal social and political equality.

sentiment. President Lincoln excused himself from receiving the Haitian agent (news had just arrived that Fort Sumter had been fired on), but he did talk to Senator Charles Sumner, who was Redpath's sponsor and the real manager of the business. Emerging from the presidential presence, Sumner laid down the lines along which the propaganda must be conducted, stressing the point that the affair must be left in the hands of white Americans, since the appearance of a Haitian delegation in Washington at that time would be inopportune.[4]

Many abolitionists were disgusted with Lincoln when he failed to make secession the occasion for a holy war against slavery, none more so than Redpath. In May, while offering to organize a John Brown raid on Cuba if Haiti would support it, he declared that he had no use for "this enslaving land," that he wished he were a Haitian rather than an American citizen.[5]

The Spanish reannexation of Santo Domingo and Haiti's open and active support of Dominican resistance had brought the two countries to the verge of war. If this circumstance suggested no more to Redpath than a raid on Cuba in the style of John Brown, Sumner had better use to make of it. He urged recognition of Haiti "as a friendly demonstration ... more effective than any declaration of the Monroe Doctrine."[6] Seward had wanted to challenge Spain on just that ground, supposing that the domestic crisis might be averted by the hoary device of a rousing foreign imbroglio (with a tempting prospect of the annexation of Cuba, much desired in the South), but Lincoln, perceiving more clearly that this policy would play into the hands of the Confederates, had tactfully rejected it. Even so, Seward adopted such a bellicose tone that, on the eve of Bull Run, the Spanish government had asked if he meant to threaten it, a question that received a soft answer on the morrow of that

[4] Redpath to Plésance, April 16, 1861, Haytian Bureau of Emigration, Official Correspondence, II. Sumner, of Massachusetts, was an ardent abolitionist with whom Redpath had been associated during the Kansas struggle (Charles Sumner, *The Works of Charles Sumner*, IV, 390, 400).

[5] Redpath to Elie, May 6, 1861, Official Correspondence, II. No white man, not even an abolitionist, could qualify for Haitian citizenship.

[6] Sumner to Redpath, June 23, 1861, *loc. cit.*

disaster.[7] If the Doctrine must be shelved for the present, it might be well to give Haiti the moral support of recognition, at least, but Sumner's scheme was no more practicable than Seward's, and nothing came of it. After Bull Run it was more important than ever to humor the loyal slave states. The Spanish affair, however, served to put Seward into friendly, if unofficial, communication with the Haitian government through its commercial agents.[8]

Sumner was compelled to advise the impetuous Redpath to stay away from Washington—the omens were not yet propitious —while that ardent spirit assured the Haitian government that Seward was the only obstacle to recognition. He even resigned his commission in order to be free to use his influence at the capital to procure the dismissal of Seward and the appointment of Sumner in his stead.[9] A month later, however, he had to admit that there was no hope for recognition "until the war assumed a different phase."[10] Seward remained in office as secretary of state.

Nine months after Lincoln's inauguration the American commercial agent at Port-au-Prince reported gloomily that Haiti had lost faith in the Republican administration. Geffrard had been led to expect immediate recognition, and his disappointment was keen. Meanwhile, the European powers, also anticipating recognition, had strengthened their representation at the Haitian capital in order to counteract the prospective increase in American influence, their simple consuls general being superseded by picked chargés d'affaires. Great Britain had called Spencer St. John from the East Indies to defend her interest. France had sent a genuine marquis, with an imposing suite. In a land where social prestige counted for so much, a mere commercial agent could make little headway against such odds.[11]

Even as the agent was pouring forth his woe, the remedy was being prepared in Washington. When Congress assembled

[7] Dexter Perkins, *The Monroe Doctrine, 1826-1867*, pp. 299 f.
[8] Notes from Haiti, I.
[9] Redpath to Plésance, July 10, 1861, Official Correspondence, II.
[10] *Idem* to *idem*, Aug. 13, 1861, *loc. cit.*
[11] Seth Webb to Seward, No. 6, Dec. 12, 1861, Cons. Let., Port-au-Prince, IV.

in December, the President judged that it was by then too late for the loyal slave states to change their minds and that something might therefore be done to hold the mutinous abolitionists in line. The session was marked by a series of acts abolishing slavery in the territories and freeing certain classes of slaves found within reach of the Federal military power. At the same time the President suggested the recognition of Haiti, and Sumner at last had the satisfaction of bringing in a bill to establish a diplomatic mission at Port-au-Prince. In urging its passage he alluded to his old contention that recognition would create a counterpoise for the Spanish occupation of Santo Domingo and strengthen the feeble position of the United States in the West Indies, but most of his remarks were directed toward the commercial aspects of the case. According to the treasury report for 1860, there were American legations in twenty-one countries of less commercial importance to the United States. American exports to Haiti were valued at $2,673,682, imports thence at $2,062,723, a trade that would be stimulated by recognition.[12] The places from which the planters had been wont to pronounce their veto were mostly vacant, but Garrett Davis, of Kentucky, rose to recite for the last time the old story of the black ambassador. The bill, he charged, was only part "of a system of measures that manifest a deliberate purpose to assail the institution of slavery in the slave States everywhere";[13] i.e., loyal as well as secessionist. His plea was hopeless. The Senate passed the bill on April 4, 1862, by a decisive vote of 32 to 7. The House concurring, 86 to 37, the President gave his assent on the fifth of June.[14] At Boston the passage was hailed as "a recognition of the Colored Man, not merely of Hayti." At

---

[12] *Congressional Globe*, 37th Cong., 2d Sess., pp. 619, 1773-1776. Sumner deliberately avoided the slavery issue until it was raised by the opposition, when he defended the bill as a tardy act of justice.

Exports to Haiti and imports thence were less than one per cent of the totals for the United States in 1860, a tremendous decline in relative importance. Nevertheless, Haitian-American commerce was more valuable than that with Russia or Venezuela, only slightly less valuable than that with Argentina, Colombia, or Chile (*Report on the Commercial Relations of the United States*, 1860).

[13] *Congressional Globe* (37.2), pp. 1806 f.

[14] *Ibid.*, pp. 1815, 2538.

Port-au-Prince, Sumner's speech was translated, and recognition was celebrated along with the news of McClellan's capture of Yorktown in the great advance on Richmond.[15]

Benjamin F. Whidden, of New Hampshire, received the first appointment as United States commissioner and consul general at Port-au-Prince,[16] and on his arrival at his post in September he was most cordially received by President Geffrard himself. But there was disappointment in the Haitian capital. With three new European chargés in town, a mere commissioner was barely distinguishable from a commercial agent. An exchange of ministers was desired. The idea appealed to Whidden too, and he informed Seward that he was assuming ministerial rank, supposing that to have been the intention of the President and that the department would correct its error by sending him the proper credentials, but by return mail (a month later) he was assured that no mistake had been made.[17] Presumably the government wished to inaugurate modestly a diplomatic mission, the very creation of which had been so long resisted, but it seems that it would have been proper to have given the first appointee a standing equal to that of his European colleagues (and competitors). If Whidden was not worthy of higher rank, a better man should have been sent. In 1866 his successor, Henry E. Peck, was made minister resident in order that he might meet Spencer St. John, the British chargé, on even terms.[18]

Whidden's chief business was the negotiation of a commercial treaty, a task which took nearly three years to complete, despite Haitian expressions of eagerness to begin. The commissioner's full powers and a copy of the commercial treaty with Venezuela were sent in December, 1862, and by May, 1863, the terms (virtually those of the Venezuela treaty) had been agreed upon, but six months later, in response to an im-

[15] Sumner, *Works*, VI, 471.

[16] Seward to Whidden, July 18, 1862, Instructions, Haiti, I. No reason for the selection is apparent.

[17] Whidden to Seward, No. 1, Oct. 1; No. 4, Nov. 4, 1862, Despatches, Haiti, I; Seward to Whidden, No. 11, Nov. 18, 1862, Instructions, Haiti, I.

[18] Seward to Peck, No. 1, Aug. 20, 1866, Instructions, Haiti, I.

patient query from Washington, Whidden explained that the formality of signing had been postponed a few days at the request of the Haitians.   In February, 1864, he was confident that the treaty would be signed eventually, but added, "I do not think they sufficiently value time."[19]   He did not explain that the delay was caused by the fact that the Haitian government had submitted the draft to the critical examination of the representatives of Great Britain, France, and Spain.   In April, France graciously waived objections raised by her agent, but Great Britain pressed for an amendment.[20]   Not until November 3, 1864, was the treaty finally signed, unamended.   Ratifications were exchanged at Washington on May 22, 1865.

The treaty made no change in the actual status of American commerce in Haiti, which had enjoyed most-favored-nation treatment since 1850, but, until Haiti was formally bound, that trade had lain at the mercy of any untoward circumstance that might provoke a renewal of the discriminations in force from 1806 to 1825 and from 1829 to 1850.   The text of the convention of 1864 was replete with both general and specific guarantees of most-favored-nation treatment.   In one particular it went further and provided that the citizens of each country, resident in the other, should not be required "to pay any contributions whatever higher or other than those that are or may be paid by native citizens"—a provision which served for forty years to secure for Americans in Haiti equality with Haitians in the matter of license fees and taxes, considerations not generally enjoyed by aliens in that country.[21]

As the treaty was being signed and ratified, Haitian-American commerce, mounting steadily since 1850, was reaching peaks

[19] Seward to Whidden, July 18, 1862, Instructions, Haiti, I; Whidden to Seward, No. 4, Nov. 4; No. 8, Dec. 6, 1862; No. 19, Feb. 6, No. 48, Nov. 7, 1863; No. 57, Feb. 27, 1864, Despatches, Haiti, I.

[20] St. John to Russell, Jan. 23, April 23, June 23, and Nov. 24, 1864, P. R. O., F. O. 35/61. The British objected to the terms regarding privateering, never of any subsequent note, but may have sought through them to obstruct the whole project. The United States was willing to yield the point (Seward to Whidden, No. 44, May 7, 1864, Instructions, Haiti, I), but the treaty was finally signed without change.

[21] Beginning in 1876, the interpretation of this article was the subject of frequent disputes, ending in the abrogation of the treaty in 1905. See below, pp. 169 f.

unprecedented since the embargo of 1806. In the fiscal year 1865 exports to Haiti were valued at $6,357,175, an increase of 180 per cent over the figure for 1821, of 955 per cent over the low ebb of 1849, of 140 per cent over the figures cited by Sumner in urging recognition. Imports from Haiti had, indeed, fallen off to $1,469,771, nearly $600,000 less than the figure for 1860, but on the whole the prospects were bright.[22]

Thus Haiti obtained the recognition of the United States, not by virtue of independence asserted and maintained, but as an incident of American civil strife. Thus mercantile interests gained the security for which they had clamored in vain since 1806, and abolitionists the satisfaction of winning recognition for a race as well as a nation. As the war for the preservation of the Union became indeed a crusade against slavery, as Abraham Lincoln set free seven times as many slaves as had Toussaint Louverture, and as Charles Sumner won for them greater civil and political rights than even Louverture had ever ventured to bestow, it might well have seemed as though Haiti and the United States, once inevitably antagonistic, were destined to be henceforth natural allies, kindred nations. Lincoln, however, had wisely observed (in 1854) that a universal sentiment, whether just or unjust, could not be safely ignored. It remained to be seen whether race prejudice could be legislated out of existence in the United States, as slavery had been.

It was notable that the Fourteenth and Fifteenth Amendments, guaranteeing the civil rights of the freedmen, disfranchising erstwhile rebels and enfranchising former slaves, were inspired by the necessities of the Republican party rather than by an awakened public conscience. The Republicans were still a minority. If the reconstruction policies of Lincoln and his successor, Andrew Johnson, were allowed to prevail, the result might be the return of the Democrats to power, since slavery, the issue which had split the majority, had been eliminated and Johnson himself was a Union Democrat. A program calculated to create an artificially solid Republican South naturally

[22] *Statistical Abstract of the United States* (1907), p. 330.

recommended itself to the leaders of the congressional majority, and so it was that a handful of sincere abolitionists, led by Sumner, were able to plot the course of what had been originally a free-soil party.   But the amendments could not have been adopted without the ratifications of the Southern States, then under Federal military control.   As late as 1868 only eight Northern states were willing to extend the franchise to negroes within their own borders (and their combined negro population was no more than four tenths of one per cent of the national total).   The more numerous the outcaste group, the more stubborn the resistance.   In 1867 the voters of Ohio smothered a proposal of negro suffrage, as did those of New Jersey.   Republican leaders in New York dared not submit the question at the polls.[23]   In Connecticut disorder and despotism in Haiti were cited as arguments against congressional reconstruction.[24] By attempting to enforce political equality before the freedmen themselves had been prepared for the responsibility and before public opinion, Northern or Southern, was ready to support the change, the radicals merely aggravated existing prejudices, sacrificed the freedmen to partisan purpose, and postponed indefinitely a genuine readjustment.   (Toussaint Louverture may have been wiser than they.)   After the bitter experience of reconstruction a South for the first time solidly Democratic proceeded to nullify the abolitionist amendments, with the tacit consent of Northern Republicans, now that they were securely entrenched in Federal power.   Holly and Bonneau[25] had been right in predicting that a social prescription stronger than conventional legislation would long survive slavery in the United States.   Whatever the relative advantages of a Southern negro sharecropper and a Haitian peasant, color prejudice would continue to complicate American attitudes toward Haiti.

[23] DuBois, *Black Reconstruction*, pp. 340 f.

[24] The New Haven *Register*, commenting upon current disorders in Haiti, observed, "That's the kind of government the Radicals are trying to establish in the Southern States."   Peck to Seward, No. 38, May 31, 1867, Despatches, Haiti, III.

[25] See above, pp. 73 f.

CHAPTER VI

ANNEXATION?

*It cannot be long before it will become necessary for this govern-
ment to lend some effective aid to the solution of the political and
social problems which are kept continually before the world by the two
Republics of the island of St. Domingo. . . . I am satisfied that . . .
annexation . . . would . . . receive the consent of the people interested.*
—ANDREW JOHNSON, December 9, 1868

THE HIGH HOPES that had attended the advent of Fabre
Geffrard to power in Haiti had not been fulfilled. Conspiracy
had been rife from the first days of his administration, the Spanish reoccupation of Santo Domingo had increased the tension,
and the result had been military dictatorship as of yore. The
disappointed advocates of parliamentary government had resorted to arms in 1863 and again in 1864, without success, but
for seven months of 1865 they held Cap Haitien against all
assaults of the government forces. While the siege was in progress, Spain gave up the reannexation of a hornets' nest, and
the Dominican congress called Buenaventura Báez from exile
to the presidency of the restored republic, to the great chagrin
of José María Cabral, who, being the provisional executive,
had anticipated his own election. The Haitian deadlock was
broken on November 9, when a British squadron bombarded the
Cape at the order of the minister, Spencer St. John.[1] Sylvain
Salnave, military leader of the parliamentarians, escaped to
Monte Cristi, where Báez took him into custody pending negotiations with Geffrard for the recognition of Dominican independence. Although William H. Seward, American Secretary
of State, then on a Caribbean cruise, attempted to bring about a
peaceful settlement between the long-hostile neighbors through
his personal good offices, the negotiations failed when Haiti

[1] This extraordinary affair is described in *Papers Relating to the Foreign Relations of the United States* (1866), Pt. II, pp. 502-507.

[91]

refused to relinquish pretensions to sovereignty over the East.[2] Instead of accepting peace, Geffrard chose to support Cabral's rebellion against Báez, who thereupon released Salnave in order that he might renew his attacks on Geffrard.[3] Báez and Salnave were speedily driven from the island, but Geffrard's triumph was not enduring. In March, 1867, his government collapsed like a house of cards, and in May, Salnave became president of Haiti. Eight months later Báez, with Salnave's help, ousted Cabral. Finally, in the spring of 1868, Salnave having shown himself to be as dictatorial as any of his predecessors, rebellion once more broke out in Haiti, led by Nissage-Saget. The ensuing struggle, complicated by a resurgence of Cabral as Saget's ally, kept the whole island in an uproar and brought the wild *cacos* and *piquets* down from the mountains to terrorize the plains. This deadlock seemed destined to last indefinitely. The island, which had known no peace since the fall of Boyer, twenty-five years before, appeared to be sinking into anarchy.

To this chaotic situation President Johnson referred in his message of December 9, 1868, and the cure which he prescribed was annexation by the United States. Contradictorily, that was precisely what most of the principals in the Caribbean battle-royal had declared that they were fighting to prevent. Geffrard had been persuaded that the United States had supported the revolt of Cap Haitien in hope of securing a naval station there and that Seward's solicitude for peace was motivated by the fact that he held the pledge of Báez for the cession of Samaná Bay. He publicly proclaimed that Báez was about to give a foreign power (the United States) a lodgment on the island and was therefore the enemy of Haiti.[4] Not many months later Báez was using the same charge against Cabral, and, in the final phase of the game, Nissage-Saget was accusing both Salnave and Báez. Actually, Salnave was willing to make such a bargain for American aid against his enemies, whom he accused of having made a deal with the British, while, as for

[2] Henry E. Peck to Seward, No. 25, Feb. 25, 1866, Despatches, Haiti, II.

[3] *Idem* to *idem*, No. 30, June 10, 1866, *loc. cit.*

[4] *Idem* to *idem*, No. 18, Nov. 18, 1865; No. 28, April 20, 1866, Despatches, Haiti, II.

Cabral and Báez, all that they were fighting for was to determine which of them should handle the proceeds of the sale of the *patria*.

But why should the United States be interested in annexing Hispaniola or any part of it? However deplorable the conditions there, they did not threaten any considerable American interest. The Monroe Doctrine was only remotely, if at all, involved.[5]

The doctrine of Monroe was the negative application of the concept of two hemispheres, one the seat of autocracy, the other dedicated to liberal republican:sm. It expressed no more than a defensive policy toward European powers. The positive application of the concept was embodied in another popular "doctrine," that of the "manifest destiny" of the United States to fulfil the divinely appointed mission of extending its beneficent institutions to all dwellers in outer darkness, from the Arctic to Cape Horn. It was not the first, nor yet the last, instance of an aggressive attitude cloaked, without conscious hypocrisy, in the guise of a *mission civilisatrice*. The faith knew no distinctions of party or section. It was particularly characteristic of the period following the Mexican War, when the rapid development of the young nation and its irresistible advance over Louisiana, Florida, Texas, Oregon, New Mexico, and California encouraged belief that there was no limit to its natural growth and that the less fortunate people of America should rejoice to be allowed to share in its prosperity and progress. During the presidential campaign of 1860 William H. Seward, the future secretary of state, saw in the "rapid decay and dissolution" of the Latin-American republics "the preparatory stage for their reorganization in free, equal, and self-governing members of the United States of America."[6]

[5] Presidents Polk and Buchanan had suggested that the Monroe Doctrine might require the benevolent intervention of the United States to clear up situations that might otherwise invite the sinister intervention of Europe, but this reasoning did not become popular until forty years later. During 1865-1874 Spencer St. John exercised strong influence on both Geffrard and Nissage-Saget, but his policy was purely negative—to prevent the United States from gaining a foothold in Hispaniola.

[6] G. E. Baker, *The Works of William H. Seward*, IV, 331 ff. Alaska and Canada were included in the vision.

The application of this philosophy to a state of anarchy in Hispaniola was plain. How could any intelligent Haitian or Dominican prefer the bloody rule of native despots to membership in the American Union? However, the continental vision of the earlier devotees of Manifest Destiny had never penetrated seaward beyond the far extremity of Cuba, where Thomas Jefferson had been willing to erect a monument inscribed "*ne plus ultra.*"[7] As might be expected, the needs of the United States, not those of the natives, belatedly manifested the destiny of the farther Antilles.

The acquisition of California directed American attention toward Hispaniola. The heart of the continent was still a wilderness, barring access to the golden coast, which could be reached most readily by way of the isthmus, but, if the navy must defend this exposed line of communication from interruption by the maritime powers of Europe, it must have a West Indian base of operations to counterbalance theirs. The need was intensified by the introduction of steam navigation, which became indispensable to naval vessels, but, by shortening the cruising radius, increased their dependence upon local depots.[8] In 1849 the United States went into the market for a West Indian coaling station, but opportunity was limited. Great Britain, France, and Spain already possessed all the likely sites, save three—Danish St. Thomas, Dominican Samaná Bay, and Haitian Mole St. Nicolas.

Until 1860 attention was focused on Samaná, since, in view of the desperate plight of the Dominican Republic, it seemed likely that a concession could be obtained in return for recognition.[9] The agent, sent in 1844 to investigate the Dominican complexion and prospects, had discovered the strategic importance and availability of the bay.[10] In 1849 Benjamin Green, charged with ascertaining the Dominican terms, learned that it

[7] A. A. Lipscomb and A. E. Bergh, *The Writings of Thomas Jefferson*, XII, 277. Jefferson conceived of the West Indies as reserved for the separate and exclusive use of negroes to be expelled from all continental America.

[8] *Annual Report of the Secretary of the Navy, 1865*, p. xv.

[9] Marcy to Cazneau, June 17, 1854, Spec. Miss., III.

[10] Hogan to Buchanan, Oct. 4, 1845, Spec. Agts., XIII.

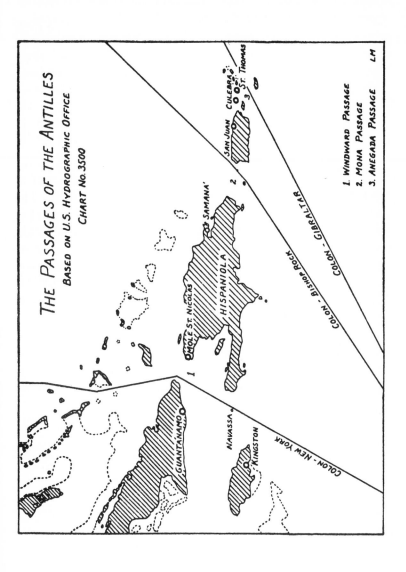

THE PASSAGES OF THE ANTILLES
BASED ON U.S. HYDROGRAPHIC OFFICE
CHART No. 3500

1. WINDWARD PASSAGE
2. MONA PASSAGE
3. ANEGADA PASSAGE

LH

could be had for any consideration that included protection from Haiti.[11] However, his mission and similar ones entrusted to Jonathan Elliott (1855) and William L. Cazneau (1853, 1854, and 1859), all failed because the American executive considered itself constitutionally unable to give the required guarantee.[12] In the circumstances, the Dominican government could not afford to alienate its European protectors by granting favors to the United States. Despairing of American aid and still fearful of Haiti, in 1861 it invited reannexation by Spain.

Recognition was the principal consideration offered by the United States for Samaná, but when the recognition of Haiti was under discussion the same tactics were not employed. The domestic situation forbade recognition on any terms before 1862 and made unconditional recognition inevitable then. The right to deposit coal for American warships at Cap Haitien was secured, but with it no territorial concession.[13] This depot and Danish St. Thomas were the only West Indian ports to which Federal cruisers might resort with assurance of being able to obtain supplies, since the sympathies of British, French, and Spanish colonial officials were with the Confederacy. Dissatisfied, the navy continued to demand an American-owned coaling station in the Antilles.[14]

By 1863 the Dominicans were in revolt against Spain. While receiving clandestine aid from Haiti, whose rulers had no desire to share the island with a powerful neighbor, the rebels were in correspondence with the American legation at Port-au-Prince, suggesting that Samaná might be had in exchange for intervention in their behalf.[15] Seward had burned his fingers on the Dominican question in 1861, and his instructions were to make

---

[11] Green to Clayton, Aug. 27, 1849, *loc. cit.*, XV.

[12] Clayton to Green, Feb. 16, 1850, Spec. Miss., I. Cazneau to Marcy, Aug. 19, 1854, Spec. Agts., XIX. The Constitution leaves the decision between war and peace to Congress; the Senate would not consent to an "entangling alliance." Such scruples must have seemed quaint in 1870 or after 1903.

[13] Whidden to Seward, No. 22, June 6, 1863, Despatches, Haiti, I.

[14] J. T. Morse, *The Diary of Gideon Welles*, II, 466.

[15] Whidden to Seward, No. 47, Nov. 6; No. 51, Dec. 5, 1863, Despatches, Haiti, I.

no official reply,[16] but Geffrard evidently had in mind the Dominican readiness to bargain with Samaná, when, on Spain's withdrawal in 1865, he proposed the neutralization of the peninsula. Seward declined to participate in a tripartite guarantee, on the ground that it was the ancient and settled policy of the United States to eschew political alliances, at the same time disclaiming any desire to disturb the peace and security of Haiti and hoping that the European powers would say as much. To the British minister he explained his policy regarding the future of Samaná itself very frankly:

The United States are sincerely desirous that the entire island of Hayti may now and henceforth remain subject exclusively to the government and jurisdiction of the people who are the dwellers and occupants thereof, and that they may never be dispossessed or disturbed by any foreign state. . . . The question, however . . . could never have been propounded at all by the government of Hayti if that government had not in some degree apprehended an inability on the part of the occupants of the island to maintain the sovereignty and independence desired. I admit that if the United States were . . . to consider these apprehensions well founded . . . then [they] might not only. be very much indisposed to see the peninsula of Samana pass into the hands of any foreign state, but . . . would deem themselves justified in considering whether they would not be authorized to seek to bring the peninsula within their own jurisdiction by just, lawful, and peaceful means.

But the Secretary assumed that the Dominicans could maintain their sovereignty and declared unequivocally that the United States did not "contemplate any proceedings to gain any possession or control within the island."[17] Although this statement did not bar the future purchase of Samaná or even the annexation of Santo Domingo, if the Dominicans so desired or were unable to maintain their independence against other powers, it truly indicated no immediate designs in that quarter, yet Geffrard's deduction from Seward's attitude was that the Ameri-

[16] Seward to Whidden, No. 32, Nov. 18, 1863, Instructions, Haiti, I.
[17] *Foreign Relations, 1865*, II, 191.

cans were secretly out to get Samaná and perhaps Cap Haitien or Mole St. Nicolas as well, and would procure the overthrow of his government, if need be, to accomplish it. In his report on the affair of Cap Haitien, St. John indicated his conviction that he had acted in the nick of time to avert the seizure of the Cape by the United States.[18]

At the moment when he denied ambition "to gain any possession or control" within Hispaniola, the Secretary of State, no longer hampered by civil war and anticipating a showdown with France over Mexico, was already seriously in quest of a West Indian naval base, but the object of his desire was St. Thomas. He met with opposition, even within the Cabinet; the Secretary of the Navy argued that with the close of domestic conflict the occasion had passed and that in the event of war with a European power that power's own islands could be seized.[19]   But Seward persevered undaunted.

While the Secretary was wooing the reluctant Danes, he was in turn being wooed by certain parties in Hispaniola. In November, 1865, Sylvain Salnave wrote from exile to accuse Geffrard of having bought St. John's intervention at Cap Haitien with a promise to cede the Mole, and to say that, if the United States would furnish him with munitions, he would repel this assault on the Monroe Doctrine, dispose of Geffrard within a month, and grant the Mole to the United States, Haitian sovereignty there being suitably guaranteed.[20]   On the heels of this offer came a proposal from Báez, through William L. Cazneau, to cede Samaná in return for aid in repelling the anticipated Geffrard-Cabral invasion.[21]   Thus Geffrard had reason to suspect both Salnave and Báez, but he was mistaken in supposing that their overtures received serious consideration in Washington.   In February, 1866, Seward informed the Danish minister of what he had been offered for intervention in the affairs of Hispaniola, but told him that he had no inclination "to follow

[18] St. John to Russell, Nov. 24, 1865, P. R. O., F. O. 35/62.
[19] Morse, *The Diary of Gideon Welles*, III, 40.
[20] Salnave to Salmon P. Chase, Nov. 11, 1865, Notes from Haiti, I.
[21] Welles, *Naboth's Vineyard*, I, 317 f.

such unprincipled advice."[22] It would obviously have been folly to treat with an exile or with a tottering government, even had there not been fair prospect of his getting what he wanted from Denmark.

During 1866 the Danish negotiations faltered. Denmark asked $15,000,000 for her unprofitable islands, and Seward was willing to give only a third as much. As hope for an agreement dwindled, the Secretary's attention was again called to Samaná Bay. Geffrard had made Cabral the Dominican president in order to defeat the schemes of Báez and Cazneau, but if Cabral, once in office, were to assume an independent attitude (dependency on Haiti being poor Dominican politics), he would have to fear both Báez and Geffrard. Consequently, in November, 1866, he asked the United States for a $2,000,000 loan in cash and munitions, offering Samaná Bay as collateral.[23] This would be virtually a sale, but when Frederick Seward was sent to negotiate, his instructions called for the outright cession of Samaná at Cabral's price or a lease including the right to fortify.[24] Cabral dared not proceed so baldly, and the deal fell through. In July, 1867, Seward informed the Cabinet that Samaná had been eliminated from consideration;[25] in October he closed with Denmark for $7,500,000.

The Danish treaty was never ratified. The Senate committee on foreign relations pigeonholed it until March, 1870, when it was reported adversely and tabled. The attitude of Charles Sumner, the committee's chairman, is difficult to fathom. He had just supported the purchase of Alaska because he deemed it a step toward the annexation of English-speaking Canada,[26] and he could hardly regard the English-speaking negroes of St. Thomas as more alien than those of Alabama. Indeed, he might be expected to wish to include them in the protection of

[22] Charles C. Tansill, *The Purchase of the Danish West Indies*, p. 21.

[23] Somers Smith to Seward, Nov. 8, 1866, Cons. Let., Santo Domingo, V.

[24] Seward to F. W. Seward, Dec. 17, 1866, Spec. Miss., II.

[25] Morse, *The Diary of Gideon Welles*, III, 124 f. In November, 1867, Cabral, whose fall was imminent, attempted to accept Seward's offer, only to be told, "Too late" (Seward to Smith, Dec. 13, 1867, Spec. Miss., II).

[26] Sumner, *The Works of Charles Sumner*, XI, 222.

the Fourteenth Amendment. It could not be said that the unwelcome rule of the United States was being imposed upon these people, who had indicated their enthusiastic approval of the transfer in a plebescite conducted by a scrupulous and disinterested government. No independent negro state would be extinguished; on the contrary, the islands, rejected, would remain subject to a European monarch. Sumner was hostile toward both Johnson and Seward, but it would have been drastic indeed to cast out the Danish negroes merely to satisfy a private grudge. A more valid explanation may lie in the fact that the House had already indicated that it would refuse to appropriate the purchase price. There was no use in precipitating a conflict between the houses when harmony was needed for the sake of congressional reconstruction. Moreover, the Senator may have felt that American expansion in the West Indies would be a threat to the independence of Haiti, the recognition of which he had sponsored. At any rate, if Sumner balked at St. Thomas, his vehement opposition to any plan involving Samaná or Mole St. Nicolas could be expected, even while his elimination of St. Thomas made such a development the more likely.

The Danish treaty was not five months old before Seward received another invitation from Hispaniola. On reaching Port-au-Prince, Gideon H. Hollister, newly appointed minister resident, had found the dictatorship of Salnave openly proclaimed and trouble brewing. Hollister, his republican sentiments outraged, filled his despatch with denunciatory rhetoric.[27] Then, less than three weeks after arriving at his post, he suddenly changed his tone, at the same time mysteriously asking for leave of absence on the ground that he had a matter of importance to communicate to Seward personally.[28] Receiving no encouragement, toward the end of June, 1868, he sent a special courier to Washington with a proposal from Salnave which he dared not put in writing.[29] According to the

---

[27] Hollister to Seward, April 8, 1868, Despatches, Haiti, III.

[28] Hollister to Seward, No. 1, April 25, 1868, Despatches, Haiti, III.

[29] *Idem* to *idem*, Private and Personal, June 29, 1868, *loc. cit.*

plan, the United States would receive the Mole St. Nicolas and three leagues of adjacent mainland in return for assuming the Haitian debt to France. Moreover, Haitian independence must be guaranteed and the government defended from both external and internal enemies.[30] Seward's disapproval was emphatic and unqualified:

> This Department does not deem it expedient to intervene directly or indirectly in the Civil War now raging in Hayti. We ardently desire the restoration there of peace, order, and good Republican government. We have no purpose or designs of acquisition or aggrandizement within the territory of Hayti.[31]

When Hollister tried to argue, the Secretary of State lost patience and declared that it was useless to examine the details of a scheme that patently amounted to a protectorate, which the executive was constitutionally impotent to establish and which Congress would never sanction.[32]

Seward was sincere in denying covetousness regarding Haitian territory. He did not reject Salnave's offer because he then had other projects in mind, for when he wrote, the Danish treaty was plainly doomed and he had no alternative plans. He did evidently despair of obtaining congressional approval, but that practical difficulty was not the fundamental consideration. It was true that hitherto he had contemplated only the acquisition of a naval station, not the assumption of a protectorate over a considerable territory and population, but, as an avowed expansionist, he would have sponsored the annexation of Haiti had he been convinced that the Haitians really desired it. The crux of the matter was that Salnave's situation, besieged in his capital, was not such as to inspire confidence in his government's stability or in its representative character. For sixty-four years the Haitians had built up a reputation as isolationists that the act of one man could not neutralize. Although Seward believed in the destiny of the United

[30] *Idem* to *idem*, Aug. 10, 1868, *loc. cit.*
[31] Seward to Hollister, No. 8, July 18, 1868, Instructions, Haiti, I.
[32] *Idem* to *idem*, No. 12, Sept. 1, 1868, *loc. cit.*

States to expand through the voluntary accession of neighboring peoples, he did not favor plucking the fruit before it was ripe.[33] Ardent expansionist though he was, his philosophy did not contemplate the annexation of civil wars.

But if not Mole St. Nicolas, what of Samaná Bay? When Salnave provoked revolt in Haiti, his ally, Báez, evidently feared the worst, for he at once dispatched Cazneau's partner, Joseph W. Fabens, to Washington to take up the Samaná negotiations where Cabral had dropped them on fleeing from office. Six months later, Fabens having made no impression on Seward and the danger of Haitian intervention steadily increasing, Báez extended the scope of his proposals until they amounted to the establishment of an American protectorate of the sort that the Secretary had just refused to consider with reference to Haiti,[34] but again Seward declined, observing that he could find no difference between this plan and Santana's overtures to Spain in 1861 except that between the United States, an American republic, and Spain, a European monarchy. "It may be doubted," he added, "whether this distinction would be regarded as moral justification."[35]

Precisely three weeks later President Johnson, with no evidence beyond these appeals from Salnave and Báez, declared himself satisfied that the people of Haiti and the Dominican Republic would welcome annexation by the United States. The hands were the hands of Johnson, but the voice was the voice of Seward. What had come over him?

It can hardly be supposed that the Secretary of State cherished any illusions about the immediate annexation of Haiti—certainly he made no move to take up the question at Port-au-Prince—but by December, 1868, it looked as though Salnave was going to win his war after all, and if there was any consistency in his nature he could hardly oppose the establishment of American influence in his neighborhood, as Geffrard had resisted the return of Spain to Santo Domingo. The allusion

[33] Albert K. Weinberg, *Manifest Destiny*, pp. 231, 249 f., 418.
[34] Smith to Seward, Oct. 24, 1868, Cons. Let., Santo Domingo, V.
[35] Seward to Smith, Nov. 17, 1868, *loc. cit.*

to Haiti in the presidential message seems to have been intended to persuade congressmen that there would be no Haitian objection to the annexation of the Dominican Republic, with the eventual annexation of Haiti deferred, in Seward's mind at least, until years of neighborly contact had disarmed fear. As for the Dominican phase of the question, for a quarter of a century every Dominican government had done its utmost to get the country annexed by some power and so much smoke must betoken some sort of fire. By December, 1868, Báez had not only maintained his position for eleven months, but was more firmly seated than ever, despite all that Cabral and Saget could do. If Báez did not truly represent the Dominican people, no one did, and, consequently, Seward may have allowed himself to be overpersuaded. Fabens, who had been at work on influential congressmen, evidently convinced him that he might hope for a favorable vote, but when General Nathaniel P. Banks, chairman of the House committeee on foreign affairs, brought in a resolution authorizing the President to establish a Dominican protectorate, it was defeated, 126 to 36. Outright annexation drew more support, but was voted down, 110 to 63.[36] This was the state of affairs when, in March, 1869, General U. S. Grant succeeded Andrew Johnson in the presidency.

During the spring and summer of that year Salnave began to lose his grip on the Haitian situation, and one September night he went secretly to the suburban residence of Ebenezer Bassett, latest American minister at Port-au-Prince, to plead for help against the French and British, who, he said, were the authors of his misfortunes, hating him because of his known friendship for the United States. Specifically, he wanted a loan of two or three million dollars, to be secured either by the customs revenues or by Mole St. Nicolas.[37] Bassett still believed that Salnave's success was the shortest road to peace, but he warned against accepting the Mole—there was no mistaking the universal sentiment against alienation of territory.[38]

[36] *Congressional Globe*, 40th Cong., 3d Sess., pp. 340, 769.
[37] Bassett to Fish, Private, Sept. 16, 1869, Despatches, Haiti, III.
[38] *Idem* to *idem*, Private No. 2, 1869, *loc. cit.*

His admonition was unnecessary, since the offer received no consideration at Washington. In December, Salnave fled from Port-au-Prince toward Santo Domingo, but he was intercepted by Cabral, who turned him over to Nissage-Saget to be shot. The victors made threatening demonstrations before the American legation, while Spencer St. John was acclaimed as patron of the revolution.[39]

Meanwhile, on November 29, 1868, the climax, approached over a quarter of a century, was reached as Báez signed a treaty of annexation with the United States. The negotiations had been conducted on the initiative of President Grant himself, rather than that of Hamilton Fish, his Secretary of State, and they had involved strange proceedings on the part of Fabens, Cazneau, and General Orville E. Babcock, the presidential private secretary, among others.[40] Two agreements were drawn up, as alternatives. The first, practically identical with Seward's counterproposal to Cabral in 1867, provided for the lease of the bay and peninsula of Samaná at an annual rental of $150,000 or the purchase of the region for $2,000,000; the second, for the annexation of the whole republic, the United States paying $1,500,000 toward the retirement of the Dominican debt. Báez was promised protection from foreign interference pending a plebescite on the question, and was advanced $147,000 in cash and munitions.[41]

It was immediately charged, and has been held since, that this military and financial support was necessary to prevent the imminent collapse of an unrepresentative government before the just wrath of its betrayed constituents, but the accusation, part of the propaganda of the time, was unwarranted. Although the transaction as a whole was tainted with fraud, that part of the convention which referred to foreign intervention meant literally what it said, for Báez had greater reason to fear foreign interference than domestic repudiation. His plebescite,

[39] *Idem* to *idem*, No. 34, No. 35, and Private No. 3, Jan. 15, 1870, *loc. cit.*

[40] For an illuminating account of these negotiations see Allan Nevins, *Hamilton Fish: The Inner History of the Grant Administration*, pp. 262-278.

[41] *Senate Executive Document No. 17*, 41st Cong., 3d Sess., pp. 98-101.

which resulted in a landslide for annexation, proved nothing, of course, but the fact remained that during the preceding two years Cabral and Company, who made political capital of the annexation issue although it had nothing to do with the real motives of their rebellion, had never come into the open without taking a beating, had never succeeded in enlisting any formidable number of Dominicans—the only way in which Dominican opinion could manifest itself.[42] Báez could handle Cabral without assistance if Cabral were unassisted, but by the end of November, 1869, Salnave was clearly done for and soon Nissage-Saget would be able to throw the whole weight of Haiti into the balance, with the moral support of France and Great Britain. The Haitians would be merely applying their own "Monroe Doctrine," the law of self-preservation as they saw it, which they would have an undoubted right to do if they were prepared to accept the responsibility, but their policy was nevertheless one of gross interference in Dominican affairs in support of a pretender so feeble that he was compelled to lurk in the bush such time as he was not actually in refuge on Haitian soil. The presence of seven American warships, which was all the promised protection ever amounted to, may have overawed some Dominicans on the coast, but in the interior their influence could hardly have been so forceful as that of the *cacos* who swarmed over the frontier. Indeed, if the previous behavior of the Dominicans is any criterion, the Haitian intervention was the one thing best calculated to influence them in favor of annexation by the United States.[43]

In the hour of victory a Haitian general, haranguing his

---

[42] Moreover, after American protection had been withdrawn, when Báez's position was perfectly plain and the Haitians were free to do all that they could to "get" him, Cabral was still unable to muster sufficient strength to stand in the open. See below, p. 109.

[43] There was precedent for the promise of protection in the annexation of Texas, with which Fabens and Cazneau were familiar. *Senate Executive Document No. 349*, 28th Cong., 1st Sess., pp. 10 f. Mexico, like Haiti, had refused to recognize the independence of a lost province and had threatened to interfere, but Texas had been unquestionably independent for nine years, the Dominican Republic for twenty-five. Moreover, Báez represented a population established for three and a half centuries, to whom the Haitians were the interlopers.

troops, cried out that instead of exterminating the Salnavists they should form a solid phalanx with them to combat the Americans, whose flag even then floated over the walls of Santo Domingo.[44] When the excitement of the moment had passed, calmer councils prevailed, but Haitian counteractivity was no less determined and vigorous for having gone underground. In obedience to instructions, Bassett warned Nissage-Saget against interference and received unqualified assurances of Haitian neutrality, the sincerity of which he did not question.[45] It was true, he said, that Haitian sympathies were with Cabral, that many of his followers were Haitians, that there was gun-running over the frontier, but he found no evidence of material aid beyond the unimportant efforts of individuals.[46] As Báez continued to complain that he had to defend himself against Haitian rather than *Cabralista* attack, Bassett was instructed to repeat his warning, whereat the Haitian government took great umbrage and demanded proofs the minister could not furnish.[47] It took him until February, 1871, to discover regular lines of supply between Haitian depots and Cabral, until April to identify Haitian regular troops operating on Dominican soil disguised as rebels.[48] The lid finally blew off when the Corps Législatif, its suspicions aroused by the meager results of its large appropriations for Cabral's benefit, threatened an investigation. The ministers of war and of foreign affairs resigned rather than faced it.[49]

[44] Bassett to Fish, No. 35, Jan. 15, 1870, Despatches, Haiti, III. This was rhetorical, but Babcock had taken possession of Samaná.

[45] *Idem* to *idem*, No. 40, Feb. 17, 1870, *loc. cit.*, IV.

[46] *Idem* to *idem*, No. 44, April 12, 1870, *loc. cit.*

[47] Bassett to Fish, No. 64, Jan. 25, 1871, Despatches, Haiti, IV.

[48] *Idem* to *idem*, Private No. 10, Feb. 7; Private No. 11, April 12, 1871, *loc. cit.* Dr. Price-Mars, who has made the first and only scholarly study of Haitian-Dominican relations, has been unable to find any Haitian evidence either confirming or refuting these specifications of material aid furnished by the Haitian government to Dominican rebels, but he considers the substance of the charge to be probably correct. It is entirely consistent with established Haitian policy as described in Price-Mars, "La diplomatie haitienne et l'independance dominicaine, 1858-1867," *Revue d'histoire et de géographie d'Haiti*, No. 32 (Jan., 1939). In 1861 Geffrard had sent his *tirailleurs* to fight the Spaniards in Santo Domingo disguised as Dominican rebels (Pierre-Eugène de Lespinasse, *Gens d'autre-fois*, p. 169).

[49] *Idem* to *idem*, No. 85, Aug. 3, 1871, Despatches, Haiti, IV.

While he was taking Haitian money, Cabral was also in correspondence with Bassett, busily hedging. He was not really opposed to annexation, he said; his record showed that. He was in arms only against the usurpation of Báez, and if he were assured that annexation would not mean his rival's perpetuation in power, that he and his followers would be secure from proscription, he would gladly submit.[50] In response to this, Fish sent word that the future governor would probably be an American and that all peaceable Dominicans would be protected.[51] Cabral declared himself satisfied, but before laying down his arms he required $150,000 to pay his debts and placate his chief adherents.[52] If the United States was really buying up venal politicians (as the opponents of annexation contended), Cabral's price was not exorbitant, but this proposition was ignored.

Neither Cabral nor Haiti could prevent the annexation of the Dominican Republic, but the United States Senate could—and did. Largely through the influence of Sumner, the treaty was rejected, twenty-eight to twenty-eight. Grant then demanded that a commission be sent to Santo Domingo to investigate the charges that had been brought against the administration, hoping thus to pave the way to annexation by joint resolution, as had been done in the case of Texas, but, although his request was granted, the attitude of the House indicated plainly that his plan could not succeed. With his party already under suspicion of domestic corruption, the President dared not strain the loyalty of his adherents any further. The commission's report was highly favorable, but Grant, having secured a personal vindication, let the matter drop.

Considered with sympathy for the people most vitally affected, the proposed annexation of the Dominican Republic could be viewed in two ways, both well expressed by Frederick Douglass, the negro secretary of the commission:

[50] *Idem* to *idem*, Private No. 5, June 14, 1870, *loc. cit.*
[51] Fish to Bassett, No. 41, July 6, 1870, Instructions, Haiti, I.
[52] Bassett to Fish, Private No. 9, Jan. 25, 1871, Despatches, Haiti, IV.

To Mr. Sumner, annexation was a measure to extinguish a coloured nation, and to do so by dishonourable means and for selfish motives. To me it meant the alliance of a weak and defenceless people, having few or none of the attributes of a nation, torn and rent by internal feuds and unable to maintain order at home or command respect abroad, to a government which would give it peace, stability, prosperity, and civilization. . . . Santo Domingo wanted to come under our government.[53]

Sumner was convinced that the Dominicans did not want to surrender their independence because he did not want them to. To him it was all a plot hatched by Cazneau, Fabens, Babcock, and others, for their own pecuniary advantage.[54] Moreover, he probably believed the propaganda furnished him in quantity by the Haitian legation, material which, according to Bassett, taxed the ingenuity, if not the consciences, of its authors.[55] On their part the advocates of the treaty did not limit themselves to the benefits to be bestowed upon the Dominicans or to their asserted eagerness for annexation. Both Manifest Destiny and the Monroe Doctrine were invoked, but, more specifically, the natural resources of the republic and the commercial possibilities were temptingly portrayed.[56] These arguments should not be allowed to obscure the fact that the original and primary objective of American policy was the acquisition of a West Indian naval base.

Even when Grant failed to exploit the commission's report no one believed that the project was dead. Stephen Preston, the Haitian minister, advised that as soon as the President had

[53] Frederick Douglass, *The Life and Times of Frederick Douglass*, pp. 359 f.

[54] They held speculative concessions the value of which would be greatly enhanced by annexation (Nevins, *Hamilton Fish*, pp. 254 ff., 275 f.).

[55] Bassett to Fish, Private No. 10, Feb. 7, 1871, Despatches, Haiti, III. Fish had evidence that the Haitian minister had spent $20,000 to defeat the treaty (Nevins, *Hamilton Fish*, p. 588). The Secretary was sufficiently vexed to write, "Mr. Preston's course . . . has not been such as to command respect or confidence in his character" (Fish to Bassett, No. 114, Aug. 31, 1872, Instructions, Haiti, I), but he felt the same way about Fabens and Babcock.

[56] J. D. Richardson, *Messages and Papers of the Presidents, 1789-1897*, VII, 61 ff. Perhaps Grant's most persuasive argument was unblushing distribution of patronage. Even the Attorney General was dismissed so that his place could be exchanged for votes (Nevins, *op. cit.*, pp. 363-368).

ANNEXATION?

been safely re-elected the treaty would be revived and forced through—therefore, let Báez be overthrown at once, while American support was withdrawn.[57] This policy was frustrated when a *Baezista* raid on Cabral's hide-out resulted in the death of a Haitian general and the utter dispersion of the rebels.[58] The Haitian press began to denounce Cabral as too expensive and too ineffectual and to urge an alliance with Báez instead, with express stipulation against alienation of territory,[59] but the Dominican president was deaf to such proposals, not daring to trust Greeks bearing gifts. In December, 1872, he leased Samaná Bay and the peninsula to a New York firm, which many supposed to be the United States in disguise, among them the fugitive Cabral. This champion of Dominican independence was still trying to make a deal in anticipation of annexation.[60]

The tension between Haiti and the United States was relieved when Grant took occasion, in his second inaugural, to declare the annexation project ended. Báez continued peacefully in office to the close of his constitutional term, when the anti-re-election issue accomplished what opposition to annexation had been unable to do. In January, 1874, he was overthrown by Ignacio María González, who had supported him in the struggle with Cabral and Nissage-Saget.[61] González terminated the concession of the Samaná Bay Company for nonpayment of rent, and, on November 19, 1874, Nissage-Saget having conveniently retired from the scene, he signed a treaty with the Haitian government of Michel Domingue requiring both states to maintain the integrity of their respective territories.[62]

If there had been any considerable public demand in the United States for the annexation of the Dominican Republic, Grant would have carried the issue to the people and no power could have thwarted him. The decisive fact was that the ex-

[57] Bassett to Fish, No. 114, Feb. 8, 1872, Despatches, Haiti, IV.
[58] *Idem* to *idem*, No. 162, Nov. 13, 1872, *loc. cit.*, V.
[59] *Idem* to *idem*, No. 164, Nov. 28, 1872, *loc. cit.*
[60] *Idem* to *idem*, No. 184, Feb. 17, 1873, *loc. cit.*
[61] *Idem* to *idem*, No. 278, Jan. 23, 1874, *loc. cit.*, VII.
[62] Jacques Nicolas Léger, *Recueil des traités et conventions de la République d'Haiti*, p. 116.

pansionists of 1870 were only a die-hard minority. Men whose attitudes had been formed in the heyday of "manifest destiny" found it difficult to readjust their views, but even Seward had observed regretfully, as early as 1868, that the attention of the majority "sensibly continued to be fastened upon the domestic questions which arose out of the late civil war."[63]   Not only was the reconstruction of the South a pressing problem, but the industrialization of the North and the settlement of the West were also matters of absorbing interest.   The completion of the first transcontinental railroad in 1869 established overland contact with California, reducing the importance of the isthmian route and removing the necessity for a West Indian naval station.   The great fleet of 1865 was sold off or scrapped until, by 1884, the navy had dwindled into insignificance and coaling stations were no longer desired.[64]   The failure of Seward and Grant to acquire Samaná Bay was attributable, not to Haitian opposition, nor even to moral indignation aroused by Sumner's eloquence, but to the utter indifference of the American people, intent upon their own affairs.

[63] Weinberg, *Manifest Destiny*, p. 245.
[64] Frelinghuysen to Langston, No. 258, Feb. 1, 1884, Instructions, Haiti, II.

CHAPTER VII

HONESTY AND HONOR

Essential as it is that the intercourse between nations should be marked by the highest honor as well as honesty, the moment that the Government of the United States discovers that a claim it makes on a foreign Government cannot be honorably pressed, that moment, no matter what may be the period of procedure, that claim should be dropped.
—THOMAS F. BAYARD, January 20, 1887

FOR NEARLY twenty years following the failure of Grant's Dominican scheme Americans took a minimum of interest in overseas affairs, and relations with Haiti followed a routine course. Consequently, the business of the legation consisted largely of claims.[1] Although those based on contract far exceeded those for spoliation, nearly all were the result of unsettled political conditions. Revolutionary governments showed an understandable disposition to repudiate the obligations of their predecessors, particularly when they were presented in the form of unpaid bills for powder and shot used against the revolutionists themselves.

No serious claims resulted from Geffrard's administration, but Sylvain Salnave left an impressive legacy of spoliation and contract cases. Those presented by American citizens amounted to $531,069.55 and an additional 13,890,514 *gourdes* of uncer-

[1] Another routine problem involved the so-called right of asylum in legations and consulates, unrecognized by international law but sanctioned by custom in Haiti, where political violence and lack of confidence in the courts seemed to justify the practice. It imposed a terrific burden on ministers and consuls, from which they would gladly have been relieved, but every effort to abolish the "right" was frustrated by the Haitian authorities themselves, who, while they might complain of the shelter afforded their enemies, wished to keep their own line of retreat open. The most serious case of this kind occurred during the presidency of Domingue, when Boisrond-Canal was for five months in refuge at the American legation. Every secretary of state condemned the practice in principle, but none was willing to place the minister in the invidious position of being compelled to refuse what his colleagues granted and local usage condoned. The problem could be solved only through the establishment of orderly processes of government, but the practice actually fostered instability by conferring immunity upon tyrants and conspirators.

tain value. Of this sum, $35,000 was demanded by James De
Long, consul at Les Cayes, for an assault upon his person, but
the minister himself eliminated the claim when he learned that
De Long had acted as a partisan in Haitian politics. There
were eleven claims for the destruction of personal effects when
Salnave burned a quarter of Port-au-Prince as a military measure and four others for pillaging by *piquets* at Miragoane and
near Les Cayes; the total for these spoliations was $38,246.64
and 63,600 *gourdes*. Seven claimants presented unpaid bills
amounting to $254,367.08 for the purchase or repair of four
warships, three of which had passed into the possession of
Saget; and there were five other contract claims for $211,455.83
and 13,826,914 *gourdes*, based on Salnave coffee bonds.[2] The
duty of the legation with regard to the spoliation claims was
plain, but Fish took care to forbid Bassett to intervene officially
in behalf of any contract claim, although permitting him to use
his unofficial good offices. Persons entering into contract with
foreign governments were supposed to calculate the risks and
adjust the rates accordingly, and they could not expect the
United States to collect their bad debts for them.[3]

As soon as a legislature could be assembled, Nissage-Saget
recommended the repudiation of all Salnave debts; his purpose
was to pass on to the legislators the onus of arranging the inevitable settlement. With equal finesse the legislature dodged
the issue by appointing a commission, which pondered the question for more than a year and reported too late for action before
adjournment in the autumn of 1871. Its plan provided for
funding the recognized contract claims with interest from 1872
and retirement of principal in ten annual instalments beginning
in 1876. The chief difficulty arose in connection with the coffee
bonds, the holders of which considered themselves the victims
of a forced loan rather than ordinary contract claimants. In
1868, when Salnave had withdrawn his depreciated hundred-
gourde notes from circulation, giving in exchange bonds prom-

[2] Bassett to Fish, No. 96, Oct. 31; No. 97, Nov. 14, 1871, Despatches, Haiti, IV.
[3] Fish to Bassett, No. 40, June 27, 1870, Instructions, Haiti, I.

ising one pound of coffee for each 3.50 *gourdes*, Haitian debtors, having no faith in the bonds, had unloaded their *gourde* notes on their creditors, who had to accept them as legal tender and make the exchange. The commission proposed to pay them the gold value of the notes at the date on which they were turned in, which was more than the coffee would have been worth at the date on which delivery was promised, but meanwhile the price of coffee had risen until the amount named in the bonds was worth ten times the exchange value of the notes in 1868. Bassett declined to support the bondholders' demand for coffee or its equivalent at current prices, considering the commission's offer to be fair enough.[4] However, as the spring of 1872 advanced, he began to lose patience. The contract claims had been accepted after *ex parte* examination by a hostile commission, but no more was offered than payment in dribblets over thirteen years and even that had yet to be passed by a legislature inclined toward repudiation.[5] As for the spoliation claims, for nearly two years a mixed commission had mulled over them without making any progress.

At this juncture the minister received a demonstration of effective claims collection. On the morning of June 11, 1872, two German warships entered the harbor of Port-au-Prince, and at noon their commander demanded that the Haitian government pay $14,550 on board by sundown. This sum was to satisfy a Salnave contract claim accepted by the commission and a spoliation claim dating from 1865, which had never been brought to the attention of the Saget administration. The minister of foreign affairs tried to open a discussion, but the Germans declared that they were "acquainted with Haitian policy and determined not to be baffled by French politeness and fair phrases." Punctually at sunset they seized the Haitian navy, and before morning the money, borrowed from a German merchant, had been paid. The German commander had been

---

[4] Bassett to Fish, No. 97, Nov. 14, 1871, Despatches, Haiti, IV.
[5] *Idem* to *idem*, No. 117, March 8, 1872, *loc. cit.*, V.

cool and deliberate, evidently acting on positive orders from Berlin.[6]

During the summer of 1872 President Saget and the Corps Législatif continued their maneuvers; each sought to fasten upon the other responsibility for the settlement of the contract claims. A legislative committee, after expressing regret that the commission had not recommended a general 90 per cent repudiation, accepted the claims it had recognized but proposed payment without interest over a period of twenty years. Then, having demonstrated that the President held no monopoly of patriotism, the legislature voted to postpone the whole question until its next session. Bassett, his patience exhausted, spoke bluntly to the foreign minister, saying that the United States did not press for the recognition of claims which Haiti deemed unjust or for faster payment than Haitian finances might warrant, but that his government did expect something to be done about the claims accepted by the commission. The cabinet, with the recent German raid in mind, laid Bassett's note before the chambers, demanding action in the present session,[7] and the Corps, having at last compelled Saget to take the initiative, found itself quite ready to legislate. On August 24, 1872, it provided that the Salnave contract claims should be paid after the French debt, the revolutionary debt of 1869, and the back pay of Salnave's army had been disposed of.[8] Having achieved this masterpiece of domestic politics, the legislature happily adjourned without having done anything about the Salnave spoliation claims, although the several mixed commissions, stimulated by the German naval visit, had finally managed to present their reports during the session.

Bassett was far from satisfied with an arrangement which discriminated against the creditors of the recognized government of Salnave in favor of the creditors of the revolution and even of the soldiers who had fought for Salnave against the present regime, and he succeeded in persuading the Secretary of

[6] *Idem* to *idem*, No. 136, June 21, 1872, Despatches, Haiti, V.
[7] *Idem* to *idem*, No. 142, July 31, 1872, Despatches, Haiti, V.
[8] *Idem* to *idem*, No. 154, Oct. 3, 1872, *loc. cit.*

State to send him an instruction declaring that the United States would not tolerate injustice toward American citizens.[9] Nissage-Saget was sufficiently impressed to call a special session of the legislature to amend the law of 1872 and to deal with the spoliations.[10] Although the mixed commissions had rejected no American claims in the latter category, they had cut the French 87 per cent and the British 90 per cent.[11] Now the foreign minister asked for an appropriation of $152,000 with which to pay this recognized debt with interest from 1870, but the temper of the legislators was such that he was glad to emerge from the debate with $115,000 for payment without interest. As soon as the French minister learned that an appropriation had been made, he demanded an instant settlement in cash, allowing the treasury no time in which to handle the funds conveniently; the British minister, hearing that his colleague had been paid, demanded equal favor; and by the time that Bassett had arrived, the treasury was empty. However, he, too, was paid out of private funds, with thanks for his courtesy in not demanding it.[12]

In view of the outburst over a relatively small sum for spoliations, there was no hope for any modification of the law concerning contract claims. Indeed, the executive and the legislature had become absorbed in the old question of ministerial responsibility, to the exclusion of all other matters. Saget refused to dismiss two members of his cabinet and brought the special session to an abrupt close.[13] He then indicated that he would quietly begin payment of the $100,000 which the commission had set as the just value of the American-held coffee

[9] Fish to Bassett, No. 125, Nov. 12, 1872, Instructions, Haiti, I. This official intervention in behalf of contract claimants was aimed only at discrimination in the mode of payment.

[10] Bassett to Fish, No. 195, March 26, 1873, Despatches, Haiti, VI; *Papers Relating to the Foreign Relations of the United States* (1873), I, 477-480.

[11] *Idem* to *idem*, No. 153, Oct. 13, 1873, *loc. cit.*, V. The French had originally claimed $442,000, the British $150,000, as compared to the $40,000 claimed by Americans. Three American claims were temporarily set aside for lack of evidence, of which one was eventually paid at a considerable reduction.

[12] *Idem* to *idem*, No. 257, Oct. 29, 1873, *loc. cit.*, VI.

[13] *Foreign Relations* (1874), pp. 583, 588.

bonds.[14]   Four of the claimants were paid in full and the fifth in part, with custom-house credits. Bassett urged that the warship claims be settled before the approaching expiration of Saget's term, but the government insisted that it must proceed cautiously, since it was violating the act of 1872. Although it would not deal with these claims as a class, it did actually pay three, totalling $128,628.23.[15]   Further action was prevented by the confusion attending Saget's last days in office.

During the brief administration of Michel Domingue (1874-1876) nothing was done to clear away the remaining Salnave claims, which amounted to $121,766.71, but three new cases were added to the list. To Boisrond-Canal the Winchester Arms Company presented an unpaid bill for $25,000, and Heuvelman, Haven & Company, of New York, another for $109,752.98, balance due on the construction of public buildings,[16] while Adrian Lazare entered a $500,000 claim for breach of contract.[17]   Lazare had undertaken to establish a national bank at Port-au-Prince, a project dear to the hearts of Domingue and his nephew, Rameau, the real ruler of Haiti during these years. The government was to provide $500,000 capital, Lazare $1,000,000. When, after an extension of time, the concessionaire was unable to produce the promised funds, the administration reluctantly cancelled the contract, but Lazare remained on excellent terms with Rameau, accepting appointment as Haitian consul general in New York and $10,000 to cover the expenses he had incurred in the promotion. It was only after Domingue had been overthrown that he discovered that he had been damaged. Bassett, with whom he had lived while in Port-au-Prince, believed that he had acted in good faith but had undertaken more than he could perform. The minister, despite his poor opinion of Rameau, considered the Haitian government to have been entirely within its rights and regarded the claim

[14] *Ibid.*, p. 591.   The bondholders had claimed $211,455.43 and 13,826,914 *gourdes.*
[15] Bassett to Evarts, No. 495, April 24, 1877, Despatches, Haiti, IX.
[16] Bassett to Evarts, No. 496, April 24, 1877, Despatches, Haiti, IX.
[17] Fish to Bassett, No. 283, Sept. 18, 1876, Instructions, Haiti, II.

as unfounded.[18]   He withheld it when presenting those of the Winchester Arms and Heuvelman, Haven companies to the commission appointed to review the "Domingue claims."

In November, 1876, the Corps Législatif created a sinking fund for the payment of recognized debts, which, at that time, amounted to $1,750,000.   Precedence was given to the old French debt, of which but $640,000 remained unpaid.   Fourth in order came the debts of the revolution of 1868 (only $12,000 by this time), followed by the remaining "Salnave claims" ($450,000).[19]   According to custom, the engagements of Domingue were repudiated, but with provision for the future consideration of all just claims (depending upon the amount of pressure exerted, said Bassett).[20]   This maneuver was really intended to fix a low starting point for haggling over the readjustment of the loan that Domingue had floated in France, a transaction saturated with fraud.   Actually, the Winchester and Heuvelman, Haven claims were accepted without any attempt at evasion,[21] and, if their payment was not so prompt, the reason was a lack of means rather than of will.

By the autumn of 1877 the claims situation which had created so many difficulties in Haitian-American relations appeared to have been cleared up.   Thanks to the friendly co-operation of Boisrond-Canal, only one case remained unsettled,[22] but if Canal congratulated himself on having removed a constant source of friction, he was destined to disappointment. The installation of a new secretary at the State Department in Washington had been an invitation to all those whose claims had hitherto been deemed unworthy of support to try again, and William M. Evarts was an easy mark for plausible adventurers.

Evarts had not been long in office when he heard from the

---

[18] Bassett to Evarts, No. 495, April 24, 1877, Despatches, Haiti, IX.

[19] Bassett to Evarts, No. 496, April 24, 1877, *loc. cit.*

[20] Bassett to Fish, No. 476, Jan. 30, 1877, *loc. cit.*

[21] *Idem* to Evarts, No. 539, Sept. 24, 1877, *loc. cit.*, X.

[22] The Oaksmith claim for $100,595.42 due on the purchase of a warship by Salnave was still pending.

lawyers of Adrian Lazare, who represented that the Haitian government itself had prevented their client from fulfilling his contract and that its cancellation was an arbitrary and unjust proceeding. The Secretary of State was impressed, but, with Bassett's condemnation of the claim before him, he hesitated to act until he had a report from John Mercer Langston, the new minister to Haiti.[23] Langston, who was not indisposed to disparage Bassett, exploited Evarts's half-conviction, declaring that his predecessor had been misleading and unfair to the claimant. In reaching this conclusion he consulted only one source of information, his private secretary, who was none other than Adrian Lazare.[24] (Indeed, one might wonder who really was the employer and who the employee, for throughout these proceedings Langston's conduct was more appropriate to a claimant's lawyer than a responsible public officer.) The minister's unqualified endorsement of his secretary's claim served to confirm the opinion of Evarts, who ordered that it be vigorously pressed. Thus, although Evarts and Langston signed the despatches, in reality Lazare at Port-au-Prince had responded to Lazare at Washington and framed the decision uttered in the name of the United States. The gullibility of the Secretary of State was the more remarkable in that he was a noted lawyer.[25]

Evarts had already instructed Langston to limit his efforts in behalf of contract claimants to the exercise of personal good offices only. To justify special consideration for Lazare, it was necessary to accuse Haiti of arbitrary injustice rather than involuntary delinquency, and this was done by citing a clause in the bank concession providing for the arbitration of disputes. The United States demanded that Haiti either satisfy Lazare or submit to arbitration.[26] Haiti protested that the clause in question was intended to apply only to the interpretation of the contract after the bank was in operation, that Lazare's failure

[23] Evarts to Langston, No. 8, Dec. 13, 1877, Instructions, Haiti, II.

[24] Langston to Evarts, No. 26, Jan. 25, 1878, Despatches, Haiti, XI; John Mercer Langston, *From the Virginia Plantation to the National Capitol*, p. 360.

[25] Langston also had some claim to legal fame. Perhaps for this reason Evarts relied on his conclusions without studying the evidence himself.

[26] Evarts to Langston, No. 8, Dec. 13, 1878, Instructions, Haiti, II.

to produce a penny when plainly required to deposit a million dollars was too obvious to require reference to a third party. The several minor issues that he had raised, long after the cancellation, could not be used to force the arbitration of the main question. The claim was described with considerable bitterness as "one of the most fraudulent of those which are so frequently brought by foreign adventurers against minor American governments,"[27] but Haitian protests and explanations made no impression whatever upon Evarts and Langston, except to increase their exasperation at Haitian stubbornness and persistence in "wrong-doing." Every argument was met with an inflexible demand for settlement or arbitration, and Langston was instructed to keep at it until Haiti gave in.[28] The result was a deadlock.

In reviving discarded claims to take the place of those happily settled by Canal, Evarts did not rest with the Lazare case. Antonio Pelletier, who had spent seventeen fruitless years in the lobbies of the State Department and the Capitol, at last discovered a sympathetic auditor.

In October, 1860, Pelletier had sailed from Mobile for a pleasure voyage in the Caribbean. "Being at that time rich and prosperous," he later explained, "I designed to visit several ports, where I had formerly navigated when poor, and where I had friends who I believed would rejoice in my prosperity and among whom I wished at any rate to exhibit the evidence of my success." The bark employed for this ostentatious excursion was an ex-slaver; the crew were later described as a gang of "rowdies and highbinders."[29] After visiting several Caribbean ports where his conduct, probably criminal, was certainly at variance with the avowed object of the voyage,[30] the captain reached Port-au-Prince in January, 1861, and there attempted to engage fifty negroes to go with him to Navassa to get a load of guano. Because of a disturbance on shipboard

---

[27] Preston to Evarts, June 9, 1879, Notes from Haiti, III.

[28] F. W. Seward to Langston, No. 58, March 12, 1879, Instructions, Haiti, II.

[29] *Senate Report No. 425*, 43d Cong., 1st Sess., pp. 1 f.

[30] A full account may be found in *Foreign Relations* (1887), pp. 595 f.

he had four of the crew lodged in jail, and they proceeded to denounce him to the authorities as a slaver. When a search of the ship revealed an unusual supply of arms, manacles, water casks, and provisions, the American commercial agent and British consul demanded that Pelletier be arrested, but the Haitian government let him go on his promise to sail at once for New Orleans. A few days later he appeared at Fort Liberté, a remote northern port, disguising his identity and again seeking to entice fifty negroes on board. The scheme might have worked, had not another member of the crew escaped to denounce him as a slaver. The "pleasure voyage" ended in a Haitian jail.

Pelletier was tried for piracy and sentenced to death, but the court of cassation ordered a new trial, which resulted in a sentence of only five years' imprisonment. In 1863 he escaped and made his way to Washington to present a claim for the wrongs he had suffered.

The American agent who attended Pelletier's trial declared that he would have called for American warships to pursue him had the Haitians released him a second time, but certain congressmen were persuaded to appeal to the Secretary of State, with the result that when Whidden sailed in 1862 he was instructed to investigate. The loathsome conditions of Pelletier's imprisonment aroused the sympathy of the commissioner, who accepted without question his story of how the Haitians had "framed" him.[31] However, Seward remained unconvinced, deciding that

proof of the citizenship of [Pelletier, a native of France] is not sufficient to warrant an interposition in his behalf. But allowing the reverse to be the fact, his conduct in Hayti and on its coasts is conceived to have afforded the reasonable ground of suspicion against him . . . which led to his arrest, trial, and conviction in regular course of law, with which result it is not deemed expedient to interfere.[32]

Pelletier presented his claim to Seward directly in 1864, without success. Four years later the House of Representatives

---

[31] Whidden to Seward, No. 11, Dec. 25, 1862; No. 46, Nov. 6, 1863, Despatches, Haiti, I.

[32] Seward to Whidden, No. 36, Nov. 30, 1863, Instructions, Haiti, I.

was induced to call for the papers in the case, but, after examining them, it dropped the subject. In 1871, Seward having retired, Pelletier's lawyers tried their luck with Hamilton Fish, with negative result. The Senate was next applied to, but the report of its committee on foreign relations ridiculed Pelletier's explanation of his voyage and questioned the authenticity of his naturalization papers.[33] On the fifth attempt the hardy mariner —or rather the lawyers who had his claim in hand—discovered Evarts.

In March, 1878, the solicitor of the State Department advised Evarts that "the proceedings of the Haitian authorities towards Captain Antonio Pelletier . . . were unwarranted by the principles of public law; were, moreover, prosecuted with a degree of harshness and cruelty inconsistent with the practices and usages of civilized nations . . . ," that the witnesses against him had been unworthy of credit, and that the evidence failed to substantiate a charge of piracy. As in Lazare's case, the Secretary of State was scrupulous enough to admit that he might be imperfectly informed, but again he prejudiced Langston's investigation by revealing a preconceived opinion. The unfavorable report of the commercial agent he attributed to partial and incorrect information, while Whidden's condemnation of the Haitian authorities he described as just.[34] (It is strange that Evarts, a distinguished lawyer, did not note that the commercial agent had been an eye-witness to many of the events in question, while Whidden's only source of information had been the same as the State Department's—that is, Pelletier himself.) As might have been expected, Langston agreed with his superior, and was thereupon instructed to press "with all energy" the claim, which by 1879 had grown to the colossal figure of $2,466,480. Evarts was "convinced that a dispassionate reopening of the case [would] result in recognition of the great wrong done." Any other result would be deplored.[35]

Instead of recoiling in dismay before the ghost of the Pel-

[33] *Foreign Relations* (1887), p. 594.
[34] Evarts to Langston, No. 23, April 12, 1878, Instructions, Haiti, II.
[35] *Idem to idem*, No. 61, March 24, 1879, *loc. cit.*

letier case, Boisrond-Canal agreeably consented to review it. No doubt he considered the claim so preposterous that an explanation and a reference to its rejection by Seward, Fish, the House of Representatives, and the Senate would be sufficient to lay it once more in the grave. He had not yet learned that when the legal firm of Evarts and Langston had once taken a case, all explanation and argument were in vain. However, at this point the discussion was interrupted by a change in administration. When the tumult subsided, Lysius Salomon was found in residence at the palace, while Boyer Bazelais had departed for a brief sojourn in Jamaica. The election had not been won without the use of artillery, and three new spoliation claims were the result.

Salomon was as determined as Boisrond-Canal had been in denying the justice of the claims of Lazare and Pelletier. It was impossible to reach an understanding in the latter case, since Evarts accepted his client's story at its face value and argued from that premise, while the Haitians had an entirely different version of what had happened. The debate was further confused by a failure to define terms, for Haitian municipal law designated kidnapping into slavery as piracy, while Evarts could find no evidence that Pelletier had committed robbery on the high seas. Langston was instructed to propose arbitration, and, if that were refused, to demand satisfaction,[36] but Salomon stalled off the minister for eight months, so that the ultimatum was not delivered until February, 1881.[37] Even then the threat had no effect, since no American warship was in sight. None came, for the new secretary of state, James G. Blaine, seems never to have learned of the wrongs of Pelletier before he was retired by the assassination of President Garfield. His successor, Frederick T. Frelinghuysen, was equally ignorant of the case until his attention was called to it by a senatorial request for the papers since 1868, a clever device of Pelletier's lawyers which capitalized their success with Evarts while drawing the veil over the opinions of Seward and Fish. Fre-

[36] *Idem* to *idem*, No. 112, June 14, 1880, Instructions, Haiti, II.
[37] Langston to Evarts, No. 356, March 3, 1881, Despatches, Haiti, XIV.

linghuysen accepted Evarts's judgment and again instructed Langston to threaten the use of force if Salomon refused to reconsider,[38] whereupon Salomon resorted to the ultimate evasion, the transfer of the discussions to Washington. A ten months' delay was gained by that expedient, but in June, 1883, Langston was directed to resume his pressure.[39] Then, just as the case seemed hopeless, fate granted another reprieve. Boyer Bazelais returned from Jamaica to lead an uprising in the South, there was rioting at Port-au-Prince in which the foreign office with all its archives was burned, and even Langston had to admit the necessity for a postponement.

Salomon found himself in a desperate plight indeed. He was having difficulty in suppressing the rebellion, while enough spoliations were being committed to promise serious trouble for the future. Not only did it seem impossible to evade much longer the Lazare and Pelletier claims, amounting to three million dollars, but the British were threatening to seize the Haitian island of Tortuga as surety for a $682,000 claim of their own. As he pondered this situation, Salomon hit upon a plan that would solve all his problems. He would foil the British and gain American support by ceding Tortuga to the United States on terms that would extinguish the American claims and strengthen his position against the rebels.[40] Frelinghuysen declined the offer, stating that the acquisition of territory overseas was contrary to American policy.[41] The Haitian president must have surmised that Tortuga was not sufficiently attractive, for he proceeded forthwith to offer the Mole St. Nicolas, pointing out its strategic importance in connection with the Panama Canal, then under construction, and predicting that the British would take it if the United States did not forestall them.[42] His second proposal was considered by the Arthur cabinet and rejected.[43]

[38] Frelinghuysen to Langston, No. 168, Feb. 27, 1882, Instructions, Haiti, II.

[39] *Idem* to *idem*, No. 212, June 13, 1883, *loc. cit.*

[40] Langston to Frelinghuysen, No. 557, May 30, 1883, Despatches, Haiti, XVI.

[41] Frelinghuysen to Langston, No. 217, June 20, 1883, Instructions, Haiti, II.

[42] Langston to Frelinghuysen, Special and Confidential, Nov. 9, 1883, Despatches, Haiti, XVII.

[43] Frelinghuysen to Langston, No. 258, Feb. 1, 1884, Instructions, Haiti, II.

By January, 1884, the rebellion had been suppressed, but that meant that Salomon must face renewed pressure on the claims issue. Believing that there was real danger that the British might seize Tortuga, ostensibly on account of the unsettled Maunder claim[44] but actually with the Panama Canal in view, the Haitian president dared not antagonize the United States, whose Monroe Doctrine he might have occasion to invoke. Consequently, Stephen Preston, his minister at Washington, was instructed to negotiate for the arbitration of the Lazare and Pelletier claims, and on May 28, 1884, Frelinghuysen signed an executive agreement providing for that solution. William Strong, a retired justice of the Supreme Court, was chosen as sole arbiter, and his separate decisions were to be considered conclusive and final.[45]

Meanwhile Salomon busied himself with the adjustment of pending minor cases. He had already paid in full the one remaining Salnave claim, for $100,595.42, which even Boisrond-Canal had dodged.[46] Six American claims totalling $100,000 for injuries to person and property during the rebellion of 1883, were settled, with relative promptitude, by the payment of $14,130.[47] By March, 1886, the spoliation claims of 1879 had also been disposed of,[48] and Salomon could maintain that his attitude on the subject was not at all recalcitrant.

[44] This claim for $682,000 was based upon a concession for the exploitation of Tortuga which each party accused the other of having violated. It was finally settled in 1887 by the payment of $154,200, under the guns of H. M. S. Canada (Foreign Relations, 1877, p. 425; Thompson to Bayard, No. 132, April 29, 1887, Despatches, Haiti, XXI).

[45] Frelinghuysen to Langston, No. 279, June 9, 1884, Instructions, Haiti, II.

[46] Langston to Frelinghuysen, No. 517, Feb. 19, 1883, Despatches, Haiti, XVI. This claim was based on the purchase of an ironclad by Salnave. The reason for the discrimination against it was that while Salnave's other ships had passed into the possession of his successors, this one had been lost at sea en route to Haiti and no hard-pressed Haitian president had been willing to "pay for a dead horse."

[47] Foreign Relations (1884), pp. 311-314, 329; (1885), p. 526; Thompson to Bayard, No. 156, Dec. 1, 1887, Despatches, Haiti, XXII. Four were settled in 1885; two others, involving disputed citizenship, in 1887.

[48] Langston to Evarts, No. 601, Dec. 17, 1883; No. 624, Jan. 22, 1884, Despatches, Haiti, XVII; Thompson to Bayard, No. 79, March 8, 1886, loc. cit., XX. These claims were reduced 67 per cent on the average (British, 79 per cent; French, 61 per cent; German, 58 per cent), so that the Americans, cut only 47 per cent, fared well. The American claims were only one per cent of the total.

On June 13, 1885, Justice Strong rendered his decision, awarding Pelletier $57,200 and Lazare $117,500 with interest from 1875. Thomas F. Bayard, who had recently taken office as the first Democratic secretary of state since 1861, knew nothing of the two cases and accepted the result of the arbitration without question. John E. W. Thompson, the new minister at Port-au-Prince, was instructed to arrange for prompt payment, and Congress was informed that, according to the terms of the protocol, the awards were final.

During the hearings the Haitians had been hampered by the loss of their archives. Not only was Lazare's the only copy of the concession available, but also it was impossible to refute his statement that on the day appointed he had been ready to produce the million dollars, which he had secured in Europe, and that he had been prevented from doing so by Rameau (long since deceased). On this assumption he had been awarded damages.[49] However, in April, 1886, Preston came forward with evidence obtained in England, which, according to his claim, he had been unable to submit to the arbiter because Frelinghuysen had refused the necessary extension of time.[50] It showed that the English firms which, according to Lazare, had put up his million-dollar capital, had actually engaged only to grant closely restricted credits for the use of the bank after it had been established. With this information at hand it was evident not only that Lazare was a consummate liar, but that the State Department and the arbiter had been rather easily duped. It is difficult to understand how either Frelinghuysen or Strong could have failed to see that the check on Lazare's alleged investors which Preston proposed to make was essential to a just decision of the case. Strong admitted that the new evidence would have altered his judgment, but held that the matter had passed from his hands to those of the Secretary of State.[51]

When Bayard began to study the case, he was amazed to

[49] *Foreign Relations* (1887), p. 616.
[50] Preston to Bayard, April 15, 1886, Notes from Haiti, III.
[51] *Foreign Relations* (1887), pp. 619 f.

discover Bassett's despatch discrediting the claim, which had been suppressed. Haitian counsel had been ignorant of its existence, and Lazare's lawyers were not expected to bring it up, but the Secretary wondered why Frelinghuysen's solicitor had failed to introduce it along with the Langston-Evarts correspondence. Lazare's statement of 1877, written when the Haitian archives were available and the American minister had been a witness to most of the proceedings in question, was so widely at variance with his testimony in 1885 that Bayard had no difficulty in reaching a decision. He refused to collect the award.[52]

In deciding the Pelletier case Justice Strong had ruled out damages for the confiscation of vessel and goods, since it had been shown that Pelletier was not the true owner, but he had allowed damages for false imprisonment, holding that Haiti had failed to prove the commission of any overt act "that amounted to piracy recognized as such by the law of nations." It was the old difficulty about definition of terms. The arbiter did not "care to inquire what the law of Hayti defining piracy may have been," since the protocol under which he acted said that the arbitration should be conducted according to the rules of international law. From this rather strained construction it was argued that there was no jurisdiction over Pelletier in the Haitian courts and that reparation was due him.[53]

Encouraged by his success in the Lazare case, in November, 1886, Preston called Bayard's attention to the Pelletier award, pointing out that whereas the American position had been based upon the assumption that Pelletier's had been an innocent voyage and the charges against him groundless, Strong, while deciding in his favor on a technicality, had taken the opposite view, saying, "It is beyond doubt that had the bark been captured and brought into a United States port when she was seized at Fort Liberté, she would have been condemned by the United States courts as an intended slaver." Should Pelletier recover damages because his evil intentions had been frustrated?

[52] Ibid., pp. 615-620.   [53] Ibid., p. 598.

Was Haiti forbidden to defend her own citizens by the application of her own law to a crime committed in Haitian waters?[54]

As in the Lazare case, as soon as the facts were brought to his attention, Bayard found himself in perfect agreement with the Haitian minister. In his opinion Haiti was within her rights in punishing one engaged in such a conspiracy, regardless of the name applied to it. For this reason and "because [Pelletier's] cause [was] of itself so saturated with turpitude and infamy that on it no action, judicial or diplomatic [could] be based," he again declined to undertake the collection of the award.[55] As might be expected, Bayard was hailed at Port-au-Prince as *chevalier sans peur et sans reproche.*

Unquestionably, successive Haitian governments made difficult the settlement of even well-founded claims, which were bound to develop so long as Haitian political conditions remained unstable. Boisrond-Canal's record was clear, but Saget and Salomon yielded only to pressure and Domingue not at all. The Corps Législatif was invariably hostile. The exigencies of domestic politics and of a depleted treasury had much to do with this attitude. Moreover, there was often reason to suspect fraud, or at least exaggeration, in claims the government dared not reject outright. Procrastination and evasion were the only defense of a weak nation under continual pressure from powerful neighbors.

American ministers, exasperated by unfulfilled promises and endless excuses, came to envy the European representatives whose governments had no scruples against employing force, or the threat of force, in order to obtain satisfaction in difficult cases, even those based on contract. No American warship visited Port-au-Prince to expedite the settlement of claims. Once, in the Lazare-Pelletier cases, Haiti was threatened, but even then it was arbitration, not payment, that was demanded and it may be assumed that British pressure on the Maunder claim had more to do with Salomon's surrender than had fear of American coercion. Despite the supposed advantages of

[54] Preston to Bayard, Nov. 18, 1886, Notes from Haiti, IV.
[55] *Foreign Relations* (1887), p. 608.

their European colleagues, the American ministers had a higher percentage of their claims paid, even though the settlements may have been longer delayed.[56]

The attitudes of successive secretaries of state on claims were indicative of the caliber of the incumbents of that high office. Seward and Fish were considerate, never abusing their superior power. Evarts and Frelinghuysen were impatient and uncompromising, superficial in their judgments, but exacting in their demands. After their regime, the advent of a man like Bayard, who could distinguish between honesty and honor, was a welcome change.

[56] Bassett settled 40 claims, Langston 38, Thompson 35, Douglass 5, Durham 8, Smythe 10, and Powell 29. They had amounted to three million dollars, but had been scaled down 40 per cent (Powell to Hay, No. 1804, June 5, 1905, Despatches, Haiti, XLVI).

CHAPTER VIII

NEUTRALITY

As it is now publicly and well known that a thoroughly disordered, if not anarchical, condition of affairs prevails in the island of Hayti, which it is not the authorized function of this or any other foreign Government to interfere with or suppress, it would be the part of common prudence for merchants in the United States to abstain from attempting to pursue commerce in that region. . . .

—THOMAS F. BAYARD, December 7, 1888

CIVIL WARS, disastrous to Haiti and to normal American commerce there, were a source of profit to some Americans, for on such occasions quantities of cast-off military equipment could be unloaded on an eager market at speculative prices. These "merchants of death" did not create the demand that they supplied—their trade could not have existed without the provocation of Haitian "Ins," the restless ambitions of Haitian "Outs" —but their services did make possible many a disturbance of the peace, prolong conflicts already begun, and thus aggravate political instability and augment its destructive effects. Moreover, the issue of a given contest could be influenced, if not determined, by the relative ability of the contending factions to obtain munitions from the United States, a fact that made the attitude of the Federal authorities on the application of the neutrality laws a matter of prime importance in Haitian politics. The American government never abused this power to foster the candidacy of any aspirant for presidential honors, but it was inevitable that it should be accused of doing so.

Until recently the laws of the United States did not restrict the exportation of munitions to belligerents or even to revolutionists, nor was there any obligation in international law to do so; it was held that the government adversely affected must protect itself by the exercise of its undoubted right to capture contraband in transit.[1] The Federal statutes, however, did for-

[1] John Bassett Moore, *A Digest of International Law*, VII, 955-973.

bid that vessels be armed or expeditions organized within American jurisdiction to commit hostilities against any "prince, state, colony, district, or people" at peace with the United States. These prohibitions operated invariably against Haitian rebels, but not necessarily against the established government, even though the rebels might argue that they represented a friendly "district or people." Recognition of a state of belligerency would be essential to the application of the law's restrictions to the activities of titular authorities, and the United States, long indignant over British recognition of Confederate belligerent rights, was indisposed to extend that favor to Haitian insurgents. The term "neutrality," as applied to the statutes, did not indicate either obligation or intent to observe impartiality between a recognized government and unrecognized parties seeking its overthrow.

During the Haitian conflict of 1868-1869 the great Federal fleet of 1865 was for sale, and both sides rushed into the market to buy, for command of the sea was of prime strategic importance in roadless Haiti. Seward ruled that there could be no objection to purchases by Salnave, although "a sale to the rebels would be another thing,"[2] but when Fish succeeded to the secretaryship he excluded Salnave from the market too, thus reducing him to a plane of legal equality with his adversaries.[3] By that time the dictator had procured enough ships to turn the tide of war in his favor; and, if the neutrality laws had been enforced against the rebels with the "due diligence" insisted upon by the United States in the *Alabama* claims, even then being pressed against Great Britain, he would probably have won, but such was not the case. The agents of Nissage-Saget were able to procure ships, armaments, and crews in the United States and to assemble them at Saint Marc without Federal interference, despite the repeated protests of the Haitian chargé.[4] Fish's only excuse was that the vessels had sailed

[2] Morse, *The Diary of Gideon Welles*, III, 424.

[3] Fish to Laroche, April 3, 1869, Notes to Haiti, I.

[4] Hollister to Fish, No. 27, March 8; No. 33, April 24, 1869, Despatches, Haiti, III. Laroche to Hoare (Attorney General), May 6, 1869; to Fish, May 15, 21, and 31, June 19 and 25, and July 19, 1869, Notes from Haiti, I.

unarmed,[5] a defense that was lame indeed beside accepted American statements of neutral duty.[6] The fact that armaments and unarmed vessels were dispatched separately, rendered the task of the Federal authorities more difficult, but fourteen years later Secretary Frelinghuysen proved that the law could be enforced. In March, 1883, the steamer *Tropic,* having cleared from Philadelphia for Jamaica with an undeclared cargo of munitions, picked up Boyer Bazelais and his followers at Inagua and landed them at Miragoane for an attack on the recognized government of Salomon. On her return to Philadelphia her officers were promptly tried and convicted of violation of the neutrality laws.[7] The rebel agents escaped unpunished, but their efforts to send further aid to Bazelais were thwarted by the vigilance of the Haitian minister and the vigorous co-operation of the Federal authorities. Preston's charges were no better sustained than were those of his less fortunate predecessor in 1869,[8] but he secured the confiscation of the *Mary E. Hogan* and of the cargo of her tender in court proceedings which established that "an expedition organized in parts, and dispatched from the United States to meet at a common rendezvous . . . and thence proceed to acts of hostility against a friendly power" was within the prohibition of the statute.[9] Deprived of anticipated succor from agents in the United States, the assault on Salomon's administration proved abortive.

In May, 1887, Salomon, having had the anti-re-election clause stricken from the constitution, entered upon a second term. Politically, his position seemed strong. The Liberals

[5] Fish to Racster, March 20; to Laroche, July 30, 1869, Notes to Haiti, I.

[6] Moore, *A Digest of International Law,* VII, 1056-1059. It may appear that Fish was not only unsympathetic toward Salnave but deliberately favoring Nissage-Saget, whose success would be a blow to Grant's Dominican plans, but that is unlikely. To forestall a claim the Secretary defended bungling local officials. There are indications that some of them may have touched rebel gold—it was a time of notorious corruption—while others may have supposed the vessels to be in the service of Cuban rebels, for whom there was a great sympathy. The Spanish minister thought so of two of them at least (Enclosure No. 2, Laroche to Fish, July 19, 1869, Notes from Haiti, I).

[7] Preston to Frelinghuysen, May 9, 1883, Notes from Haiti, III; Davis to Preston, June 1, 1883, Notes to Haiti, I.

[8] Preston to Frelinghuysen, July 17, 1883, Notes from Haiti, III.

[9] Moore, *A Digest of International Law,* VII, 897.

were demoralized and leaderless, never having recovered from the debacle of 1879 and the military disaster of 1883. Many particularly among the foreign merchants, favored him as representing political stability, but among the *élite* there were mutterings about black dictatorship and the life presidency. Salomon, himself a Southerner, made his second inauguration the occasion for a cabinet reorganization favoring the North, the black stronghold. As Dr. John E. W. Thompson, the American minister, observed, no revolution could hope to succeed without the adherence of that section.[10]

In the spring of 1888 it was rumored that Salomon would resign on account of ill health and would cause François Manigat to be elected as his successor. As commander in the field against Bazelais, Manigat had acquired a reputation for barbarity and mulattophobia. Consequently, a remnant of the Liberals united with a disgruntled Nationalist faction to support the rival candidacy of François Denys Légitime, who was accounted a man honorable, humane, and, though black, without prejudice of color. Salomon compelled both Manigat and Légitime to leave the country, but Thompson predicted that trouble was only temporarily averted, that a sanguinary conflict was impending.[11] He charged that his French and British colleagues, Seismaisons and Zohrab, were fostering conspiracy against the government to which they were accredited. Both were imperialists convinced of Haitian incapacity for self-rule and, Thompson believed, deliberately fomenting internal discord in order to prepare the ground for European intervention. The French legation served as a safe headquarters for the partisans of Légitime. There on July 7, Seismaisons and Zohrab, in the presence of ex-President Boisrond-Canal, tried in vain to induce the American minister to join them in demanding the resignation of Salomon.[12]

[10] Thompson to Bayard, No. 94, July 2, 1886; No. 137, May 17, 1887, Despatches, Haiti, XXI. Thompson was right. Every president, from the fall of Salomon to the American intervention, was from the North save three, whose tenure was brief on account of the hostility of that section.

[11] *Papers Relating to the Foreign Relations of the United States* (1888), I, 884 ff.

[12] Thompson to Bayard, Confidential, July 16, 1888, Despatches, Haiti, XXII.

During July a fifth of Port-au-Prince was laid waste by a series of fires, for which the adherents of Légitime were presumably responsible.[13] Soon thereafter revolution broke out, not at the capital, but at Cap Haitien, where General Seide Thélémaque[14] pronounced against the government. The North responded with enthusiasm, and Salomon, realizing that the end had come, embarked for New York on August 10, 1888.

Thélémaque's uprising had overthrown the government, but the friends of Légitime had no idea of permitting their own well-developed conspiracy to be sidetracked by the Northern general. They had the inestimable advantage of being already at the capital, while Thélémaque was still far away. Disclaiming personal ambition, Boisrond-Canal promptly took possession of the government, while Légitime hurried home from Jamaica. It was evidently intended that Canal should hold an election that would elevate Légitime to the presidency, but the first task of the Port-au-Princiens was to keep Thélémaque's army out of the capital. The French minister undertook to do this, acting without warrant in the name of the diplomatic corps and urging upon the Northern commander that it would be dangerous to bring so many men into the partially ruined city during the yellow fever season. He was unable to prevent Thélémaque from entering Port-au-Prince with eight thousand troops, but, by threatening that the diplomatic corps would refuse clean bills of health to ships clearing from the port, he did finally persuade him to send away all save six small divisions of regulars.[15]

On Thélémaque's arrival a provisional government was set up in which he was included, together with Boisrond-Canal, Légitime, Florvil Hyppolite, and three others. The elections

[13] The events of July-October, 1888, are narrated in detail in *Foreign Relations* (1888), I, 897-937, which account will be followed here, except as otherwise noted.
Incendiarism was a customary revolutionary procedure. Instead of antagonizing the populace, it almost invariably prodded them into overthrowing the government in order to save their homes from being burned.

[14] Thélémaque was a Northern mulatto who had risen to prominence under Salnave, and, although excluded from office by Saget, had served without interruption under Domingue, Canal, and Salomon.

[15] All the diplomatic officers at Port-au-Prince were also consuls general. Thompson protested against this, since there was no sickness actually present.

for a constituent assembly began on September 17, and ten days later it was apparent that Thélémaque had made a clean sweep of the North, the Northwest, and the Artibonite and that only Port-au-Prince had gone solidly for Légitime. All during September 28 the tension was high at the capital, and at night-fall the break came. The Légitimist garrison in the palace opened fire on the nearest Northern division, a confused strug-gle ensued in the darkness, and Thélémaque was killed.

Of course each side accused the other of aggression. It was claimed that Thélémaque's men had been advancing silently on the palace, the garrison of which had fired only in self-defense, but the American minister reported that when the shooting began he had happened to be in conversation with the commander of the division in question, who had been reclining before the door of his quarters (no very aggressive attitude). Thompson, if not pro-Thélémaque, had at least been strongly anti-Légitime ever since that meeting at the French legation on July 7, but his story was more plausible than that of the palace commandant. The latter may well have been sincere—it is notorious that in the dark a nervous sentinel will see the very thing for which he is on watch—but if anyone premeditated an attack, it was Légitime, whose men admittedly fired the first shots. He was desperate, while the existing political situation was entirely satisfactory to Thélémaque. Moreover, the mili-tary situation was just the reverse. Being first on the ground, the Légitimists held the palace, the arsenal, and the forts. They had artillery, of which the Northern army had none, and a *mitrailleuse*, which was regarded with particular awe. Thélé-maque's forces were scattered, in no position to defend them-selves, much less to attack. Whether they had been tampered with or knew not which way to turn in the darkness and con-fusion, four of his divisions stood idle, while the other two were being cut to pieces. In the morning they went over to Légitime, and their commanders testified that Thélémaque had planned a coup.

One by one, the Northern members of the provisional government resigned and went home, although Canal and Légitime begged them to stay and preserve an appearance of solidarity. News came that Jacmel had repudiated the rump administration and that St. Marc had driven out a Légitimist commandant with cries of *"à bas les Port-au-Princiens."* Next came a manifesto from Cap Haitien denouncing Légitime as a murderer and threatening civil war in the event of his election.[16] Despite these warnings—indeed, in haste because of them— thirty-three of the eighty-four recently elected delegates convened at Port-au-Prince and, on October 16, 1888, named Légitime provisional president of the republic. The disaffected regions, crying "no quorum," denied the validity of these proceedings and formed a provisional government of their own at Cap Haitien, choosing Florvil Hyppolite as their leader.[17] The situation thus created was not unlike that which had existed in the days of Pétion and Christophe.

As had Boyer Bazelais, Légitime considered himself the champion of republican government against military autocracy, yet was himself unwilling to submit to the popular will. The "Protestants," conscious that the dead Thélémaque was still the stronger candidate and that his political heirs would prevail in a reasonably free election, offered to submit to any president chosen by the full membership of the constituent assembly meeting anywhere save at Port-au-Prince, but Légitime spurned their proposal, since he dared not submit his candidacy to the whole body of constituents and to do so would admit the imperfection of his present title. Thompson quoted him as having declared to him personally, "If they want a civil war, I will give them a civil war. I have more resources than they and

[16] The consular corps at the Cape attested the unanimity of the North and begged the diplomatic corps to persuade Légitime to withdraw in the interest of peace, but of course Seismaisons and Zohrab would not consent to have their candidate eliminated by the demise of his rival, while Thompson would no more agree to act thus against Légitime than he would to demand Salomon's resignation in Légitime's interest (Thompson to Bayard, No. 224, Nov. 24, 1888, Despatches, Haiti, XXII).

[17] Hyppolite, son of a minister of Soulouque, had been secretary of war under Salnave, had been instrumental in securing the election of Canal over Bazelais in 1876, and with Légitime and Thélémaque, had supported Salomon in 1879.

will see the country totally destroyed before I allow these ignorant people to put me down."[18] The temper of the remark
reveals that the conflict was but another round in the long
struggle between the Francophile mulatto *élite,* an aristocracy
of wealth and culture as much as color, and their traditional
opponents.[19] Men aligned themselves on that issue, regardless
of their private opinions as to what had happened on the night
of September 28. Both sides presented lengthy arguments on
fine points of constitutional law, but, as is generally the case,
these were intended to rationalize a stand already taken and did
not represent the real considerations involved. The *élite* felt
justified in employing any means to save themselves from a
dictatorship founded on popularity with the masses.

Légitime claimed the recognition of the world as the heir
of Boisrond-Canal's provisional government and therefore the
rightful ruler of all Haiti. On the recommendation of his
patrons he received the prompt recognition of France and Great
Britain, and subsequently that of Italy and Portugal. He controlled the capital, the regular army and navy, and all the
machinery of government, with every appearance of *de facto*
power. He charged that his opponents were no more than a
disappointed faction, devoid of popular support, rebels against
a regime established according to the forms of law. On their
part, they were out of diplomatic contact with the world, and
their administration was obviously a hastily improvised affair.
They frankly admitted being a revolutionary organization and
never pretended to represent more than a portion of the Haitian
people. Should not the United States, then, recognize Légi-

---

[18] Thompson to Bayard, No. 216, Oct. 18, 1888, Despatches, Haiti, XXII. The
additional remark, "Before I retire, I prefer to see the country go into the hands of
foreigners," was the point of the direct quotation. Thompson thought that it gave
substance to rumors that Légitime and Seismaisons were about to re-establish French
control over Haiti.

[19] Emmanuel Edouard, in his *Essai sur la politique intérieure d'Haiti,* p. 31, finding mulattoes in Hyppolite's entourage, holds the issue to have been sectional rather
than social or racial. Sectionalism was obviously present; moreover, the leadership
of both "parties" had always been of the socially elect. These factors, complicating
the fundamental cleavage, have been discussed above, pp. 19 f. The point here is
that although Légitime was a Nationalist, the Nationalist spirit, principles (so far as
the party had any formulated program), and following were rather with Hyppolite.

time as entitled to the same consideration as that shown Salomon in 1883 and enforce the neutrality laws exclusively against the insurgent, Hyppolite—or should Légitime's claims be critically examined?

Despite the imposing façade, the imperfect foundations of the government at Port-au-Prince were plainly apparent, and a majority of the powers represented there, including the United States, Germany, and Spain, declined to be rushed into premature recognition. That Boisrond-Canal accepted Légitime as his successor meant little, in view of the relationship of the two even before the fall of Salomon. Although a provisional government headed by Canal—and including Thélémaque—had, at one time, been universally accepted in Haiti, it had itself been extraconstitutional and revolutionary and any title derived from it must be so. Moreover, the withdrawal of a majority of its members brought its authority, such as it was, into question. It had existed simply to bring together a constituent assembly, but Légitime could muster not even a quorum of that body, except by packing. Preston argued that it was none of Bayard's business to count the votes by which Légitime had been elected, that he must accept Légitime's de facto possession of the capital without presuming to inquire into Haitian domestic affairs. If that were presumption, it would be gross interference indeed for the United States to decide that one of two equally revolutionary factions was the true government of Haiti and favor it accordingly. Bayard held that "the only thing to do was to await the progress of events and defer any formal recognition until it could be given to an established government evidently representing the will of the Haitian people,"[20] a policy heartily approved by the "Protestants" but one to which no legitimate exception could be taken. If Légitime were all he claimed to be, he could afford to wait for recognition until he had pacified the country. If, on the other hand, Bayard's policy operated to Hyppolite's advantage, it could only be that the Haitians themselves preferred Hyppolite, and that Légitime's chances of survival de-

[20] *Senate Executive Document No. 69*, 50th Cong., 2d Sess., pp. 234-235.

pended upon his ability to impose on foreign powers before his enemies had time to mobilize their strength. That Hyppolite should benefit from impartiality did not make it any less impartial.

From Bayard's policy on recognition it followed that due precautions would be taken to enforce the neutrality laws and prevent American territory "from becoming the base of supplies for either of the warring factions,"[21] but, since the laws applied only to arming vessels and organizing expeditions, they did not erect a barrier to the shipment of munitions, as articles of commerce, to either party. The remedy of capture in transit was plainly beyond the power of Hyppolite, who possessed no navy, but Légitime did have two gunboats, soon supplemented by three armed Haitian merchant steamers, and Bayard conceded to him the right to bar all commerce with the "Protestants" if he could establish an effective blockade.[22] Although this policy seemed to favor Légitime, at the outset a case arose in which Bayard was alleged to have betrayed an animus against the Port-au-Princien government.

On October 4 an American liner, the *Haytian Republic*, sailed from New York on her regular voyage to Haitian ports. As a common carrier she took on passengers and freight at Cap Haitien and Port-de-Paix for Gonaives and Saint Marc. Her cargo happened to include men and munitions en route to the Artibonite front, but the vessel was not diverted from her regular commerce into Hyppolite's control, nor was she liable for this act after its completion at Saint Marc.[23] By the same token she was not liable for having, unknown to her master, transported two revolutionary agents as passengers to Miragoane

[21] President Cleveland to Congress, Dec. 3, 1888, *Foreign Relations* (1888), p. xiv. Both factions being unrecognized, the operation of neutrality laws did not depend upon formal recognition of a state of belligerency (Moore, *A Digest of International Law*, VII, 1077-1084).

[22] *Foreign Relations* (1888), I, 990. In 1869 Fish had held that revolutionists whose belligerency had not been recognized could not establish a valid blockade, but his successors adopted the view that a blockade instituted by such a party should be respected if effective, the very fact of their ability to establish an effective blockade being taken to prove them entitled to belligerent rights, at least to that extent (Moore, *A Digest of International Law*, VII, 785-788).

[23] Moore, *A Digest of International Law*, VII, 410.

and Les Cayes. On October 19 she sailed from Jacmel on her return voyage, bearing four passengers for Gonaives, and a day later she entered St. Marc unmolested, there learning for the first time that Légitime had proclaimed a blockade of the port on October 15. Coming out next morning, she was stopped by the gunboat *Dessalines* and taken as a prize to Port-au-Prince.[24]

The capture of the *Haytian Republic* meant more to Légitime than the enforcement of his blockade. The four passengers from Jacmel were that arrondissement's duly elected delegates to the constituent assembly, en route to join their colleagues gathered at Gonaives in opposition to Légitime's "constituent assembly" at Port-au-Prince. The membership of the latter body having, by devious methods, been increased to forty, Légitime could, with the addition of the unwilling Jacmel delegation, at last claim a quorum. On December 16, 1888, he was elected constitutional president of Haiti, three hardy Jacmelites venturing to vote in the negative.[25] It is not surprising that the "Protestants" failed to regard the December election as any more valid than that of October.

In violation of the treaty of 1864, Légitime set up an extraordinary commission to try the case of the *Haytian Republic*.[26] This body based its decision on unsworn and often contradictory testimony founded on hearsay. It condemned the ship for having transported rebel troops and supplies from Cap Haitien to Gonaives (although she was not liable for this act at the time of her capture, if ever), for having put herself in the rebel service for the purpose of inciting rebellion in the South (although she had visited the Southern ports in the prosecution of a scheduled commercial voyage), for having actually brought about the rebellion at Jacmel (although it had occurred before she sailed from New York), and for having

[24] *Foreign Relations* (1888), I, 932–935. The *Dessalines* had sighted the *Haytian Republic* as she entered Saint Marc, but was too far away to intercept her or give the notice of blockade required by international law.

[25] Thompson to Bayard, No. 236, Dec. 18, 1888, Despatches, Haiti, XXIII; Preston to Blaine, March 28, 1889, Notes from Haiti, V.

[26] Article 28 required that prize cases be heard before regularly established courts. Articles 24 and 27 had already been violated in the capture of the vessel.

violated the blockade of Saint Marc (although she had received
no notice of it and had found the port unguarded).[27]   On
learning of the capture of the *Haytian Republic*, Bayard had
cabled Thompson to "protest instantly." When the decision
of the "prize court," together with the official record of its
proceedings, was communicated to him, he demanded the immediate restoration of the vessel to her owners, his decision
being based as much upon the Haitian minutes as upon the
reports of American officials.[28]   Two warships had to be sent to
Port-au-Prince before the demand was complied with.[29] The
outcome of the affair was, of course, a blow to Légitime's
prestige, but he seems to have "asked for it." Undoubtedly
Hyppolite would have experienced the same treatment had the
situation been reversed. If Bayard was uncompromising, he
showed greater forbearance than did the American press. Republican editors roasted the administration for its supineness in
allowing Légitime to hold the vessel for two months, while
the Democratic papers were reduced to crediting Bayard with
remarkable patience and magnanimity.[30]

Légitime's blockade was never effective. With only two
gunboats to begin with and six at most, he had undertaken to
close seven ports scattered along some two hundred miles of
coast, a manifest impossibility. The blockading vessels spent
much of their time hovering between ports, unable to bar entrance to any. Because of the limited capacity of their bunkers
they could not remain at sea more than a few days, and frequently all of them were seen anchored at Port-au-Prince.[31]
During November twenty-eight Norwegian, German, British,
Italian, and Dominican ships entered at Cap Haitien alone.
American consuls, shipmasters, and merchants bombarded Washington with complaints that the failure of the government to
declare the blockade ineffective and to protect shipping from
interference by roving gunboats was ruinous to business,[32] but

[27] *Foreign Relations* (1888), I, 962-971.
[28] Bayard to Preston, Dec. 8, 1888, Notes to Haiti, I.
[29] Moore, *A Digest of International Law*, VII, 117.
[30] *Public Opinion*, VI (1888), 494.
[31] *Senate Executive Document No. 69* (50.2), pp. 112, 223 f.
[32] *Ibid.*, pp. 148-149, 167-169, 177-179.

in spite of—perhaps because of—the obvious interest of American commerce, the Secretary of State was overscrupulous in his efforts to give the Légitime faction no ground for protest. When called upon to say definitely whether the blockade was entitled to respect, he gave an evasive answer, the substance of which was that each case that might arise would be judged upon its merits. To him it seemed that "it would be the part of common prudence for merchants in the United States to abstain from attempting to pursue commerce in that region."[33] Admiral Luce, in December, first stated categorically that he would protect any American vessel molested by a Haitian gunboat under color of a blockade that had never been effective and had now manifestly ceased to exist.[34] In February, Bayard finally ventured to express the same opinion.[35]

American merchants did not follow Bayard's advice to steer clear of Haiti. The Clyde Line did indeed drop Cap Haitien from its schedule, but it carried quantities of munitions to Monte Cristi to be relayed to Hyppolite's base of operations at Ouanaminthe.[36] Preston complained bitterly that the "rebellion" was sustained by New York speculators, but in this observation the pot called the kettle black, since Légitime also made considerable purchases of munitions in that quarter, not the least evidence of which were the unpaid bills presented to Hyppolite as contract claims at the end of the war.[37] The real importance of this indiscriminate traffic in munitions lay in the fact that, if Hyppolite could obtain arms at all, Légitime's initial advantage in the possession of the Haitian arsenal and regular army would be neutralized, leaving the issue to be decided by men rather than artillery.

Although the United States did not forbid the shipment of

[33] *Ibid.*, p. 201.

[34] *Ibid.*, p. 262. He had found the entire blockading squadron at anchor at Port-au-Prince.

[35] Moore, *A Digest of International Law*, VII, 792 f.

[36] Ouanaminthe, on the frontier, was nearer to Monte Cristi than to Cap Haitien. The Dominican government was sympathetic toward Hyppolite.

[37] *Senate Executive Document No. 69* (50.2), p. 261. Haustedt to Bayard, Dec. 7, 1888; to Blaine, March 5, 1889, Notes from Haiti, IV-V. Durham to Foster, No. 94, July 15, 1892, Despatches, Haiti, XXVI.

munitions to Haiti, the Federal authorities recognized their obligation to prevent the arming of vessels in American ports for the service of either party. Since Légitime already had a navy, this restriction fell exclusively upon Hyppolite in practical effect, but he was able to evade it. In January, 1889, the steamer *Mercedes* cleared from New York under the Dominican flag. She had been purchased by Leoncio Julia, Dominican consul, with funds supplied by Hyppolite's agents, and, after receiving her armament at Samaná, she passed into Hyppolite's service as the *Jacmel*. No suspicion was held against the *Mercedes* when she cleared, no complaint having been made against her, but in February the *Carondelet*, laden with munitions, was seized by the Federal authorities, at Preston's behest, and charged with being part of a hostile expedition organized in the United States. Julia, however, claimed the cargo as property of the Dominican Republic, and, neither Preston nor the United States being able to produce evidence to contradict him, the court dismissed the case.[38] The *Carondelet* sailed away to Samaná and ultimately became a unit in Hyppolite's navy. In the case of a third steamer, which cleared under Dominican registration as the *Conserva*, a Federal court ruled that the evidence showed she was to be dispatched from New York to Samaná in a condition unfit for the commission of hostilities, to be delivered to the Dominican government; that the use to which she might thereafter be put by that government was a matter for which it and not the United States would be responsible; and that a well-founded suspicion that ultimately she would be employed in the service of Hyppolite would not justify a finding that she had been fitted out in New York in violation of the statute.[39] Even if the judgment of the court were to be challenged, it could not be held that it was subject to the influence of the Federal executive, whose representatives had faithfully presented all the evidence that could be mustered. The United States could not control the policy of the Dominican Republic.

[38] Preston to Bayard, Jan. 25; to Blaine, March 11, 1889, Notes from Haiti, V.

[39] Moore, *A Digest of International Law*, VII, 904. The *Conserva* sailed in March, but there is no indication that she ever reached Hyppolite.

In any case, these ships did not break the blockade, which had been declared ineffective before the first of them sailed from New York, nor did they exert any appreciable influence upon the outcome of the war. During May, 1889, after five months of reported victories, Légitime met with crushing defeat on every front, and Hyppolite advanced to the gates of Port-au-Prince. Early in August the South joined the winning side, and only the capital was left to the "constitutional president." On August 22 he resigned, and on September 9 the full membership of the constituent assembly, in session at Gonaives, unanimously elected Florvil Hyppolite to the presidency of Haiti.[40]

When the "Protestants" entered Port-au-Prince, many regarded it as a triumph for the United States as well as for Hyppolite. Since the affair of the *Haytian Republic* the local press had taught them that the Northern leader had sold out to the Yankees. Hyppolite was indeed friendly and grateful, but the United States had aided him only to the extent of not interfering in Légitime's behalf, a policy of impartiality that stood in pleasant contrast to the attitude of France and Great Britain. Bayard's decisions to recognize an effective blockade and to bar both parties from obtaining warships had actually been to Légitime's advantage. The policy which had enabled Hyppolite (and Légitime) to purchase munitions in the United States had been established by Jefferson nearly a century before. Bayard's only favors, if they could be called that, had been to admit belatedly the patent ineffectiveness of Légitime's blockade and to decline, with obvious propriety, to recognize Légitime prematurely, thus permitting the Haitian people to determine their own future without the interference of the United States.

Had it not been for munitions imported from abroad the poorly armed "Protestants" might well have been overcome, but these supplies merely put them on even terms with their adversaries, averting their defeat. It took something more to

[40] *Foreign Relations* (1889), p. 497.

achieve the victory, and with that the United States had no connection whatever.

In any war, military strategy, or the lack of it, must have some bearing on the result. In October, 1888, the circumstances compelled Hyppolite to assume the defensive, and the initiative lay with Légitime. He proved incapable of using it, scattering his forces in the pursuit of diverse objects. Seven months later he had nothing to show for his efforts. His left wing had surrounded St. Marc and Gonaives, his right had slipped

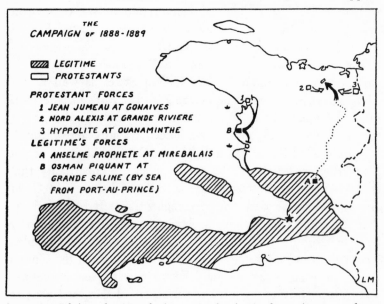

THE
CAMPAIGN of 1888-1889

▨ LEGITIME
▭ PROTESTANTS

PROTESTANT FORCES
1 JEAN JUMEAU AT GONAIVES
2 NORD ALEXIS AT GRANDE RIVIERE
3 HYPPOLITE AT OUANAMINTHE
LEGITIME'S FORCES
A ANSELME PROPHETE AT MIREBALAIS
B OSMAN PIQUANT AT
  GRANDE SALINE (BY SEA
  FROM PORT-AU-PRINCE)

into the Plaine du Nord through the back door, but no place of importance had been taken and no Northern force had been defeated in battle. In fact, Hyppolite, allowed seven months of grace in which to organize and equip his militia, was stronger than ever and ready to strike. He fell upon Légitime's isolated right wing at Le Trou and annihilated it, then rushed in victorious strength to the relief of Gonaives, and routed his enemies in that quarter. The pursuit met no check until it reached the suburbs of Port-au-Prince.[41] To sound strategy in destroying Légitime's armies in detail, Hyppolite owed his victory.

[41] I am indebted to Dr. Price-Mars, formerly of Grande Rivière du Nord, for confirming and supplementing inferences drawn from Preston to Blaine, March 30,

Generalship, however, would have been to no avail unless supported by men of sufficient conviction to stand steadfast for seven months during which the tide of war had seemingly set against them, men in sufficient numbers to strike a decisive blow. In the last analysis the Haitian people themselves must be considered to have determined the issue. In 1889 a majority of them elected the man of their choice by the only procedure that their political experience had yet developed.

1889, Notes from Haiti, V; Thompson to Blaine, No. 282, May 15; No. 285, May 20, 1889, Despatches, Haiti, XXIII; Goutier to Wharton, No. 969, June 21, 1889, Cons. Let., Cape Haytien, XVI.

CHAPTER IX

THE MOLE AFFAIR

Neither the records of the Navy or State Department will give you an adequate idea of the situation. . . .
—WILLIAM P. CLYDE, October 7, 1890

In THE SPRING of 1889, when the victorious Northern armies were marching on Port-au-Prince, there was organized at the Haitian capital a Ligue pour le maintien de l'independance nationale, a propaganda agency created to spread the idea that Florvil Hyppolite owed his success solely to aid rendered him by the United States in exchange for a promise to cede the Mole St. Nicolas. Légitime's last hope had been to hold on until nationalistic reaction against his rival could be stirred up by this means. Only five years had elapsed since the Arthur administration, rejecting Salomon's offer to cede this same Mole St. Nicolas, had loftily declared, "The United States have never deemed it needful . . . to maintain impregnable fortresses along the world's highways of commerce,"[1] but on March 4, 1889, a new president had been inaugurated out of whose first official utterance the Ligue had been able to pick a text. Reversing his immediate predecessors, Republican and Democratic alike, Harrison had declared that the navy needed overseas coaling stations. The context showed that he was thinking primarily of Samoa.[2] Nevertheless, it was true that the announced policy of the incoming administration reflected an awakened interest in the navy and in Caribbean affairs.

As long as the isthmian transit had been important to the United States, the Federal executive had favored a strong navy and had sought a West Indian coaling station, but with the

[1] Frelinghuysen to Langston, No. 258, Feb. 1, 1884, Instructions, Haiti, I. The rejection of the Danish and Dominican treaties was cited to prove it.
[2] James D. Richardson, *A Compilation of the Messages and Papers of the Presidents, 1789-1919*, IX, 10 ff.

completion of the transcontinental railroad the search had been abandoned and the navy had been allowed to deteriorate. Even before the national authorities lost interest, the American people had become absorbed in domestic rather than overseas affairs, as the experience of Seward and Grant had showed. But, as 1889 approached, the problems of Southern reconstruction were shelved, the West was won, the industrialization of the North was fairly accomplished, and, with American public opinion becoming more sensitive to foreign stimuli, Frenchmen had undertaken to build a canal at Panama, attracting attention once more to the Caribbean. President Hayes had given prompt warning that "the policy of this country is a canal under American control," and a movement had been launched to restore the navy to a state of respectability. The demand for a naval base to guard the West Indian approaches to the isthmus lagged behind the demand for a new navy, but with the inauguration of Harrison the old search was resumed, with St. Thomas, Samaná Bay, and Mole St. Nicolas still the only possibilities.

Frederick Douglass, one of the most distinguished negro Americans of his day, had used his influence in favor of Harrison in the election of 1888, and as a reward he was appointed minister to Haiti, reaching his post in October, 1889. In December he complained that the U. S. S. *Yantic* had been making an unauthorized survey of the harbor of Mole St. Nicolas, an act embarrassing to Hyppolite because it played directly into the hands of the Ligue. The Minister explained that

in view of the numerous articles which have appeared . . . in American journals, relative to an alleged purpose of the United States to gain some sort of a foothold at the Mole, and in view also of what appears to me to be an extreme sensitiveness of the Haytian people generally on the subject of any possible alienation of their territory, it is but natural that . . . those opposed to the existing administration should avail themselves of the circumstance to try to create the impression, particularly among the less favored classes, that already the preliminary steps have been taken to "sell the country to the Americans."[3]

[3] Douglass to Blaine, No. 17, Dec. 9, 1889, Despatches, Haiti, **XXIV**.

In July, 1890, Douglass was granted a three months' leave of absence, but it was December before he returned to Port-au-Prince. James G. Blaine, Harrison's secretary of state, had detained him in Washington, finally sending him back to Haiti with instructions to open negotiations for the lease of Mole St. Nicolas as a naval coaling station. Although Douglass had favored Grant's project for the annexation of the Dominican Republic and did not feel that any harm would come to the negro population of Haiti through closer association with the United States, he was also aware of Haitian sensitiveness regarding the Mole and hardly knew how to begin. Antenor Firmin, Hyppolite's minister of foreign affairs, relieved his embarrassment by being the first to broach the subject. In the course of an informal New Year's call, Firmin complained that the New York *Sun* had published a statement that during the late civil war Hyppolite had definitely promised the Mole to the United States. With some heat the Minister denied the existence of any such promise, denouncing the report as Ligue propaganda. Douglass assured him that the State Department entertained no such impression; that, on the contrary, his government would welcome an opportunity to open negotiations for a lease. At that point they were interrupted by other callers, and Firmin left without making a reply.[4]

On January 25 Admiral Bancroft Gherardi arrived at Port-au-Prince with instructions to secure the lease of the Mole.[5] Aware that he had been virtually superseded, the minister's first impulse was to resign,[6] but he remained to second Gherardi loyally. His task was a thankless one, since if they succeeded, Gherardi would get the credit, and if they failed, Douglass would bear the blame.

Three days later Gherardi and Douglass called on Hyppolite and Firmin. The Admiral reminded the President "of services rendered, . . . and of certain promises made by the

[4] Douglass to Blaine, Private and Confidential, Jan. 5, 1891, Despatches, Haiti, XXV.

[5] Blaine to Gherardi, Jan. 1, 1891, Instructions, Haiti, III.

[6] Frederick Douglass, "Haiti and the United States," *North American Review*, CLIII (1891), 342

Haitian Provisional Government which now it was the desire of the Government at Washington to have fulfilled."[7] As evidence of the bargain he produced a document purporting to be a copy of the proposals of Frederick Elie, an agent sent by Hyppolite to the United States in January, 1889, wherein it appeared that Elie had offered sundry commercial privileges and the cession of Mole St. Nicolas in exchange for the breaking of Légitime's blockade and the free export of munitions. Firmin at once denied that Elie had been authorized to treat concerning the Mole and asked whether Gherardi considered that he was presenting a treaty to be enforced or the friendly request of one power to another. The Admiral had to admit that his paper was no treaty, signed and sealed, but he argued that the Hyppolite government owed its very existence to the services faithfully rendered by the United States in accordance with the understanding reached with Elie, and he warned that if his request were refused, his government would force the fulfillment of the moral obligation. Firmin protested that the lease of the Mole would provoke a revolution, but Hyppolite agreed to submit the question to his cabinet.[8]

It never occurred to the doughty Admiral that the Haitians would dare resist him, but he grossly underestimated his opponents, who had evidently taken his measure. When he visited Firmin privately at his home, the Minister spoke enthusiastically of the government's desire to improve the country and its willingness to grant all the best concessions to American capital. Thus drawn out, Gherardi observed that as long as the Mole remained in Haitian hands any revolutionist could use it to purchase the favor of the United States, while if Hyppolite should cede it now, the United States would keep him in power despite any outcry that might be raised. His host was visibly affected by this combined threat and bribe, but when he asked how much territory was wanted, the Admiral declined to discuss such details until the lease had been agreed to in principle. Haiti must sign a blank check. Gherardi was immensely

---

[7] Douglass to Blaine, No. 123, Jan. 29, 1891, Despatches, Haiti, XXV.
[8] Gherardi to Blaine, No. 1, Jan. 31, 1891, loc. cit.

pleased with himself, lightly suggesting in his report to Blaine that if Hyppolite were, by any chance, blind to the "manifest destiny" of the Mole, he would gladly seize it by force.[9] At the same time Douglass was reporting that the presence of three United States warships at Port-au-Prince was provoking considerable apprehension among the people. Gherardi had obtained permission to hold target practice in the bay.[10] The cabinet would deliberate to the booming of the big guns!

The cabinet took its time, but the light did not dawn on Gherardi until, three weeks after his arrival, Firmin blandly asked to see his full powers for the negotiation of the necessary treaty. The answer that he was an admiral did not prove acceptable—a frantic cablegram had to be dispatched to Washington.[11] Three weeks later the desired full powers arrived, but Gherardi delayed another six weeks before presenting them and calling for a categorical answer.[12] During that interval every warship available was ordered to Port-au-Prince,[13] and as they began to arrive, Douglass ventured to express his disapproval of naval diplomacy to Blaine:

I think it clearly my duty to state to you that the presence in this harbor . . . of five of our war vessels and the knowledge that others are soon to join them, coupled with a general vague information that negotiations are pending . . . concerning some matter in regard to which the Haitian people are unduly and perhaps unreasonably sensitive, has created a feeling of apprehension, anxiety, and even of alarm beyond anything of the kind that I have ever before personally known to exist here.

The Minister gave warning that if Hyppolite submitted to Blaine's demands his government would fall "under the crash of popular condemnation."[14] On April 22, 1891, Haiti for-

---

[9] Gherardi to Blaine, No. 2, Feb. 7, 1891, Despatches, Haiti, XXV.

[10] Douglass to Blaine, No. 126, Feb. 9, 1891, *loc. cit.*

[11] Gherardi to Blaine, Telegram, Feb. 16; No. 3, Feb. 21, 1891, *loc. cit.*

[12] Douglass to Blaine, No. 155, April 21, 1891, *loc. cit.*

[13] Ramsey to Gherardi, April 8, 1891, Cipher Messages Sent, Navy Department MSS.

[14] Douglass to Blaine, No. 154, April 21, 1891, Despatches, Haiti, XXV.

mally declined to accede to the request of the United States for the lease of the Mole St. Nicolas.

Gherardi had been "hoist by his own petard." In justifying the decision of his government Firmin presented a lengthy argument on the unconstitutionality of the proposed lease, but his most telling point was addressed to the presence of seven American men-of-war in the port. It had, he said,

made a most unfortunate impression on the entire country. . . . Haiti could not enter negotiations without appearing to yield to foreign pressure and to compromise, de facto, [her] existence as an independent people; so much the more so as several American journals in an undivinable object [were] making a deceiving propagandism tending to cause it to be believed that there were certain engagements [between Hyppolite and the United States for the cession of the Mole].

The Minister of Foreign Relations thereupon denied the authenticity of the Elie paper and, in the most diplomatic language, accused the Secretary of State of falsification.[15]

Without defending their document or Blaine's reputation, the two plenipotentiaries merely expressed their regret at Haiti's decision. Douglass inquired whether the negotiations might be reopened after the withdrawal of the ships, but he received a negative answer.[16] Such was the popular clamor that Hyppolite was compelled to publish assurances that no territory would be leased.[17] Firmin was so roundly denounced for having entertained Gherardi's proposals for even a moment that he had to resign, despite his brilliant diplomatic victory,[18] while in the United States Douglass was made the scapegoat for Gherardi, with the result that he too resigned.[19] Except for recriminations in the press, the Mole affair ended with startling abruptness. Gherardi's bluff had been called, and there had been nothing behind it, for the fact was that an administration

[15] Firmin to Douglass and Gherardi, April 22, 1891, enclosed in Douglass to Blaine, No. 156, April 23, 1891, Despatches, Haiti, XXV.

[16] Douglass to Blaine, No. 161, May 2, 1891, loc. cit.

[17] Idem to idem, No. 159, May 2, 1891, loc. cit.

[18] Douglass to Blaine, No. 162, May 7, 1891, loc cit.

[19] Idem to Wharton, No. 180, July 30, 1891, loc. cit.

dependent on negro votes[20] could not afford to drive Douglass too far[21] or to employ the *ultima ratio regum* against the Black Republic. Gherardi's imposing naval parade trailed off over the Haitian horizon and was seen no more. The defeat was ignominious, but to have made good the threat would have been despicable.

The American press accepted the Blaine-Gherardi story of the Elie promises without question and hysterically accused Hyppolite of bad faith, ingratitude, and insolence, yet a dispassionate examination of the American case would have revealed obvious defects. Assuming that such a bargain had been struck, its impropriety is manifest, but, on the face of the document itself, there was grave reason to doubt that anything of the sort had occurred. A copy of the undated, unsigned, and unratified proposals of a minor agent was no proof that such proposals had ever been made, much less that an agreement had been reached. Moreover, if he really believed that he held Hyppolite's pledge, why had Blaine waited sixteen months after the fall of Légitime and then instructed Douglass to open negotiations for the lease of the Mole as though no pledge existed?

Blaine's admirers endeavored to meet these objections by explaining that it was Bayard, his Democratic predecessor, who had made the corrupt bargain, but that, since the United States had faithfully performed its part, he felt justified in calling upon Hyppolite to discharge his moral obligation, after generously allowing him sixteen months in which to consolidate

[20] The negro vote had been Harrison's margin of victory in 1888. Although he had obtained an electoral majority of 233 to 168, Cleveland had actually received a popular plurality, which a slight shift in votes in certain pivotal states (of only 6,500 in the single state of New York, for instance) would have made an electoral majority.

The strangely sudden collapse of the American effort was explained in some Haitian quarters as the result of the puissant diplomatic intervention of France, but that was sheer romance. The France of 1891 would not have rushed in where the France of 1867 feared to tread. The Quai d'Orsay still remembered what had happened to Gambetta in 1882 and to Ferry in 1885 when they ventured to shift their gaze from Alsace-Lorraine to extra-European affairs.

[21] Douglass took great pains to dissociate Harrison from the machinations of his secretary of state (*Lecture on Hayti*, pp. 12 ff.; "Haiti and the United States," *passim*), but it would be impossible to do so if Harrison let Blaine go too far.

his power.[22] However, it has been shown in the preceding chapter that no Elie paper is necessary to explain Bayard's policy with regard to Légitime's blockade and to the export of munitions during the Haitian civil war. Elie's commission was dated December 28, 1888; he could not have reached Washington until sometime in January. Légitime's blockade was declared ineffective by Admiral Luce in December, before Elie had sailed, and Bayard's ratification of that decision in February needs no explanation beyond the established fact of the blockade's ineffectiveness. The policy of the United States regarding the exportation of munitions had been established before Hyppolite was born, and Bayard had explained it to Preston in October, 1888, three months before Elie's arrival at Washington.[23] Consequently, the "service" rendered by the United States cannot be considered as being, in any sense, part of a bargain with Elie for the Mole St. Nicolas.

The only "Protestant" emissary received by Bayard was Dr. Nemours Auguste, who called at the State Department on December 21, 1888, to argue against the recognition of Légitime and to urge a policy of strict impartiality between the two factions, a policy which Bayard had already adopted. Alluding to a report that Légitime had pledged the Mole to France, Auguste declared categorically, "We, to whom the Mole St. Nicolas belongs, could not either promise it or sell it," but he did suggest that commercial privileges, such as a special reduction of tonnage dues and of customs duties on textiles, might be had in return for American favor. Bayard held that even discussions of this character must "await the event,"[24] but, Nemours Auguste having departed for Paris, Frederick Elie was sent to Washington expressly to keep alive this idea of a

[22] This view is taken by Alice Felt Tyler, whose *Foreign Policy of James G. Blaine* is the standard work on that subject, but her account (pp. 91-98) appears to have been based entirely on Preston's note to Blaine, April 18, 1889, which, with evident special pleading, damns the Democrats for political effect. Preston was an eloquent advocate, but Bayard's correspondence with him, bound in the same volume, would have shed more light on the subject.

[23] *Papers Relating to the Foreign Relations of the United States* (1888), I, 990.

[24] *Senate Executive Document No. 69*, 50th Cong., 2d Sess., pp. 234-238.

commercial arrangement as a counterpoise for any temptations that might be offered by Légitime. Elie was not received.

The Blaine-Gherardi case depends upon the assumption of a continuity in American policy in 1888-1891, which, in fact, was totally lacking. Bayard was not interested in the Mole St. Nicolas or any other Caribbean naval base;[25] Blaine, his successor, was. Bayard had shown a high sense of *noblesse oblige* in American relationships with defenseless neighboring republics,[26] but Blaine's Pan American policy had a pecuniary motive. Bayard's personal character was above question, but the same could not be said of the "plumed knight" of "Mulligan letter" fame. If anyone exploited Haitian distress to make a deal for Mole St. Nicolas, it could not have been Bayard and must have been James G. Blaine.

In 1891 Hannibal Price, Haitian minister to the United States, writing under a pseudonym, did accuse Blaine of bargaining with Légitime for the Mole.[27] Such a charge, coming from a partisan of Hyppolite, is open to suspicion, but a series of curious circumstances tend to support it. According to Firmin, on March 27, 1889, Elie wrote to warn him that Blaine was eager for a coaling station and that "the day M. Preston offers the least concession we will be sacrificed."[28] The next day Preston, who was making desperate efforts to secure the recognition of Légitime by the new administration, informed Blaine that Légitime would consider a proposal for "closer relations" with the United States.[29] For some reason Admiral Gherardi, reporting Hyppolite's advance on Port-au-Prince in

[25] He had opposed the annexation of the Dominican Republic because it would launch the United States upon the "trackless sea of imperialism" (*Congressional Globe*, 41st Cong., 3d Sess., p. 194). Although he defended established American interests in Samoa, he consistently avoided new overseas ventures, rejecting in 1885 a treaty of alliance with Nicaragua, negotiated by Frelinghuysen.

[26] See below, p. 177.

[27] Hannibal Price, *The Haytian Question*, pp. 31 f.

[28] Antenor Firmin, *Diplomates et diplomatie*, p. 57. One might suspect that right then, with or without authority, Elie made his proposals in order to forestall Preston, were there not reason to believe that Blaine did not discover their existence until December, 1890, as will be shown.

[29] Preston to Blaine, March 28, 1889, Notes from Haiti, V. He also offered a treaty pledge against alienation of territory, but in such a way as to make "closer relations" appear as an alternative.

cipher and at unusual length for a cablegram, described the
Northern army as "the enemy."[30] On August 2 Gherardi reported that Légitime could hold out indefinitely.[31] On August 7
Preston wrote to Blaine, "When news of Hyppolite's retreat
is officially received I will have important communications to
present to you, but deem it perhaps safer to postpone making
them until official news reaches here."[32] What could this important communication be that it was safer for Preston to withhold until he could be sure that Hyppolite had not entered
Port-au-Prince and the Haitian presidency? In 1898 Solon
Menos, who had been Légitime's minister of foreign relations,
boasted that his party had chosen to succumb rather than to
accept Blaine's offer of a rescue in exchange for Mole St.
Nicolas.[33] In view of Preston's note of August 7 one may
suspect that the offer was not so much rejected as accepted too
late.

In any event, Blaine gave no indication that he was aware
of any contract between Elie and himself or his predecessor.
For more than a year after the fall of Légitime his hopes were
based entirely on the relations between Hyppolite and William
P. Clyde, president of the West India Steamship Company.
During the war Clyde had transported quantities of munitions
to Monte Cristi. The freight bill must have been large in
proportion to the extent, importance, and risks of the service,
but Hyppolite, without a treasury, could not pay unless he won
and then perhaps only by means of a concession such as Clyde
already held from the Dominican Republic. If the United
States could trade on Hyppolite's obligations to Clyde, the
Mole St. Nicolas might yet be won as part of the proposed
concession.

Clyde was on terms of peculiar intimacy with Harrison's
secretary of the navy, Benjamin F. Tracy, whose law firm he

[30] Gherardi to Tracy, June 30, 1889, Cipher messages received; No. 21, July 15,
1889, Serial 5738, Reports of squadron commanders, North Atlantic, Navy Department MSS. He evidently deemed it important to get the full details of Légitime's
reverse to Washington in all haste and secrecy.
[31] *Idem* to *idem*, No. 26, Aug. 2, 1889, Serial 6707, Reports, North Atlantic.
[32] Preston to Blaine, Personal, Aug. 7, 1889, Notes from Haiti, V.
[33] Solon Menos, *L'affaire Lüders*, p. 234.

retained as counsel and for whom personally he traded on the stock exchange.[34] While the Haitian civil war was still in progress, he had employed this influence to protect his stake in Hyppolite, but his intercession, occurring after the "Protestant" victory in the field, contributed nothing to that success and seems rather to have been designed to head off any last minute rescue of Légitime by Blaine. What Clyde had to offer was not definite enough to halt the correspondence between Washington and Port-au-Prince, but it was remembered as a hedge against Légitime's defeat. "If our government," Clyde had said, "will go wisely about it and will permit itself to cooperate with intelligent and judicious commercial interests, we can secure anything, in my opinion, which we could in decency ask."[35] This idea was the key to the second phase of Blaine's drive on Mole St. Nicolas, but, obviously, Hyppolite was to be snared. No one yet claimed that he had pledged the Mole to anyone.

Légitime had hardly resigned before Gherardi cabled that a new minister should be sent out to attend to the Mole affair[36] —and Blaine knew what that now meant. Thompson was still at Port-au-Prince and he enjoyed Hyppolite's confidence, but the business in hand was too delicate to be entrusted to a Democrat. The Secretary of State, alarmed by the urgency of the message, offered to recall Thompson and leave the legation in Gherardi's charge,[37] but the Admiral hastened to explain that he had meant only to expedite the arrival of a minister having full knowledge of and sympathy with the purpose of the administration.[38] That purpose was not to apply openly for the lease of the Mole, but to bring official pressure to bear in favor of a concession to the Clyde Line, a private interest. Since the

[34] Clyde to Tracy, Dec. 28, 1889, Sept. 9, 1892, Tracy MSS, Library of Congress. See also *idem* to *idem*, Oct. 29, 1889; Jan. 6, Feb. 17, April 24, and June 13, 1890; and May 19, 1891, for a series of gifts, including St. John's book on Haiti, and a series of interventions to influence the assignment of naval officers, the appointment of midshipmen, and the labor policies of the Brooklyn Navy Yard.

[35] Clyde to Tracy, May 31, 1889, Tracy MSS.

[36] Tracy to Blaine, Aug. 26, 1889, Misc. Let.

[37] Blaine to Gherardi, Telegram, Sept. 4, 1889, Instructions, Haiti, III.

[38] Gherardi to Blaine, Telegram, Sept. 9, 1889, Despatches, Haiti, XXIII.

appointment of a new minister was still further delayed (by wrangling in Washington as to who he should be), Gherardi, unable to restrain himself longer, did put in an oar, obtaining from Hyppolite assurances that something nice would be done for Clyde.[39] The conspirators agreed that the situation was "delicate but promising." They were on "the right road," but "a mistake would ruin everything."[40]

The first mistake was the appointment of Frederick Douglass as the new minister. That might be necessary to discharge Harrison's political obligations, but it was unfortunate for the Blaine-Tracy-Clyde-Gherardi plans.[41] Douglass was not opposed to the extension of American influence in Haiti, but he could appreciate the Haitian point of view, and Blaine dared not reveal to him the true policy of the State and Navy Departments. Douglass gave the Clyde concession all proper support, but he declined to resort to the species of bribery that Clyde considered necessary to the attainment of his more extreme demands.[42] Before Douglass had been at Port-au-Prince a month, Clyde and Gherardi were in Washington insisting upon his recall and the appointment of John S. Durham in his stead. Blaine realized that the change could not be effected abruptly, but he promised that Durham should have Douglass's place just as soon as it could be decently arranged.[43]

Gherardi finally put through the Clyde concession. With the coming of cold weather the North Atlantic squadron returned to the West Indies. At the moment it was rumored that France would support Légitime in a counter-revolution, and the Admiral seized the opportunity to suggest to Hyppolite that it was "a fitting time to draw closer the commercial interests" of Haiti and the United States.[44] Within a month the

[39] Clyde to Tracy, Personal, Oct. 6, 1889, Misc. Let.
[40] Idem to idem, Oct. 29, 1889, Tracy MSS.
[41] Several New York newspapers, presumably inspired by the conspirators, opposed Douglass's confirmation by the Senate, urging that a white minister be sent to Haiti (Booker T. Washington, Frederick Douglass, p. 298).
[42] Douglass, "Haiti and the United States," p. 455.
[43] Clyde to Tracy, Nov. 19, Dec. 4, 1889, Tracy MSS. Durham, recently appointed consul at Santo Domingo, was also a gentleman of color, but evidently one more acceptable to Clyde, for reasons best known to him.
[44] Gherardi to Tracy, No. 57, Dec. 19, 1889, Reports, North Atlantic.

concession had been granted, consisting of a subsidy of $290,000 for the maintenance of a semimonthly steamship service to New York for five years, renewable at $50,000 a year thereafter.[45] It contained no mention of Mole St. Nicolas, nor did Gherardi believe that any effort should be made to get possession of that site for the present, but he had no doubt that it could be done in the near future, now that the wedge had entered.

In March, Douglass was disturbed by the too frequent visits of Gherardi's warships and by speculation in the Haitian and American press "as to alleged designs of the United States upon the integrity of Haiti,"[46] but Clyde considered the situation promising for both private and public interests. At his suggestion Gherardi was called to Washington for a council of war.[47] In July, Douglass, the marplot, was allowed to come home on three months' leave. Then, on August 16, Clyde telegraphed that he must see Tracy and Blaine on urgent business. He had suddenly informed the Haitian government that his concession must include a ninety-nine-year lease of Mole St. Nicolas as a coaling station, "under the express condition that no war vessel be permitted to enter there with the exception of American ships," and he had been turned down cold.[48] Not only the great plan, but the concession itself was in jeopardy.

Douglass's return to Port-au-Prince was delayed for two months, while Blaine, Tracy, Clyde, and Gherardi, in frequent conferences, tried to figure out what to do next. Blaine had Hannibal Price, Hyppolite's minister, on the carpet, but accomplished nothing by attempting to browbeat him. Clyde insisted that Price be confronted by Gherardi in person, since "their pledges to our Government . . . were made to and through Admiral Gherardi, and in his knowledge is the only record of all that did take place,"[49] but in doing so he exposed the pitiful weakness of the case. Hyppolite's expression to Gherardi of

[45] So wrote Gherardi to Tracy, Jan. 22, 1890 (Serial 1097, Reports, North Atlantic), but Clyde subsequently claimed that his concession was worth $470,000 (Clyde to Tracy, April 21, 1891, Tracy MSS).
[46] Douglass to Blaine, No. 46, March 13, 1890, Despatches, Haiti, XXIV.
[47] Clyde to Tracy, March 20 and 24, 1890, Tracy MSS.
[48] Idem to idem, Aug. 16, 1890, loc. cit.; Price, The Haytian Question, p. 36.
[49] Clyde to Tracy, Oct. 15, 1890, Tracy MSS.

good will toward Clyde could not be considered as a binding engagement with the United States to grant any sort of concession to the Clyde Line, much less to surrender the Mole St. Nicolas. Clyde himself had no pledge of that sort from Hyppolite. With nothing on which to base such a claim save Hyppolite's good will, he had acted on Gherardi's tall tales of a pledge to the United States, as represented in the Admiral's person, tales that seemed plausible in conjunction with Gherardi's yarn of how he himself had made Hyppolite president as part of the bargain.[50] In all the excitement, all the plotting and planning, no one mentioned a contract between Bayard and Elie[51]—because no one supposed that such a thing existed.

Douglass finally sailed for Haiti in December with instructions to open a negotiation for the lease of Mole St. Nicolas by the United States, a straightforward course and Blaine's last desperate alternative. By December 23 it was decided that Gherardi had better manage the affair, but even at that late date there was no idea of building a case on any "Elie proposals," the existence of which had not yet been discovered— or invented. It was only on a clue furnished by Clyde on January 8 that the materials out of which that all-important document was composed were discovered among the reports of the Cap Haitien consulate.[52]

Those papers disclosed that on February 14, 1889, the State Department had advised Stanislaus Goutier, the consul, that his No. 934 had failed to arrive, and had instructed him to send a duplicate. In reply Goutier had explained that the missing despatch had been withheld at Hyppolite's request. Rebuking the consul for having confidences with the local authorities which he could not share with his own government, the department had ordered that the despatch be forwarded at once, and

[50] *Ibid.* This assertion proves the absurdity of the whole fabrication. Gherardi had reached Haiti only in April, 1889, after American policies regarding the civil war had been established for months. He did nothing there not his plain duty in carrying out those policies.

[51] Clyde to Blaine, Oct. 7 and 8, 1890, Misc. Let.; Clyde to Tracy, Aug. 16, Sept. 18 and 30, Oct. 3, 15, and 31, Nov. 6, 20, 25, and 28, and Dec. 23, 1890, Tracy MSS.

[52] Clyde to Tracy, Dec. 23, 1890; Jan. 8, 1891, Tracy MSS.

on April 4, 1889, No. 934, dated December 27, 1888, had finally reached Washington.[53]

Goutier's No. 934 contained, verbatim, the text of the paper which Gherardi later presented as a copy of the "proposals" of Frederick Elie. In it the consul told how Hyppolite, desperate because of the aid which France (or rather Seismaisons) was rendering Légitime, had decided that his only hope lay in enlisting the aid of the United States. To the commercial favors which Elie had been authorized to offer (lower tonnage on American vessels and lower duties on American textiles) he would add the use of Mole St. Nicolas as a coaling station, asking in return only that the blockade be broken, the free export of munitions be permitted, and that European powers be compelled to keep hands off. In his anxiety he had laid these terms before Goutier, asking his opinion as to the outcome, but the consul had given him no encouragement.[54] Before No. 934, reporting all this, could be despatched, a cablegram from Nemours Auguste had arrived saying that France would not recognize Légitime, whereupon Hyppolite had asked Goutier not to report their conversation and had sent Elie off with no authority to offer more than the commercial concessions originally proposed.[55]

No. 934, reaching Washington only in April, 1889, and apparently unknown to Blaine until January, 1891, evidently had no influence upon American policy, either during the civil war or for sixteen months after its close. Whoever first received it must have noted from Goutier's covering despatch that the proposals in it had been null before it left Cap Haitien. Whoever found it in 1891 must have noted the same thing. Yet, although the discovery took place three weeks after it had been decided to send Gherardi to Haiti, when the admiral arrived there, his whole case was based on a copy of an extract

[53] Rives to Goutier, No. 359, Feb. 14; Goutier to Rives, No. 943, March 6; Adee-to Goutier, March 18, 1889, Cons. Let., Cape Haytien, XVI.

[54] Goutier to Rives, No. 934, Dec. 27, 1889, Cons. Let., Cape Haytien, XVI.

[55] Goutier to Rives, No. 949, March 13, 1889; idem to Adee, No. 962, April 16, 1889; idem to Wharton, No. 969, June 21, 1889, Cons. Let., Cape Haytien, XVI; idem to Quincy, No. 1088, Nov. 1, 1893, loc. cit., XVII.

of Goutier's No. 934, falsely labeled as a copy of the proposals of Frederick Elie. The dishonesty of that proceeding was so obvious that it must have been realized at the State Department, if not by the Admiral himself.

Invalid as it was, the document presented fine possibilities for blackmail. Hyppolite would know what had happened, of course, but how could he explain? If it became public that he had, for an instant, considered such an idea, the Ligue would raise a whirlwind and the government would fall. Firmin escaped from that dilemma by giving Gherardi enough rope to hang himself and by giving Blaine the lie, a course at once so adroit and so bold as to have been unanticipated. He must have counted on Harrison to restrain the two, yet even so it was a desperate gamble, for the uproar in Haiti was such that Firmin himself was driven from office and Hyppolite was nearly overthrown.

Clyde did not at once give up hope, for he had information of an impending revolution that would either bring Hyppolite to his knees or put a more complacent Haitian in his place, depending on how Blaine chose to call the play.[56] On May 28 there was an *émeute* at Port-au-Prince, suppressed with such panicky severity that the metropolitan press, already in a frenzy of disappointment, found in it something to scream about.[57] Durham, who had visited Légitime at Kingston before the outbreak, was speedily transferred to Port-au-Prince as minister. Nevertheless, Hyppolite survived the crisis, and Clyde's Man Friday had to admit that no revolution could succeed while he lived.[58] Several attempts at assassination failed.

Blaine also remained sanguine, despite his rebuff. In the summer of 1891 he expressed the opinion that all of the Greater Antilles were fated to fall into the possession of the United States.[59] (The lease of Mole St. Nicolas would have been, then, but a step in the march of Manifest Destiny toward

[56] Clyde to Tracy, April 21 and 24, May 4 and 27, 1891, Tracy MSS.
[57] *Public Opinion*, XI (1891), 196, 272, 323, 379. The Philadelphia *Record* suggested that the assassination of Hyppolite would be a public service.
[58] Durham to Blaine, No. 38, Jan. 29, 1892, Despatches, Haiti, XXVI.
[59] Blaine to Harrison, Aug. 10, 1891, Harrison MSS, Library of Congress.

the annexation of Haiti.) During 1891-1892 Durham tried his hand at leasing Samaná Bay, but, although Ulises Heureaux, the Dominican dictator, was willing and the United States Congress appropriated $250,000 for the first payment, in the end the deal failed because of the clamor among the Dominicans.[60]

The Harrison administration was universally unlucky in its attempts at expansion. The best that it could do was a treaty for the annexation of Hawaii, which Cleveland, returning to power in 1893, threw into the wastebasket.

Had Blaine, Tracy, and Gherardi been called to account for their unscrupulous methods, they would have argued that their critics lacked a sense of proportion. For want of a coaling station, such as might have been established at Mole St. Nicolas, the United States might, some day, meet with a disaster costly in blood and treasure. They would, therefore, have been derelict in their duty had they neglected to employ any available means, fair or foul, to gain possession of that site. The idea that the interests of a million or two Haitians should be permitted to outweigh those of the sixty-three million Americans for whose security they were responsible would have appeared absurd to them. No jesuitical defense, however, could disguise the fact that the Mole affair was one of the more unsavory episodes in the history of American diplomacy.

[60] Blaine to Durham, No. 5, Santo Domingo Series, Jan. 28, 1892; Foster to Durham, No. 37, Santo Domingo Series, Aug. 6, 1892, Instructions, Haiti, III. Durham to Blaine, Personal, April 25, 1892; to Foster, No. 82, Oct. 29, 1892, Despatches, Dominican Republic, II.

CHAPTER X

COMMERCIAL PENETRATION

Your legation has . . . called the attention of our merchants to the great possibilities of trade with this Republic, and that it was due that the greater part of the incoming and outgoing trade should go to the States and that this would be the case if there was a serious attempt on our part to cultivate the same. . . .

—WILLIAM F. POWELL, October 23, 1905

IN 1891 Hannibal Price suggested that the United States could gain more from Haiti by cordiality than by the tactics employed in the Mole affair.[1] He referred particularly to the important commerce at stake, and to support his argument, he produced figures from the *Exposé général*[2] for 1890, indicating the relative value of Haitian-American trade in that year as follows:

	Imports	Exports
United States[3]	$ 6,454,601	$ 2,289,292
France	917,994	8,437,500
Germany	1,930,773 ⎫	
Great Britain	662,191 ⎬	3,518,987
Others	95,580 ⎭	
	$10,061,139	$14,245,779

Thus, according to Haitian statistics, American trade with Haiti was 36 per cent of the total (French, 38 per cent; others, 26 per cent), but, unfortunately for Price's argument, that trade was only four tenths of one per cent of the total for the United States.[4] Commercially, Americans were hardly aware of Haiti's existence.

[1] Price, *The Haytian Question*, p. 45.
[2] *Exposé général de la situation de la République d'Haiti*, a government publication embodying the president's annual message and accompanying documents.
[3] The corresponding American figures were $5,335,068 and $2,421,221 (*Statistical Abstract of the United States*, 1907, p. 330).
[4] *Ibid.*, pp. 284, 330.

Eighteen-ninety was a better than average year in Haitian commerce, but the proportions shown in Price's figures were fairly indicative of its character. In order to meet the interest and retirement charges on the external debt, held in France, it was necessary to maintain a large excess of exports over imports. The bulk of the exports, chiefly coffee, went to Le Havre, and from Europe (and increasingly from Germany) came most of the manufactured articles imported, but, as in colonial times, the United States held a virtual monopoly of the trade in provisions and lumber. Since Haiti, devoted to a one-crop economy, did not feed itself, imports from the United States not only exceeded those from all other countries combined, but were less subject to the adverse effect of local depressions.

From 1865 to 1890 the activity of the Federal government in behalf of commerce had been limited to the protection of shipping and resident merchants from unjust exactions and discriminatory regulations.[5] Equal competitive conditions for American citizens having been obtained, it was assumed that the government's duty was done and that the sale of goods must depend upon private initiative. By 1890, however, with the American flag disappearing from Haitian ports,[6] with American merchants still limited to their natural monopoly, and with German rather than American manufactures supplanting those of France and Britain, the Federal authorities undertook the active promotion of sales by seeking exclusive competitive advantages for American goods. This undertaking was but the application to Haiti of a general change in commercial policy.

[5] Reams of paper and gallons of ink were expended in this service, much of it pointlessly. For six years the legation labored to obtain the discontinuance of a Haitian practice held to discriminate against sailing vessels (mostly American) in favor of steamers (mostly European), only to discover at last that the majority of American shipmasters believed they would be driven out of business if the *status quo* were altered (Thompson to Bayard, May 3, 1888, Despatches, Haiti, XXIV; *Papers Relating to the Foreign Relations of the United States,* 1891, pp. 650-657; 1894, pp. 351-354). See also the case of the consular fees, *ibid.* (1878), pp. 415, 427, 445; (1879), pp. 583-596.

[6] As long as sailing vessels could operate there profitably, the American flag was a common sight in Haitian waters, but by 1898 the schooners had disappeared and the four steamship lines to New York were European (*Report on the Commercial Relations of the United States,* 1900, p. 357; Powell to Hay, No. 1536, Sept. 14, 1904, Despatches, Haiti, XLIII; No. 1685, March 15, 1905, *loc. cit.,* XLIV).

As the industrialization of the United States had progressed, the character of American imports had changed, the proportion of articles of European manufacture decreasing while that of raw materials, particularly those of tropical origin, increased. At the same time American manufactures were seeking to enter foreign markets where those of Europe had hitherto held sway. It became apparent that if a competitive advantage for American manufactures in these markets could be purchased by granting free entry to tropical products which Americans wanted and which did not compete with American agriculture, the United States would gain something for nothing. Latin America was evidently the most promising field in which to make the attempt. Under the inspiration of James G. Blaine the first Pan American conference was called to meet at Washington in 1889 to consider proposals for an American customs union, suitably embellished with talk of continental neighborhood, friendship, arbitration, and peace. When that scheme failed, Blaine arranged for a modification of the McKinley Tariff by means of which he hoped that he might yet accomplish his purpose. Sugar, molasses, tea, coffee, and hides were placed on the free list, but the president was empowered to impose retaliatory duties on imports of those commodities from any country which subjected American products to duties deemed to be "reciprocally unjust or unreasonable."

The fact that 87 per cent of the imports from Latin America entered the United States duty free, while only 10 per cent of Latin-American imports from the United States were so favored, was cited in justification of the act, but there was another side to the question. American goods had to meet stiff European competition in Latin America, but the Latin Americans had no competitors in the United States except each other. If all came to terms, none would gain any advantage thereby, while the United States reaped substantial benefits. If any of them, for whatever reason, found it impossible to grant the desired concessions, it would be driven from the American market. Thus Blaine set out to promote neighborliness with a club. Concessions were obtained from Brazil, the Dominican Republic, Spain and Great Britain (for their West Indian possessions), and the five republics of Central America. Only three states—Colombia, Venezuela, and Haiti—when informed that their tariffs were unreasonable, refused to come to terms.[7]

Even in the fiscal year 1890, before coffee was put on the free list, only seven hundredths of one per cent of American imports from Haiti were dutiable,[8] while Haitian imports from the United States were charged all that the traffic could bear. At Washington this situation was regarded as a flagrant example of reciprocal injustice. Haiti, however, was an exception to the general rule in that the United States already enjoyed a favorable balance of $2,913,847 in that trade, in contrast to an adverse balance of $142,000,000 in trade with Latin America as a whole. Under the most inviting conditions the United States bought little from Haiti, and the only probable effect of a reciprocity agreement would be to increase the American share in the Haitian market without any corresponding advantage to Haiti. Moreover, the Haiti government could not afford to curtail its customs revenue, virtually its sole resource. It neglected to respond to Blaine's overtures, and on March 18, 1892, President Harrison proclaimed the imposition of retaliatory duties on Haitian hides, molasses, sugar, tea, and coffee.

In 1890 Haiti had stood fourth among Latin-American consumers of American goods; her purchases were exceeded only by those of Mexico, Brazil, and Argentina, countries many times her size. If Blaine did not succeed in expanding this market, neither did his retaliatory measures destroy it, the reports of the next Democratic minister[9] to the contrary notwithstanding. American exports to Haiti did drop sharply in the fiscal year 1892, a fact attributable to indignation over the Mole affair rather than to a proclamation issued near the close of the period, but they rose again during the next two years. When the plunge from $5,743,935 in 1894 to $2,455,966 in 1899 occurred, the cause was hard times in Haiti on account of low coffee prices at

---

[7] J. Laurence Laughlin and H. Parker Willis, *Reciprocity*, pp. 209-213.
[8] *Statistical Abstract* (1907), p. 330.
[9] *Foreign Relations* (1894), pp. 335 f.

Le Havre, a circumstance that bore more heavily upon European than upon American exporters.[10]

The Harrison proclamation did have an immediate and drastic effect on Haitian exports to the United States. They had risen from $2,421,221 in 1890 to $3,243,454 in 1891, coffee entering duty free, but they fell to a mere $736,021 in 1893, the first fiscal year in which the retaliatory duties had full effect.[11] At the same time American importation of Brazilian coffee more than doubled.[12] More Haitian coffee reached the United States in the fiscal year 1894, while the Brazilians fought a civil war, but the gain could not be held after peace had been restored at Rio. Although the returns for 1891 may suggest that Haiti might have profited by free access to the rapidly expanding American market for coffee, no serious damage was done to her established export trade, which had long been oriented toward Europe. The only people Blaine succeeded in punishing for the "unreasonableness" of the Haitian authorities were the four or five Americans who were engaged in raising Haitian coffee expressly for the American market.[13] Even so, after the bitterness of the Mole affair, it was regrettable that Price's plea for cordiality should have been answered in the spirit of commercial retaliation.

Cleveland's victory over Harrison in 1892 gave promise of tariff reform, but Henry M. Smythe, the new minister to Haiti, suggested that Harrison's proclamation be revoked at once, on the ground that this favor, coupled with Cleveland's popularity on account of the Lazare-Pelletier decision, would restore political as well as commercial good will. On its part the Haitian government argued that the proclamation was a violation of the most-favored-nation clause of the Treaty of 1864, since the listed commodities continued to be imported duty free from Mexico and Argentina in the absence of any tariff concessions from

[10] In 1898 the total of Haitian imports was only 39 per cent of what it had been in 1890, but the American share had risen from 64 per cent to 67 per cent (*Commercial Relations*, 1899, I, 537).

[11] *Statistical Abstract* (1907), p. 330.

[12] Laughlin and Willis, *Reciprocity*, pp. 218 f.

[13] Durham to Blaine, No. 50, Feb. 19, 1892, Despatches, Haiti, XXVI.

them.[14] The President, however, was unwilling to act in advance of legislation then pending. The Wilson-Gorman Tariff was notoriously a bitter disappointment to him. Incidentally, instead of removing the special duty on Haitian coffee, it levied a duty on all imports of that commodity. Haiti was unable to compete with Brazil on these terms, much less when the Republicans in 1897 revived the reciprocity idea and made another arrangement with the latter country.

Blaine's scheme to gain ascendancy over Haiti by leasing Mole St. Nicolas had ended in fiasco. His hardly more subtle endeavor to establish commercial dominion by beating down the Haitian tariff had resulted only in the erection of a second barrier by the United States, so that the last state of Haitian-American commerce was worse than the first. In 1897, however, McKinley sent to Port-au-Prince a minister who believed that there was a third way, as yet untried. William F. Powell labored earnestly to promote trade by sheer salesmanship. His purpose was to drive European goods from the Haitian market, to make the republic an economic dependency of the United States, not primarily for the sake of commercial gain, but as a measure of strategic security.[15]

Powell's method was to advertise the Haitian market in the United States, advising exporters on how to appeal to it, and to advertise American wares in Haiti. He argued that there was no reason why American manufactures should not compete successfully with those of Europe if American manufacturers made an effort to please the Haitians. Hitherto that elementary principle of salesmanship had been neglected. Flour, pork, beef, cod, soap, lard, and butter, the chief imports from the United States,[16] had sold themselves, but American shoes and textiles were not popular because not designed to the Haitian taste, Americans complacently regarding it as a fault in the Haitians that they did not prefer American styles to their own. The English took care to provide the bold, clear prints in vogue

[14] *Foreign Relations* (1894), pp. 335 f. Presumably the Mexican and Argentine tariffs had not been deemed unreasonable.

[15] Powell to Loomis, Aug. 23, 1905, Despatches, Haiti, XLVI.

[16] *Commercial Relations* (1899), I, 537.

with the ladies of Port-au-Prince and to make their bolts of a size convenient to Haitian retailers. Most disadvantageous was the American practice of limiting credit to sixty days, while their European competitors allowed six months, enabling the retailer to pay for goods out of the proceeds of their sale.[17] In order to arouse the mercantile community, the minister wrote extensively to trade journals and chambers of commerce and spent his time on leave carrying his message directly to merchants and manufacturers.[18]

Thanks to Powell's efforts, American-manufactured goods at last found a place in the Haitian market. The United States became the chief source of ironware, machinery, furniture, wagons, and saddlery.[19] A spectacular advance was made in the sale of textiles, for in 1893 Great Britain had commanded four fifths of that trade, but in 1903 the United States dominated it in the same degree.[20] All told, the American share of Haitian imports had risen from 67 to 73 per cent,[21] but the Minister was disturbed by a decline in the sale of provisions, even though it did not benefit any European rival. Because of continued hard times the poorer Haitians were eating less, and that homegrown stuff.[22]

After his strenuous efforts to promote trade, it was ironic that Powell should have been compelled to witness the Haitian abrogation of the commercial treaty of 1864. The occasion for this decision was a dispute over the interpretation of Article 5, which read:

The citizens of each of the high contracting parties, residing or established in the territory of the other, shall be exempt from all compulsory military duty by sea or by land, and from all forced loans or military exactions or requisitions; nor shall they be compelled to pay any contributions higher or other than those that are or may be paid by native citizens.

[17] *Ibid.* (1897), I, 749 ff.
[18] Powell to Hay, No. 1855, Oct. 23, 1905, Despatches, Haiti, **XLVI**.
[19] *Commercial Relations* (1902), I, 93.
[20] *Ibid.* (1903), II, 241.
[21] *Ibid.* (1899), I, 537; (1904), I, 607.
[22] Powell to Hay, No. 1855, Oct. 23, 1905, Despatches, Haiti, **XLVI**.

The American contention was that "contribution" here meant all taxes, fees, and other payments to the state not covered by the prohibition against forced loans, military exactions, and requisitions, an interpretation sustained by the context and by the customary use of the word in both French and English legal parlance. The Haitian counter-argument was that "contributions" was used in the sense of "military exactions," but the fallacy of such reasoning is immediately apparent on the face of the article. If military exactions were already absolutely prohibited, what logic would there be in establishing that Americans should pay none higher or other than those paid by native Haitians? The point had been argued in 1876, 1878-1879, 1893, and 1897-1900, but each time the Haitian government had finally submitted to the American interpretation.[23]

On each occasion the question had been raised by an attempt to enforce a Haitian law of 1876 designed to promote the development of a middle class by reserving for it a commercial field free from foreign competition. Aliens were forbidden to trade outside the open ports, to buy directly from producers, or to sell at retail. Incidentally, the fees for wholesalers' licenses, which were the only ones foreign merchants could obtain, were considerably higher than those charged for licenses to engage in retail trade. The law was never enforced except to the extent of requiring foreigners to pay the higher fee for licenses under which they were actually permitted to sell at retail. This was so much the case that in all the long history of the dispute there was nothing to indicate that the issue was not simply whether Haiti could, under the treaty, charge Americans more than Haitians for retail licenses. When the question came up again in 1903, Powell once more invoked Article 5 and succeeded in having Americans assimilated to natives for the time being, but the Haitian government decided to do away with

[23] Bassett to Fish, No. 473, Sept. 16, 1876, Despatches, Haiti, IX; Langston to Evarts, No. 25, Jan. 25, 1878, loc. cit., XI; Evarts to Preston, June 13, 1879, Notes to Haiti, III; Durham to Gresham, No. 235, Aug. 28, 1893, Despatches, Haiti, XXVI; Smythe to Gresham, No. 16, Dec. 13, 1893, loc. cit., XXVIII; Powell to Sherman, No. 81, Nov. 12, 1897, loc. cit., XXI; Foreign Relations (1898), pp. 387-397; Powell to Hay, No. 821, Oct. 10, 1900, Despatches, Haiti, XXXVI.

the obnoxious clause under which they claimed that privileged character.

In May, 1904, Jacques Nicolas Léger, Haitian minister at Washington, submitted a draft of a new commercial treaty, but Secretary of State John Hay ignored the matter for nine months. He then indicated that Léger's convention was entirely acceptable save for Article 3, which substituted the most-favored-nation principle for the guarantees regarding "contributions" found in Article 5 of the old treaty. It was futile for Léger to dispute Hay's interpretation of the term, but he could argue with reason that Article 3, as he had written it, was still of more value to the United States than to Haiti, since Americans had to meet competition there, while Haitians never settled in the United States, "for well known reasons."[24] Hay insisted on the abstract point that under a most-favored-nation clause a hypothetical Haitian merchant in New York would enjoy equality with natives in respect to taxes and license fees, while Americans in Haiti would not, a situation which the United States refused to accept.[25] The State Department was content to see the treaty lapse because it knew that, considering the balance (or unbalance) of power in the Caribbean in 1905, Haiti would never venture to revive the pre-recognition discriminations against the United States. A most-favored-nation clause was no longer necessary, but if, by holding out, Article 5 could be preserved, that would be so much to the good. The Haitians, also, could do without a treaty, for the most-favored-nation clause had never been of much value to them, none at all since Harrison's proclamation in 1893, and to be rid of Article 5 was something gained. In September, 1905, the Haitian government announced that American merchants would thenceforth be required to obtain wholesaler's licenses, like other aliens.

The effort to create a Haitian middle class was resumed with new vigor in 1907 when Sténio Vincent, mayor of Port-au-Prince, gave notice that the act of 1876 was really going to be enforced at last. The foreign mercantile houses clamored

<hr/>

[24] Léger to Hay, No. 1209, Feb. 24, 1905, Notes from Haiti, VI.
[25] Memorandum, Van Dyne to Adee, March 1, 1905, Notes from Haiti, VI.

that they would be driven out of business, that it was a rare day for them when their total sales amounted to the minimum prescribed by law for a single transaction, while the diplomatic corps rather extravagantly demanded time in which to announce to the world that Haiti had closed her ports to foreign commerce. As a result of all this uproar, the law was again abandoned, the only result of the attempt at its enforcement being to shake down, at the rate of ten dollars each, those foreign merchants who did not already have retailer's "patents" in addition to their wholesaler's ones. The commune did a brisk business supplying them with the licenses required by law for the sort of trade in which they had been engaged, without license, for years, although the same law forbade that they be licensed to engage in that trade at all. That was considered to be a fair compromise. Meanwhile the desired social reform was indefinitely postponed.[26]

Curiously, just as the ratification of the commercial treaty of 1864 had been followed by a decline in Haitian-American commerce, so its abrogation was followed by a boom. However high the percentage of Haitian imports of American origin in 1905, their actual value had fallen to the lowest ebb since the dark days of the Salnave war—$2,297,080—but from that point they climbed steadily to a $7,271,999 peak in 1912.[27] This increase was merely the effect of the return of a relative degree of prosperity to Haiti. However, even as American sales increased in volume and value, the American share of the market actually declined to a normal 60 per cent, more or less, for Haitians with money to spend sought European luxuries as well as American necessities. Obviously commercial penetration had failed as a means to strategic control.

[26] Foreign Relations (1907), pp. 728-742.
[27] Statistical Abstract (1907), p. 330; (1917), pp. 369, 766.

CHAPTER XI

THE MONROE DOCTRINE

Chronic wrongdoing, or an impotence which results in a general loosening of the ties of civilized society, may . . . ultimately require the intervention of some civilized nation, and in the Western Hemisphere . . . the Monroe Doctrine may force the United States . . . to the exercise of an international police power.
—THEODORE ROOSEVELT, December 6, 1904

AT THE OPENING of the twentieth century the Caribbean interests of the United States were greater than ever, and the desire to render them secure by dominating that region, at least to the extent necessary to prevent the intrusion of any formidable and ambitious power, had correspondingly increased. A formula was devised to suit the occasion, and, in order that it might gain popular acceptance, it was presented as a corollary of that article of American political faith known as the Monroe Doctrine, yet actually the "corollary" was in many respects the antithesis of Monroe's famous pronouncement.

In 1823 President Monroe, considering the possibility that the "Holy Alliance" might follow up its antirevolutionary interventions in Italy and Spain by attempting to subdue Spain's former colonies in America, declared that the United States must regard any effort of the European powers "to extend their system to this hemisphere as dangerous to our peace and safety." In warning the allies against "interposition for the purpose of oppressing . . . or controlling" American republics, he not only pointed out the American practice of abstention from purely European affairs, but stated, with reference to Spanish America as well, that it was "still the true policy of the United States to leave the parties to themselves." There would be no departure from this attitude except under the provocation of an overt act of European intrusion, and then the American intervention would be directed against the European powers responsible.[1]

Monroe's declaration was framed with reference to a particular situation, but it was based squarely on the teachings of the founding fathers.[2] Consequently, it came to be regarded as the classic expression of a traditional American attitude. However, not until a generation had passed did Americans become conscious of "Monroe Doctrine" as a name to conjure with, and then it was employed, not in the spirit of Monroe, but in the service of "manifest destiny," that other scion of the two-hemispheres concept. During the forties and fifties "Monroe" became the rallying cry of statesmen whose primary concern seems to have been to keep European, especially British, hands off territories marked for acquisition by the United States. This association resulted in the transmutation of Monroe's policy, defensive toward Europe and noninterventionist toward neighboring republics, into a warrant for expansion wherever Hispanic American disorder and impotence suggested the necessity of the benevolent intervention of the United States to forestall the sinister intervention of European powers.[3] As late as 1870 Grant argued that the doctrine imposed the duty of annexing the Dominican Republic, since if the option were not exercised, the United States could not reasonably object to the sale of Samaná to some European power.[4] Through the agency of Manifest Destiny the Monroe Doctrine became a shibboleth, but after the decline of expansionism it regained its original sense of static defense against European intrusion.

In 1823 Haiti was not numbered among the revolutionary republics whose independence the United States had recognized and wished to defend, nor is there any doubt that the party then in power would have welcomed the reconquest of that particular

---

[1] J. D. Richardson, *A Compilation of the Messages and Papers of the Presidents*, II, 209.

[2] The concept of two hemispheres, one the domain of despotism, the other the home of liberty, and the idea of nonintervention in foreign politics.

[3] Polk applied this reasoning to the case of Yucatán in 1848 and Buchanan to that of Mexico in 1858 (Richardson, *A Compilation of the Messages and Papers of the Presidents*, IV, 399, 582).   [4] *Ibid.*, VII, 100.

colony by its former sovereign.   Even in the era of Manifest
Destiny, when Washington was so sensitive to European influence in America that an Anglo-French blockade of distant
Buenos Aires was roundly denounced as a flagrant violation of
the principles of Monroe,[5] the United States encouraged these
same powers to threaten a blockade of Port-au-Prince and offered
no objection to their establishment of virtual protectorate over
the Dominican Republic.[6]   Except for domestic circumstances,
Seward might have responded to Haiti's appeal for support in
1861, but the Spanish had abandoned Santo Domingo before he
recovered freedom of action.   The interference of Spencer St.
John in Haitian politics from 1865 to 1874 provoked no protest.   Not until the French began to dig a canal at Panama did
the United States become sufficiently apprehensive of European
designs in the Caribbean to extend the protection of the Monroe
Doctrine to Haiti, and then the application was purely negative.

On four occasions between 1884 and 1891 European powers
were warned to stay out of Haiti.   Shortly after Frelinghuysen's
rejection of Salomon's offer to cede La Tortue or Mole St.
Nicolas to the United States, Preston left Washington for Paris,
and during the summer of 1884 the suspicion grew that he was
making a similar offer to France, a suspicion confirmed by certain
papers Langston succeeded in extracting from the Haitian foreign office (if they were indeed authentic).[7]   Immediately the
attention of the Quai d'Orsay was called "to the fact that the
acquisition of Haytian territory by France would conflict with

[5] J. R. Clark, *Memorandum on the Monroe Doctrine*, p. 121.   There had been
no objection to British mediation in this same region in 1828, after the United
States had declined to act on account of the traditional policy of nonintervention.

[6] Clayton did send Green to check European influence at Santo Domingo, but he
seems to have been more interested in securing Samaná for the United States than
in defending any abstract principles.   Green's attitude, certainly, was more anti-
Haitian than anti-European.   See above, p. 57.   Webster's tripartite intervention
was criticized as a departure from the Monroe Doctrine (*Democratic Review*, 1853,
p. 185), but to have opposed France and England would have been to defend
Haiti, which was the opposite of what the United States wished to do.   Even the
Pierce and Buchanan administrations acquiesced in the Anglo-French domination of
Hispaniola, which, while it prevented the United States from acquiring Samaná, did
serve to protect the Dominicans from Haiti.

[7] Langston to Frelinghuysen, No. 696, Dec. 24, 1884, Despatches, Haiti, XVIII.

the principles of our public policy known as the Monroe Doctrine."[8] Two years later the British were the villains. Screaming "Remember Suez," certain French journals had accused "perfidious Albion" of planning to use the Maunder claim as a pretext for seizing La Tortue in order to dominate the Panama Canal until the time was ripe for stealing it.[9] The Haitian government was sufficiently worried to ask whether it might rely upon American support, and Bayard considered it worth while to instruct his minister in London "to remonstrate . . . against . . . any measure . . . which would violate the well known principles of the Monroe Doctrine."[10] During the civil war of 1888-1889 rumors that Légitime had bought the support of Seismaisons with a pledge to cede Mole St. Nicolas and La Gonave to France were so persistent that Bayard sent another warning to Paris and Blaine obtained a denial from the Quai d'Orsay.[11] When, after the vigorous suppression of the conspiracy of 1891, there was talk of a European intervention led by France, the American press paused in its denunciations of Hyppolite long enough to say that no European power could touch him without the unlikely consent of the United States.[12] Times had changed in the forty years since the tripartite intervention in 1851.

In Haiti the doctrine was interpreted as a "tacit alliance of the American nations," and from it Hannibal Price derived the corollary that the United States, in denying the American republics European political support, became morally bound to respect their territorial integrity and independence.[13] His con-

[8] Frelinghuysen to Morton, No. 698, Feb. 28; No. 700, March 2, 1885, Instructions, France, XXI. The French denied everything. Morton to Bayard, No. 744, April 2, 1885, Despatches, France, XCVI.

[9] Thompson to Bayard, No. 121, March 5, 1887, Despatches, Haiti, XXI. Had the French never heard of Jamaica or Santa Lucia?

[10] Bayard to Phelps, No. 546, Feb. 24, 1887, Instructions, Great Britain, XXVIII.

[11] Bayard to McLane, No. 414, Dec. 21, 1888, Instructions, France, XXI; Blaine to Thompson, No. 166, June 11, 1889, Instructions, Haiti, II. Later, at Hyppolite's behest, Blaine asked for and received assurances that Seismaisons would not be sent back to Port-au-Prince. Reid to Blaine, No. 128, Jan. 23, 1890, Despatches, France, CIV.

[12] Public Opinion, XI (1891), 272.

[13] Price, The Haytian Question, pp. 5, 37.

clusion was in accord with the sentiments of American anti-imperialists, as expressed by Bayard in an *obiter dictum* in his report on the Pelletier case.[14] According to him:

> The United States has proclaimed herself the protector of this Western World, in which she is by far the strongest power, from the intrusion of European sovereignties. . . . She has announced that she would cherish, as it becomes her, the territorial rights of the feeblest of these states, regarding them not merely as in the eye of the law equal to even the greatest of nationalities, but, in view of her distinctive policy, as entitled to be regarded by her as the objects of a peculiarly gracious care.

This interpretation of the Monroe Doctrine in terms of *noblesse oblige* had been received at Port-au-Prince with even greater delight than that derived from his decision not to collect the Pelletier award.[15]

Blaine's rapacious policy, a repudiation of the glowing, though perhaps historically inaccurate, pronouncement of his predecessor, defeated its own purpose, for instead of binding Haiti to the United States it forfeited the good will won by Bayard and compelled Hyppolite to seek European support, but after the return of Cleveland to the White House the Haitian President again regarded the Monroe Doctrine as a safer reliance than a Europe "in the throes of colonization fever."[16] The Haitians found as much cause for satisfaction in the attitude of Cleveland's second administration as they had in that of the first. Interposing between Great Britain and Venezuela, Secretary Olney declared that the states of America were "friends and allies" of the United States,[17] while Port-au-Prince applauded the spectacle of the strongest American

---

[14] *Senate Executive Document No. 64*, 49th Cong., 2d Sess., p. 15.

[15] Thompson to Bayard, No. 136, May 16, 1887, Despatches, Haiti, XXI.

[16] Durham to Gresham, No. 229, Aug. 5, 1893, Despatches, Haiti, XXI. Hyppolite ventured to suggest that Cleveland invite the European powers to join the United States in guaranteeing Haitian territorial integrity and independence (Goutier to Wharton, No. 1066, April 25, 1893, Cons. Let., Cape Haytien, XVII), but nothing came of it. The United States had consistently avoided such engagements in the past, on the ground that they would constitute an "entangling alliance."

[17] *Papers Relating to the Foreign Relations of the United States* (1895), I, 558.

republic disinterestedly shielding a weaker neighbor from the alleged aggressions of a mighty world empire.[18]   Interest in the actual course of events would seem to have diverted Haitian attention from another line in Olney's remarkable exposition of the Monroe Doctrine.   "Today," he wrote, "the United States is practically sovereign on this continent and its fiat is law upon the subjects to which it confines its interposition." His statement would have satisfied the most ardent devotee of Manifest Destiny.

Two years later the Haitians suffered a rude disillusionment. In September, 1897, Emil Lüders, a German, claiming some peculiar extraterritoriality for his Port-au-Prince livery stable, attempted to prevent by force the arrest of a Haitian employee charged with petty larceny, and was sentenced to thirty days for assault and battery.   He appealed, and was granted a new trial, at which additional charges were brought against him and he was sentenced to a year's imprisonment and a five-hundred dollar fine.   On learning of what had happened the German Kaiser was deeply moved—Lüders had been a soldier in the Supreme War Lord's own regiment—and therefore he wrote personally to President Simon Sam and demanded the release of Lüders, the removal of the judges, the imprisonment of the police, and the payment of an indemnity of five thousand dollars for each day that his man had spent in jail.   Unfortunately, although a letter from the All Highest himself could not be delivered into the hands of clerks, the German chargé, accredited only to the foreign office, could not gain access to the wary President until, like a process-server, he cornered him at a public reception.   Simon Sam refused to receive it except through the foreign office, and the fat was in the fire.   If he gave way, there might be a revolution, but if he did not there would certainly be another visit from a German squadron.[19]

The Haitian preparations for defense consisted of the re-

[18] Antenor Firmin, *M. Roosevelt et la République d'Haiti*, p. 168.   In 1895 British military power was immensely superior to that of the United States, but British hands were "very full in other quarters of the globe."
[19] Powell to Sherman, No. 55, Oct. 21, 1897, Despatches, Haiti, XXX.

lease of Lüders,[20] an offer to arbitrate the other German demands, and an appeal to the United States for help in the name of the Monroe Doctrine. They were insufficient. Although Léger argued that he was "the natural protector of the Island," President McKinley would undertake no more than mediation with the consent of both parties,[21] which, considering the German mood, meant nothing at all. On December 6 two German cruisers appeared at Port-au-Prince, and President Sam was given three hours in which to decide whether he would listen to a public reading of the imperial letter and pay an indemnity of twenty thousand dollars or face a bombardment. Urged to submit by all the diplomatic corps save Powell, who could offer no hope of American support, he yielded.

Powell poured forth his indignation to the Secretary of State.

I think [he wrote] that our Government is rapidly losing its influence with the people of these small republics, they look to the United States as their protector from unjust aggressions . . . they expected as well as the representatives of other powers an enforcement of the Monroe doctrine, they expected to see the arrogance of the German Emperor checked strongly but firmly, this could have been readily done, if our Government had given Germany thus to understand that no coercion shall ever take place by a stronger upon a weaker state on this side of the Atlantic. The people so well as the Haitian Gov. feels that in their sore distress the country to which of all countries they looked for aid failed to respond to their cry of need. This is the first time in my life, I have ever had cause to be ashamed of being an American.[22]

The American press shared Powell's hot exasperation,[23] indicating that he and Bayard were not the only ones who cherished a sentimental regard for the Monroe Doctrine, conceiving of

[20] As a favor to the American minister. Powell was reprimanded for this face-saving intervention, but he justified it on the ground that the Germans might provoke an antiforeign frenzy dangerous to Americans (idem to idem, No. 56, Oct. 22, 1897, loc. cit.).
[21] Memorandum, Sherman to McKinley, Oct. 20, 1897, Notes from Haiti, V.
[22] Powell to Sherman, No. 109, Dec. 6, 1897, Despatches, Haiti, XXXI. In his agitation the minister forgot his grammar and punctuation.
[23] Tansill, Purchase of the Danish West Indies, p. 380.

it as something more than a cloak for ulterior aims, but the statesmen at Washington, about to wage a "glorious little war" against decrepit Spain "in the name of humanity" and for such rights of small nations as did not conflict with the ambitions of larger ones, remained quite cool. The *Revue des Deux Mondes*, observing with satisfaction that "the Monroe Doctrine, yesterday so intransigeant and arrogant, showed itself all of a sudden of the most easy composition," asked whether this was out of regard for the German-American vote or because, in the interest of its designs on Cuba, the United States dared not antagonize Germany.[24]   Perhaps the McKinley administration did know what it was about.

Contrary to Powell's predictions, no revolution occurred, but friends of the government did approach him with a plan for a treaty that would have placed Haiti definitely under American protection.   The minister's drooping spirits quickened, and he began to write excitedly of naval stations.[25]   Secretary of State John Sherman, however, was not tempted.   The United States, he said, had constantly avoided the idea of an all-American alliance

in the conviction that in any such system "the United States would necessarily be its protector and the party responsible to the world, while the Spanish-American States would get the benefits of a system of mutual protection which the United States did not need." Moreover, protectorates over our neighbors have never been advocated in our foreign policy, being contrary to the principles upon which this government is founded. A protectorate, however qualified, assumes a greater or less degree of responsibility on the part of the protector for the acts of the protected state, without ability to shape or control these acts, unless the relation created be virtually that of colonial dependency. . . .[26]

In Sherman's conception of the Monroe Doctrine none of the knight-errantry of Bayard and Olney was evident, but neither was there any sense of responsibility for the conduct of Carib-

[24] Powell to Sherman, No. 154, Jan. 21, 1898, Despatches, Haiti, XXXI.
[25] *Idem* to *idem*, No. 134, No. 135, Dec. 24, 1897, *loc. cit.*
[26] Sherman to Powell, No. 97, Jan. 11, 1898, Instructions, Haiti, III.

bean republics, "with paramount intervention of the protector in the domestic concerns of the protected community." Sherman was seventy-five, seven months older than the Monroe Doctrine itself. His was the generation that had defeated the expansionist schemes of Seward and Grant, but in the spring of 1898 he was an anachronism.[27]

Barely launched at the time of the Mole affair, the movement for naval expansion and Caribbean control had gathered momentum during the nineties. The economic and psychological influences which had produced the new European imperialism in the preceding decade were beginning to be felt in the United States. Unlike the earlier American expansionists, who had contemplated the admission of their neighbors to equal partnership in the Union,[28] the latest generation thought only in terms of colonial dominion, overseas commerce, and the prestige of world empire. Chief among the advocates of a "large policy"—a concept of a "new manifest destiny" extensive enough to include the Philippines—were Henry Cabot Lodge, senator from Massachusetts, and Theodore Roosevelt, assistant secretary of the navy. Their philosophical guide was Captain A. T. Mahan, discoverer of the influence of sea power on history, who throughout the decade proclaimed the need for naval bases in Hawaii, Samoa, and the Antilles.[29] Although the basic motive of the new expansionism was economic,[30] the chief consideration, so far as the Caribbean was concerned, was not the economic value of the Caribbean lands but the military security of the trade routes through the prospective isthmian canal. In 1897 Mahan surveyed the region, indicated the

[27] Sherman had been opposed to the annexation of the Dominican Republic, and in 1897 he was still an anti-imperialist (*Recollections of Forty Years*, II, 1216), even though he was constrained to sign an annexation treaty with Hawaii against his own convictions.

[28] See above, p. 93. All the territories acquired before 1890 had been nearly vacant lands, open to settlement from the older states, but those now coveted were detached, tropical, and already crowded with unassimilable populations.

[29] *The Interest of America in Sea Power*, a collection of magazine articles published between 1890 and 1897.

[30] However, big business was so slow to catch the vision that at first it actually opposed the war with Spain and the assumption of colonial burdens destined to follow from it (Julius W. Pratt, *Expansionists of 1898*, pp. 230-278).

strategic importance of the Windward Passage, and, ignoring the Mole St. Nicolas, picked Guantánamo Bay as the most desirable site for an Antillean naval station.

A few months later the United States seized not only Guantánamo, but also Cuba and Puerto Rico,[31] and in 1903, Roosevelt, as president, "took Panama." An American canal, guarded by a naval base in the Windward Passage, was thus assured, but the gentlemen of the "large policy" were not satisfied. In 1902 they endeavored, unsuccessfully, to purchase the Danish West Indies, not because a naval harbor in that quarter was any longer needed—Culebra Island, off Puerto Rico, would suffice[32]—but simply in order to make certain that Germany could never acquire St. Thomas.[33] As had other imperialists before them, they had discovered that the occupation of a given area for defensive purposes might necessitate the occupation of adjacent areas in order to defend the original acquisition. Thus "self-defense" reveals infinite expansive possibilities.

The inescapable fact was that the Panama Canal constituted a vital interest which the Federal authorities were in duty bound to protect to the full extent of their ability. Adequate provision of Caribbean naval stations was only half the task. No formidable naval power could be permitted to effect a lodgment within striking distance of Panama or the Windward Passage. To appreciate the strategic considerations involved, one must forget the immense power of the modern American navy and remember both its relative inconsequence and the limitations of all war craft thirty-five years ago.[34] The new

[31] I do not suggest that the United States cynically attacked Spain in order to grab Guantánamo, on the advice of Mahan, but, events taking the course they did, the advocates of the "large policy" knew what they wanted, while most Americans had not thought the matter through.

[32] Although St. Thomas has belonged to the United States for twenty years, Culebra is still the advance base of the navy's Caribbean "war games."

[33] Admiral Bradford to Hay, Sept. 28, 1898 (quoted in A. L. P. Dennis, *Adventures in American Diplomacy*, p. 271), presents the logical basis of the attempted purchase.

[34] In 1903 the world's navies were constituted as follows:

	Great Britain	France	Germany	Russia	Italy	United States	Japan
Battleships	48	28	28	18	17	11	7
Cruisers	132	50	41	22	21	29	33
Other types	238	306	134	134	171	59	87

navy of 1898 had not been able to prevent even Cervera's pitiful squadron from reaching its Caribbean base nor could a fleet that had not dared to attack the antique defenses of Santiago hope to seize the Caribbean harbors of a first-class power before that power's own navy could arrive on the scene, as Welles had suggested with the American naval strength of 1865 in mind.[35] Given a local base, the British, French, or Germans could have met the United States in the Caribbean on better than even terms, provided the European political situation permitted the absence of their fleets from home waters— and naval strategists, paid to anticipate the worst, could not assume that such a condition would never arise.

Actually, Great Britain and France were not feared. The British, compelled to consider the rise of two new navies, had concentrated against the Germans and abandoned the Caribbean to the United States. Great Britain could not be deprived of her many Antillean stations, but in their dismantled condition they were not formidable. On the other hand, Germany, with no overseas stations of her own, but with well-known imperial ambitions, might logically be expected to take advantage of an unguarded opening, and any Caribbean base which Germany might acquire would surely be highly fortified. Because the Danish treaty of 1902 had been designed to thwart Germany, Americans not unnaturally, though mistakenly, attributed its defeat in the Danish parliament to German influence and conceived an exaggerated notion of the imminence of the German menace.[36]

The Monroe Doctrine in its purely negative sense, and the nontransfer principle traditionally associated with it, covered the case—it was well known that the United States would resent

[35] See above, p. 98. There may have been good strategic reasons for not exposing the fleet to damage while the hostile navy remained intact, but these only reinforce the point. The army's Santiago campaign had not been such as to inspire optimism.

[36] In *The Purchase of the Danish West Indies*, pp. 373-453, Prof. Tansill has shown that Germany was not responsible for the defeat of the treaty. Von Tirpitz did covet Caribbean naval stations, but in the existing state of European tension the Wilhelmstrasse hesitated to challenge the Monroe Doctrine (Alfred Vagts, *Deutschland und die Vereinigten Staaten in der Weltpolitik*, II, 1410-1524). Any relaxation of that tension might well lead to a more aggressive German policy in the Americas.

and probably resist any attempt to obtain a Caribbean naval
base from Haiti, say, or Denmark—but what could the United
States do in the face of a *fait accompli?* It seemed wiser to
apply an ounce of prevention in dealing with minor powers
than to measure out a pound of cure for the intrusion of an
empire. At only three points could the Antillean line of defense be broken, St. Thomas, Samaná Bay, and Mole St.
Nicolas, the same three that had been the hope of American
naval strategists in the days before the United States took
over the possessions of Spain. Let the United States buy
out Denmark, if possible, and secure such control over the
republics of Hispaniola as to be able to prevent a voluntary
cession and to remove all pretext for forcible European intervention. Thus, as in the time of Polk and Buchanan, men
began to think of the Monroe Doctrine as authorizing them
to forestall rather than simply to resist European exploitation
of the disorder and impotence of Latin-American states, but their
objective was merely a negative strategic control, not outright
annexation. Even such limited interference in the affairs of a
recognized sovereign would be difficult to justify as a measure
of self-defense against a remote contingency, but if Americans
could persuade themselves that the states concerned would
receive benefit rather than harm thereby, their consciences would
be set at rest. In the circumstances Americans were as good as
persuaded.

Experience with Cuba had indicated the technique by means
of which the strategic interests of the United States could be
protected without the assumption of colonial burdens. The
Teller amendment, adopted at the outset of the war with
Spain, had promised Cuba to the Cubans, but the Platt amendment of 1901 had made American withdrawal contingent upon
Cuban consent to American intervention whenever needed to
maintain a stable government and upon a Cuban pledge not to
contract an excessive public debt or to enter into any other
engagement tending to permit the lodgment of any third power
in the island. It was felt that these terms, which eliminated
every pretext for European intrusion, imposed no hardship

upon Cuba, while the sanitary and other reforms inaugurated by the brief post-war occupation had conferred substantial benefits upon the Cuban people. It followed that, should the occasion ever arise, to "Cuba-ize" Hispaniola in any appropriate degree would be to serve the interests of Haiti and the Dominican Republic as well as those of the United States.

Because, after all, there was no Treaty of Paris giving the United States a clear warrant to arrange the affairs of Hispaniola, the American interventionists found it necessary to reinforce their argument by showing that in proceeding thus they would be discharging a solemn duty to the world at large, and on this point the British, eager to cultivate American good will, proved very helpful. Since 1895 they had contended that if the Monroe Doctrine forbade Great Britain to defend threatened interests in the Americas, then it must impose upon the United States the burden of compelling disorderly Latin-American republics to live up to their obligations.[37] This argument had the curious effect of transforming the idea of an American interest in safeguarding Latin America from European interference into the idea of an American duty to protect European interests from Latin-American interference, but in his annual message of 1904 President Roosevelt publicly adopted it as his own.[38] Beginning with the assurance that "if a nation shows that it knows how to act with reasonable efficiency and decency in social and political matters, if it keeps order and pays its obligations, it need fear no interference from the United States," he went on to declare that "chronic wrong-doing, or an

[37] As early as 1887 James Anthony Froude, lamenting the decline of British power and prestige in the Caribbean, had argued to this effect (*The English in the West Indies*, p. 345). In 1895 the London *Chronicle* had suggested the same idea (J. Fred Rippy, *Latin America in World Politics*, p. 117), and Lord Salisbury had incorporated it in his reply to Olney (J. B. Moore, *A Digest of International Law*, VI, 562). When, in 1901, Britain surrendered substantial rights (and with them the hegemony of the Caribbean) for no express equivalent, there seems to have been a tacit understanding that the United States would not employ the strategic advantage to the prejudice of British interests (Rippy, *op. cit.*, p. 123). The final withdrawal of British forces in 1904 coincided with Roosevelt's public adoption of the British idea.

[38] Philippe Buneau-Varilla had suggested a Roosevelt Doctrine of this sort, as a complement to that of Monroe, but Roosevelt presented his policy as a corollary (Weinberg, *Manifest Destiny*, pp. 426 f.).

impotence which results in a general loosening of the ties of civilized society" would, in the Caribbean at least, result in a visit from the United States in the role of an international policeman. The logical connection between this "international police power" and the doctrine of Monroe was expounded in a later message.[39]

It has for some time been obvious that those who profit by the Monroe Doctrine [the Caribbean republics] must accept certain responsibilities along with the rights it confers; and that the same statement applies to those who uphold the doctrine. . . . The justification for the United States taking this burden and incurring the responsibility is to be found in the fact that it is incompatible with international equity for the United States to refuse to allow other powers to take the only means at their disposal of satisfying the claims of their creditors and yet refuse, itself, to take such steps.

Thus Roosevelt's warrant for intervention was presented as a corollary of the Monroe Doctrine, although apparently there were more points of contrast than of resemblance between the two ideas. Far from assuming any "international police power" for the United States, Monroe's purpose had been to warn a self-appointed squad of international policemen to stay out of the American neighborhood. His message was directed exclusively toward Europe, and so far as it gave any indication of a policy in inter-American relations, it was one of nonintervention. Whether or not Roosevelt's preventive measures were justified as one phase of a larger Panama policy, as a "pretension to special prerogatives by virtue of special duties involved in the peculiar mission of a nation with preeminent capacities," they savored less of Monroe than of the "new manifest destiny."[40]

The advocates of a "large policy" were following Sherman's logic to the opposite conclusion. Since they had decided that circumstances compelled them to protect Hispaniola from every possibility of European intrusion, they were bound to assume a "paramount intervention . . . in the domestic concerns

[39] *Foreign Relations* (1905), p. 334.
[40] Weinberg, *Manifest Destiny*, p. 415. See *ibid.*, pp. 428-431, for a cogent discussion of the Roosevelt ideology and the influence of the ideas of his former teacher, John W. Burgess, concerning the civilizing mission of the Teutonic nations.

of the protected community." They did not feel, as Sherman had, that this was a violation of the principles upon which the United States had been founded. On the contrary, they told themselves that they were upholding a cherished American principle, the Monroe Doctrine.

The Roosevelt "corollary" was not the product of mere abstract speculation. In 1902, when Great Britain, Germany, and Italy employed force against Venezuela to compel the settlement of certain claims, it was feared in Washington that Germany might be seeking to obtain a Caribbean leasehold similar to Kiauchau. That episode was safely closed, but if a recurrence of the situation, with its dangers of a collision, were to be prevented, some positive procedure must be developed. The President's message of 1904 was framed with specific reference to conditions in the Dominican Republic. That unhappy country, in the throes of political disintegration, was actually bankrupt, its overlapping obligations to creditors of half a dozen nationalities inviting intervention on the Hague principle of "first come, first served." Early in the year the Dominican government requested American assistance in untangling its fiscal affairs and staving off threatened European interference,[41] but Roosevelt, while maturing his plans, declined to act until after the presidential election. His message in December was followed by the negotiation of a treaty in which the United States undertook the readjustment of the Dominican debt and the collection of the customs. When the Senate refused to sanction this arrangement, the customs receivership was established anyhow, by executive agreement, while the debt was scaled down 46 per cent under supposedly Dominican auspices, although no doubt the feat was made possible only by the implicit support of the United States. There was no discrimination in favor of American claimants, who protested.[42] In 1907 the Senate was persuaded to regularize the *fait accompli* by consenting to a modified treaty bringing the customs receivership openly under

[41] However, the Dominicans did not propose a customs receivership until virtually compelled to do so (*Foreign Relations*, 1905, I, 298).

[42] *Ibid.*, I, 377.

the aegis of the United States. A fifty-year loan of twenty million dollars was floated in New York for refunding the readjusted debt. The immediate results of the intervention were good, for the improvement in the customs service was such that the Dominican government's share of the revenue actually exceeded the entire amount previously collected, while the foreign creditors were pacified. At the same time the warring factions were curbed, and an unfamiliar peace reigned in the land.[43]

Evidently Roosevelt's conviction of a civilizing mission and the clamor of American economic interests were not without influence upon his Dominican policy,[44] but to ascribe that policy primarily to economic imperialism[45] is to confuse the means with the end and to ignore its obvious relationship to the problem of the security of the Panama Canal, dear to the President's heart. American investors in the Dominican Republic called loudly for intervention, but that does not prove that it was designed expressly to serve them. They were used in the preliminary proceedings, but the ultimate arrangements were certainly not drawn to their specifications. American economic interests may have benefited from the establishment of order under American auspices but they received no special favors. Roosevelt's agents may have thought of Egypt as they negotiated at Santo Domingo, but other powers had sought control of Egypt primarily on account of its strategic relationship to another canal.

Roosevelt did exaggerate the danger of European intervention, in order to link his policy with the magic name of Monroe. In 1904 various powers were making threatening gestures, but the outbreak of the Russo-Japanese War and the establishment of the *entente cordiale* (maturing French designs on Morocco)

[43] Howard C. Hill, *Roosevelt and the Caribbean*, pp. 157-169; Dana G. Munro, *The United States and the Caribbean Areas*, pp. 104-112.

[44] An examination of Roosevelt's motives and the influences brought to bear on him may be found in J. Fred Rippy, "The Initiation of the Customs Receivership in the Dominican Republic," *Hispanic American Historical Review*, XVII (1937), 419-457.

[45] See Melvin M. Knight, *The Americans in Santo Domingo*, pp. viii, 18-23.

heightened the European tension to such a degree as to make any intervention in the face of American opposition inconceivable. By the same token, European opposition to American intervention would be impossible. The spring of 1905 presented an unusually favorable opportunity for securing a negative control over Samaná Bay, and this consideration, rather than any of those openly avowed, seems to have been Roosevelt's primary motive.

The implications of the Roosevelt policy for Haiti were plain. The Black Republic had not followed its eastern neighbor into political and financial collapse, but its condition was shaky. The hopes of its intellectuals, based on the twelve-year peace under Hyppolite and Simon Sam,[46] had been shattered by a resurgence of praetorianism in the person of the octogenarian Nord Alexis.[47] That even the years of peace had not been years of good government was soon revealed when it was discovered that Simon Sam, his ministers, and their French and German accomplices in the Banque Nationale had defrauded the treasury of $1,257,993 in the consolidation of the floating debt.[48] The aged President showed a certain courage in prosecuting these influential persons, at the risk of domestic disturbance and foreign complications, but his own administration was honeycombed with corruption.[49] The bank endeavored to coerce the government by depriving it of credit. Exchange soared, to the distress of the common people, already afflicted by crop failures.[50] From Paris came suggestions of a tripartite

[46] See Frederic Marcelin, *L'haleine du centenaire*, pp. 23 f. Hyppolite died in 1896, and was succeeded by his secretary of war without disturbance of the peace.

[47] There were three candidates in 1902. When Nord Alexis, secretary of war, employed force to defeat Antenor Firmin in the Cap Haitien primary, the latter denounced the election and set up a revolutionary regime at Gonaives. The attempt failed. Alexis then executed a surprise march on Port-au-Prince, where he was acclaimed president by the army and the populace. He ordered the two remaining candidates to withdraw. His subsequent election by the National Assembly was a meaningless formality (Powell to Hay, "I," Jan. 17, 1903, Despatches, Haiti, XXXIX).

[48] Republic of Haiti, *L'affaire de la consolidation;* Powell to Hay, No. 1595, Dec. 26; No. 1598, Dec. 27, 1904, Despatches, Haiti, XLIII.

[49] *Idem* to *idem,* "W," March 5, 1904, *loc. cit.,* XLI; No. 1617, Jan. 11; No. 1813, June 14, 1905, *loc. cit.,* XLVI.

[50] *Idem* to *idem,* No. 1479, Aug. 1, 1904, *loc. cit.,* XLII.

control of Haitian finance by the governments of France, Germany, and the United States.[51] Conspiracy was held in check only by the very multiplicity of the conspiring factions. How long the senile president could rule over such disruptive forces, political and financial, was problematical. If a break came, the example of the Dominican Republic showed what the fate of Haiti would be.

The élite were aware of the danger, and many a Jeremiah called the people to repentance. As early as 1893 Leonidas Laventure had foretold, with prophetic insight, that the Monroe Doctrine would be transformed into a colonial policy and that the blow would fall when the eventual European war broke out.[52] As time passed, the emphasis shifted from the need for vigilance to the need for reform from within as a guard against reform from without. Emmanuel Edouard had argued that unless Haiti redeemed herself a white protectorate would be inevitable.[53] Frederic Marcelin, observing that if Haiti would preserve her independence she must take into account the effect of the Spanish-American War upon the Caribbean situation, presented the same argument with a new urgency.[54]

Actually, the United States had no such designs on Haiti as these men feared. During the electoral disturbances of 1902 the metropolitan press did raise a clamor for intervention, but when Léger nervously inquired as to the intentions of the government, he was assured that nothing of the sort was contemplated, although it was pointed out to him that Haiti had better settle down, for her own good and to avoid international complications.[55] The intervention in the Dominican Republic, following hard upon the consolidation scandal at Port-au-Prince, raised a new alarm, especially since foreign merchants made it plain that they thought a similar intervention would do Haiti

---

[51] Powell to Hay, "B," Sept. 19, 1903, Despatches, Haiti, XL.

[52] Haiti: le danger de la patrie, pp. 20-26.

[53] Essai sur la politique intérieure d'Haiti, p. 46.

[54] Une évolution nécessaire (1898); L'haleine du centenaire (1901); Le passé (1902), pp. 15 f.

[55] Memorandum, Oct. 2, 1902, Notes from Haiti, VI.

no harm,[56] but another inquiry by Léger elicited fresh assurances from Hay.[57]

The Government of the United States of America has no intention of annexing either Haiti or Santo Domingo, and no desire of acquiring possession of them, either by force or by negotiations, and . . . even if the citizens of either of these Republics should solicit incorporation into the American Union, there would be no inclination on the part of the National Government, nor in the sphere of public opinion, to agree to any such proposal. Our interests are in harmony with our sentiments in wishing you only continuous peace, prosperity, and independence.

So saying, Hay seems to have represented accurately the American attitude, but when he spoke of incorporation he begged the question. Haiti would never be annexed, but, if peace and prosperity should persistently avoid the Haitian shore, there was every likelihood that the United States would intervene in some degree in an effort to induce their return. This intervention would be undertaken precisely because, incorporation being out of the question, a peaceful, prosperous, and securely independent Haiti became essential to American security in the Caribbean.

Throughout his administration Theodore Roosevelt adhered to this attitude. He and Elihu Root, Hay's successor as secretary of state, believed that it would be well to "Cuba-ize" Haiti, ostensibly for reasons of humanity, basically for reasons of strategy, but their program did not include annexation. Their hands were stayed by lack of an appropriate occasion and by lack of public support in the United States for such a policy. Roosevelt was somewhat piqued about it, observing:

Now in Haiti what we need is something that will show our people that this Government, in the name of humanity, morality, and civilization, ought to exercise some kind of supervision over the island; but this should be done as a part of our general scheme of dealing with the countries around the Caribbean. . . . I would have interfered . . . in Haiti already, simply in the interest of civilization, if I could have waked up our people so that they would back a rea-

---

[56] Powell to Hay, No. 1641, Feb. 8, 1905, Despatches, Haiti, XLIV.
[57] Hay to Léger, Feb. 9, 1905, Notes to Haiti, II.

sonable and intelligent foreign policy which should put a stop to crying disorders at our very doors. Such a policy would be a little in our own interest, but much more in the interest of the peoples in whose affairs we interfered.[58]

Root was more concerned with Haitian than with American opinion. He realized that

The Haitians are suspicious of us. They are densely ignorant and really believe that we want to gobble up their country, and we have to be very careful about volunteering any interference in their affairs lest we be met with an outcry of protest. Of course, they have some pretty good reasons for doubting the advantages of too close an association between the United States and a black man's government. I have been watching every move in Haiti for several years very closely in the hope that a situation would arise in which we could be of material help to them and in which we could give that help in such a way as to establish the right sort of relations. . . . For any positive step I think we must wait for the "psychological moment."[59]

However, even Root did not recognize in the revolution of 1908 the psychological moment. When the American minister suggested that anarchy prevailed at Port-au-Prince, the Secretary replied flatly, "The United States has no idea of intervening in Haiti."[60]

The Haitian reaction to more intimate American-Dominican relations was in marked contrast to that of 1870. There was considerable excitement, but no determined effort to defeat the project. The press attacked the validity of the *modus vivendi* in legalistic fashion,[61] but no one undertook to grapple with actualities in the spirit of Nissage-Saget. Although there was systematic smuggling on the unmarked frontier,[62] a would-be Cabral, General Espaillat, was actually deported by the Haitian authorities.[63] The situation differed in many important respects

[58] Roosevelt to William B. Hale, Dec. 3, 1908, quoted from State Department MSS in Philip C. Jessup, *Elihu Root,* I, 554.
[59] Root to Albert Shaw, Dec., 1908, *ibid.*, p. 555.
[60] *Ibid.*, p. 557.
[61] Powell to Hay, No. 1650, Feb. 15, 1904, Despatches, Haiti, XLIV.
[62] Bonaparte to Hay, July 11, 1905, Misc. Let.
[63] Powell to Hay, No. 1692, March 22, 1905, Despatches, Haiti, XLIV.

from that of a generation before. A co-operative scheme of financial administration presented a less vulnerable target than plain annexation. Although the United States Senate had shown coolness toward the Roosevelt plan, no negrophile Charles Sumner led the fight in Washington. The Anglo-French sympathy enjoyed in 1870 was also notably lacking in 1905. Nissage-Saget had been encouraged by Geffrard's ultimate success against Spain, but recent events in Cuba and Panama had had a different moral effect upon his successors. The followers of Nissage-Saget had been sustained by confidence in their ability to fulfill the promises of 1843, of 1859, and of 1867, but the atmosphere of 1905 was one of disillusionment. A government conscious of its own shortcomings was not eager to challenge American efforts at rehabilitation next door for fear of attracting unwelcome attention to itself.

Within Haiti there was, in fact, division of opinion. Foreign merchants were not the only ones prepared to believe that a thorough cleansing and a new start might be for the public good. No Haitian could openly advocate American intervention, but there seems to have been an undercurrent of sentiment in that direction, though of necessarily uncertain proportions. Back in 1893 Laventure had deplored the existence of an annexationist party.[64] During the crisis of 1902 there were rumors that certain ardent young men had threatened to provoke American intervention rather than submit to the dictatorship of Nord Alexis.[65] Powell, who was of course no foe to the idea, thought that he detected a growing sentiment for annexation or a protectorate, as the only means of ending habitual strife and establishing prosperity and progress.[66] As men of property or merely as government employees, the élite had nothing to gain by chronic disorder and instability. Only among them could be found men of sufficient education to appreciate their country's predicament. In the days of Nissage-Saget they had been in

[64] *Haiti: le danger de la patrie*, p. 20.

[65] Powell to Hay, No. 1122, July 21, 1902, Despatches, Haiti, XXXVIII.

[66] *Idem* to *idem*, No. IIII, July 7, 1902, loc. cit. He noted that but for the lack of confidence engendered by discriminations against negroes in the United States this idea would have been more widespread.

fact a ruling caste, naturally jealous of foreign interference, but since the debacle of 1879 every president had been a black autocrat deriving his strength from his hold over the ignorant masses. The necessity for some degree of literacy in the public service had prevented the total exclusion of the *élite* from office—they lived on the country, as of old, and some attained positions of great influence beside the throne—but in a state of dependency and insecurity they had occasion to wonder whether their traditional attitude any longer represented their true interest. Young patriots among them genuinely desired to remedy the evils that beset the land. They would have preferred reform from within—they did not wish to "sell the country to the Americans"—but any of them who gave way to despair became potentially a secret friend of intervention.

In 1905 there appeared a book dedicated to the blacks of Haiti and extreme in its denunciation of the mulattoes. It was called *Haiti, vivra-t-elle?*, and its frontispiece depicted a sickroom.[67]

"A very grave case, recovery hardly probable," said the mulatto doctors.

"Pardon," replied the blacks, "the patient can perhaps be saved if we combine our efforts."

A later scene, with the patient visibly failing.

"Ah, if we had only known," exclaimed the distracted blacks.

"Superfluous vows, tardy regrets, futile imprecations, the patient is irremediably lost," said the mulattoes. "We must call the Americans."

In the same year there appeared another work on the same subject, written by Antenor Firmin, in exile at St. Thomas.[68] He accepted Roosevelt's assurances that any nation capable of governing itself had nothing to fear, citing the American withdrawal from Cuba to prove the point. He stressed Booker T. Washington's dinner at the White House for the benefit of those

[67] A. Charmant, *Haiti, vivra-t-elle? Étude sur le préjugé des races: race noire, race jaune, race blanche, et sur la doctrine de Monroe.*

[68] *M. Roosevelt, président des États-Unis, et la République d'Haiti.*

who feared American race prejudice. Roosevelt's message of December 6, 1904, he pronounced to be "inflexible logic." He saw no danger of annexation, since the United States, possessed of Guantánamo, had no need of Mole St. Nicolas. America's interest now was to insure continued Haitian possession of the Mole by building up the strength and stability of Haiti as a guarantee of her independence. Intervention would come only if the republic fell into anarchy, and would intervention be such a misfortune in that case? Haiti could escape the bitter experience by reforming herself, and in that way alone. Firmin's question was, "*Haiti, marchera-t-elle?*"

Chapter XII

DOLLAR DIPLOMACY

It is . . . essential that the countries within that sphere shall be removed from the jeopardy involved by heavy foreign debt and chaotic national finances and from the ever-present danger of international complications due to disorder at home. Hence the United States has been glad to encourage and support American bankers who were willing to lend a hand to the financial rehabilitation of such countries.
—William Howard Taft, December 3, 1912

While we desire to encourage in every proper way American investments in Haiti, we believe that this can be better done by contributing to stability and order than by favoring special concessions to Americans. —William Jennings Bryan, December 19, 1914

Roosevelt's Dominican venture was his only undertaking of that kind, but the Taft administration attempted to apply the debt-refunding and customs-receivership technique to other Caribbean republics.[1] Their corollary of his corollary was that if it were well to intervene when Latin-American turbulence had produced a political and financial crisis, it were better to lend aid to avert that contingency. It was hoped that financial rehabilitation would result in economic improvement and political stability, thus lessening the danger of international complications, but the State Department, without undue optimism, was more particularly interested in transferring the foreign debt of those countries from Europe to New York, so that, if the worst came to the worst, the United States could insist upon the exclusive right of intervention with better countenance. Obviously, the substitution of American for European bankers would not relieve a Caribbean republic of "the jeopardy involved by a heavy foreign debt," but it would relieve the United States of considerable anxiety. This policy, vigorously pursued

---

[1] Treaties negotiated for this purpose with Honduras and Nicaragua in 1911 were rejected by the Senate (Munro, *The United States and the Caribbean Area*, pp. 216-221).

by Secretary Knox, was called "dollar diplomacy" on account of President Taft's reference to the substitution of dollars for bullets in American foreign relations. Although he regarded it as an evidence of philanthropy, the idea still carried a connotation of conquest. As John Bassett Moore had observed in 1898, "to get control of the financial resources of the country is only the next step to taking control of the country itself."[2]

Since bankers are of necessity interested in profits rather than in international politics, dollar diplomacy cannot be divorced from economic exploitation, but the State Department was evidently thinking of financial control as a means of political influence, and, in the Caribbean at least, such influence was desired primarily for reasons of naval strategy. There is reason to believe that in that quarter the initiative lay with the department rather than with the bankers, and that it was only by giving the fullest assurances of protection that it could overcome the reluctance of substantial capitalists to invest in Caribbean states.[3] The evidence of its efforts to induce unwilling American capital to enter Haiti seems to confirm that supposition.[4]

Just as Washington was beginning to think in terms of dollar diplomacy, many Haitians were coming to the conclusion that their country's problems could be solved only through the introduction of foreign capital. Frederic Marcelin, minister of finance to Nord Alexis, had publicly adopted that view,[5] which was also held by Antenor Firmin, the existing government's bitterest opponent.[6] All Haitians were bound to regard with dismay the shoestring speculators who had repeatedly victimized them,[7] but these men wished to attract responsible capitalists because they believed that only through economic development could political stability be attained and American

[2] Memorandum, Moore to Adee, May 9, 1898, in Vagts, *Deutschland und die Vereinigten Staaten in der Weltpolitik*, p. 1789.

[3] Huntington Wilson, "The Relation of Government to Foreign Investment," *Annals of the American Academy of Political and Social Science*, LXVIII (1916), 298-311.

[4] See below, pp. 200 f. [5] *Une évolution nécessaire*, pp. 6-30.

[6] Firmin, *M. Roosevelt . . . et la République d'Haiti*; Tribonien Saint-Justé, *La mort de l'illustre M. Antenor Firmin*, p. 2. [7] See above, p. 22.

intervention avoided.   Other Haitians, however, saw foreign capital as a Trojan Horse, to be regarded with suspicion.   They sensed the idea expressed by Elihu Root in 1908, when he said that, were American interests in Haiti as considerable as those in Cuba, disorder there would certainly lead to intervention;[8] accordingly, they clung to their traditional exclusiveness, even though it meant economic stagnation with its attendant political ills.

When William F. Powell took over the legation at Port-au-Prince in 1897, he found no American investment in Haiti except in mercantile establishments.   Agricultural development, such as had occurred in Cuba, was effectively barred by the constitutional prohibition of alien ownership of real estate.[9]   Powell's best efforts as a one-man chamber of commerce failed to bring about any considerable investment in other productive enterprises.   In 1899 the Haitian Exploration Company, of New York, obtained a concession for the development of the copper deposits at Terre Neuve, and several Americans undertook the exploitation of the cabinet woods of La Tortue and La Gonave.[10]   In 1900 the aerial railway of the Compagnie Haitienne, constructed in 1898 to carry dyewood from the heights into Port-au-Paix, was purchased by the American Dyewood Company, of Boston.[11]   That was all, but it was as much as any other foreign investment in Haiti except the French bank.

Powell believed that American capital could be profitably and strategically invested in railways, since Haiti had only a dozen miles of track and no roads worthy of the name.[12]   His efforts in this direction were spectacularly rewarded, though the principal concession was rather in the nature of an old-fashioned speculation.

[8] Scott Nearing and Joseph Freeman, *Dollar Diplomacy*, p. 262.

[9] Even under the Spanish regime American properties in Cuba had been valued at fifty million dollars.

[10] Powell to Hay, No. 637, Aug. 28; No. 675, Dec. 15, 1899, Despatches, Haiti, XXXV; No. 787, May 30, 1900; No. 857, Jan. 25, 1901, *loc. cit.*, XXXVI.

[11] *Idem* to *idem*, No. 794, June 11, 1900, *loc. cit.*

[12] It required four days on horseback or two days by steamer to reach Cap Haitien, only 180 miles from Port-au-Prince.   To reach Jacmel, thirty-nine miles across the mountains, took twenty-four hours' traveling overland or three days by sea (*idem* to *idem*, No. 786, May 30, 1900, *loc. cit.*).

The first Haitian railway contract had been granted in 1876 to an American for a line from Port-au-Prince eastward to the Dominican frontier. The construction never got beyond the city limits, and the enterprise, operated as an urban tramway for several years, was finally abandoned about 1890.[13] In 1896 the concession was given to certain Haitians, with the promise of an annual subsidy as soon as the line had been extended at least as far as the suburbs of Turgeau and Petionville. They turned the tramway over to a German firm and did nothing about new construction, so that the government was forced to grant another concession for the construction beyond the city limits. The net result of all this was that in 1901 the German minister extorted half a million dollars in "damages" for the concessionaries of 1896 and their German associates—$100,000 for unpaid (and unearned) subsidy and $400,000 because of the duplicate concession—on top of which they forced the government to buy back its own tramway, for the grant of which it had received nothing.[14] Starting anew after this sad experience, the government gave the concession to a mixed syndicate controlled by three Americans, and within two years—twenty-seven years after the original contract—the forty-mile Chemin de Fer de la Plaine du Cul-de-Sac was pushed to completion, fortified by an annual subsidy and a government guarantee of 6 per cent interest on the construction bonds.[15]

In July, 1904, Rodolphe Gardere, a Haitian, received a concession for a railroad from Gonaives to Hinche and promptly sold his rights to Louis Dalmas and Edward Blanton, Philadelphians, for $50 cash and $62,500 in stock. Powell was jubilant, for the line would open up virgin hinterland, till then closed to foreigners. His joy was turned to dismay when the Corps Législatif unanimously refused to sanction the concession.[16]

[13] Bassett to Fish, No. 419, Jan. 19, 1876, Despatches, Haiti, VIII; Durham to Gresham, No. 211, Jan. 24, 1893, *loc. cit.*, XXVII.

[14] Powell to Hay, No. 983, July 29, 1901, Despatches, Haiti, XXXVII; No. 1024, Nov. 24, 1901, *loc. cit.*, XXXVIII.

[15] *Report on the Commercial Relations of the United States* (1904), I, 608.

[16] Powell to Hay, No. 1471, July 23, 1904, Despatches, Haiti, XLII; No. 1546, Sept. 17, 1904, *loc. cit.*, XLII.

Some of the legislators may have been jealous of Gardere's windfall, some may have doubted the ability of Dalmas and Blanton to fulfill the contract, many had sincere objections to dragging the Trojan Horse within the gates, but today young Haitians are taught that the most serious opposition to the development of a national railway system came from politicians who foresaw that it would at last give the national government an effective control over the provinces, facilitating the suppression of incipient revolutions and breaking the sinister power of the *cacos*.[17]   Ignoring the legislature, Nord Alexis proceeded to grant a new and more valuable concession to "a Haitian corporation with its main offices in Philadelphia," and thus, after a year's delay, Dalmas and Blanton secured authority to extend the Gonaives-Hinche line to Port-au-Prince, connecting with the Cap Haitien-Grande Riviere Railway recently completed under British auspices, on which they held an option.[18]   As a result, the entire railroad system of Haiti was brought under American control, although all save eighty miles of it existed only on paper and the legality of the key concession was open to doubt.

Powell, whose ambition was to secure such control over Haitian economic life that "they would unknowingly be forced into closer connection with us, and . . . our influence in the Republic would become paramount and permanent,"[19] realized that the most effective form of penetration would be to capture the national bank, a French corporation chartered in 1880 with extensive command over the fiscal affairs of the government. Golden opportunity presented itself when the consolidation scandal made a reorganization inevitable, but the minister's strenuous efforts in that direction were fruitless.   No shoestring speculation would suffice, and, such was the lack of confidence in the Haitian government, particularly in the Haitian courts, that responsible American capitalists could not be induced to enter the country in the absence of ironclad guarantees of sup-

---

[17] J. C. Dorsainvil, *Manuel d'histoire d'Haiti*, p. 351.
[18] Powell to Root, No. 1853, Oct. 21, 1905, Despatches, Haiti, XLVI.
[19] *Idem* to Loomis, Aug. 23, 1905, *loc. cit.* Cf. Moore to Adee, May 9, 1898, above, p. 197.

port.[20] Powell, the agent of McKinley and Roosevelt, had no Philander C. Knox behind him.[21]

Knox became secretary of state in 1909, a few months after Nord Alexis had been overthrown by Antoine Simon. Upon Simon devolved the task of reorganizing the national bank in the heyday of dollar diplomacy, but in the ensuing scramble the Haitians were spectators rather than participants. The French regarded themselves as Haiti's predestined bankers, but both Germany and the United States demanded a share. The Germans would have excluded the Americans, but the French would not consent to German participation unless the United States were also represented. Knox wished to eliminate European interests altogether, but he could not escape valid French and German claims to consideration. In the end, 6 per cent of the bank stock went to Germany, 15 per cent to three American houses of close German affiliation, 5 per cent to the National City Bank of New York, and the remaining 74 per cent to France, with the exception of a few shares actually held in Haiti.

The reorganization included a 5 per cent loan of $16,000,000, on which the government netted only 72.3 per cent. The money was to be used to settle accounts with the old bank, refund the internal debt, and retire the fiduciary currency. Ten million francs were reserved for the last purpose, to be administered by the bank, which was to have a monopoly of note issue. The debt service was also under the control of the bank, which, as the sole depository of the Haitian treasury, was to receive the revenue as it came in, hold it intact until the end of the fiscal year, and then make available to the government what

[20] *Idem* to Hay, "J," Dec. 20, 1903, *loc. cit.*, XLI; No. 1768, June 1, 1905, *loc. cit.*, XLVI. These despatches show that as late as 1905 it was the legation that was seeking to enlist indifferent bankers, not the bankers who were pressing the department to make Haiti safe for investment.

[21] Although the State Department had been "interested" in promoting the investment of American capital in Haiti since 1898 (Memorandum, Cridler to Moore, Sept. 1, 1898, on Livingston's No. 913, Aug. 20, 1898, Cons. Let., Cape Haytien), Powell had to act "without the hand of the . . . Administration appearing" in order to "avert any unfavorable criticism" (Powell to Hay, No. 1768, June 1, 1905, Despatches, Haiti, XLVI).

was left after the service of the loans of 1875, 1896, and 1910 had been met.[22]

In 1910 the National Railroad, of which James P. Mac-Donald was now the prime mover, was also reorganized, receiving a new fifty-year concession in which the Haitian government guaranteed 6 per cent interest on its bonds up to a value of $35,000 per mile of constructed track. A loan of half a million dollars to the railroad by the National City Bank tied it in with the American interest in the Haitian national bank.[23]

These arrangements had hardly been completed when revolt broke out in the *caco* country, led by Cincinnatus Leconte, ex-minister of public works and ex-convict (he had been found guilty of complicity in the consolidation frauds), whose cry was that Simon had sold the country to the Yankees, but who seems to have been a fit representative of those who feared that, if Haiti were to have sound finance and real railroads at last, their racket would be ruined. On his second attempt, in the summer of 1911, he overthrew Simon, but exactly a year later he and the presidential palace were blown up. He was succeeded by Tancrede Auguste, another consolidation convict, who died within nine months, presumably of poisoning. The next president was Michel Oreste, the first civilian ever to attain that office, which he lost within nine months. The revolt had been launched in the *caco* country by Davilmar Theodore, but, as it followed the traditional route to the capital via Cap Haitien, Gonaives, and St. Marc, it was hijacked by Oreste Zamor. Theodore returned to the hills and started around again. Haiti was evidently entering the path which the Dominican Republic had trod ten years before.

Bankruptcy lay on the road toward anarchy. The Haitian government's income was not sufficient to meet the ordinary budget, service the foreign debt, and pay the expenses of an annual revolution as well. Resort was had to internal loans, with steadily diminishing returns. The $674,000 issue of 1911,

[22] United States Senate, *Hearings before a Select Committee on Haiti and Santo Domingo*, I, 105 f.; Davis, *Black Democracy*, p. 144.
[23] Millspaugh, *Haiti under American Control*, pp. 21 f.

netting 81 per cent, was followed by another for $609,000 in 1913 at 78.8, another for $712,000 in 1914 at 60, and a fourth in June, 1914, for $525,000 at 56. German merchants were the chief subscribers; the proceeds were distributed among the *caco* chiefs. Customs receipts pledged to the service of the foreign debt were diverted to the repayment of these party obligations, with the result that in 1914 the amortization of the loans of 1875 and 1896 went into default. The deficit rose from 25 per cent of receipts in the fiscal year 1913 to 60 per cent in 1914; there was no prospect for further borrowing, external or internal; and the bank, which had been making advances to the government as a matter of accommodation, refused to do so any longer. Zamor then decreed that the monetary reform administered by the bank should be suspended and funds pledged for that purpose made available for current expenses, but the bank refused to comply, holding to the terms of the 1910 loan agreement. Nothing was left save the printing press, but the issue of fiat money was a plain violation of the bank contract.[24] Chronic disorder had brought Haiti to the verge of bankruptcy. French, German, and British as well as American interests were involved. It had ceased to be a matter of dollar diplomacy, strictly speaking, and had become a case for the "international policeman."

At this time the Democrats returned to power at Washington under the banner of the "New Freedom." Woodrow Wilson and William Jennings Bryan, his secretary of state, repudiated the imperialism of McKinley, Roosevelt, and Taft, even as they opposed the "predatory interests" in the domestic sphere, but their very idealism led them to a conception of a manifest destiny to make the Caribbean (and, later, the world) safe for democracy. They might renounce the ideology of dollar diplomacy, but something of "international police power" was left, with a new emphasis on the defense of the American peoples from native despotism. The President regarded himself as not merely the friend, but the champion, of constitutional government in America, "because in no other way [could] our neighbors, to whom we would wish in every way to make

[24] Davis, *Black Democracy*, pp. 149 f.; Jones, *The Caribbean since 1900*, p. 140.

proof of our friendship, work out their own development in peace and liberty."[25]   In that case, his Calvinist conscience would have little difficulty in persuading him that something ought to be done about any ex-convict who, with his *caco* mercenaries, might deny the Haitian people their right to constitutional self-government.

Significantly, the first step in the Wilson administration's approach to the Haitian problem was to obtain from Michel Oreste a promise that no other power would be permitted to gain a foothold at Mole St. Nicolas.[26]   Despite the well-known Haitian sentiment against alienation of territory, experience had shown that governments hard pressed politically or financially were not always immune to the temptation to mortgage that asset.   Bryan also acted to defend "vested interests," regardless of his attitude toward dollar diplomacy.   In September, 1914, he interceded to arrest foreclosure proceedings against the National Railroad.[27]   He took up the cudgels for the National Bank, even though the Haitians questioned his right to interfere in the affairs of a French corporation whose concession forbade recourse to diplomatic intervention.   When it was feared that the Haitian government might seize the pledged funds held by the bank, unarmed marines were landed to escort half a million dollars on board the U. S. S. *Machias* for transfer to the National City Bank in New York.[28]   These measures may have seemed necessary for the defense of various American interests, but they contributed nothing toward clearing up the chaotic situation that had placed American investments in jeopardy and had exposed the Mole to alienation.

When the administration addressed itself to the fundamental problem, its thought was naturally influenced by Dominican

[25] *Congressional Record*, 63d Cong., 2d Sess., p. 43.

[26] *Foreign Relations* (1914), pp. 339 f.   German private interests reputed to have government support were seeking a concession there.

[27] *Ibid.* (1915), pp. 538-548.   Zamor, wishing to escape the guarantee of interest on the railroad bonds, charged nonfulfillment of contract, construction being behind schedule.   The railroad's answer was that it could not build in the midst of chronic disorder.

[28] *Ibid.* (1914), pp. 334-382; (1915), pp. 496-521.   After this the government did remove $67,000 from the bank.   It also decreed the creation of a new bank and transferred the treasury service to various merchants.

experience. In January, 1914, American representatives were instructed to protest against the seizure of customs houses by revolutionists and to warn *de facto* authorities of "the necessity of complying with national obligations with respect to assignment of customs funds for the payment of definite debts." In February it was hinted that the United States would gladly assist Zamor in the administration and collection of customs.[29] Nothing came of this, however, and by June the bank controversy had reached a crisis. In the opinion of the American minister, Bailly-Blanchard, the bank had suspended its advances to the government in order to deprive it of the means of carrying on its operations and so force it to ask for American assistance, which would inevitably mean a customs receivership.[30]

On June 23 the Haitian situation was discussed by the Cabinet, and on June 25 Wilson directed Bryan to draw up a tentative convention with Haiti along the lines of that with the Dominican Republic.[31] On July 2 the draft was transmitted to the legation at Port-au-Prince. The only variation from the model was the addition of provision for a financial adviser who should "generally exercise the functions of a comptroller of accounts."[32] On July 25 the German chargé at Washington indicated that his government would expect to share in the proposed customs control, but Bryan made it plain that the United States would insist upon an exclusive privilege.[33] Just what success Bailly-Blanchard had with Oreste Zamor is not clear, but the rumor of negotiations was used by his opponents to undermine him. That something was in the wind may be indicated by the fact that the State Department so much preferred to discuss customs control with him than with his successor that eight hundred marines were dispatched to Port-au-Prince to sustain a government that had irremediably fallen before they appeared.[34] Zamor had been able to delay Davilmar Theodore's arrival at the capital less than nine months.

[29] *Ibid.*, pp. 336-339.   [30] *Ibid.*, pp. 345 f.
[31] Ray Stannard Baker, *Woodrow Wilson: Life and Letters*, IV, 451.
[32] *Foreign Relations* (1914), pp. 347-350.
[33] *Senate Report No. 794*, 67th Cong., 2d Sess., pp. 31 ff.
[34] *Foreign Relations* (1914), p. 355. The minister was authorized to use his discretion as to the employment of this force.

Appalled by six violent changes in administration in six years and impressed by the baneful influence of the *cacos* on Haitian political life, the State Department came to feel that a truly representative government was as sorely needed as financial untanglement. Accordingly, in early November it suggested arrangements for an election under the neutral supervision of the United States.[35] It may appear that in this scheme a government which only a few days before had been willing to use force to restore a fallen regime and keep Theodore out may have been seeking another means to accomplish that purpose and secure an administration that would accept a customs convention, but the advantage to Haiti in breaking the dizzy succession of *caco*-supported factions and setting up a national government with some promise of stability is obvious. There could be no hope of any solution of Haiti's problems if the vicious cycle were allowed to run its course uninterrupted.

The plan came to naught when Bailly-Blanchard reported that Davilmar Theodore was definitely "in" for the time being. The State Department then tried the doubtful expedient of refusing to recognize him unless he came to terms. Specifically it wanted the customs convention proposed on July 2, a settlement of the bank and railroad controversies, and Haitian pledges to give full protection to all foreign interests and never to lease the Mole St. Nicolas or any other potential naval station to any European power. Theodore, and Louis Borno, his foreign minister, were willing to give the desired assurances and to arbitrate all outstanding disputes, but they refused to consider a customs convention—Borno had barely escaped violence at the hands of irate senators when he informed them of the American proposals. Instead, they suggested a new loan, offering concessions in exchange. Meanwhile Bryan had suddenly shifted his ground, saying that recognition would be considered on its merits, since the United States had no desire to extort a customs convention from an unwilling government. What was wanted, he added, was not concessions, but stability

[35] *Ibid.*, pp. 355-358.

and order.[36] These negotiations, like those with Zamor, got nowhere, for Theodore's days were numbered. He had campaigned a full year for an office that he was able to hold less than four months.

The new president was Vilbrun Guillaume Sam, another consolidation convict elevated by the *cacos*. In his advance along the well-trod revolutionary path he was escorted by the United States Navy in the person of Admiral W. B. Caperton, not for the purpose of supporting him, but in order to prevent fighting and looting in the port towns.[37] If he could not have stability, Bryan meant to require at least a relative degree of order.

Sam had hardly reached Port-au-Prince when J. F. Fort and C. C. Smith appeared as special emissaries of President Wilson to see what could be done about a customs receivership. Ulrick Duvivier, the foreign minister, took a leaf from Firmin's book, asking to see their credentials, a request which gave them their answer. Two months later Paul Fuller arrived with full powers and a draft treaty omitting the offensive customs matter, but pledging Haiti not to alienate the Mole and to arbitrate all foreign claims. In return the United States would defend Haiti from external attack and support the established government against insurrection. The treaty was acceptable to Sam, with one significant proviso: if American forces were ever landed in Haiti, they must be withdrawn "at the first demand of the constitutional authorities." Moreover, in his urgent need of financial assistance, he introduced the customs question himself. If the United States would facilitate the entrance of sufficient capital to refund the debt, reform the currency, and ensure the full economic development of the country, Haiti would consult the lenders on the choice of the higher customs officials.[38] This

---

[36] Ibid., pp. 359-371. Then and later (below, pp. 243, 252) Borno showed that he regarded a loan and the investment of American capital as prerequisite to stability. Theodore fell for lack of funds with which to pay his *cacos*.

[37] *Hearings*, pp. 64, 286-292.

[38] H. M. Wriston, *Executive Agents in American Foreign Relations*, p. 513; *Foreign Relations* (1915), pp. 464-468; *Hearings*, pp. 35-37.

made Sam (or Duvivier) something of a dollar diplomat, but one jealous of Haitian independence. Apparently both sides were at last in a mood to seek an effective compromise, but at this point fate interrupted the negotiations, and when they were resumed, the situation had been profoundly altered.

As Sam was approaching Port-au-Prince, Dr. Rosalvo Bobo, one of Theodore's ministers, had headed for the *caco* country to launch the next revolution. By June, Bobo was threatening Cap Haitien, and Admiral Caperton was recalled from Vera Cruz to guard against fighting in the ports once more. At Port-au-Prince, Sam rounded up so many suspects that the prison was crowded with members of the *élite*. On the night of July 26 there was an attack on the palace, whereupon the prison guard proceeded to massacre 167 unfortunates in cold blood. This act turned a feeble conspiracy into a popular uprising. Sam took refuge in the French legation, but on the morning of July 28, 1915, when the U. S. S. *Washington* was seen entering the harbor, the President of Haiti was dragged from under the bed and lynched.

The *Washington* was boarded by the diplomatic representatives of France, Great Britain, and the United States, who came to say that the French legation had been violated, that the city was in the possession of the mob, and that Admiral Caperton should take control. That night American marines bivouacked in Port-au-Prince. They were there on account of the utter collapse of self-government in a land where the strategic interests of the United States could not permit such a condition to exist. They would have been present had there been no bank, railroad, or any other American investment in Haiti. This action was not "dollar diplomacy," but "international police power."

CHAPTER XIII

"THE MARINES HAVE LANDED. . . ."

*Cooperation is possible only when supported . . . by the orderly
processes of just government based upon law, not upon arbitrary or
irregular force. . . . We hold . . . that just government rests always
upon the consent of the governed. . . . We shall lend our influence of
every kind to the realization of these principles in fact and practice. . . .*
—WOODROW WILSON, March 11, 1913

*United States has now actually accomplished a military intervention
in the affairs of another nation. Hostility exists. . . .*
—ADMIRAL CAPERTON, August 19, 1915

ON THE MORNING of July 27, 1915, the readers of the New
York *Times* learned, under a four-column head, that a German
submarine had sunk the American freighter *Leelanaw*. They
were also informed of wholesale violence in Europe—the British pounding at the Dardanelles, the Germans driving toward
Warsaw—but they would have searched their paper in vain for
an indication that anything had happened or might happen at
Port-au-Prince. Next day, indeed, there was mention of a
massacre in Haiti, but the *Leelanaw* sinking still dominated the
front page. On the twenty-ninth of July the featured story
dealt with the impending execution of a condemned murderer,
and the lynching of a Haitian president rated only one column
in which it was noted that the marines had landed and had the
situation well in hand. On July 30 the Russians were in full
retreat, the condemned man had died denouncing the prose-
cutor, and it would have required a diligent search on page 9
to discover that Haiti was still in the news. On the last day
of the month the killing of two sailors by *caco* snipers did make
the front page, but in Poland the Russians had slain their
thousands, the Germans their tens of thousands, and Hinden-
burg was at the gates of Warsaw.

If this were true of a great metropolitan daily, one may

imagine how much Haitian news was being reported at Gopher Prairie. Even those disinterested Americans who happened to note that the marines had landed somewhere in the Caribbean had no fixed opinions as to what should be done next and no idea that the occupation would last more than a few days. The news despatches from Port-au-Prince had said something about customs control and the Platt amendment, but even the *Times* assumed that the marines would keep order until Dr. Bobo arrived and would then be withdrawn. Evidently the initiative lay with the government rather than with public opinion, which was prepared to accept any course that might be adopted.[1]

At the moment the State Department as well as the general public was absorbed in the *Leelanaw* sinking and the European cataclysm, but it had developed a fairly definite idea of what it wanted in Haiti. It had already shown that it would protect vested interests from arbitrary interference pending the settlement of their claims and that it desired sufficient control over Haitian collections and disbursements to assure the faithful execution of the bank contract and loan agreement. Despite earlier aspersions on dollar diplomacy, it was returning to the idea that the replacement of European with American capital would simplify the situation. The object of its policy, however, was not to expose Haiti to American exploitation, much less spoliation, but rather to promote Haitian political stability, which would entail financial rehabilitation and economic development. This solicitude was not pure altruism, but the advantage sought had to do with Caribbean strategy rather than the profit motive. Of course the vested interests, such as they were, existed in hope of profits, and Americans, with an exaggerated notion of Haitian resources, expected the intervention to open up a new field of economic opportunity,[2] but if there existed any doubt as to the government's motive, the contemporaneous purchase of the economically worthless Danish West Indies at an exorbitant price should have dispelled it. The

---

[1] Two weeks later *The Literary Digest* reported that all comment on the intervention in the American press had been favorable.

[2] See W. A. MacCorkle, *The Monroe Doctrine in Its Application to the Republic of Haiti*, p. 25.

anxiety of the State and Navy Departments lest Mole St. Nicolas slip from Haiti's feeble grasp into stronger hands was a matter of record. There was no immediate prospect of such a coup by any European power, but the war could not go on forever. A victorious Germany might be free to pursue American ambitions hitherto suppressed. If Germany were eliminated by defeat, Great Britain might become less tolerant of the hegemony of the United States in the Caribbean, where an Anglo-French alliance could still make itself formidable. That fleet "second to none" was not yet in being, and who, in 1915, could foresee the utter exhaustion of the eventual victors? Discretion suggested that the opportunity be seized to end, once and for all, dangerously chaotic conditions in Haiti, and that could be accomplished only by a permanent occupation, extinguishing Haitian independence, or by a long-term, but definitely limited intervention to reorganize and strengthen the Haitian state. There could be no doubt of American preference for the latter alternative.

Even the choice of the milder course involved the Wilson administration in an awkward paradox. In 1913 the President had said that co-operation was possible only with governments based on the consent of the governed rather than upon "arbitrary and irregular force." By that he had meant to condemn the sort of rule from which *caco*-ridden Haiti suffered, but, when he intervened to break the revolutionary cycle, he too employed arbitrary force. However well intended and beneficial the measures adopted to solve the Haitian problem, they were inherently defective because founded on the coercive presence of a foreign marine brigade. In the circumstances of July 28, 1915, it was inevitable that there should be a landing to restore order, establish a reform administration, and secure a suitable treaty as a basis of future co-operation, but it is unlikely that anyone in Washington anticipated a twenty-year military occupation. Instead, it seems to have been expected that, the *cacos* being restrained, a respectable Haitian administration could be installed that would receive the consent of the governed and would co-operate under the protection rather than the compulsion of the principles of the Platt amendment, without the continued presence of American armed forces.[3]

Such slight resistance as the marines encountered was offered by simple-minded *cacos*. The *élite*, stunned by the culminating disaster foretold by all the national prophets, either remained passive or welcomed the intervention in genuine relief.[4] Some even spoke out to tell their countrymen that their humiliation was the consequence of their own faults.[5] As Charles Moravia expressed it: "We are not at war with the United States. We are at war with Humanity, whom we have not ceased to offend for a century. The Americans are the enemies of a sovereign, Despotism, and occupy the country to prevent his restoration."[6]

As the dismay engendered by the *cacos* was dispelled by the marines, dismay at the presence of a foreign military force increased, but many Haitians were realistic enough to accept the inevitable and to collaborate with the United States. It would be too simple an explanation to describe them all as sycophants, attributing a monopoly of patriotism to those whose assumed an attitude of hostility, just as it would be too simple to regard them all as disinterested statesmen, classing the opposition as disappointed office-seekers who would gladly change their tune for a place on the payroll. Undoubtedly the attitudes of many in both parties were determined by considerations of private fortune rather than of the public good, for that was inevitable in a class which knew no source of livelihood save the treasury. Others, long advocates of the reforms sought by the United

[3] In the early stages of the intervention the United States gave assurances that the marines would be withdrawn as soon as a stable government had been established in Haiti (*Foreign Relations, 1915*, pp. 479-481). This condition proved to be a rather elastic one, but at the time it seems to have been intended to mean as soon as the desired treaty had been put into operation.

[4] Dantès Bellegarde, *Pour une Haiti heureuse*, II, 5; Timothée Paret, *Dans la mêlée*, p. 102.

[5] Jules Rosemond, *La crise morale et civique*; Gabriel Le Rouge, *Ou vivre libres et respectés ou mourir lamentablement décimées par la guerre civile*. Later Jean Price-Mars, in *La vocation de l'élite*, courageously exposed the deficiencies of that class in an effort to rally them as an effective influence for the preservation of Haitian nationality despite the fact of an alien occupation.

[6] In *La Plume*, Aug. 25, 1915, as quoted in Le Rouge, *op. cit.* Ironically, in 1926, Moravia spent some time in "preventive arrest," without indictment or trial, having ventured to criticize the regime he thus hailed in 1915.

States, may have come to believe that they could not be attained except through American aid. As the event was to prove, some were ready to imperil Haitian independence in order to gain a political advantage over their fellow citizens, but the fact remains that the question was one on which even true patriots could differ. Ten years before some had feared that the introduction of foreign capital would lead to intervention, while others, equally patriotic, had argued that only by that means could stability be achieved and intervention averted. Instability having resulted in intervention, some might hold that independence could be saved only by a refusal to collaborate with the intruder, while others might believe that independence was surely lost unless a Haitian government officered by Haitians were kept in existence, however limited its authority.[7] Presumably the motives of individuals were confusingly mixed; each persuaded himself that his course was in the public service, while his selfish interest was very plain to his critics. Few could have been utterly cynical, but also few showed themselves ready to make personal sacrifices for the sake of their convictions. Would the proportion have been greater in any other society?

Since the United States preferred to act in collaboration with a native Haitian government, the first order of business was the election of a new president. In the normal course of events the National Assembly would have chosen Bobo, just as five months before it had elected the man who had driven Bobo from office, not because it wanted him, but in fear of the *cacos*. The situation, however, required a man free of revolutionary connections, one identified with national rather than

[7] In 1916 the Dominicans rejected terms which the Haitians had been required to accept, with the result that for eight years American naval officers administered the Dominican government and the sovereign existence of that republic was reduced to a legal fiction indeed. Haiti escaped that. However, the Dominican situation proving intolerable, the military occupation was ended there ten years before the marines were withdrawn from Haiti. But who could have anticipated in 1915 the unprecedented withdrawal of a world power from a territory in which its military authorities were the only government? It required positive action in Washington to restore self-government in Santo Domingo, but it would have required a further initiative to destroy it entirely in Haiti.

factional interests. Admiral Caperton cast about for a non-partisan candidate, but ex-President Légitime, Jacques Nicolas Léger, and Solon Menos refused to run. Finally, he discovered Philippe Sudre Dartiguenave, president of the Senate. Marines protected the Assembly from *caco* interference, but it may be doubted whether the electors cast their ballots in any greater sense of freedom. Dartiguenave received 94 out of 116 votes.

In the long view of Haitian history the most notable fact concerning the new president was not that he was elected in the presence of United States marines, but that he was a Southern mulatto, the first to hold that office since 1879. Restraining the *cacos*, the Americans had indeed worked a revolution in Haitian politics, the influence of which would be felt long after the last marine had been withdrawn. It is unlikely that Admiral Caperton grasped the full significance of what had happened, but evidently some of the *élite* knew an opportunity when they saw one and needed no American advice on how to vote.

Dartiguenave entered office more or less committed to the recognition of an American right of intervention like that enjoyed in Cuba, to the establishment of a customs receivership along Dominican lines, and to the acceptance of a financial adviser,[8] but he meant to drive a close bargain, surrendering no more real control to the United States than he could avoid. Although the Haitian and American objectives were divergent and Haitians were notoriously adept at stalling, there had never been a time when so many of them realized the need for a new departure and were ready to accept some degree of foreign guidance. Therefore it was at least possible that a workable agreement could be reached with a modicum of tact and patience.

[8] According to Caperton, Dartiguenave, in the presence of other legislators, had said that the chambers would agree to the cession of Mole St. Nicolas, the right of intervention, customs control, and anything else the United States required (*Foreign Relations*, 1915, p. 431). Before the election the State Department indicated that it expected customs control and such financial control as it deemed "necessary for an efficient administration" (*ibid.*, p. 479). Under fire in 1922, the American officers concerned testified that there had been no pre-election bargain (*Hearings*, pp. 317-364), but during the treaty negotiations in 1915 the State Department cited a "previous understanding" (*Foreign Relations*, 1915, p. 437). Apparently there was a tacit agreement in general terms, with no specifications as to the details.

Three months later all hope of genuine co-operation had been destroyed, partly by Secretary Lansing, who demanded that the Haitians accept without discussion a treaty more extreme than anything they had been led to anticipate and simultaneously directed the Navy to take over certain functions without waiting for Haitian consent, and partly by Admiral Caperton, who, largely on his own initiative, transformed a temporary interposition at Port-au-Prince into a formal and unlimited military occupation of the entire republic. These acts were not capricious—there was an apparently sound reason for each of them—but, with the benefit of hindsight, their wisdom may be questioned. If it had been worth while to set up the hand-picked Dartiguenave administration, it should have been worth while to treat it as something better than *cacos* to be coerced, or puppets to be manipulated, in order to retain the confidence and co-operation of those Haitians best disposed toward the United States. The result of the arbitrary measures adopted was a system that had neither the virtues of a treaty regime based on true agreement nor those of a clean-cut military administration like that established at Santo Domingo, but only the bad features of both.[9]

The treaty draft presented to Dartiguenave a few days after his election went beyond all previous proposals to any Caribbean state, combining pertinent features of the Platt amendment with the terms of the Dominican customs receivership and including additions to that instrument which were even then being urged, unsuccessfully, upon the Dominican government. It provided that the United States should "appoint" a general receiver and all the customs service personnel, who should collect the revenues and apply them, first, to the expense of the receivership; second, to the service of the debt; third, to the

[9] A bona fide treaty regime would presuppose Haitian co-operation, but would restrict the activity of the United States. An open military government like that at Santo Domingo would be based on force, but would allow the United States freedom of action. The regime in Haiti left the United States embarrassingly restricted by a treaty, but was actually based on force, thereby antagonizing all Haitians, even those who wished, or professed to wish, to co-operate.

maintenance of a constabulary; and, finally, to the ordinary expenses of the Haitian government. Haiti was forbidden to increase the debt or to reduce the customs revenue without the consent of the United States. Additional provisions suggested by Dominican experience were for a financial adviser with extensive powers, and for the creation of a native constabulary officered by Americans. The bank and railroad controversies were covered by provision for the future negotiation of a protocol for the settlement of all foreign claims. Under the supervision of American engineers, Haiti was to undertake "such measures as in the opinion of the United States" might be necessary for sanitation and public improvement, a considerable enlargement of a familiar provision in treaties with Cuba and Panama. Although both Dartiguenave and Bobo had offered the cession of Mole St. Nicolas, the United States did not seek possession of that site, but its future security was provided for in terms reminiscent of the Platt amendment, Haiti being required to agree not to surrender jurisdiction over any territory, by sale, lease, or otherwise, to any foreign power except the United States, "nor to enter into any treaty or contract with any other foreign power . . . that [would] impair, or tend to impair," the independence of the republic, and also to recognize in the United States "authority to prevent any and all interference" with the operation of the treaty, "as well as the right to intervene for the preservation of Haitian independence and the maintenance of a government adequate for the protection of life, property, and individual liberty."[10]

Not only was the language of the draft, leaving everything to the discretion of the United States, offensive to Haitian pride, but the Haitian cabinet, while ready to accept it in the main, felt that some of its provisions required discussion and modification. The State Department, fearing that discussion was meant to serve no purpose save evasion and delay, justified its demand for immediate acceptance by the contention that Dartiguenave had signed a blank check which the United States

[10] *Foreign Relations* (1914), pp. 347-350; (1915), pp. 431-433.

had filled in with commendable restraint.[11]   The prompt agreement it required was not forthcoming.

Without waiting for the Haitians to come to terms, the State Department had Admiral Caperton instructed to take over the customs houses and restore the treasury service to the National Bank, depositing the revenue in his own name, in trust for the Haitian government but not subject to its order.   This procedure was considered to be urgently necessary to prevent the dissipation of the national income by self-appointed local authorities, Bobo partisans who had not recognized Dartiguenave, but obviously the solution went beyond the requirements of that particular situation.   Caperton was authorized to expend the funds thus collected for the immediate organization of a native constabulary and for the relief of distress among the unemployed (including disarmed *cacos*) through a public works program.[12]   Unfortunately, although the admiral was able to set the proletariat to work repairing roads and telegraph lines and giving urban Haiti the clean-up of a century, he had no money for the unemployed *élite* or even for the government whose only considerable source of income had been seized.   The unnamed purpose of these measures seems to have been to show the Haitian cabinet that the United States would put the treaty into operation whether they agreed to it or not, and to persuade the *élite* that they would fare better with the treaty than without it.

On July 28 American forces were landed simply to protect foreign lives and property.   By August 8 this interposition had developed into an informal occupation of the capital and its environs, at the request of the Department of State, and on August 18 Lansing directed that the customs houses be seized and an armed guard furnished for the protection of the American collectors.[13]   This appears to be as far as the initiative of Washington went toward the establishment of a military occupation in Haiti, which leaves to Admiral Caperton by far the

[11] *Foreign Relations* (1915), p. 437.   See above, p. 214 n.
[12] *Ibid.*, pp. 518 f.   [13] *Ibid.*, pp. 478 f., 518.

greater share of responsibility for the development. Where Lansing appears to have contemplated the posting of a small guard at the customs houses, Caperton assumed that their protection entailed the establishment of the same degree of control over the municipal administration of all the port towns of Haiti as that already exercised at Port-au-Prince.[14] To render that occupation secure, it became necessary to clear the surrounding countryside of armed *cacos*, and that in turn required the occupation of the *caco* homeland far in the interior. This sequence, beginning with a mission to guard the customs houses and ending with the occupation of Hinche, as distant from any customs house as it is possible to get in Haiti, was typical of military logic, but that it was contrary to the policy of Caperton's political superiors is attested by the ineffectual efforts of the Secretary of the Navy to restrain his headstrong admiral.[15]

From a strictly military point of view Caperton's decisions were unimpeachable, but politically they were penny wise and pound foolish. Their immediate effect was to coerce the Haitians into submission, but they completed the work begun by Lansing in destroying any good will toward the United States that may have existed in Haiti. Even those unsympathetic toward the *cacos* were bound to regard the increasing reliance of the United States upon military measures and the

[14] But Washington had desired military control of the capital in order to influence the presidential election and treaty negotiation, considerations not applicable to other towns.

[15] Josephus Daniels made it perfectly plain that he was opposed to an advance into the interior and that he was dismayed at the number of Haitian casualties—some two hundred were killed during the campaign—but he had to rely on the judgment of his commander on the ground; and, consequently, while he begged Caperton to desist, he issued no categorical order. The admiral, in a tone of injured innocence, explained that he was engaged in nothing more than "protective patrolling," but at each clash his patrols were found deeper in the interior. Caperton's tone revealed clearly his impatience of civilian control—if it could be called that. When Daniels finally became insistent, Caperton made great show of submitting to the mistaken judgment of his superior as soon as he had completed his contemplated operations (*Foreign Relations*, 1915, pp. 486 ff.). Daniels had to accept successive *faits accomplis*, since to recall the marines would entail tremendous loss of face. It may be said in Caperton's behalf that Lansing had already set him an example in forcefulness, and that, as the responsible military commander, he would naturally give primary consideration to the military situation unless instructed in more certain terms than Daniels ventured to employ.

expansion of the occupation over the whole republic with fear and suspicion. Despite the formalities of election and treaty negotiation they found themselves confronting, not a simple landing to protect lives and property, but foreign military government.

In addition to the actual fact of the American occupation, Admiral Caperton, on his own initiative, had formally proclaimed the subordination of Haitian civil authority to his martial rule.[16] This condition, originally applicable only to the occupied area about Port-au-Prince, was extended with the American advance to include the entire republic, subordinating the national as well as municipal administrations. Because native Haitians continued to occupy the offices of state, instead of being supplanted by American naval officers, as was done in the Dominican Republic in 1916, and because the proclamation referred to "martial law," some writers have tended to confuse it with a declaration of martial law in the domestic sense. This interpretation is erroneous.[17] Although the absence of a formal state of war made the situation anomalous, Caperton was acting in conformity with the provisions of international law and of the United States *Rules of Land Warfare* for the government of foreign territory occupied by a belligerent.[18] On his "authority as Commanding Officer of the Forces of the

[16] In announcing his intention to the Secretary of the Navy, Caperton wrote as one justifying his own plans rather than as one acting on instructions (*Foreign Relations*, 1915, p. 484). Since military occupation automatically constitutes military government and is held to be self-evident, requiring no proclamation (W. E. Birkhimer, *Military Government and Martial Law*, p. 61), it may be argued that the formal announcement was of no significance, but Caperton himself indicated that he expected it to make his control more regular and effective.

[17] Great confusion results from the use of "martial law" for all forms of military jurisdiction over civilians, and therefore the term is preferably confined to domestic occasions, as distinguished from those occurring on foreign soil and within the domain of international law, which are better described as military government.

[18] War Department, *Rules of Land Warfare, 1914*, pp. 105-117. As distinguished from martial law, which presupposes a disorderly condition with which the civil authority is unable to cope, these rules contemplate a situation sufficiently stabilized to allow civil government to function under the control of the military occupant, and make it incumbent upon him to permit native officials to enforce their own law so far as their activities do not conflict with those of the occupying force, which, in the last analysis, is vested with the powers of government "in all its functions and branches" (*ibid.*, p. 108).

United States in Haiti and Haitian waters" and "in accordance with the law of nations," he declared himself "invested with the power and responsibility of government in all its functions and branches," but he denied intent to interfere with such proceedings of the constitutional authorities as did not affect his own operations and invited them to remain at their posts.[19]

Later the judge advocate general of the navy drew a herring across the trail by ruling that the Haitian government had not been "displaced," since Dartiguenave had requested a declaration of martial law.[20] This decision begged the question, for Caperton acted on his own authority, not that of the Haitian president (then unrecognized). Dartiguenave declared no martial law himself, but this argument served to confirm the impression that somehow Caperton was only carrying out the wishes of the Haitian government in enforcing martial law of the domestic type—a legal impossibility and a complete misconception of the true situation. The quality of the Haitian "request" may be judged by the repeated protests of the Haitian legation against Caperton's "threats" to declare martial law and against the declaration itself.[21]

While Admiral Caperton was forcibly taking the situation in hand, the State Department was laboring to establish a treaty relationship that must depend on consent and co-operation for success. The foreign minister, Pauleus Sannon, declared that if the Secretary of State insisted on the acceptance of his draft without modification, the government would resign, but Lansing called the bluff by replying that, unless Dartiguenave were quick about it, the United States would consider whether to set up a military government "until honest elections could be held" or to allow the administration to pass directly to some other faction more willing to participate in a revolution-proof regime.[22]

[19] Much of the proclamation was taken verbatim from that of Admiral Fletcher at Vera Cruz on April 26, 1914, or else was copied from the same form. See H. A. Smith, *Military Government*, p. 112.   [20] *Hearings*, pp. 69 f.

[21] *Foreign Relations* (1915), pp. 485 f. These protests may have originated with the Foreign Minister rather than the President, but according to the envoy they came from Dartiguenave personally.

[22] *Ibid.*, pp. 436-438. The first alternative evidently referred to an exclusively military administration like that subsequently established in the Dominican Republic,

This prospect, fearful to patriots and unbearable to politicians, split the cabinet. Sannon continued to insist that the financial advisership be omitted and that the customs-house patronage be left to Haiti, but his position had been undermined by his colleague, Louis Borno, and by Dartiguenave, both of whom gave private assurances that the substance of the American demands would be conceded if the phraseology were altered to save Haitian face.[23] On September 3 Caperton proclaimed "martial law," and it became evident that only a signed treaty could save the Haitian government from destruction.[24] Four days later Sannon resigned rather than participate in Dartiguenave's surrender.

That surrender was more apparent than real, for Dartiguenave and Borno, who took Sannon's place, liked the treaty no better than had Sannon and were determined to employ guile where open resistance had proved too perilous. Borno threatened to resign unless the draft were rewritten "in the attempt to concede all the United States demands but to do so in a manner less humiliating to the Haitian people, and also to avoid certain points which in the opinion of the Government are not possible under the Haitian Constitution." Lansing, who interpreted this proposal to mean the acceptance of the substance of the original draft, approved a revision of the phraseology,[25] thereby indicating that he either failed to note or meant to ignore that Borno had proposed two things, one of them an alteration in the meaning as well as the wording of certain cardinal passages. These changes were now phrased ambiguously, so as not to give

but one intended to be only transitory. Caperton was authorized to set up a military government—*if* the cabinet did resign.

[23] *Ibid.*, pp. 438 f. Sannon's counterproposals were made on Aug. 28 and 30, but Borno and Dartiguenave had given their assurances on Aug. 24, the date of Lansing's reply to Sannon's refusal to accept the treaty without modification.

[24] It was pretended that the proclamation was for Dartiguenave's benefit, but taken in conjunction with Lansing's instruction of Aug. 24, it was a distinct threat. At the time Caperton boasted to a subordinate that he had procured the dismissal of Sannon by "exercising military pressure at propitious moments," but when called upon to explain that expression in 1922, he evasively "supposed" that it had reference to pressure against the *cacos* in order to protect Dartiguenave from coercion by them (*Hearings*, p. 353).

[25] *Foreign Relations* (1915), pp. 442-445.

the game away, and the revision was accepted at Washington as part of the general face-saving process. Thus there was no meeting of minds in the final draft. Obviously the United States would interpret the treaty in conformity with the intent of the original proposal, the meaning of which was well understood by the Haitian cabinet—witness Sannon's resignation—but it is also evident that the Haitians intended to dispute every step of the way, insisting that Borno's ambiguous language meant precisely what Sannon had proposed openly without success. Lansing may have been caught napping, but it was typically Haitian to pit words against actuality. However, for the time the Americans were satisfied, and the government had survived the immediate crisis.

A treaty signed was not a treaty ratified, and the conduct of the Americans since the presidential election had made ratification more rather than less difficult. Stronger pressure had to be applied. When Dartiguenave complained that he was without funds for current expenses and arrears of salaries, he was told that no money would be available until after the chambers had acted, when he might hope for a $100,000 advance from the customs revenues and perhaps a loan.[26] On October 6 the Chamber of Deputies proceeded to give its assent, subject to an "interpretive commentary" which held that the Haitian president could refuse to appoint officials nominated by the United States, that he could remove the receiver general for cause, that all customs-service employees except those in the receiver general's office were to be Haitians "exclusively and directly" appointed by their president, and that the financial adviser was to be a mere adviser, subordinate to the minister of finance, not a "comptroller placed above the executive and legislative powers"[27]—in short, that the treaty was one to which even Pauleus Sannon should have been able to give his approval. The Senate remained obdurate, and on November 10 Admiral Caperton was instructed to let it be known that the United States intended

[26] Ibid., pp. 447 f. Later the government was granted a weekly dole of $25,000 (Hearings, p. 383).

[27] Foreign Relations (1916), pp. 322-325.

to retain control of Haiti whether the treaty were ratified or not and would proceed forthwith to complete the pacification of the country, meting out to opponents the treatment which their conduct merited.[28] Overnight the Senate decided that the treaty was quite acceptable. On February 28 the United States Senate gave its consent, unanimously and without debate, but the exchange of ratifications was delayed until May 3 by Borno's unsuccessful efforts to have the Haitian "interpretive commentary" accepted as reservations.[29] Meanwhile the Haitian government had received the promised $100,000, but had learned that there could be no loan until it had settled its dispute with the bank.

The Haitians who had signed and ratified the treaty primarily in order to escape foreign military government even if it meant surrender to a certain degree of civilian supervision were dismayed as months passed with Admiral Caperton's naval appointees continuing to collect the customs, dispense the public funds, and control municipal administration, public works, sanitation, and other civil functions in addition to ordinary police duty. Even after the belated arrival of regularly appointed treaty officials the officers of the occupation and the gendarmerie showed "reluctance" to turn over to them "the functions that properly would come within their cognizance."[30] When, finally, all the treaty services had been organized and the gendarmerie had shown itself capable of maintaining order, it was expected, on the basis of American assurances, that the marines would be withdrawn, to return only in the event of fresh disturbances, as had been the case in Cuba, but instead the military regime was continued in the sense that for nearly twenty years the ultimate authority in Haiti was vested in the senior American naval officer rather than in the president of the republic and was

[28] *Ibid.* (1915), p. 458.
[29] *Ibid.* (1916), pp. 325-327. Lansing denied that the commentary was binding on the United States, since it had not been submitted to the American Senate.
[30] *Annual Report of the Secretary of the Navy, 1920*, p. 232. The gendarmerie was organized at once, but was not brought under even nominal Haitian control until September, 1916. A financial adviser was appointed in July, and a general receiver took over the customs service in August. Although the first treaty engineer was appointed in July, 1916, the gendarmerie did not relinquish control of sanitation until December, 1917, of public works until 1920.

derived from Caperton's proclamation of "martial law" rather than from the treaty or the Haitian constitution.

Caperton's successors exercised their overlordship from their capital at Santo Domingo, where they were personally discharging the functions of the Dominican presidency.[31] Their viceroys for Haiti were the commanding officers of the marine brigade, who ruled the land by ruling the Haitian president rather than by taking his office themselves. The gendarmerie, nominally a treaty service subject to presidential control, but actually a subsidiary of the occupation, relieved the marines of police duty, so that the military government came into direct contact with the people only through the provost courts, which continued to enforce "martial law."[32] However, on occasion the brigade commander revealed his absolute power to intervene in any phase of Haitian affairs without reference to any treaty provision.[33]

The treaty officials, as distinguished from those of the military occupation, were employees of the Haitian government, but the text of the original draft showed that it had been intended that they should act independently, as agents of the United States, and this they proceeded to do, over Haitian protest. Unfortunately, if the president of the republic were not to supervise and co-ordinate their activities, then no one was authorized to do so except, by inference, the president of the United States, who was too busy trying to solve the problems of the world at large to have time for those of Haiti. The State Department should have acted for him in matters pertaining to the application of the treaty, but presumably because it lacked personnel qualified to deal with problems of internal administration, it confined itself to supervision of the financial adviser,[34]

[31] When military government was proclaimed in the Dominican Republic, it was intended that it should be like that in Haiti—that is, a native administration under military control—but when no Dominican could be found willing to co-operate, naval officers were appointed to the various constitutional offices.

[32] Their activity was restricted largely to censorship of the press.

[33] For instance, see below, pp. 230 f.

[34] The financial adviser, who considered himself responsible to the chief of the Latin-American Division of the State Department, spent most of his time in Washington, leaving his office in charge of the general receiver and handling special cases by correspondence (*Hearings*, pp. 1351 f., 1396, 1404 f., 1408 f.).

handing over the customs receivership to the War Department's Bureau of Insular Affairs[35] (the nearest approach to a colonial office in the structure of the Federal government), and leaving the nonfinancial services to the Navy, which inevitably experienced great difficulty in distinguishing them, in practice, from the affairs of the marine occupation.[36]

The situation was worse confounded by the fact that, between 1915 and 1922, there were four secretaries of state and six chiefs of the Latin-American Division in Washington, four senior naval officers at Santo Domingo, and six marine brigade commanders and six chiefs of the gendarmerie in Haiti,[37] with a correspondingly rapid turnover in other offices. A most delicate task was being imposed upon men who were strangers to each other and unfamiliar with the situation. If these Americans were unable to work together in harmony, it is not remarkable that ignorance of the language, color prejudice, and military predilections prevented them from establishing cordial relations with their Haitian colleagues. According to one former treaty official, "a more confused, disorganized, and unsatisfactory state of affairs could hardly be conceived."[38]

As a consequence of these inauspicious circumstances, the seven years of Dartiguenave's administration were more remarkable for ceaseless friction than for constructive achievement. Haiti enjoyed comparative tranquility, and the more obvious measures of sanitation and public improvement were undertaken, but little was accomplished toward remedying the basic

[35] *Report of the Receivership of Customs, 1918-1919*, p. 3. The treaty, providing for reports to both the Haitian government and the state department, said nothing about supervision and control.

[36] It was expressly agreed that the gendarmerie should be "subject only to the President of Haiti," to be controlled by him through the Ministry of the Interior (*Foreign Relations*, 1916, p. 335), but such was the intimate relationship between the functions of the police and the responsibilities of the occupation that the marine commandant continued to consult the marine brigade commander and sometimes took orders directly from him (*Hearings*, pp. 418 f., 623-625, 702). The engineer and surgeon in charge of public works and sanitation were naval officers, but they had many conflicts of jurisdiction with the marines (above, p. 223 n.; below, p. 226 n.). Whatever the theory, the Secretary of the Navy was not far beside the point when he spoke of the "naval administration of Haiti" (*Annual Report, 1919*, p. 140).

[37] *Senate Report No. 794* (67.2), p. 25.

[38] Millspaugh, *Haiti under American Control*, p. 70.

causes of past disorder. The financial problem, which had seemed all-important in 1914, remained unsolved—indeed, under American control Haiti went into default on interest as well as amortization payments. Haitian critics made much of this, but, in fact, it was attributable to factors beyond American control: the chaotic condition of Haitian finance in 1915 and the European war. Although collection was measurably improved, French war restrictions on the importation of coffee and the shortage of ocean tonnage so reduced Haitian commerce and Haitian revenue that, had the debt service been met, nothing would have been left for domestic expenses. No loan could be had until a settlement was reached with the bank, and even when a claims protocol and loan agreement were finally negotiated in 1919, execution was delayed for three more years. Meanwhile Haiti passed from the desperate economic straits of the war period into a post-war inflation ending in the universal collapse of 1920-1921.[39]

While the promised financial and economic benefits of intervention remained unrealized, the United States steadily encroached upon the remnants of Haitian independence. In applying the treaty the Americans not only enforced the ideas embodied in their original proposals, as opposed to those of the Haitian interpretive commentary, but they also read certain afterthoughts into the text.[40] More ominously, they procured the suppression of the legislature and a revision of the constitution according to their specifications. However, it must be

[39] *Report of the Financial Adviser-General Receiver, 1923-1924*, pp. 55-57; Millspaugh, *Haiti under American Control*, pp. 82-85.

[40] For instance, the treaty gave no hint of an American control over telephones and telegraphs, but even before it had been signed Admiral Caperton had assumed such control as a military matter of course and the occupation was loath to give it up. Therefore Lansing argued that those services were properly included among the "public improvements" to be undertaken by American engineers for the "development of natural resources," at the same time proposing that the works thus described in Article XIII be entrusted to the gendarmerie organized under Article X. Haitian denial that telephones and telegraphs came under the jurisdiction of any treaty service were unavailing, but they did succeed in excluding them from the gendarmerie agreement of August 24, 1916, yielding them to the treaty engineer in a separate protocol of the same date. Despite these explicit terms, the gendarmerie retained control of the services in question (*Rapport de M. Louis Borno*, p. 196; *Foreign Relations*, 1916, pp. 328-336).

noted that what happened in this connection was as much a result of old-fashioned intrigue of Haitian against Haitian as of disposition on the part of the United States to impose its will by force.

Haitian constitutional provisions regarding parliamentary government had never been effective, but a hostile legislature could at least embarrass the executive as long as he permitted it to exist. The debate on ratification had warned the Americans that their interpretation of the treaty could not be enforced without a collision with the legislative power, which could make itself dangerous by providing a rallying point for the disaffected. Dartiguenave also favored a reorganization that would make the legislative body more manageable.[41] Moreover, the State Department was prepared to insist upon the removal of the prohibition of alien ownership of real estate, regarding it as a barrier to the development of Haitian resources contemplated in the treaty. In this it promoted the interests of Americans who hoped to profit by investment in Haiti,[42] but it could also have claimed strong Haitian support for its argument. Although the prohibition had been cherished since the days of Dessalines, some Haitians were advocating its repeal as early as 1860,[43] and many recent publicists had condemned it as an anachronism.[44]

In April, 1916, Dartiguenave, fearing impeachment by a legislature representative of the old regime, dissolved the Senate and called on the Deputies to serve as a constituent assembly. His decree was enforced by the gendarmerie, although the marine brigade commander, Lieutenant Colonel Littleton W. T. Waller, was personally opposed to the dissolution.[45] The deputies refused to act; consequently, nothing could be accom-

[41] *Hearings*, p. 415. It was also necessary to provide for the substitution of the gendarmerie for the old army, and so forth.

[42] B. H. Williams, *Economic Foreign Policy of the United States*, p. 34; Davis, "Notes on Haiti and Santo Domingo," *Pan American Magazine*, March, 1917.

[43] Bonneau, *Haiti: ses progrès, son avenir*, p. 80.

[44] Notably Marcelin, *L'haleine du centenaire*, pp. 51 ff.; *Une évolution nécessaire*, pp. 19-30. Marcelin suggests that the prohibition survived less on account of genuine conviction than because of the fright of all politicians at the partisan cry, "*On vend le pays aux blancs*."

[45] *Hearings*, pp. 23-27, 415-421. The American naval officers involved have insisted that at this point the initiative was Dartiguenave's.

plished until after the regular elections held in January under supervision of the marines and gendarmerie.[46] Meanwhile Dartiguenave submitted a draft constitution to the State Department and received thence several suggestions for its modification.

The new Assembly, meeting in April, 1917, evinced implacable hostility toward these American proposals, particularly that regarding real estate, and proceeded to draw up a constitution of its own directly counter to the known desires of the United States. Dartiguenave was playing a double game, subtly inciting legislative resistance[47] while at the same time suggesting to Americans the feasibility of suppressing the legislature and governing with an appointed council of state.[48] Apparently he wished the Assembly to provoke the Americans to its own destruction, leaving him free of legislative restrictions while the United States bore the onus of the act. However, the new brigade commander, Colonel Eli K. Cole, was recommending that Dartiguenave be suppressed along with the Assembly.[49] Having reported that dissolution alone could prevent the passage of the anti-American constitution and having received authority to act on his own discretion, avoiding the use of force if possible, he called on the President for the promised decree. Dartiguenave held back, hoping to force Cole to issue the order himself, but when he learned that in that case the executive would share the fate of the legislature, he signed. Major Smedley D. Butler, commandant of the gendarmerie, thereupon dispersed the Assembly.[50]

After further consultation between President Dartiguenave, Captain Knapp (the senior naval officer), the chargé d'affaires,

[46] *Ibid.*, pp. 625 f. Judging by the results, this election, conducted by Colonel Waller, was the fairest ever held in Haiti.

[47] *Ibid.*, p. 696. He submitted the correspondence with Washington along with the draft, providing ammunition for those who wished to denounce American dictation. [48] *Ibid.*, p. 699.

[49] Ibid., pp. 1784 f. The recommendation was made six months after the Navy had taken over the administration of the Dominican Republic.

[50] *Ibid.*, pp. 536-538, 698-703. Two hours before the dissolution Cole had received an order from the Navy Department to "take no action until arrival of State Department message," but, in view of the imminence of the passage of the unwanted constitution, he had decided that it was his duty to press for the decree. Dartiguenave's capitulation saved him from having to act on his own responsibility.

and the brigade commander in Haiti, and the State and Navy Departments in Washington, a constitution was finally drawn up.[51] Although it permitted resident aliens to own real estate and contained a special article validating the acts of the occupation, the main body of its text varied from that of the constitution of 1889 only on the democratic side.[52] The joker was in a series of transitory articles which authorized the president to name the year of the first legislative election and to govern meanwhile with an appointed council of state for a legislature. On June 12, 1918, this document was submitted to a plebescite and, with the officers of the gendarmerie frankly electioneering for a favorable vote, was accepted, 69,337 to 335. The only suspicious feature of the count was the strength of the opposition, for, while elaborate precautions were taken against disorder, repeating, and the like, it was patent that only affirmative votes were wanted.[53] The whole proceeding was farcical, in that the electorate was called upon to pass on a constitution based upon the premise that, for the present at least, the electorate was incapable of selecting representatives capable of passing on such questions.

Having used the Americans to rid himself of all potential Haitian opposition, Dartiguenave now prepared to "take a new attitude" toward the United States, to grapple with the occupation in earnest.[54] There would be no more concessions, but rather a demand for freedom of action. Alas, it also occurred to the occupation authorities that the moment when Dartiguenave stood alone was a propitious one for grappling with him, and before he knew it, the United States had won a veto power over all his actions that would have been difficult to find in either the treaty or the constitution.

[51] *Ibid.*, pp. 628, 696, 718. In 1920 Assistant Secretary of the Navy Franklin D. Roosevelt boasted that he was the author of the Haitian constitution (New York *Times*, Aug. 19, 1920).

[52] *Foreign Relations* (1918), pp. 487-502. It reduced the presidential term from seven to four years, provided for popular rather than indirect election of senators, and required plebescites on constitutional amendments. Among the guarantees of individual liberty were freedom of assembly and of the press and trial by jury in political as well as criminal cases.   [53] *Hearings*, pp. 43, 77, 192 f., 566 f., 1508 f.

[54] Bellegarde, *Pour une Haiti heureuse*, II, 25.

Before any treaty existed the United States had revealed a tendency to exploit power over the purse to accomplish larger objects than strict financial regularity. Once the treaty was in effect the Haitians had argued that they could spend their small share of the revenue as they chose. Adhering to the letter of that document, they held that the financial adviser could only "devise . . . , aid . . . , inquire . . . , enlighten . . . ," and "recommend" to the minister of finance "improved methods of . . . applying the revenues," the minister's obligation to "lend efficient aid" to give effect to the adviser's proposals being regarded as subject to discretion. From the several American treaty projects and the Dominican experience that lay behind this feature of them, plainly the United States meant the "adviser" to be a comptroller empowered to prevent an increase of the floating debt through Haitian misapplication of funds.[55] In October, 1918, the adviser, Addison T. Ruan, demanded that the council of state pass a bill forbidding the minister of finance to make out vouchers for payment by the bank without obtaining his visa. When the council refused, on the ground that the proposal was contrary to both the constitution and the treaty, Colonel John H. Russell, by virtue of his authority as military governor under the occupation, ordered the bank to stop all payments to the Haitian government. A three months' deadlock ensued, during which Ruan even refused to pay the funeral expenses of the Haitian minister at Washington, and a provost court severely punished a Haitian editor for printing a report that the adviser had been recalled; but finally, Dartiguenave submitted.[56] The power claimed under the treaty may have been necessary to establish a pre-audit system deemed indis-

[55] *Foreign Relations* (1914), pp. 347-350; (1915), pp. 431-433; Munro, *The United States and the Caribbean Area*, pp. 119-124.
[56] *Hearings*, pp. 1435 f.; *Documents diplomatiques* (1921), p. 33; F. L. Buell, *The American Occupation of Haiti*, p. 353. Ironically, the report was correct in the sense that Ruan had resigned, but Lansing declared that the punishment—three months' suspension and a $600 fine—fitted the crime (*Hearings*, p. 175). Borno, who had given the tip, was driven from the cabinet. Dartiguenave tried to send him to Washington as minister to lay the situation before Lansing directly, but the United States would not accept him (Bellegarde, *Pour une Haiti heureuse*, II, 94).

pensable and salutary by the Americans, but it is obvious that it was open to abuse for the attainment of any desired object. However, so far as coercion by withholding funds is concerned, Colonel Russell's intervention shows that the power existed in the fact of the military occupation, apart from any interpretation of the treaty.

In August, 1918, the American minister required Dartiguenave to agree to submit to him all projected legislation "bearing upon any of the objects of the treaty" for the "information" of the United States and "discussion" between the two governments, if necessary. In July, 1919, the minister protested the enactment of certain laws, unrelated to the treaty according to the Haitians, on the ground that they had not received his approval.[57] The council of state continued to pass laws without reference to the legation and to ignore some suggestions of the financial adviser, John A. McIlhenny, until, in July, 1920, that officer stopped payment on the salaries of the president, cabinet, and council.[58] The State Department let it be known that there would be no paychecks until eleven laws had been repealed or modified and four enacted, and again Dartiguenave was forced to surrender,[59] the American administration in Haiti acquiring a virtual right to initiate and veto legislation of any character. At the same time American officials declared invalid all pre-occupation laws which were, in their opinion, out of harmony with the treaty,[60] and ignored the decisions of Haitian courts, while Haitians whose conduct did

[57] *Documents diplomatiques* (1921), pp. 5 f., 15 f., 21. He claimed that in November, 1918, Dartiguenave had agreed to submit all legislation, in order to avoid misunderstandings, but, according to the Haitians, they had rejected the minister's proposal to that effect.

[58] This was considered to be no more than a strict application of the priorities of payment established by the treaty, which had hitherto been waived, since otherwise there would have been no funds available for the Haitian government (*Hearings*, pp. 797 f., 1430 ff.).

[59] *Ibid.*, pp. 79-81, 1444 f. However, Dartiguenave successfully refused to comply with McIlhenny's suggestion that he be given control of the import and export of foreign currency. He was supported on this issue by the French and British legations, the Royal Bank of Canada, and the American Foreign Banking Corporation (Charles P. Howland, *Survey of American Foreign Relations, 1929*, p. 141; below, p. 245 n.). [60] *Documents diplomatiques* (1921), p. 200.

not meet with their approval were subject to trial in the provost courts of the occupation.[61]

Unable to cope with the American officials in Haiti, supported as they were by an armed occupation, Dartiguenave made frequent, but fruitless, appeals to Washington. These failing, his minister in Paris tried to gain access to President Wilson at the peace conference, but he was shunted off by Lansing.[62] No heed was paid to the angry protests of the Haitian administration because it was realized that it did not represent either the peasants or the majority of the *élite*. Although called upon to renounce sterile dissension and unite in a common effort, the members of that class, divided and demoralized, continued to revile each other as vigorously as they denounced the treaty regime, depriving their country of any authoritative spokesman.[63] In the end it was the humble *cacos* who made the voice of Haiti heard.

Even in the days when Cincinnatus Leconte had led his *cacos* against Antoine Simon it was understood that improved communications would extend the power of the ruling authority at Port-au-Prince and ruin the revolutionary profession. Admiral Caperton had lost no time in setting the unemployed to work on the roads. Later, when no relief funds were available, someone thought of the *corvée*, which had existed in Haitian law since colonial times, but had not been consistently enforced for generations.[64]

At first there was little complaint, but as construction entered sparsely settled districts abuses crept in.[65] Perceiving the

---

[61] Buell, *American Occupation*, pp. 354 f.; below, p. 242.

[62] *Documents diplomatiques* (1921), pp. 41, 53, 84, 173, 177.

[63] Price-Mars, *La vocation de l'élite*, pp. iii, 73-80; Bellegarde, *Pour une Haiti heureuse*, II, 5; Paret, *Dans la mêlée*, pp. 102-105.

[64] The legal requirement in 1916 was three days' labor a year on the roads in the peasant's home district, but it had never been invoked within the memory of man except as a threat by local chiefs to coerce individuals (Price-Mars, *La vocation de l'élite*, p. 40; Antoine Michel, *Avènement du Général Geffrard à la présidence d'Haiti*, p. xii). In 1907 a "general" had undertaken to use this tactic on a negro American resident in Haiti, precipitating a minor diplomatic incident (*Foreign Relations*, 1907, pp. 742 f.).

[65] Men were compelled to work outside their districts and for longer than the prescribed time. Most of the abuses were attributed to Haitian gendarmes, habituated

growing discontent and the opportunity it afforded the critics of the treaty regime, the commandant of the gendarmerie ordered the *corvée* discontinued on October 1, 1918, but the order was not immediately obeyed in remote districts of the *caco* country. There Charlemagne Peralte was able to organize armed resistance,[66] and by March, 1919, the situation had become so serious that marines had to be sent to reinforce the gendarmerie. The force available for field service was limited,[67] and, consequently, the guerrilla warfare dragged on for months. Charlemagne was killed in October, but his successor, Benoit Battraville, in a last desperate effort, actually penetrated the city of Port-au-Prince before dawn on January 15, 1920, and so made headlines in the United States.[68] In this startling fashion Americans suddenly learned that all Haitians were not full of gratitude toward the United States government for its kindly and helpful interest in their affairs.

The insurrection had affected only a quarter of the country. The number of *cacos* actively hostile had never been more than a few thousand, but two thousand Haitians had been killed on their native soil, as compared to seven marines and twenty-seven gendarmes,[69] and wild rumors of atrocities were abroad in the land. Here was propaganda material more effective than questions of treaty interpretation, and the *élite* made the most of it. Some of the charges were unfortunately true, but many more

---

to impressments and military irresponsibility under the old regime, but agitators were enabled to talk of a restoration of slavery by the whites (*Hearings*, pp. 83 f., 479, 483 f., 494 f., 497-502, 530 f., 533, 556, 559-565, 599, 627 f., 653-661, 1253 f.).

[66] Charlemagne was an irreconcilable *caco* chief who had been convicted by a provost court of complicity in an attack on the gendarmerie in 1917, a generally quiet year, before the storm had risen over the *corvée*. He escaped during the summer of 1918 and made himself leader of the disaffected.

[67] Of the one thousand marines and two thousand gendarmes, the greater portion were required for garrison and police duty. There were supposed to be five thousand *cacos* in the field, with perhaps twelve thousand more subject to Charlemagne's orders.

[68] The repulse of this attack virtually ended the revolt, over three thousand *cacos* surrendering during the next few weeks. Benoit was killed in May, and by midsummer the country had been pacified once more.

[69] Clyde H. Metcalf, *History of the United States Marine Corps*, p. 401. Some eleven thousand *cacos* were reported captured or surrendered.

were not.[70] Considering that war is not a cordial relationship and that this campaign was conducted under the most difficult conditions, with a minimum of superior control, the marines in general behaved very creditably.[71] The several official findings to this effect have been described as a "liberal coat of white-wash," but they are supported by the fact that the mass of Haitian peasants did not regard the marines as the fiends in human form described by the *élite*. Many investigators made this significant observation, but the most notable of them was Senator William H. King of Utah, who saw "nowhere the slightest evidence of their being repressed or existing in a state of terror."[72] His testimony is credible, because he assumed the mantle of Sumner as Haiti's champion in the United States Senate.

There had been some public discussion of American relations with Haiti in 1917,[73] but the nation, girding itself for the

[70] Every sort of atrocity was alleged, but some of the acts attributed to marines may have been committed by *cacos*, who lived off the country and resorted to the old Haitian practice of impressment. The *Rules of Land Warfare, 1914*, p. 130, prescribed death as the penalty for civilians rising in arms against a military occupation. The offenses proved had to do with the summary execution of prisoners, done in violation of orders (*Hearings*, pp. 465-471, 551, 588, 598, 661, 1830). Every investigating agency acknowledged that there had been isolated instances of this, but denied that the improper or criminal conduct of a few individuals warranted the general charges against the marine brigade as a whole. See *Senate Report No. 794* (67.2), pp. 11-23; *Annual Report of the Secretary of the Navy* (1920), pp. 245-320.

[71] Of necessity, operations against the guerrillas were carried on by small detached patrols, generally led by enlisted men, remote from control or succor, alone in a wild country and momentarily expecting to be ambushed. No mark distinguished hostile *caco* from peaceful peasant, and, with one's own life at stake, there was a strong temptation to give oneself the benefit of any doubt. Had the marines not shown remarkable restraint, the havoc in the hinterland must have been greater. Such unfortunate occurrences as took place were no more than was to be expected in the circumstances. The responsibility for these circumstances, rooted in a military occupation of foreign soil, rested not with the marines, but with their political superiors.   [72] *Hearings*, p. 239.

[73] Oswald G. Villard pointed out the inconsistency between the situation in Haiti and the lofty principles proclaimed in Wilson's war message ("The Rights of Small Nations in America," *Annals of the American Academy of Political and Social Science*, LXXII, July, 1917, 165-171; "Our Relations with Haiti and San Domingo," *Proceedings of the Academy of Political Science*, VII, 1917, 412-417). He was answered by Edwin M. Borchard, who frankly championed economic imperialism regardless of "the rights of small nations" and "the consent of the gov-

great crusade in Europe, gave no heed. In 1920 the war was over, leaving some Americans still inspired by ringing phrases about the rights of small nations and the others weary of military adventures overseas and anxious for a return to "normalcy." Moreover, a presidential campaign was under way, with the Republicans eager to exploit any issue that might embarrass the administration. In the circumstances Benoit Battraville's raid on Port-au-Prince was perfectly timed to capture American attention. In May a negro "University Conference on Mexico and the Caribbean" assailed the intervention and reopened public discussion.[74] In response to a protest of the National Association for the Advancement of Colored People the Republican candidate denounced Wilsonian tactics in Haiti.[75] The great sensation, however, was caused by the publication of a confidential letter from the commandant of the Marine Corps to the commander of the marine brigade which spoke of "practically indiscriminate killing of natives." A press that had begun to miss its accustomed ration of war news seized on that choice morsel and made the most of it.[76] There followed a series of investigations,[77] all of which resulted favorably for the marines and the intervention, but the clamor was only intensified thereby.

erned" ("Commercial and Financial Interests of the United States in the Caribbean," *loc. cit.*, pp. 383-391).

[74] David Y. Thomas, *One Hundred Years of the Monroe Doctrine*, p. 253. See Otto Schoenrich, "The Present American Intervention in Santo Domingo and Haiti," *Journal of International Relations*, XI (1920), 45-62; and Col. George C. Thorpe, U. S. M. C., "American Achievements in Santo Domingo, Haiti, and the Virgin Islands," *loc. cit.*, pp. 63-86, the former accusing, the latter defending. See also Samuel Guy Inman, *Through Santo Domingo and Haiti*, and J. Dryden Kuser, *Haiti: Its Dawn of Progress after Years in a Night of Revolution.*

[75] New York *Times*, Aug. 31, 1920.

[76] General George Barnett made this sensational deduction from the remarks of a defense counsel at a court martial. It was not sustained by subsequent investigation. How such a document fell into the hands of the press during a political campaign was never satisfactorily explained.

[77] Notably those of Admiral Knapp, General Lejeune, and a naval court of inquiry headed by Admiral Mayo, and that made by Carl Kelsey at the request of the Latin-American Division of the State Department. The reports of the first three may be found in *Annual Report of the Secretary of the Navy, 1920*, pp. 222-240, 245-311, and 312-320, respectively. For Dr. Kelsey's findings see "The American Intervention in Haiti and the Dominican Republic," *Annals of the American Academy of Political and Social Science*, C (March, 1922).

Oswald Garrison Villard allied *The Nation* with the National Association for the Advancement of Colored People[78] and the Union patriotique d'Haiti, forming the Haiti-Santo Domingo Independence Society to carry on the agitation. These groups demanded the immediate re-establishment of constitutional government, immediate withdrawal of the marines, and the negotiation of an equitable treaty.

In December, 1920, and February, 1921, Representative Oscar Bland (Republican, Indiana) and Senator Hiram Johnson (Republican, California) demanded congressional investigations, but the election was over and the "lame duck" session was not interested. However, in May, Sténio Vincent arrived with a memoir of the Union patriotique,[79] and *The Nation* proceeded to build a fire under the Republican Congress. As a result, a Senate committee composed of Medill McCormick (Republican, Illinois), Philander Knox (Republican, Pennsylvania—of "dollar diplomacy" fame), Tasker Oddie (Republican, Nevada), Atlee Pomerene (Democrat, Ohio), and William H. King (Democrat, Utah) was appointed to investigate the situation in Haiti and Santo Domingo. After lengthy hearings at Washington and in Haiti, the committee decided against the abrogation of the treaty or the withdrawal of the marines. Endorsing the policy of intervention, it sought to strengthen the treaty regime by recommending measures designed to correct its deficiencies.[80]

Curiously enough, while the Republican majority found itself well pleased with the fact of the Wilsonian intervention and critical only of the execution of that policy, it was the Democratic senator from Utah who stood forth as Haiti's champion. He was supported by the Popular Government League, which held that the intervention was in the exclusive interest of bankers and promoters, and by the Foreign Policy Association, under whose aegis twenty-four lawyers (including

[78] See James W. Johnson, "Self-Determining Haiti," *The Nation*, Aug. 25-Sept. 25, 1920.

[79] The memoir may be found in *The Nation*, May 31, 1921, or in *Hearings*, pp. 5-33. It was signed by Pauleus Sannon, Sténio Vincent, and Perceval Thoby.

[80] *Senate Report No. 794*, 67th Cong., 2d Sess.

Felix Frankfurter) signed a brief condemning the occupation on legal as well as moral grounds.[81] However, despite all the pressure the Haiti-Santo Domingo Independence Society could bring to bear, when Senator King, seconded by Borah and Norris, sought to kill the occupation by amendment to the naval appropriation bill, he was defeated, nine to forty-three.[82] Thereafter it was evident that the occupation would be maintained during the life of the treaty, and that the result of the agitation and investigation would be greater rather than less interference in Haitian affairs.[83]

[81] Foreign Policy Association, *The Seizure of Haiti by the United States.* See also E. H. Gruening, "The Conquest of Haiti and Santo Domingo," *Current History,* XV (1922), 885-896.

[82] *Congressional Record,* LXII, 8940-8974.

[83] At the same time arrangements were being made for the withdrawal of the marines and naval administration from the Dominican Republic, leaving only the customs receivership established in 1907 and an unofficial financial adviser.

CHAPTER XIV

RECONSTRUCTION

The American people will not consider their duty under the treaty discharged if . . . there are not placed within reach of the Haitian masses, justice, schools and agricultural instruction. The treaty itself makes no provision to consummate these things, necessary [in order to increase] the buying power and well-being of the people . . . as under American guidance or control they have so marvelously increased in Cuba and Porto Rico during the last generation.
— SENATE COMMITTEE, June 26, 1922

As a candidate President Harding had been shocked by Wilsonian interference in the domestic affairs of Haiti, but in 1922 his administration prepared to strengthen and expand the Wilsonian system of control. A reconstruction of Haitian life in all its aspects was to be undertaken with businesslike directness and dispatch, for the benefit of the masses and regardless of the sensibilities of the parasitical *élite*. The end justifying the means, no strict construction of treaty terms was to be permitted to hinder this good work, which would increase Haitian buying power as well as Haitian well-being.

The first step was to carry out the recommendations of the Senate committee designed to replace Democratic confusion (the result of a conflict between principle and practice) with Republican efficiency. At Washington control was centralized in the Department of State; the Bureau of Insular Affairs was relieved of its functions in connection with the customs receivership, and the jurisdiction of the Navy was confined to the personnel of the marine brigade. Senator McCormick suggested that the disorganization in Haiti be remedied by sending thither a high commissioner with diplomatic powers, to whom "all American officials appointed under the treaty, as well as the commandant of the Marine brigade, should look for direction and guidance"; in February, 1922, such an officer was appointed to supervise the treaty services.[1] One of his first acts was to require treaty officials to transmit their correspondence with Washington, the Haitian government, or each other through his office. In budgetary matters he ruled over rival American-directed services and dealt separately with the Haitians. This system may have given needed co-ordination to the American effort, but it divorced American "advisers" from the departments which they were supposed to advise and created two distinct governments in Haiti connected only by contact between the Haitian president and the high commissioner.[2]

In suggesting this reorganization Senator McCormick had assumed that the high commissioner would be a civilian,[3] but instead President Harding appointed General John H. Russell, then commanding the marine brigade. Russell's character and ability were generally recognized, and his Haitian experience was probably greater than that of any other individual available, but he was a novice in business, finance, and civil administration and it was the consensus that the desired spirit of "co-operation and accommodation" could be attained only by minimizing the military character of the intervention. Moreover, he had ordered the bank to withhold funds from the government in 1918, he had led the campaign against the *cacos* in 1920, and, as a Georgian and a marine, he represented all that the *élite* had found distasteful in the first phase of the intervention. The unadvertised consideration that overcame all these objections was that as long as military government was to be maintained in Haiti, it would be impossible to vest

[1] *Messages and Papers of the Presidents*, XVIII, 9110. While Bailly-Blanchard remained titular minister to Haiti until his death in 1925, he was actually kept on special duty in Washington. The high commissioner's appointment was not submitted to the Senate for confirmation despite his diplomatic character, on the ground that he was a treaty official (H. M. Wriston, *Executive Agents in American Foreign Relations*, pp. 803 f.). That office could be read into the treaty only by reference to a clause empowering both parties to take such steps as might be necessary to ensure the complete attainment of its objects, a provision intended originally to permit the United States to support the treaty regime with military force if need be (*Foreign Relations*, 1915, p. 433).

[2] Millspaugh, for two years financial adviser-general receiver, gives a penetrating discussion of relations between the high commissioner, treaty officials, and Haitian authorities in *Haiti under American Control*, pp. 101-108.

[3] *Hearings*, pp. 1475 f.

in a civilian functions superior to those of the brigade commander, and only by utilizing a marine general as high commissioner could the brigade and the treaty services be brought
under unified control. This meant that while ostensibly the
treaty services were being co-ordinated by the legation, actually
they were being incorporated into the military government, the
legation serving as a façade.

To keep the continued rule of force decently concealed was
possible because Haitians of the official party were astute enough
to perceive that the disappointing result of the senatorial investigation left them no alternative save to co-operate with as good
grace as possible. Consequently, no occasion arose for an
overt exercise of "military pressure" as of yore. Dartiguenave's
term expired a few months after Russell's appointment, and
he failed of re-election, although he was an avowed candidate
and had himself selected the electors, his council of state.[4] Louis
Borno was chosen in his stead. The new president had once
opposed the Americans vigorously enough to be driven from
the foreign office by Colonel Russell (in 1918), but before the
arrival of any marines in Haiti he had shown his willingness
to co-operate with the United States for Haitian reconstruction
under adequate guarantees; the treaty of 1916, to which the
Haitian government owed its continued existence, bore his sig-
nature; and, having been convinced that more was to be gained
by conciliation than by resistance, he was eminently qualified to
defend Haitian interests while carrying out such a policy. The
personal benefit derived by Borno and his associates from their
new attitude is obvious, but it can also be soundly argued that
their realistic program was more to the advantage of Haiti than
any other would have been in the existing circumstances.[5]

---

[4] This result was so remarkable as to give rise to charges of bribery, but, without
passing on that question, it may be shown that no such hypothesis is needed to explain
Dartiguenave's rejection. Although the occupation did not exert overt pressure, as
in 1915, the Haitian councillors were intelligent enough to see that a reorientation
of policy was in order and that Dartiguenave, by the bitterness of his resistance in
1918-1922, had disqualified himself.

[5] See Damase Pierre-Louis, *Les mensonges de notre démocratie*, pp. 183-192;
Paret, *Dans la mêlée*, pp. 103-105.

Borno's government followed the pattern of dictatorship established since 1916. The members of the legislative council of state held office at his pleasure, and successive even-numbered years were allowed to pass without the election of a National Assembly. In justifying his decision to call no election in 1926 the President said:

> Our rural population, which represents nine-tenths of the Haitian people, is almost totally illiterate, ignorant, and poor; . . . it is still incapable of exercising the right to vote, and would be an easy prey of those bold speculators whose conscience hesitates at no lie.
>
> As for the urban population, . . . those of its members who are capable of expressing an intelligent vote . . . have for a long time for the most part renounced their electoral right. . . . The remainder is a small group of professional politicians, with their followers of every sort, who are mainly illiterate.[6]

Then, having replaced eighteen of the twenty-one members of his council, Borno had them re-elect him for another four-year term.[7]

Absolute control of the executive and legislative functions did not suffice to protect the president from the annoyance of an unprecedented independence in the judiciary and the press. Enjoying an unaccustomed security by virtue of the occupation, they condemned all its works without restraint. The courts not only delighted to contradict the administration in their interpretation of the treaty and the laws, but many of their judgments against the state seemed to bear little relation to the evidence. In such cases the financial adviser refused to allow the payment of awards on the ground that the treaty forbade the Haitian government to increase its debt without the previous consent of the United States, a quibble that made the situation doubly intolerable. Haitian journals, conducted in the French tradition as organs of opinion rather than as publishers of news, sometimes incurred official enmity by telling criticism, but more often were simply scurrilous. Protected by constitutional guar-

---

[6] *Report of the American High Commissioner, 1925*, pp. 5 f. The high commissioner endorsed this policy.

[7] Buell, *The American Occupation of Haiti*, p. 386.

antees of free expression and trial by jury, they could not be restrained through the Haitian courts, which would not convict an editor no matter how libelous his attacks on the authorities. The provost courts, unhampered by any bill of rights, could and did, but their jurisdiction was limited to incidents that could be construed as incitement to rebellion. Borno's gendarmerie sometimes held editors in "preventive arrest" without any trial at all, but that was embarrassing.[8]

It was decided therefore to amend Mr. Roosevelt's too liberal constitution in such a way as to permit the removal of judges, the restriction of the freedom of the press, and the denial of jury trial in press cases. Thirteen changes designed to strengthen the executive power were accepted by the council of state in October, 1927. Borno, simultaneously ruling that the people were still unfit to elect a legislature, submitted these complex questions to a plebescite, as the constitution required, and carried them by a vote of 177,436, to 3,799, amid taunts that "if people . . . are considered capable of voting on . . . amendments they cannot read, surely they are capable of choosing their representatives from men they can see and hear, and whose character they have known for years." At any rate, dictatorship had been made scrupulously constitutional.

Centralization of power in the hands of Russell and Borno, and close co-operation between them amounted to a "joint dictatorship." Unfortunately, it also made each partner liable for the debts of the other.[9] Borno could not hold the allegiance of Haitians hostile toward the occupation. Americans striving to serve Haiti without reference to politics lost their neutral character and found themselves identified with single faction, suspect to all articulate members of the community outside the government circle.

Dictatorship, whether practiced as military government or encouraged in Borno, was a strange method for teaching democ-

[8] See Davis, *Black Democracy*, pp. 255-263, and Millspaugh, *Haiti under American Control*, pp. 90, 113 f., for extensive discussions of this situation.

[9] Clarence Streit, "Haiti: Intervention in Operation," *Foreign Affairs*, VI (1928), 626.

racy. Actually, Americans had come to recognize that democracy could have no real existence in Haiti in the prevailing circumstances.[10] It might be retained as a theoretical goal in the distant future, but the immediate task was to push reconstruction by the most effective means at hand. Peace, internal improvements, and increased production would stimulate commerce and augment revenue, providing funds for further development, especially in education, until eventually the living standards and political understanding of the Haitian masses had been raised to a point that would permit the introduction of truly representative government.[11] Whether all that could be accomplished before the expiration of the treaty was a question that went unanswered. The acts and attitude of treaty officials gave the impression that they assumed the occupation would continue indefinitely.[12]

Prerequisite to reconstruction was the reorganization of Haitian finance, still in a state of confusion after seven years of American supervision.[13] Since the days of Theodore and Sam, a number of Haitians had been eager for a new loan to refund the old debts and develop the country. The first article of the treaty, requiring the United States to aid, by its good offices, the development of Haitian "agricultural, mineral, and commercial resources" and the establishment of Haitian finances "on a firm and solid basis" had originated with Borno, not in Washington or New York, and according to the "interpretive commentary" it meant an immediate loan.[14] In 1917 the life of the treaty was extended ten years, to 1936, in order "to offer

[10] *Report of the American High Commissioner, 1923*, p. 11.

[11] *Senate Report No. 794*, 67th Cong., 2d Sess., p. 24.

[12] *Report of the President's Commission* (1930), p. 8. In 1920 Admiral Knapp expressed the opinion that it would take "at least a generation to have in Haiti sufficient men of a high enough standard of ethics to provide personnel for an honest administration and a background of honest population for its support" (*Annual Report of the Secretary of the Navy, 1920*, p. 319).

[13] The debt service remained suspended until 1920, but all arrears of amortization and interest were then paid up (*Senate Report No. 797*, 67.2, p. 9).

[14] *Foreign Relations* (1915), p. 442; (1916), p. 322. Here "aid" evidently meant more than furnishing a general receiver, financial adviser, and engineers, already provided for in the American draft and in other articles of the treaty.

to the capitalists the serious guaranty which they claim of an uninterrupted stability" during the period of the projected loan,[15] but, largely on account of the exigencies of the war, none could be floated. In 1919, when the claims protocol required by the treaty was finally signed, it was agreed that for the funding of the obligations recognized by the claims commission, for refunding other debts, and for constructive expenditure Haiti should issue a thirty-year loan of forty million dollars, but the execution of that plan was blocked by controversies between Dartiguenave and McIlhenny, so that nothing was accomplished before 1922.

The trouble arose from problems connected with the reorganization of the Banque Nationale. In 1917 the National City Bank of New York had bought out other American interests, and in 1919, with the active encouragement of the State Department,[16] it obtained exclusive control by acquiring the rights of the Banque de l'Union Parisienne for some $1,400,000. After much controversy, in 1921 the Banque Nationale was rechartered as a Haitian corporation, and its concession was modified somewhat in favor of Haiti. Its commission for the treasury service was reduced from 1½ to 1 per cent, and profit on the subsidiary coinage was to be credited to the government. During the negotiations the State Department suggested that the bank be required to pay the government interest on its deposits, but the Haitians themselves surprisingly rejected that idea, inflicting upon their treasury the loss of some $80,000 a year.[17] In this application of "dollar diplomacy" the United States did not sacrifice Haiti to the National City Bank, but, on the contrary, secured for Haiti more favorable terms than had

[15] Article XVI allowed this if the purpose of the treaty had not been fully accomplished, but Haitian critics protested that extension within the first year of the treaty's life was premature. It was prerequisite to the admittedly essential loan, however.   [16] *Hearings*, pp. 105, 119.

[17] Paul H. Douglas in *Occupied Haiti* (ed. Emily Greene Balch), pp. 48 f. Their idea was that if no interest were required the money would have to be kept in Haiti, as in a safety deposit vault. As a result, the financial adviser had to transfer treasury reserves to New York to obtain interest, receiving none on current funds deposited in Haiti.

ever been enjoyed before, guarding Haitian interests against all save the Haitians themselves.[18]

As soon as Borno entered office the necessary legislation was enacted to put the protocol of 1919 into execution. On the basis of competitive bids a Series A 6 per cent loan of sixteen million dollars was awarded to the National City Company, which offered 92.137 and sold the bonds to the public at 96.50. Of the $15,039,945 thus realized, $4,129,701 and $2,160,857 went to the National Bank and National Railroad, respectively, in payment of claims (both being controlled by the lender); $6,037,650 went to refund the three French loans, which had been worth $21,470,618 at the 1915 rate of exchange; and $2,411,737 was applied to public works, $300,000 being retained for amortization.[19]

Meanwhile an issue of five million dollars in Series B bonds was authorized to refund the unpaid balance on previous internal loans and to fund a portion of the awards of the claims commission. The loan was floated by the National City Company on the same terms as Series A, except that the bonds were payable in Haiti and subject to Haitian income tax. Only the amount of $4,234,042 was actually issued, of which $1,883,262 was applied to the first purpose.[20] The commission's report was delayed until 1926, while it considered 73,269 claims, of

[18] A possible exception to this statement may be found in the effort of Mr. McIlhenny in 1920 to secure control of the import and export of foreign currency. Although it was plausibly argued that this was intended to place a wholesome curb on speculation, the Royal Bank of Canada and others contended that the real purpose was to give the National City Bank a monopoly of banking in Haiti. In any event the United States gave way on the question. See above, p. 231 n.

[19] Report of the Financial Adviser-General Receiver, 1923-1924, pp. 82 f. In 1922 McIlhenny was blamed for having "lost" a million dollars by not refunding before the franc had recovered from the war (Senate Report No. 794, 67.2, p. 9). Later he was criticized for not waiting for further depreciation of the franc, the critics enjoying the benefit of hindsight (Douglas, in Occupied Haiti, p. 42). They also neglected to consider the reasons for delay at first and for immediate action after 1922. As it was, the depreciation of the franc was a valuable windfall for Haiti. However, the holders of 50,506 bonds of 1910 held out for 26,934,000 gold francs—and are still holding out (Foreign Bondholders Protective Council, Annual Report, 1936, p. 572).

[20] Report of the Financial Adviser-General Receiver, 1923-1924, p. 84; 1926-1927, p. 92; 1927-1928, p. 105.

which those coming within its jurisdiction amounted to $29,-485,901. It allowed only $3,526,170, less than 12 per cent, payable one third in cash and two thirds in bonds.[21]   Thus nearly all outstanding claims against Haiti were settled and either paid out of Series A or refunded in Series B.

The problem of the interest guaranteed on the bonds of the unprofitable National and Plaine du Cul-de-Sac Railroads remained to be solved.   The National City Bank had loaned $500,000 directly to the National Railroad and by 1922 had acquired 70 per cent of the $3,544,582 in outstanding bonds by purchase from French holders below par even in depreciated francs.   The road per se was a poor investment, its average gross revenue from 1914 to 1922 being only $85,000, less than half the cost of operation, not counting interest and amortization charges amounting to $248,121 a year, but guaranteed by the government.   Yet despite this anemic condition, Roger L. Farnham, a vice-president of the National City Bank, was allowed a $24,000 salary as receiver and Sullivan & Cromwell, attorneys for the receivership, got $20,000 for their services, together more than half of the victim's gross income.[22]   In 1923, when the entire bond issue could have been bought up for $800,000, disposing of the whole problem, the financial adviser elected to pay the receiver $2,160,857 as arrears of interest out of the Series A loan.[23]   It has been estimated that

[21] As follows:

	Claims	Claimed	Allowed
American	157	$ 6,037,675.73	$ 455,729.90
Haitian	72,133	14,888,728.29	1,615,154.39
French	572	16,307,642.65	756,071.53
British	177	1,345,634.45	176,638.51
Italian	52	186,054.57	21,004.21
German	178	1,163,492.27	501,571.54
	73,269	$39,929,277.96	$3,526,170.08

The commission was limited to the period 1899-1916, and, consequently, $10,443,-326.91 of the total claimed above did not come within its jurisdiction (Howland, *Survey of American Foreign Relations, 1929*, p. 141). This table, found in *Report of the High Commissioner, 1926*, p. 8, is frequently cited without noting that fact.

[22] After reorganization Farnham continued to receive $18,000 a year as president, although he remained in New York and gave the road no more attention than an absentee landlord.

[23] Douglas, in *Occupied Haiti*, pp. 42-45.

the National City Bank or its clients made two million dollars profit through this payment and the appreciation of the bonds,[24] and, against the answer that it would have been unethical to avoid payment of interest by purchasing bonds depreciated by deliberate nonpayment of interest, it is argued that the concession was fraudulent in the first place. However, the 1910 contract seems to have been made in good faith, whatever the character of that of 1904. Moreover, it may be doubted whether the Series A loan could have been so successfully floated had not the National City Company been assured of getting a return on its railroad holdings thereby.

Past difficulties having been cleared up, an effort was made to free the Haitian treasury of this incubus by making the railroad amount to something more than a paper speculation profitable only to bankers. The bondholders gave up $600,000 of the accrued interest, which was to be spent on new construction in the hope of increasing operating revenue, and at the same time a majority of them exchanged their railroad securities for 75 per cent of their face value in Series C government bonds, the railroad assuming responsibility for interest and amortization charges whenever its net income would permit.[25] In practical effect this was the same as the former guarantee, but with the amount involved reduced, to the benefit of the Haitian treasury, and the discharge of the government's obligation made automatic instead of the subject of an annual wrangle. The new line into the Artibonite was opened late in 1925, but the railroad still failed to prosper because of the competition of busses on Haiti's thousand miles of new highway.[26]

The financial adviser's most bitter controversy concerned the government's guarantee of interest on the bonds of the Plaine du Cul-de-Sac Railroad, which was also operating at a loss. Together with the Port-au-Prince wharf, electric plant, and tramway, it belonged to the Haitian Corporation of America and

[24] Douglas, "The American Occupation of Haiti," *Political Science Quarterly*, XLII (1927), 230, 383.

[25] *Report of the Financial Adviser-General Receiver, 1923-1924*, p. 88.

[26] *Ibid.*, *1925-1926*, p. 95.

had come to be little more than a private line to that company's sugar plantations. The Plaine du Cul-de-Sac sought to compel the government to pay both interest and operating deficit, while after 1925-26 the financial adviser refused to pay any subsidy at all. Finally, in 1929, an agreement was reached whereby the railroad surrendered its claim to an annual subvention in return for the payment of a substantial sum.[27]

On January 1, 1924, the offices of financial adviser and general receiver were combined, and for the next ten years they were held in turn by W. W. Cumberland, former superintendent of customs in Peru (1924-1927); A. C. Millspaugh, former administrator general of Persian finances (1927-1929); and S. de la Rue, former financial adviser of Liberia (1929-1933). The first two followed a policy of reducing the debt more rapidly than the amortization schedules required, so that in 1928 it appeared possible that it might be entirely liquidated by 1943 instead of 1953. At the same time they built up a cash reserve of four million dollars, partly because, with revenues unprecedentedly large, debt reduction had to be curtailed, since Haitian bonds were selling above par.[28] Here was something new indeed in Haitian finance! In 1928 Millspaugh guardedly suggested that it might be better to spend surplus funds on internal development rather than on amortization in excess of contractual obligations, and in 1930 his successor, de la Rue, definitely adopted that policy. During six years the public debt of Haiti had been reduced from $24,210,000 to $16,541,000 or a net debt of $12,565,000 if the cash reserve were deducted.[29]

Other financial measures had to do with the reform of Haiti's lopsided tax structure. Ninety per cent of the national income was derived from an antiquated tariff which bore heavily

[27] Millspaugh, *Haiti under American Control*, pp. 133 f. A heated controversy over wharfage was also involved in this.
[28] *Report of the Financial Adviser-General Receiver, 1927-1928*, p. 105-109. Cumberland had justified the maintenance of a large reserve by showing that Haiti could not borrow without unreeling much red tape, and that Haitian income was subject to serious fluctuations, since it was derived largely from the customs, and trade depended on one crop. However, he had considered $1,400,000 to be ample (*ibid.*, *1923-1924*, pp. 70, 78; *1924-1925*, p. 80).
[29] Millspaugh, *Haiti under American Control*, p. 125.

on necessities, lightly on luxuries, favoring the *élite* at the expense of the peasants, and which laid heavy duties on exports, discouraging industry and doubly burdening the peasants. However, because of the dependence of the government upon that single source, it was felt that revision could not be attempted until an internal revenue had been developed. After years of discussion, a project to create an internal revenue service under the administration of the general receiver of customs was passed in 1924, the financial adviser having consented to an increase in the salaries of councillors of state. No new taxes were imposed until 1928, but administrative improvement resulted in increasing the yield of the old taxes from $379,434 in 1921 to $830,658 in 1927.[30] On the strength of that a new tariff was put into effect in 1926.[31] It did not eliminate the export duties, but new excise taxes were levied on alcoholic beverages and manufactured tobacco in 1928, with the proviso that export duties might be lowered in proportion to their yield. Despite difficulties in enforcement, they produced half a million dollars, and the duties on coffee were reduced accordingly.[32] Recourse to a land tax was also discussed, in the hope of stimulating production by bringing neglected acreage into use, but the idea had to be abandoned on account of the ignorance of the peasants and the prevailing confusion as to surveys and titles.[33]

Technical details of accounting and budgetary procedure were improved after 1923, and commendable economy was practiced in the financial administration.[34] Above all, the task was performed with absolute honesty. Critics of the regime would

[30] *Report of the Financial Adviser-General Receiver, 1923-1924*, p. 51; *1927-1928*, p. 55.

[31] *Ibid., 1925-1926*, p. 31. It established higher duties on luxuries as compared to necessities, and placed protective duties on articles that could be produced in Haiti, but were not. In 1928 and 1929 certain exemptions were granted to encourage education and agriculture.

[32] *Report of the Financial Adviser-General Receiver, 1927-1928*, pp. 57, 67; *1928-1929*, p. 55.

[33] *Report of the High Commissioner, 1929*, p. 19.

[34] Out of savings in funds allotted to administration means were found for much new construction, including a modern building for the ministry of finance, which must otherwise have come out of the general budget or not have been built at all. Repair and maintenance was also provided.

have been delighted to discover a good, resounding scandal, and many of them, recalling Teapot Dome as well as *L'affaire de la consolidation*, were prone to assume that there must be one hidden somewhere, but, despite charges hurled on mere suspicion, the financial administration's record was clear.[35]

The Gendarmerie, the Direction Générale des Travaux Publiques, and the Service National d'Hygiène made steady progress under the high commissioner. The Gendarmerie, known after 1928 as the Garde d'Haiti, numbered three thousand men at that date and accounted for 15 per cent of the budget. Its functions included urban and rural police, prison administration, fire protection and the coast guard, and its officers served as financial advisers (supervisors) to communal governments.[36] The public works administration, dispensing 16 per cent of the budget, constructed and maintained highways, trails, and communication systems, erected numerous public buildings, improved streets and parks, built wharves and lighthouses, renovated municipal water works, repaired ancient irrigation systems, and made various surveys. The influence of its labors may be illustrated by such facts as an increase in the number of telephone subscribers at Port-au-Prince from 450 in 1924 to 1,200 in 1929, while the number of automobiles in Haiti increased from virtually none in 1915 to three thousand in 1929, including commercial trucks and passenger busses.[37] The work of the public health service, with only 9 per cent of the budget at its disposal, was the most generally appreciated of all American activities. It found an appalling proportion of the Haitian people debilitated by yaws and syphilis, malaria, hookworm, and malnutrition.[38] Aided by the Rockefeller Foundation,[39] it established

[35] *Report of the President's Commission* (1930), p. 12.
[36] Millspaugh, *Haiti under American Control*, p. 112.
[37] *Ibid.*, pp. 158-160. In *The Nation*, in March, 1927, Prof. Rayford Logan undertook to "debunk" the pretensions of the public works administration, especially as to the roads. These were admittedly of hasty, low-cost construction, not to be compared with primary routes in the States, but, considering the condition of Haitian "roads" in 1915, physical handicaps, and financial limitations, they marked a creditable achievement.
[38] *Report of the High Commissioner, 1927*, Appendix IV, p. 47; Kent C. Melhorn, *Health of Haiti*, p. 59.
[39] The Foundation conducted a medical survey of Haiti in 1924-1925, and in

twelve modern hospitals, with a total admission of more than 10,000, and 147 rural clinics, where 1,341,596 treatments were given in the fiscal year 1929.[40] The public health service also examined and vaccinated school children, distributed quinine, drained swamps, watched over water supplies, attended to street cleaning and garbage disposal, improved markets and slaughter houses, constructed public and private latrines, and carried on a general campaign of sanitation. Its work was handicapped by illiteracy, superstition, and apathy, but its magic was even more impressive than that of the *hougans*, and it also introduced to the masses the novel idea that the government might be the servant rather than the master of the people.

From the first, it was understood that the treatment of Haiti's disease, as distinguished from the treatment of its symptoms, would not have begun until means were found to increase production, exports, national wealth, and revenues, creating employment, raising living standards, and providing funds for education and further development. In 1913 the value of Haitian exports, as compared to those of Antillean areas under American influence, had been as follows:

	Total[41]	Per capita
Cuba	$165,207,000	$63.54
Puerto Rico	48,597,000	40.50
Dominican Republic	10,470,000	15.00
Haiti	11,316,000	5.66

The economy indicated by those figures left many Haitians unable to maintain themselves, even according to the prevailing low standards, and the activities of the Service d'Hygiène were calculated to increase the overpopulation unless new sources of employment were developed. Seasonal migration to Cuba and the Dominican Republic had afforded some relief, for even those who returned to Haiti had enjoyed a wage-scale five times

1926 it provided funds to equip a medical school and to enable Haitians to pursue postgraduate studies in France, Canada, the United States, and Puerto Rico.

[40] Melhorn, *Health of Haiti*, pp. 10, 17. There were four other hospitals, two pertaining to the Garde d'Haiti, one to the marine brigade, and one civilian.

[41] *Statistical Abstract* (1922), p. 730.

that at home, and, furthermore, it is estimated that there had been a net loss of fifty thousand emigrants in the decade from 1912 to 1921.[42]

Since the emigrants were seeking employment on the American sugar plantations in the neighboring republics, one solution for the problem seemed to be to bring American plantations to Haiti.[43] When Borno inserted Article I into the treaty, it was evidently his purpose to engage the United States to encourage the investment of American capital in Haitian "agricultural, mineral, and commercial" activity as well as in financial reorganization, and the amendment of the constitutional provision regarding alien ownership of real estate was clearly directed toward the same end.

Results, however, were meager. The only new capital to enter Haiti before 1923 was sunk in an ambitious, but unsuccessful, project to raise castor beans for aviation purposes and later to cultivate long-staple cotton. In 1923 the Haitian-American Corporation, established before the intervention, reorganized as the Haitian Corporation of America, with $3,000,000 capital. Its properties included the Compagnie d'éclairage électrique, lighting both Port-au-Prince and Cap Haitien, the Compagnie haitienne du wharf de Port-au-Prince, the Plaine du Cul-de-Sac Railroad, and the Haitian-American Sugar Company. Operating without benefit of agricultural concession, enjoying the enmity rather than the favor of the government and the financial adviser, by 1930 it had acquired 24,000 acres, half of the total controlled by Americans, and

[42] Douglas, in *Occupied Haiti*, p. 77.

[43] It was recognized that the solution must be agricultural. A geological survey had revealed that the mineral resources of Haiti were negligible, except for the abandoned copper mines of Terre Neuve, reopened by the Haiti Mines Corporation of New York, which issued $3,500,000 in first mortgage bonds. The dyewood problem was one of reforestation rather than exploitation, although the Logwood Manufacturing Corporation and the American Dyewood Company continued their activity. Manufacturing offered little promise, despite the growth of local industries behind a protective tariff. (American capital was invested in the Société commerciale d'Haiti at St. Marc and the Usine de manteque de Port-au-Prince, makers and exporters of cotton-seed cake.) Fisheries were neglected. Efforts to promote tourism produced no significant results.

was giving employment to a thousand Haitians in its fields and sugar mill alone. Its assets were valued at $10,896,000; its bonded indebtedness, at $2,996,531. In 1923 also the Haitian Pineapple Company was launched by the California Packing Corporation, with 1,000 acres and plans for a million-dollar investment, including a cannery. By 1926 the United West Indies Company and the North Haiti Sugar Company had entered that field with relatively small investments. In 1927 the Haitian Agricultural Corporation and the Haitian-American Development Corporation leased limited areas of public land for the cultivation of sisal. The 14,000 acres obtained by the latter had been unproductive for a century, but in 1930 a thousand peasants had found employment there.[44]

The fears of those who had supposed that the removal of constitutional barriers would result in the expropriation of the native farmer had not been realized, for the hitherto idle lands being brought under cultivation by American enterprise constituted less than one per cent of Haiti.[45] Alas, by the same token only some 2 per cent of Haiti's agricultural exports in 1930 were produced on plantations[46]—hopes as well as fears were left unrealized. Although American direct investments had increased from four million dollars in 1913 to fourteen million in 1930, American capital entering the Antilles still found neighboring countries more attractive than Haiti.[47] According to the financial adviser, there was no hope of substantial

[44] Robert W. Dunn, *American Foreign Investments*, p. 135; Max Winkler, *Investments of United States Capital in Latin America*, pp. 214-216; Millspaugh, *Haiti under American Control*, p. 152 f.

[45] Douglas, in *Occupied Haiti*, p. 74. Of the 50,000 acres under American control, only 13,000 were owned outright, the rest being leased (Millspaugh, *loc. cit.*).

[46] Millspaugh, *op. cit.*, p. 154.

[47] The figures in 1930 were: Cuba, $1,989,957,000; Dominican Republic, $69,322,000; Jamaica, $21,941,000; Haiti, $14,191,000 (U. S. Department of Commerce, Trade Information Bulletin No. 731, pp. 18 ff.). The total American investment in Haiti—$30,743,000—was only one-half of one per cent of that in Latin America as a whole. Cf. Mexico, 28 per cent; Cuba, 27 per cent; Argentina, 11 per cent; Brazil, 8.5 per cent; Chile, 7 per cent; and Panama, 0.65 per cent; Dominican Republic, 0.43 per cent; Nicaragua, 0.43 per cent (Winkler, *Investments in Latin America*, pp. 278, 284). These figures, and those for 1913 (p. 275) reveal the absence of any significant relationship between investment and intervention, either as a cause or effect.

progress until there was greater confidence in Haitian courts and less uncertainty regarding titles.[48]

During this period Haitian foreign commerce did increase, but not enough to constitute a fundamental development. Haiti still depended on a single crop and a single market, though perhaps to a slightly less degree.[49] Beginning at $6,590,000 in the depression year 1920-1921, the value of exports rose to $22,667,000 in 1927-1928, but even so the per capita foreign commerce of the Dominican Republic, Puerto Rico, and Cuba was three, eight, and nine times that of Haiti, respectively, and their trade was growing more rapidly.[50]

If plantation agriculture, sustained by foreign capital, skilled management, technical methods, and efficient marketing was not to be the answer to the problem, then the only hope lay in the development of an industrious peasantry trained in more effective methods of small-scale farming. Many, fearing that the plantation system would create a rural proletariat, preferred the latter course. They cited the fact that sugar plantations operated by American corporations had not produced any substantial improvement in the lot of the Cuban and Puerto Rican

[48] *Report of the Financial Adviser-General Receiver, 1925-1926*, p. 100; *1926-1927*, p. 108; *1929-1930*, p. 81. Some 3,700,000 acres, nearly half the country, were public domain, and much of the remainder consisted of the plantations abandoned by the forefathers of the *élite*. Most of this land had reverted to bush. Most of the peasants, descendants of former sharecroppers, were simply squatters, cultivating small garden patches and gathering wild coffee. Everywhere titles and boundaries were uncertain. While it was recognized that this chaos must be reduced to order, for the protection of peasants as well as of foreign investors, it proved impossible to reach agreement on any project of law.

[49] In 1918 the United States took 81 per cent of Haitian exports (France 0.5 per cent), but by 1924 the American share had reverted to a prewar 9 per cent and France was taking 66 per cent as of yore. France bought 80 per cent of the coffee crop that year, 60 per cent in 1929. Haitian imports from the United States also declined from 93 per cent in 1919 to a normal 70 per cent in 1929 (*Report of the Financial Adviser-General Receiver, 1928-1929*, pp. 5, 173; Trade Information Bulletin No. 264, pp. 7 f.).

[50] *Report of the High Commissioner, 1928*, p. 33. The commerce of Haiti and her neighbors may be compared as follows in Winkler, *Investments in Latin America*, p. 277. (Figures in millions.)

Total Commerce	1913	1927	Increase Per Cent	Trade with United States 1913	1927	Increase Per Cent
Cuba	$304.2	$580.0	92	$206.5	$414.2	103
Haiti	19.4	31.0	60	6.9	12.3	78
D. R.	19.7	59.0	199	11.5	28.5	148

agricultural workers.[51]   In the Dominican Republic, where ten times the Haitian acreage had been brought under the plantation system and the sugar crop was worth as much as the entire annual export of Haiti, a favorable balance of trade was a mockery, being counterbalanced by the outward flow of interest payments, dividends, salaries to American employees, and the like, while native labor received starvation wages.[52]   In Haiti the American regime had striven to promote both types of agriculture, but the failure of the plantation system made the future wholly dependent on the success of its efforts with the peasants.

The attempt to develop a self-reliant yeomanry, the traditional mainstay of any commonwealth, became the responsibility of the Service Technique de l'Agriculture et de l'Enseignement Professionnel, a new treaty service organized in 1924 as a bureau in the Ministry of Agriculture.   Its functions were to provide "higher agricultural education for the training of experts, research workers, teachers of farm schools, and farm advisers; rural farm schools . . . ; advice to adult farmers . . . ; direct aid . . . through animal clinics and demonstrations . . . ; experiments in all phases of agricultural activity; . . . and vocational industrial education."[53]   While seeking to improve the cultivation of coffee, the Service Technique made strenuous efforts to persuade the peasants to diversify their crops.[54]   It sought to stimulate and instruct adult farmers through fairs, bonuses, demonstration farms, and visits from agents similar to the county agent familiar in the States.[55]   Future farmers were

[51] Buell, *American Occupation*, p. 330. See Jones, *The Caribbean since 1900*, pp. 186-192, for an account of the situation in Puerto Rico.

[52] Knight, *The Americans in Santo Domingo*, pp. 139 ff.

[53] *Report of the High Commissioner, 1924*, p. 32.

[54] It set up a coffee experiment station and ten demonstration farms, procured the planting of two million new trees by offering a bonus, and obtained the enactment of a standardization law in 1929. Despite the emphasis on diversification and the plantation production of sugar and hemp, the proportion of coffee in Haitian exports increased from 61 per cent in 1916-1921 to 75 per cent in 1921-1926 and 79 per cent in 1927-1928, but the peasants were exporting some corn and had increased their production of tobacco to the point of satisfying the domestic demand (*Reports of the High Commissioner and of the Financial Adviser-General Receiver*).

[55] In 1927 thirteen agents made four thousand visits (*Report of the High Commissioner, 1927*, pp. 20, 55). After a disastrous hurricane in 1928 the Service Tech-

reached through seventy rural schools, and ten industrial schools were also established for the benefit of the same class in the towns.[56]

It was necessary to build from the ground up, for the native regime had never provided schools worthy of the name for these people, and it speedily became apparent that with severely limited funds it would be impossible to reach them all before 1936.[57] All that could be hoped for was to begin the development of a middle class of progressive farmers and artisans between the peasants and the *élite*, and to train native teachers and agents to carry on the work after American direction had been withdrawn. A central school of agriculture was established at Damien for the latter purpose, but a significant difficulty immediately appeared. Until the new rural schools had prepared country boys for an agricultural high school established in 1929 and it had prepared a class for Damien, the École Centrale must depend for students upon the graduates of the classical *lycées*, sons of the urban *élite*, who detested manual labor and rural life, many of them coming to Damien only for the sake of the scholarship offered and with dubious intent to devote their lives to the service of the masses. Even when students of peasant stock became available, the result would be doubtful, for the natural tendency of an educated country boy would be to go to town and try to establish himself among the *élite*.

The program of the Service Technique, and especially its educational efforts, corresponded with the recommendations of innumerable Haitian publicists,[58] yet no phase of American activity in Haiti received such bitter condemnation from the *élite*. There were several reasons for this paradox. First, it was

---

nique also carried out a resettlement project involving three thousand families (*ibid.*, *1929*, p. 80).

[56] In addition to technical instruction, these schools gave basic courses of a general nature (*ibid.*, *1925*, p. 41).

[57] In 1930 the enrollment in Service Technique schools was only 9,349, out of an estimated school-age population of four hundred thousand.

[58] See particularly Joseph Justin, *Étude sur les institutions haitiennes* and *Les réformes nécessaires*; Bellegarde, *Pour une Haiti heureuse*, I, 100 ff.

an encroachment, for even a committee of United States senators favorable to intervention had admitted that no express warrant for it could be found in the treaty.[59] Moreover, the *élite* perceived that in the future a substantial yeomanry would be less easy to exploit than had been an ignorant peasantry in the past,[60] while for the present they feared, with reason, that the masses might become more loyal to their American benefactors than to their unsympathetic former masters, strengthening the treaty regime and leaving the opposition suspended in mid-air.[61] Any Haitian Liberty Leaguer could see that the peasants would hardly choose to "shoot Santa Claus." Finally, the American invasion of the educational field, one of the few functions left to the native government under the treaty, precipitated a conflict paling the differences of opinion between Burghardt DuBois and Booker T. Washington.[62] Vocational education, the need for which had long been recognized in theory, if not in practice, became identified with alien domination.[63] To Haitian

[59] *Senate Report No. 794*, 67th Cong., 2d Sess., p. 24. Later, authority to appoint an "agricultural engineer" was read into Article XIII, the authors of which seem to have contemplated the "development of natural resources" through the building of roads, irrigation systems, and other public works only. Direct agricultural instruction depended more particularly on Article I, which had not been in the American draft but had been inserted by Borno for the very different purpose of facilitating the investment of American capital in plantations.

[60] In "Education in Haiti," *Journal of Negro History*, XV (1930), 410-419, Prof. Rayford Logan brings out the interesting point that although Haitian intellectuals had been able to conceive of an ideal educational system, various rulers had deliberately sabotaged their efforts in order to keep the masses ignorant and submissive, citing Thomas Madiou (*Histoire d'Haiti*, III, 262), Mark Baker Bird (*The Black Man*, p. 144), and others to that effect.

[61] Dr. Price-Mars, recognizing the part of the *élite* in creating existing class antagonism, urged them to combat this menace by revealing a sense of social responsibility in themselves, striving to relieve the masses of poverty and ignorance in order to establish social solidarity as a defense against alien domination (*La vocation de l'élite*, pp. 51 ff.).

[62] In the first flush of freedom many American negroes preferred to emphasize liberal studies, disdaining vocational education as somehow associated with a servile status. Others, taking a realistic view of the situation, recognized that vocational training could better serve the actual needs of the greater number of their people. It took these Americans a generation to perceive that the two systems might complement rather than conflict with each other.

[63] In the opinion of eminent authority the treaty officials had correctly analyzed pressing needs, but had erred in permitting the rise of two distinct and rival school systems (*Report of the United States Commission on Education in Haiti*, by Dr. Moton and others, p. 59). The Americans could not claim control over all schools

alarmists, the Service Technique was not only mobilizing the masses against the classes, intensifying the deplorable divisions of Haitian society, but it was also seeking to capture the minds of the Haitian youth, robbing Haiti of her soul.[64]

There could be no severer critics of the Haitian educational system than the successive ministers of public instruction themselves.[65] Of 350,000 school-age children in 1905, only 30,000 were in any kind of school, and more than a third of them were being taught by the church.[66] Rural education was virtually nonexistent except as an item in the budget and a convenient system of petty patronage. All teachers were ill-paid, but some were actually illiterate. The urban *lycées*, comparable in curriculum to the classical academies of the ante-bellum South, were more respectable, but their methods of instruction were not intellectually stimulating,[67] and those of their graduates who showed literary merit owed it to native ability rather than to the character of their training. Every effort to establish vocational schools had failed. Educational opportunity beyond the high-school level was confined to schools of law and medicine, "limited in scope and inadequate as to standards."[68] Such talented ministers of public instruction as Dantès Bellegarde might draw up impressive plans, but they could not overcome apathy, lack of funds, and the vicious influence of the spoils system.[69]

----

and, in view of the Haitian record in rural education and attitude toward vocational training, they were unwilling to leave what they considered to be a vital program to Haitian direction—hence the division instead of sympathetic co-operation.

[64] The Service Technique would answer that it was trying to bridge the gap, not to widen it, and that as for the Haitian soul, the Haitian youth needed nothing so much as reorientation, the graduates of the *lycées* having very nearly destroyed Haiti's individual existence, which could be saved only by men trained in the vocational schools.

[65] See almost any *Exposé général*, or Logan, "Education in Haiti," pp. 410 f.

[66] *Exposé général, 1905*, p. 82.

[67] According to Price-Mars (*La vocation de l'élite*, pp. 68 ff.), the object was to engrave as many *connaissances* as possible on the mind of the child without regard to whether they were assimilated, or in keeping with the needs of Haitian society, or of value in developing character and a sense of responsibility. Recitation exercised memory at the expense of other faculties, with a resulting "verbomania" and loss of realism.

[68] *Report of the Commission on Education in Haiti*, p. 53.

[69] As minister to Nord Alexis, Bellegarde proposed to raise salaries, procure better teachers, and promote rural, vocational, normal, and girls' schools, but he

American writers have united in criticizing Lansing for "forgetting" to include education in the treaty, not caring to recognize, perhaps, that in 1915 no one yet contemplated so thorough an intervention in Haitian domestic affairs as was in progress a decade later. The State Department took no active part in the matter until 1921, although American officials in Haiti had previously interested themselves in educational questions. In 1918 Bellegarde entered Dartiguenave's cabinet and renewed his efforts to improve the Haitian school system, but the financial adviser, McIlhenny, impressed by the politics-ridden character of the system as it then stood, refused to sanction increased appropriations for salaries and normal schools unless American inspectors were appointed.[70] To the Haitians, who refused his terms, it appeared that he was preventing the correction of the very abuses of which he complained, using them as an excuse for a new encroachment, but the fact that he did approve grants to support normal courses at church schools shows that his only concern was to guard against misapplication of educational funds in the traditional Haitian manner. In 1920 an American adviser in the Ministry of Public Instruction,[71] convinced that the majority of Haitian teachers were ignorant spoilsmen, insisted that their number be reduced from thirteen hundred to four hundred and that American inspectors be appointed, whereupon his resignation was demanded and received.[72] At this point the State Department, prompted by the marines, proposed the appointment of an educational adviser with the status of a treaty official, an idea which Dartiguenave

was overthrown by palace intrigue before aught was accomplished (Bellegarde, *Pour une Haiti heureuse*, I, 100 f.). He was also a member of the Oreste administration, which, in its short life, succeeded in building up a considerable fund for education, only to see it squandered by Zamor for "military expenses."

[70] *Ibid.*, II, 74, 178, 181, 188, 201, 204, 208, 212, 219; Logan, "Education in Haiti," pp. 453-455.

[71] He was a Mr. Bourgeois, French-speaking county school superintendent from Louisiana, appointed by Dartiguenave in 1917. In June of that year Dartiguenave had promised the officials of the occupation that he would employ American advisers in the departments of agriculture and public instruction if he were permitted to rule with a council of state instead of an elected legislature (*Hearings*, pp. 699, 1349).

[72] Bellegarde, *op. cit.*, p. 239.

rejected.[73]   Even Borno refused to surrender the established school system when consenting to the creation of the Service Technique.[74]

Thus distinct and rival systems came into being, but the Americans, who held the purse-strings, continued to believe that funds granted to the native school administration would be misspent, and, consequently, it was their policy to "absorb" Haitian-directed schools as rapidly as those of the Service Technique could be developed, holding appropriations for the one at a minimum while constantly increasing those for the other.[75]   In 1928-1929, when $977,252 was spent on education, 58 per cent of that sum was allotted to vocational schools.[76]   While undoubtedly a much greater proportion of Haitian children had more need for vocational than for academic instruction, it was an awkward fact that at that time there were nearly nine times as many pupils in the poverty-stricken Haitian system.[77]   Although the number of its students had increased 42 per cent since 1925, its income had actually decreased 11 per cent since 1924.[78]   In the circumstances Haitian-directed education could not be expected to improve, and the *élite* were bound to regard the Service Technique with jealousy and resentment.

[73] *Hearings*, pp. 86, 1349, 1351, 1477; *Documents diplomatiques* (1921), pp. 233-237.

[74] In 1918 a Haitian project for agricultural schools (under Haitian control) was opposed by the marines and failed to receive the approval of the legation (*Documents diplomatiques*, p. 84).   According to Bellegarde, the purpose of the Americans was to stifle Haitian initiative and claim all the credit for themselves (Bellegarde, *Pour une Haiti heureuse*, II, 242), but it seems evident that the reason was the same as that for McIlhenny's refusal to provide funds for normal schools under Haitian direction.

[75] An example of this tendency may be found in the case of the medical school. Evicted from its quarters to make room for a nurses' school under Red Cross auspices, it struggled along with meager appropriations until taken over by the Service d'Hygiène in 1926, after which it became relatively prosperous under American direction (Bellegarde, *Pour une Haiti heureuse*, II, 215; Logan, "Education in Haiti," p. 450).

[76] *Report of the Financial Adviser-General Receiver, 1928-1929*, pp. 80, 84.   In 1929-1930 the Service Technique administered 65 per cent of the educational budget (*Report of the Commission on Education in Haiti*, p. 73).

[77] This meant an expenditure of approximately $50.00 per capita in the American-directed schools and $4.50 in the Haitian.   Of the four hundred thousand children of school age, three fourths were not in either system.

[78] Logan, "Education in Haiti," p. 442; Millspaugh, *Haiti under American Control*, p. 164 n.

The vast majority of Haitians, for whose benefit the program of reconstruction was designed, were peasants hardly able to comprehend it. That primitive mass could not be transformed in eight short years. To the articulate minority, the *élite*, the intervention brought only discontent. Close control over government funds and their expenditure for constructive enterprises rather than for the maintenance of a ruling class deprived them of their accustomed means of livelihood and caused genuine distress. The development of commerce afforded them no relief, since it was largely in foreign hands, and temperament and tradition forbade their participation in new productive enterprises. Apart from financial considerations, exclusion from office wounded their pride and racial sensitiveness, while the presence of foreign white troops in the Caserne Dessalines was a constant reproach.

An eloquent spokesman of this class was Dantès Bellegarde, whose personal experiences in the Ministry of Public Instruction had increased his bitterness. To him the intervention launched in 1915 to assist in the development of a strong and self-reliant Haitian state had for its evident purpose the destruction and absorption of the moral and economic forces of his country.[79] His people had been seduced by promises of peace and prosperity, but submission to dictatorship brought no real peace. For fourteen years nothing had been done to establish a government truly stable because firmly rooted in popular consent. The Americans had not even made Haiti prosperous. Then Bellegarde reached the heart of the matter: "*Exportation n'a pas augmenté; mais les expertes américaines sont importés en nombre de plus en plus considérable.*" The civil service was being overrun by Americans,[80] many of whom looked like spoilsmen rather than experts to Bellegarde. The more numerous they became, the more difficult it would be ever to get rid of

[79] In Bellegarde's opinion the intervention had been undertaken, without legal or moral pretext, in the interest of American bankers. The argument here presented in brief is taken from *L'occupation américaine d'Haiti.*

[80] By 1929 the percentage of Americans in the Haitian civil service had decreased, but their actual number had increased. This was a result of expansion in the treaty services, with the appointment of Haitians to subordinate positions (Millspaugh, *Haiti under American Control,* pp. 172 f.).

them. They were more to be feared than marines, for they advanced inperceptibly toward the permanent subjugation of Haiti through the inherent tendency of bureaucracies to expand and perpetuate themselves. Inspired by color prejudice, they assumed the intellectual and moral inferiority of all Haitians, refusing to allow them to handle their own money,[81] although the record of graft and corruption in the United States did not encourage blind confidence in the integrity of American office-holders. They prepared Haitians for subordinate positions only, with the object of depriving the nation of initiative and dignity. They, of all people, dismissed every protesting Haitian as a disappointed office-seeker, when it was patent that the treaty regime existed primarily to make jobs for them.

Had Bellegarde been familiar with Southern history he might have referred to the treaty officials and their native allies as "carpetbaggers" and "scalawags." That analogy, like any other, requires qualification, but it goes far toward explaining the attitude of the *élite*. The differences between the situation of the occupied South in 1867-1870 and that of occupied Haiti are too obvious to require elaboration. Moreover, the scandals which attended Southern reconstruction found no parallel in Haiti. Whether or not they were guilty of occasional errors in judgment, the personal integrity of the treaty officials is established beyond cavil. Although American methods of teaching democracy, 1915-1930, may have been peculiar, at least no one thought of electing a legislature composed of peasants and agents of the Service Technique, the *élite* being specifically excluded. However, there were certain resemblances. The marines were there to impose the will of Washington regarding the reconstruction of the state. Even though they might be free of the characteristics that gave the name of "carpetbagger" its sinister connotation, the treaty officials were nevertheless outlanders who had come to thrust the native ruling class aside and reorganize the community in the interest of hitherto exploited agricultural

---

[81] In 1929 the debt service absorbed 24.5 per cent of the budget; the American-directed departments, 58.7 per cent; the Haitian-directed departments, 16.8 per cent (*ibid.*, p. 174). The Haitian departments were subject to the financial adviser's budget control and pre-audit.

labor. The natives who forfeited the respect of their caste in order to co-operate did so from patriotic motives, according to Washington, "for pelf," according to the *élite*. The former rulers, unable to oppose force to force, were none the less determined to regain control. A true and lasting solution of Haitian problems could not be imposed from without, said Bellegarde. That could come only through the efforts of the Haitians themselves.[82] And in time Americans began to tire of the endless reconstruction of Haiti, as before the North had wearied of the eternal Southern problem.

[82] *Pour une Haiti heureuse*, II, 3; *L'occupation américaine d'Haiti*, p. 11.

CHAPTER XV

HAITIANIZATION

*Your commission [recommends] that the President declare that the
United States will approve a policy . . . providing for an increasingly
rapid Haitianization of the services, with the object of having Haitians
experienced in every department of the Government ready to take over
full responsibility at the expiration of the existing treaty.*
—THE PRESIDENT'S COMMISSION, March 26, 1930

T HE EXCITEMENT attendant upon Louis Borno's re-election in
1926 led to a revival of agitation on the Haitian question in
the States. An investigating committee, organized by the
Women's International League for Peace and Freedom, stated
its point of view:

The most disconcerting aspect of the whole affair is that it is
possible to do what has been done in Haiti, directly contrary as it is
to all our principles and professions, without its ever being proposed
or debated beforehand, and with so little realization in the United
States that it had been done.

They found the problem

to consist not in individual instances of misused power, but in the fact
of the armed occupation of the country. Any good done by high-
minded officials does not touch this bottom fact, and by men's reaction to this fact will their opinions as to Haiti be shaped.

Their own reaction was to recommend progressive steps toward
restoring the country to its natives, especially the election of a
legislature.[1]

During the next three years many voices were raised in
criticism and defense. It was asserted that the intervention had
drifted from its charted course; that to build on a scale that

---

[1] Emily Green Balch and others, *Occupied Haiti*. Besides contributing to that
report, one member of the committee, Professor Paul H. Douglas, surveyed the subject in "The American Occupation of Haiti," *Political Science Quarterly*, XLII
(1927), 228-258, 368-396.

would require generations for success was to invite disaster in 1936; that present policy prepared the *élite* for subordinate roles only and threatened to transform the peasants into a landless proletariat.[2] Even a representative of the new plantation interest questioned the wisdom of military control over civil affairs and of excluding qualified natives from responsible office.[3] The high commissioner's defense consisted in part of the *argumentum ad hominem* that the critics of the regime were either Haitian politicians deprived of spoils, or American businessmen foiled in their designs to exploit the peasants, or sentimentalists with no conception of the practical difficulties of the situation.[4] He was supported by at least one scholarly observer, who held that the true story of the intervention bore little resemblance to the superficial accounts of noisy agitators, and that a premature withdrawal would sacrifice all that had been thus far accomplished.[5] A highly qualified critic, pointing out that the task undertaken could not possibly be completed within the duration of the present treaty, suggested that Haiti be persuaded to accept *civilian* tutelage extending beyond 1936.[6]

By 1929 interest had been aroused to such an extent that both the critical Foreign Policy Association and the more conservative Council on Foreign Relations deemed it timely to publish surveys of the Haitian situation.[7] The same rising tide floated a new series of romantic works on Haiti which, while they contributed little to the current discussion, did serve to attract further interest.[8] However, the efforts of Senator King to bring the occupation to an end by congressional action in

---

[2] Streit, "Haiti: Intervention in Operation," *Foreign Affairs*, VI (1928), 615-632.

[3] Davis, *Black Democracy*, pp. 270 f., 288 f.

[4] Buell, *The American Occupation of Haiti*, p. 391.

[5] Charles E. Chapman, "The Development of the Intervention in Haiti," *Hispanic American Historical Reveiw*, VII (1927), 299-319.

[6] Millspaugh, "Our Haitian Problem," *Foreign Affairs*, VII (1929), 556-670; "Haiti under American Control," *Current History*, XXXI (1930), 919-926. Dr. Millspaugh had resigned the financial receivership after a conflict of jurisdiction with General Russell.

[7] Buell, *The American Occupation of Haiti*; Howland, *Survey of American Foreign Relations, 1929.*

[8] Niles, *Black Haiti*; Vandercook, *Black Majesty*; and Seabrook, *The Magic Island.*

1926, 1928, and 1929 were summarily defeated.[9] With immediate withdrawal eliminated from consideration, the remaining alternatives were: (1) a continuation of present policies in order to accomplish the maximum material progress in the next few years, at the risk of the collapse of the highly technical system when American direction was suddenly withdrawn in 1936; (2) a gradual tapering off of American control with the progressive Haitianization of the treaty services, even at the cost of reduced efficiency; (3) a decision to retain control indefinitely until Americans were satisfied that a new generation of Haitians were prepared to run their country as Americans thought it should be run.

The answer to the Haitian question depended less on Haitian factors than on the American attitude toward Caribbean interventions in general. That issue was being extensively debated by 1928,[10] for while President Coolidge was resolutely "following the path of his predecessors," the considerations that had shaped their policy no longer applied. The strategic insecurity felt by Roosevelt, Taft, and Wilson had given way to confidence as the sixth-place fleet of 1903[11] had grown into one that no navy afloat could venture to challenge in the Caribbean.[12] The termination of the war, instead of releasing the victors to try their strength in overseas adventures, had left them shaken and more deeply entangled in European affairs

[9] *Congressional Record*, LVII, 4082; LXIX, 7047; LXXI, 107. President Borno refused to permit Senator King to enter Haiti on the ground that he had made "a false and offensive declaration" against the president and had "made himself the agent in the United States of the worst element of disorder in Haitian politics" (New York *Times*, March 13, 1927).

[10] "Recent Aspects of Our Relations with Latin America," a symposium in the *Annals of the American Academy of Political and Social Science*, CXXXVIII (July, 1928), 54-81; Beman, *Selected Articles on Intervention in Latin America*; *Foreign Affairs*, VI (1928), 541-586; Buell, *The United States and Latin America*; Howland, *Survey of American Foreign Relations, 1929*.

[11] See above, p. 182 n.

[12] Distribution of naval tonnage in 1928, in thousands:

	United States	Great Britain	Japan	France	Italy
Battleships	526	580	301	195	134
Aircraft carriers	79	107	63	22	0
Cruisers	75	304	143	105	67
Destroyers	329	212	92	54	59
Submarines	53	28	42	23	8

than ever, while the unsuspected might it had revealed in the United States gave assurance that American susceptibility regarding the Antillean passages would be respected. In the popular mind European intervention in that region was no longer conceivable. Although some feared the consequences to the Caribbean states themselves if American tutelage were withdrawn,[13] to many more the political and financial confusion that had formerly prevailed there was half forgotten, and it had come to appear that the continued use of marines was a cause of unrest rather than a cure. Experience had made the men of 1928 less sanguine than Wilson regarding Caribbean democracy. Its realization in Haiti was evidently a matter of generations rather than of years. If, in Nicaragua, ballots had been substituted for bullets with remarkable success,[14] to have to endure the hullabaloo being raised by and in behalf of Sandino was a high price to pay for the privilege of performing that service. Whatever the earlier influence of economic imperialism, by 1928 its promises had been discredited. Although American investment in and commerce with Latin America increased 350 per cent and 118 per cent, respectively, between 1913 and 1929, bankers and merchants preferred to seek fortune in such lands as Argentina, Brazil, and Chile, avoiding those where the very fact of intervention was evidence of uninviting conditions in normal times.[15] Not only did that policy fail to produce anticipated economic benefits; the hostility it engendered in Latin America[16] hindered economic activity in

[13] The withdrawal of the marines from the Dominican Republic in 1924 had not been followed by any untoward consequence, but their withdrawal from Nicaragua in 1925 had been followed by a civil war leading to their return in 1927.

[14] See Munro, *The United States and the Caribbean Area*, pp. 254-270.

[15] In 1913 the only Latin-American states to attract more than 5 per cent of the total United States investment in that region were Mexico and Cuba, while Haiti, the Dominican Republic, and Nicaragua drew less than 1 per cent. In 1928 the bulk of the greatly increased investment was distributed among Mexico (28 per cent), Cuba (27 per cent), Argentina (11 per cent), Brazil (9 per cent), and Chile (7 per cent), and Haiti, the Dominican Republic, and Nicaragua still drew less than 1 per cent each (Winkler, *Investments of United States Capital in Latin America*, pp. 275, 278, 284).

[16] See C. H. Haring, "South America and Our Policy in the Caribbean," *Annals of the American Academy of Political and Social Science*, CXXXII (July, 1927), 146-152. As early as 1920 it had been observed that Caribbean interventions had been for

those regions where American interests were larger and reward of success greater. Observing that "never before in our history have we had fewer friends in the Western Hemisphere," even the self-confessed author of the Haitian constitution was prepared to admit that "intervention as we practiced it in Santo Domingo and Haiti was not another forward step. It is not that assistance of some sort was not necessary; it was the method which was wrong."[17]

Latin-American clamor over both Haiti and Nicaragua and the rising tide of domestic anti-imperialism threw the Coolidge administration on the defensive. Abandoning the language of the *mission civilisatrice*, it fell back on the legal right to protect the lives and property of nationals abroad.[18] It was considered a masterly defense when Charles Evans Hughes checked a threatened demonstration of Latin anti-interventionism during the Pan American Conference at Havana in 1928, insisting on the right of the United States to judge for itself the necessity for interposition. To show the innocence of American intentions, he declared:

It is our desire to encourage stability in the interest of independence. . . . We would leave Haiti at any time that we had reasonable expectations of stability. . . . We are endeavoring . . . to assist in the establishment of conditions for stability and prosperity, not that we may stay in Haiti, but that we may get out at the earliest opportunity.[19]

---

years "a most serious handicap to the Pan American influence and prestige of the United States" (*Current History*, XIII, 348).

[17] Franklin D. Roosevelt, "Our Foreign Policy: A Democratic View," *Foreign Affairs*, VI (1928), 583.

[18] Ogden Mills, "Our Foreign Policy: A Republican View," *loc. cit.*, p. 569. The flaw in this argument was that although the United States had originally entered both Haiti and Nicaragua to protect lives and property, its efforts had developed into political intervention rather than legal interposition. See Howland, *Survey*, pp. 299, 320-329.

[19] *Reports of the Delegates of the United States of America to the Sixth International Conference of American States*, pp. 14 f. Hughes had made a statement to the same effect when secretary of state in 1923, but from Bellegarde's point of view it seemed evident that such declarations were pure hypocrisy (*L'occupation américaine*, pp. 3 ff.). Walter Lippmann recognized them as a true expression of the American attitude ("Second Thoughts on Havana," *Foreign Affairs*, VI, 1928, 541-554) but argued that, instead of stifling discussion and insisting on an exclusive privilege, the

These words meant no more than Lansing's promise of 1915 that the marines would be withdrawn as soon as stability was assured, but Lansing had been leading an advance, while Hughes was fighting a rear-guard action.

When Herbert Hoover, the secretary of commerce, became president-elect late in 1928, he significantly chose to convert the necessary journey from his California home to Washington into a good-will tour of Latin America. On reaching the White House he set to work to moderate the Caribbean policy of his predecessor as rapidly as one president decently could that of another of his own party.

While Hoover was contemplating the appointment of a commission to review the Haitian problem and recommend a solution, the opposition party in Haiti took steps to force his hand. To be of any benefit to them, action must be taken before 1930, since the president chosen then would be in office at the expiration of the treaty in 1936. Borno's failure to keep his promise to permit the election of a National Assembly indicated that he meant to control the choice through his hand-picked council of state. Since Haiti was beginning to feel the effects of the general depression, it was easy to use the new excise taxes and coffee standardization law to stir up the gullible peasants.[20] However, unrest in the Southern countryside during August, 1929, was quickly allayed by agents of the Service Technique, and the *élite* found that if they would precipitate a crisis they would have to work through the "white-collar" class. On October 31 there was a student strike at the central agricultural school,[21] followed by strikes in the Port-au-Prince customs

United States should make it clear that the task of keeping order in the Caribbean was an affliction rather than the gratification of covetous ambition by demanding that Latin America assume a share of the burden. Such a policy should quiet the storm of criticism, since the Latin Americans were injured in pride rather than in interest, but the administration was not ready to make so radical a departure from precedent. In *Manifest Destiny*, pp. 447-450, Weinberg discusses the nationalistic interpretation of "international police power" and its later modification.

[20] The excise was actually of benefit to the peasants, since it compelled the *élite* to share in the tax burden and made it possible to reduce export duties bearing on producers. The standardization law penalized indolence, but rewarded industry.

[21] The grievance was that 20 per cent of the scholarship fund had been allotted to wages for students working on demonstration farms. This was a boon to peasant

house, the general receiver's office, and the Service Technique. With the mob aroused, General Russell invoked martial law on December 4. Then, as the United States Congress assembled, fifteen hundred excited peasants were organized in a march on Cayes, the order to halt was ignored, the marine detachment fired, and ten Haitians were killed.[22]

The President's commission[23] arrived at Port-au-Prince on February 28, 1930, with instructions to find a way to liquidate American responsibilities in Haiti that would at the same time assure stability.[24] General Russell advised them that the maintenance of order required that something "be done to allay popular sentiment and find a way out of the electoral impasse"[25]—that is, that the "Outs" be let in. Addressing itself to this problem, the commission drew up an extraconstitutional plan that was accepted by Borno, the opposition, and Hoover. It provided that a neutral candidate nominated by the opposition and acceptable to Borno should be elected president by the council of state, with the understanding that after having seen to the election of a National Assembly he would resign in favor of a president chosen by that body.[26] The opposition nominated five men, of whom Borno chose Eugene Roy, a private banker with a reputation for integrity and impartiality. Other candidates having appeared, his election was accomplished only after the United States had indicated that it would recognize no one else and Borno had replaced ten councillors of state.[27] Roy was

---

lads, but intolerable to sons of the *élite* who, while posing as students of agriculture, were too proud to engage in manual effort.

[22] *Report of the High Commissioner, 1929,* pp. 7-13; New York *Times,* Dec. 8, 1929.

[23] Composed of Cameron Forbes, former governor general of the Philippines; Henry P. Fletcher, career diplomat, delegate to the Pan American conferences of 1923 and 1928, and Hoover's adviser on his good-will tour; Elie Vezina, secretary of L'union St. Jean Baptiste d'Amérique; James Kerney, editor and former adviser to President Wilson; and William Allen White, renowned Kansas editor. At the same time it was announced that another commission headed by Dr. R. R. Moton, of Tuskegee, would investigate Haitian education.

[24] *Report of the President's Commission,* pp. 1 f.

[25] Henry P. Fletcher, "Quo Vadis, Haiti?" *Foreign Affairs,* VIII (1930), 543.

[26] *Commission Report,* pp. 5-7.

[27] New York *Times,* April 14-22, 1930; Fletcher, "Quo Vadis, Haiti?" *Foreign Affairs,* VIII (1930), 544-546.

inaugurated quietly on May 15, 1930, and five months later a National Assembly controlled by the opposition groups was elected. On November 19 it chose Sténio Vincent to serve the unexpired portion of the 1930-1936 term.[28]

Having disposed of the Haitian political crisis, the President's commission turned its attention to the question of American policy during the remainder of the life of the treaty. Finding that the physical presence of the marines was not objected to so much as the formal occupation and military government,[29] they recommended that the brigade be left in Haiti for the present, but that the office of high commissioner be abolished and a civilian be appointed as minister with supervision over other American officials. They suggested further that the intervention be limited "definitely to those activities for which provision is made for American assistance by treaty or specific agreement"; that there be "an increasingly rapid Haitianization of the services, with the object of having Haitians in every department of the Government ready to take over full responsibility at the expiration of the existing treaty"; and that the new minister "be charged with the duty of negotiating . . . further modifications of the existing treaty and agreements providing for less intervention in Haitian domestic affairs." President Hoover adopted the policies recommended by the commission, General Russell resigned on November 1, 1930, and Dr. Dana G. Munro, then chief of the Latin-American Division of the State Department, was appointed to succeed him.

With the bitterest critics of the treaty regime in office and their impatience to extend their control over the American-directed services intensified by the fact that the end of the intervention was in sight, the new minister's task was a most delicate one, relieved only by the moderation shown by President Vincent and his successive foreign secretaries on their translation from opposition to positions of responsibility. Pauleus Sannon,

[28] New York *Times*, Nov. 20, 1930. Vincent had been president of the Senate at the time of its dissolution in 1917, and had represented the Union patriotique before the committee of inquiry in 1921.

[29] *Commission Report*, p. 9. The marine brigade payroll was an important item in the commercial life of Port-au-Prince.

restored to the foreign office, quickly produced plans for the Haitianization of all the services except the Garde in the space of one or two years, but he indicated that the government had no desire to wreck them or to turn out the Haitians trained in them, and he was willing to enter into a full discussion of the whole matter. Progress was delayed by several controversies regarding the current work of the services and by a Haitian political crisis in the spring of 1931.[30]

Meanwhile American authorities had concluded that failure to agree on other points need not delay the complete Haitianization of the public works and public health services, in which there were already available mature and experienced men who would profit little from further training in subordinate positions, and of the Service Technique, which had been demoralized by the events of the autumn and winter of 1929.[31] On August 5, 1931, an agreement was signed by Dr. Munro and Abel N. Léger, the new foreign minister, providing for the withdrawal of all American officials from those services on October 1. The United States also consented to abrogate the agreements of 1918 requiring that legislation be submitted to the legation for approval and that payments receive the formal visa of the financial adviser, the government recognizing its obligation to hold expenditures within the limits of appropriations made in accord with him.[32] On the same date the military occupation was technically ended, although the marine brigade remained in Haiti.

The issues left for future settlement concerned the Haitianization of the Garde, the withdrawal of the marines, and the reorganization of the financial administration. The United States was unwilling to commit itself regarding the first two questions until the work of Haitian officers advanced to positions of responsibility in the Garde had been observed, but if all went well there could be no serious delay on that account. The financial question was more difficult, for the Haitians wished to take over the entire administration, leaving only an American

[30] See below, p. 280.
[31] Munro, *The United States and the Caribbean Area*, pp. 184 f.
[32] *Executive Agreements Series, No. 22.*

"fiscal agent" with powers of inspection but no authority, an arrangement the United States was unable to accept because it departed from the provision of the loan contract promising the bondholders that, after the expiration of the treaty and until the complete retirement of the loan, the collection and allocation of the hypothecated revenues would be controlled by an officer nominated by the United States. Haitian lawyers challenged the validity of the 1919 protocol, on which the loan contract was based, but it was indisputable that without that promise Haiti could never have obtained funds, the need for which was not open to question.

Both governments were anxious to bring the intervention to an end and after thirteen months of discussion they were willing to make concessions in order to reach an agreement. On September 3, 1932, Munro and a new foreign minister, Albert Blanchet, signed a treaty designed to be a final settlement of all questions at issue. It was agreed that the Garde should be completely Haitianized by December 31, 1934, and that the withdrawal of the marines should be accomplished within thirty days thereafter. Provision, however, was made for a "military mission" to complete the training of the Garde, having powers of inspection but no authority to act except by recommendation to the commandant or the president. It was also recognized that if unforeseen disturbances "or other difficulties" arose, it might not be possible to carry out the agreement. On the same date the financial adviser-general receiver was to be replaced by a "fiscal representative," whose functions would continue until automatically ended by the retirement of the 1922 loan. He was to collect the customs duties with the assistance of a personnel appointed on his nomination, inspect the internal revenue service, which otherwise passed into exclusively Haitian control, and audit all disbursements. The Haitian government was pledged to balance its budget, but it regained the important right to allocate available funds as it saw fit without foreign interference.

When the treaty was submitted to a National Assembly,

already hostile toward the President for reasons of domestic politics,[33] it was bitterly assailed on the ground that the military provisions were nullified by the strings attached to them and that the fiscal arrangement would extend and perpetuate American financial control.[34]   These criticisms, in part at least the result of distortion for political effect, were altogether unrealistic.   Many points raised were based upon a comparison of the new treaty with the interpretive commentary of 1915 rather than with the actual situation.   Any consideration of the attitude of President Hoover and that of his probable successor would have shown that the United States, far from seeking a pretext to keep marines in Haiti, was as anxious to get them out as the Haitians were to see them go, and that no more financial control was desired than the loan contract required, nothing less being possible until the loan was paid off.   However, it must also be recognized that the Haitians had been taught to be suspicious by seeing what strange afterthoughts could be read into the treaty of 1915.   Such fears could not be banished while a single American official retained any shadow of authority in the Haitian government.

The Haitian administration, admitting that the treaty did not fulfill its aspirations, could only urge that its terms were the best that could be obtained after months of effort and that it was a substantial advance toward the ultimate goal, but on September 15 the National Assembly rejected it unanimously. President Vincent then asked if the United States would put the protocol regarding the Garde and the marines into effect as an executive agreement, leaving the financial question for future settlement, but he was informed that the terms regarding the fiscal representative constituted the maximum concession possible and that the marines would not be withdrawn until they were accepted.[35]   President Hoover's term expired with the situation still dead-locked.

The Haitians may have hoped for better things from "good neighbor" Roosevelt, but he, too, recognized an "unescapable

[33] See below, p. 281.
[34] Davis, *Black Democracy* (1936 ed.), pp. 265-267.
[35] Munro, *The United States in the Caribbean Area*, pp. 190-193.

obligation" to the bondholders. The executive agreement signed by Norman Armour and Albert Blanchet on August 7, 1933, was substantially the same as the protocols attached to the rejected treaty, although the date for the Haitianization of the Garde, withdrawal of the marines, and inauguration of the fiscal representative was advanced to October 1, 1934, and those features of the previous arrangement which had drawn most criticism were modified or eliminated.[36] The Haitians continued to press for greater financial freedom, but in December, 1933, President Roosevelt rejected President Vincent's request for an immediate withdrawal of supervision. At the same time he did indicate that he would welcome any arrangement with the bondholders that would relieve the United States of its unwanted responsibility. Discussions continued, and on April 7, 1934, after a conference between the two presidents at the White House, it was announced that the basis of an agreement had been reached.[37] In token of good will the marines were withdrawn ahead of schedule in July and August, exactly nineteen years after the fateful landing at Bizoton.

The scheme for ending American financial supervision, in its official character at least, was that Haiti should purchase control of the Banque Nationale, reorganizing the board of directors to include representatives of both the government and the bondholders, and that the bank should then relieve the fiscal representative of his duties, receiving all revenues and executing the loan contracts. The National City Bank was glad to sell out for one million dollars, but trouble developed in another quarter. There were to be six directors, two representing the government, two appointed by the Haitian president from among five nominees of the fiscal agent of the Series A loan (the National City Company), and two appointed in the same way from among five nominees of the Foreign Bondholders Protective Council.[38] In May, 1935, the Council was

---

[36] *Executive Agreement Series, No. 46.* The customs-house personnel was to be exclusively Haitian.

[37] Davis, "Haiti and the Good Neighbor Policy," *Literary Digest,* April 28, 1934.

[38] A corporation formed in 1933 under official inspiration and in imitation of the British Council of Foreign Bondholders.

asked for nominations, but it held that the plan was detrimental to the interest of the bondholders, depriving them of the official American financial control promised in the bond, and it therefore refused to co-operate. The board of directors was completed by selection from among five nominees of the four directors already appointed, but the bank could not supersede the fiscal representative in the face of the bondholders' objections without a new executive agreement, which the Council promised to oppose and to which the United States could not consistently subscribe.[39]

Thus the American intervention in Haiti came to an end, except for the presence of the fiscal representative and his staff, acting in behalf of Haiti's creditors rather than of the United States. By 1936 the balance due on the debt had been reduced to nine million dollars and with its approaching extinction even that slight degree of supervision would be removed.

The Haiti the departing Americans left behind them was obviously neither the Haiti of 1915 nor what that Haiti might have become had it continued to evolve along the path it was then following. Any tourist could observe the works of "sanitation and public improvement" accomplished under American direction. The Service d'Hygiène and the Service Technique had made contributions to Haitian life of a nature unknown before their inception. Haitian bonds were selling at par, and there was good prospect that within a few years the republic would enjoy the rare distinction of a nation free of debt.

It was true that these were superficial improvements imposed by alien forces; that no fundamental change had been wrought in the economic, social, and political character of the community; that the basic problems of 1915 were still the problems of 1935. No power on earth could have solved them in a dozen years, although the Americans had optimistically essayed to do so in 1922, perhaps assuming that their time was really unlimited. The Americans, however, had made a beginning and had set an example, if not of democratic procedures,

[39] Foreign Bondholders Protective Council, *Annual Report, 1935*, pp. 123 f. De la Rue, the last financial adviser, had remained as fiscal representative.

at least of benevolent despotism and social service. The future would depend on whether the *élite*, chastened by their experience and challenged by an opportunity unequalled in all Haitian history, proved capable of breaking with the errors of the past and leading the community along the way now open before it, or whether, in their antipathy toward all things American and their susceptibility to old temptations, they permitted themselves and the community to turn back into the wilderness.

CHAPTER XVI

HAITI LIBRE

The commission is under no delusions as to what may happen in Haiti after the convocation of the elected legislative assembly and, to a greater extent, after the complete withdrawal of the United States forces. . . . The educated public opinion and literate minority are so small that any government formed in these circumstances is liable to become an oligarchy.

—THE PRESIDENT'S COMMISSION, March 26, 1930

Not only did the Forbes commission anticipate that a free Haitian government must tend toward oligarchy, but it also held that "until the basis of the political structure were broadened by education—a matter of years—it must necessarily be more or less unstable and in constant danger of political upheavals."[1] The commission was right on the first point; only partially so on the second. Dartiguenave had been a Southern mulatto, the first to attain the presidency since the Liberal debacle of 1879.[2] Borno, Roy, and Vincent were all mulattoes of Port-au-Prince. Nearly forty years of domination by Northern blacks had ended in the still greater debacle of 1915,[3] the Port-au-Princien oligarchy was in power, and the chances were that it could stay indefinitely. Not only had the revolutionary cycle been broken by the marines, but the days when a *caco* had been a match for a government soldier were over. The Garde d'Haiti was technically a constabulary rather than an army, but modern weapons and training made it the most efficient military force that the republic had ever possessed and improved means of communication enabled it to concentrate rapidly at any threatened point. There could be no resurgence of cacoism,

[1] *Commission Report*, p. 2.

[2] Michel Oreste, a *griffe* of Jacmel, might be counted an exception, but he lasted less than nine months and fell because of Northern hostility.

[3] That this group could produce worthy men was proved by Florvil Hyppolite and Antenor Firmin, but the average had not been high, as the state of Haiti in 1915 is sufficient to demonstrate.

for no popular uprising could succeed unless it were universal, a condition which wise statesmanship could prevent. The only danger was of a coup d'état by the Garde itself, against which there was no defense save discipline and the character of its officers.[4]

Their supremacy assured, how have the Port-au-Princien oligarchy made use of their opportunity? Was Sténio Vincent to be a Boisrond-Canal, failing through his reluctance to employ forceful measures, or a Fabre Geffrard, belying his promises of reform in a dictatorship that prepared the way for a Sylvain Salnave and national disaster, or a Jean Pierre Boyer, presiding over peace and stagnation; or was he, perhaps, to set a new standard for Haitian presidents?

A partial answer may be found in the prefaces of Antoine Michel, the most productive of Haitian historians, whose works give evidence of close study and balanced judgment. Seven of his volumes present a detailed exposition of factional politics in the Liberal era between the rise of Geffrard and the tragic failure of Boyer Bazelais (1859-1879).[5] In 1913 the author confidently informed his readers that his generation would give a new orientation to the Haitian mind, that it would not participate in public affairs without showing its firm resolution to avoid the errors of the past.[6] In 1932 he observed that nineteen years had elapsed since he had challenged the generation of Sténio Vincent to present a concrete program and that none was yet forthcoming. Seymour Pradel might speak of "future struggles of emancipation tending to procure for the laboring classes a proper proportion of privileges too long reserved to the minority," but Salomon had expressed that idea in 1843, and its repetition in 1930 showed only that nothing had changed.

[4] In the Dominican Republic, Rafael Trujillo, commandant of the marine-trained constabulary on the withdrawal of the marines in 1924, made himself president in 1930 and has since become as ruthless a dictator as Spanish America has ever produced. President Vincent lost no time in exiling Demosthenes Calixte, marine-chosen commandant of the Garde d'Haiti.

[5] *Avènement du Général Fabre Nicolas Geffrard à la présidence d'Haiti* (1932); *La XIVe législature* (4 vols., 1932-1933); *L'emprunt de trois millions de piastres* (1934); *Salomon jeune et l'affaire Louis Tanis* (1913).

[6] *Salomon jeune,* p. vii.

It was not sufficient to denounce the obvious evil; a remedy must be found.[7] The youth should condemn politicians who deceived the people, violating principles to attain power in order to abuse it, resorting to dictatorship because incapable of executing a program for the development of democracy.[8] His fear of new deceptions, he explained, impelled him to write these histories. Caius Lherison might accuse him of corrupting the youth by telling them of former corruption, but Lherison had an undoubted interest in preventing them from understanding Dorsainvil's question: "Did the United States execute in the country an expedition of chastisement?" Haitians should have the courage to admit the errors of the past and to attack the problems of the day. Had not the time come for the rulers to prove by acts and not by discourse that they were sincere in their desire for a *"Haiti heureuse"*?[9] Of course it was easier for the historian in his study to demand that something be done than it was for practicing politicians in cabinet to devise an immediate cure for the abuses of generations, but there is an indication here that there were Bourbons in the government of the Haitian restoration.

In truth, the political history of post-occupation Haiti did follow a traditional pattern. Before the Forbes commission the opposition had made much of Borno's iniquity in ruling without an elected legislature. Like Geffrard, Salnave, and Nissage-Saget, Vincent had entered office at least morally committed to the principle of a parliamentary regime, and, like them, in practice he was impatient of legislative opposition—perhaps with some reason—and disposed to assert executive omnipotence. He had been in office less than six months before he was in conflict with the Assembly which had elected him.[10] A new legislature composed of his followers was chosen in regular course in Jan-

---

[7] *La XIVᵉ législature,* I, viii-ix.   [8] *Ibid.,* III, xviii.

[9] *Ibid.,* IV, XI-XII, referring to J. C. Dorsainvil, *Le problème de l'enseignement primaire,* pp. 146-148.

[10] Munro, *The United States and the Caribbean Area,* p. 185. This resulted in a cabinet reorganization, in which Pauleus Sannon was removed from the foreign office. See above, p. 272.

uary, 1932, yet again within six months he was at odds with them. As a patriotic gesture the American-made constitution of 1918, as amended in 1928, had been revoked, but the new one bore a remarkable resemblance to it, concentrating power in the executive. Assemblymen, aroused by presidential opposition to proposals to lengthen their terms, increase their pay, and augment legislative authority at executive expense, denounced Vincent for retaining powers that he had condemned in Borno and took revenge by defeating the projected treaty of 1932.[11]

As the expiration of Vincent's term approached, the tension increased, and the plan to purchase the Banque Nationale provided an issue. The measure was blocked by the inflexible opposition of a senatorial majority, which contended that the National City Bank had fleeced Haiti already and had no moral claim to another million dollars.[12] Their stand was consistent with the position the Vincent party had taken while in opposition, but it forced on the president the unhappy alternative of violating the constitution or breaking his covenant with Roosevelt, whereby Haiti had procured the early withdrawal of the marines and hoped to be relieved of the unwelcome assistance of the fiscal representative. In February, 1935, an inspired Chamber demanded that the issue be carried to "the people," who sustained the administration by a vote of 454,357 to 1,172. The recalcitrant senators were then declared to be "in rebellion to the will of the people" and expelled from office.[13] The moment was seen to be ripe for a revision of the constitution "more adequately to provide for the needs of the situation," and in June a new version, containing special provision for the prolongation of Vincent's mandate for an additional term of five years,[14] was overwhelmingly approved by "the people." The character of the *régime plébescitaire* may be judged by the declaration that the legislative and judicial powers exist to assist

[11] Munro, *The United States and the Caribbean Area*, p. 191.

[12] Hubert Herring, "Haitian Troubles Continue," *Current History*, XLII (1935), 78.

[13] Davis, *Black Democracy* (1936 ed.), p. 270.

[14] That is, until 1941. The constitution under which he had been elected had forbidden re-election.

the president, functioning under his authority.[15]   Even so, observers generally agree that Sténio Vincent does not have it in him to become a despot of the same stamp as his neighbors, Fulgencio Batista and Rafael Trujillo—which is to his credit.

That Vincent should resort to dictatorship did not mean that he was indifferent to the social and economic problems of his country any more than it had in the case of Borno, but whereas Borno, until 1929, had benefited from a rising tide of world prosperity, Vincent had entered office in the midst of general depression. Falling revenues enforced the curtailment of expenditures, and, even though the large reserves amassed by Cumberland and Millspaugh covered the annual deficit, no funds were available for ambitious projects for relief or development.[16]

Although Vincent's government was in a sense a dictatorship of the *élite*, he based his power on the Garde and on officially controlled plebescites, and it was his own class, disgruntled by the subordination of the legislature, that he had most to fear politically. For that reason it was expedient that some provision be made for them. They were experiencing hard times, made the more bitter by the disappointment of hopes raised in 1930. The occupation, while separating them from the payroll for fifteen long years, had taught them new wants. Their numbers were increasing out of proportion to the ability of the community to sustain them in the style to which they aspired. The government could not employ them all, the overcrowded professions did not pay, they scorned to participate in productive

[15] Pan American Union, "The New Constitution of Haiti," *Bulletin*, LXIX (1935), 799-804. The president was authorized to dissolve the legislature and govern by decree, the repeal of his acts requiring a two-thirds vote of a subsequent legislature. The presidential election was taken from the Assembly and given directly to "the people," and the prohibition against re-election was dropped. The chamber of accounts was suppressed. Many personal guarantees were omitted.

[16] The Haitian budget, 1930-1936, may be summarized as follows (in millions of dollars):

	1930	1931	1932	1933	1934	1935	1936
Revenue	7.7	6.3	5.6	7.5	7.4	6.0	6.9
Expenditure	8.4	7.4	6.8	6.7	7.4	8.5	7.3

(Foreign Bondholders, *Report*, 1936, p. 572.)

activity, and they were excluded from commerce by foreign competition. It was to meet this problem that the president revived a project in which he had been interested as mayor of Port-au-Prince twenty-eight years before.[17] In October, 1935, aliens were required to pay a higher license fee to engage in retail trade, and were entirely excluded from certain branches, notably the sale of textiles.[18] It was hoped that this measure would keep in Haiti some of the profits of distribution, would provide a new field of dignified activity for the unemployed *élite*, and would ultimately result in the creation of a mercantile class more interested in the maintenance of stability than in gaining office by revolution.

It was seen that the fundamental problem was still that of increasing agricultural production,[19] and that it must be done by stimulating peasant proprietors rather than by the plantation system. Articulate Haitians were hostile toward the development of alien-owned plantations and lacked both the means and the inclination to engage in such enterprises themselves. Moreover, the American ventures launched during the twenties had all failed except the sugar estates of the Haitian Corporation of America in the Plaine du Cul-de-Sac and the sisal plantation of the Haitian-American Development Corporation near Fort Liberté in the Plaine du Nord. Progress would therefore depend on the success of the National Service of Agriculture (the former Service Technique) in arousing peasant ambition and increasing peasant skill, but of necessity its educational efforts could have only gradual effect.

The government's most striking achievement in this direc-

---

[17] See above, pp. 171 f.

[18] Great Britain, Department of Overseas Trade, *Report on Economic Conditions in the Dominican Republic and in the Republic of Hayti, 1936*, pp. 28-30.

[19] The volume of the chief Haitian exports in significant years has been estimated as follows, in millions of pounds:

	1791	1904	1929	1934
Sugar	177.2		10.4	49.0
Coffee	73.9	89.0	63.0	74.9
Cotton	6.8	3.0	10.5	11.7
Dyewoods		155.6	46.0	39.0

The population has been estimated as half a million in 1791; three million in 1934.

tion resulted from a contract made with the Standard Fruit Company in an effort to promote diversification. In return for a monopoly of the banana trade the company engaged to purchase the entire Haitian crop at a regulated price and to aid the agricultural service in expanding and improving peasant cultivation of the fruit.[20] The peasants responded to this new opportunity with such alacrity that Haitian exports of bananas jumped from an average of 1,600 stems in 1927-1931 to 1,363,176 stems in 1937-1938, and in value from three thousand to two million *gourdes*. Even greater returns anticipated in the latter year were prevented by unprecedented drought and destructive windstorms.[21]

Coffee continued to be the Haitian staple, but the trade was conducted along traditional lines, so that Haiti derived no benefit from the natural advantage of being the nearest producer to the world's greatest consumer, the United States. Haitian coffee was still largely uncultivated and was prepared for market by primitive methods long since abandoned by every other exporter of commercial importance. In consequence, even while Caribbean "mild" coffees were gaining in American and world favor, the Haitian product was steadily losing ground until it could find ready acceptance only at Le Havre, and its dependence on that market became a matter of necessity rather than of choice.[22] This condition was due to the ignorance and shiftlessness of the peasants, but also to the indifference of coffee merchants, who cared not how low prices might fall so long as they could take their usual profit and pass the poor return on to the producers.

In March, 1936, the Haitian coffee trade was stirred out of its complacent lethargy by French denunciation of the Franco-

[20] Great Britain, Department of Overseas Trade, *Report on Hayti, 1936*, pp. 28, 42.

[21] *Rapport du représentant fiscal, 1935-1936*, p. 29; *1937-1938*, pp. 42, 121. The company itself undertook the cultivation of a 2,500-acre plantation in the Artibonite and the construction of wharves, etc., at St. Marc and Cayes (*ibid., 1935-1936*, pp. 44-46).

[22] Jones, *Caribbean Backgrounds and Prospects*, pp. 112-118.

Haitian commercial convention, virtually closing the French market to Haitian products.[23] In this emergency merchants were ready enough to co-operate with the government in raising standards to meet the requirements of more exacting markets. In consultation with the New York Coffee and Sugar Exchange, the agricultural service established a testing station at Port-au-Prince and began the construction of concrete drying platforms for the use of peasants, while traders took a new interest in decorticating machinery and modern coffee washing plants were set up. As a result of these measures, the 1937-1938 crop, while reduced in quantity by unusual climatic conditions, was the best in quality ever produced in Haiti, and nearly nine million kilos (35 per cent) found a market in the United States, with a fair prospect of further development.[24] In forcing these advantageous changes, it appeared that the loss of the Havre market, despite its initial inconveniences, might prove a blessing in disguise.

Even while revolutionary changes in the production and marketing of the traditional staple were being promoted, Haitian economy received additional benefit from progress in diversification, the proportion of coffee to total exports declining before the rise of cotton, sugar, sisal, and bananas.[25] Besides the new banana trade, plantation production of sugar and sisal continued to increase, only cotton suffering a check, attributable to the appearance of the boll weevil.[26] Viewing the general

[23] This was ostensibly because of the law barring aliens from certain branches of retail trade, but actually because of an adverse balance of trade intolerable to the new mercantilism prevailing in Europe. To save the tottering franc, the French cut off all trade with Haiti—a commentary on current economic tendencies.

[24] *Rapport du représentant fiscal, 1935-1936*, pp. 29-30, 49 f.; *1937-1938*, pp. 33-38. Although there may be a glut of ordinary coffees, the demand for higher grades of the mild type is increasing. The soils and high altitudes of Haiti are well suited to the production of superior arabica coffee.

[25] Volume of Haitian exports in millions of kilos:

	1917-26 average	1927-31 average	1932-36 average	1937	1938
Coffee	30.6	31.8	30.8	24.8	25.1
Cotton	3.2	4.7	5.9	5.4	4.7
Sugar	4.6	9.7	26.7	31.4	33.5
Sisal	.1	.3	4.6	6.2	7.2
Bananas (millions of stems)			.2	1.3	1.4

[26] *Rapport du représentant fiscal, 1937-1938*, pp. 38-45.

advance in export production, the fiscal representative concluded that Haiti was at last beginning to receive a return on capital invested during the period of intervention.[27]

These developments brought about a closer commercial association of Haiti and the United States than had existed even in the days of occupation. The transfer of Haiti's banking from Paris to New York, the pegging of the *gourde* to the dollar, the negotiation of one of Secretary Hull's reciprocity agreements, and the autarchic maneuvers of various European states had had their influence, but the opening of an American market for Haitian coffee and increasing production of sugar, sisal, and bananas were the decisive factors. The latter were quite as important as the shift in the coffee trade.[28] In 1935-1936 France had taken 47 per cent of Haitian exports and the United States only 14 per cent, a proportion deemed normal for generations,[29] but in 1937-1938 the United States took 43 per cent, Great Britain 14 per cent, Belgium 13 per cent, and France only 12 per cent. The United States had thus displaced France as Haiti's chief market. At the same time the United States continued to supply the greater portion of Haiti's import needs (54 per cent), as compared to 15 per cent from Great Britain, 6 per cent from Germany, and 5 per cent from Japan.[30]

Although the government was making gradual progress in improving the quantity and quality of Haitian agricultural production, its achievement was unhappily offset by a decline in prices determined by factors beyond Haitian control. Depression had dogged the steps of Sténio Vincent from the first, but in 1937-1938 the value of Haitian exports fell far below even

[27] *Ibid., 1935-1936*, pp. 14 f. Production was handicapped by drought in 1937 and 1938, but even so, gains were made except in cotton and coffee.

[28] In 1937-1938 the United States took 35 per cent of Haitian coffee exports (Belgium 24 per cent, France 11 per cent, Denmark 11 per cent); 44 per cent of sugar exports (Great Britain 52 per cent); 94 per cent of sisal exports; and all of the bananas. Cotton exports went to Great Britain (45 per cent) and France (38 per cent).

[29] Cf. 59 per cent to France and 17 per cent to the United States in 1890. The abnormal World War years were the only exception.

[30] *Rapport du représentant fiscal, 1937-1938*, pp. 5-13.

the depressed average for 1932-1936.[31] Only bananas showed
a greater increase in value than in quantity. Cotton prices were
the lowest since 1933, sugar continued to be unprofitable to
even efficient producers, and the low return for sisal threatened
to curtail production. But the most severe blow fell when
Brazil abandoned coffee valorization in November, 1937, and
coffee prices plummeted.[32]

In order to move the coffee crop at all, the Haitian government was compelled to reduce export duties on that commodity,
sacrificing anticipated revenue at a time when its income was
already curtailed by the depressed state of business. Permanent
benefit might be expected from the emergency to the extent that
it forced revision of an unwholesome tax structure,[33] but the
immediate consequence was an unbalanced budget.

At this point the excellent credit previously established
stood Haiti in good stead. Amortization of the 1922 loan had
proceeded so far ahead of contractual requirements that, were
the contractual terms adhered to in the future, it would be
extinguished nine years in advance of the prescribed date (in
1944 instead of 1953). In the circumstances the bondholders
agreed to a temporary reduction of amortization payments to a
nominal figure, being perhaps pleased to prolong the life of so
secure an investment. The arrangement was sanctioned by an
accord between Haiti and the United States dated January 13,

[31] Value of Haitian exports in millions of *gourdes*:

	1917-26 average	1927-31 average	1932-36 average	1937	1938
Coffee	53.7	59.3	29.5	23.4	17.3
Cotton	7.4	8.0	6.1	7.7	5.3
Sugar	2.1	2.2	2.8	3.9	3.7
Sisal		.2	1.9	3.8	3.2
Bananas			.3	1.9	2.0
Total	74.4	77.8	43.4	44.8	34.7

[32] *Rapport du représentant fiscal, 1937-1938*, pp. 5, 39-42. The volume and value
of 1937-1938 exports may be compared to those of 1936-1937 as follows:

	(Per Cent) Volume	Value		(Per Cent) Volume	Value
Bananas	+ 3	+ 7	Coffee	+ 1	− 26
Sugar	+ 7	− 4	Cacao	+ 9	− 31
Sisal	+ 17	− 15	Cotton	− 13	− 31

[33] *Ibid.*, pp. 55-59. Cf. above, pp. 11, 248 f.

1938.[34]   In July, 1938, to relieve unemployment and to stimulate production, the government launched a program of public works to be constructed by the J. G. White Engineering Corporation and to be financed by means of a credit advanced by the semi-official Export-Import Bank of Washington.[35]   Haitian borrowing since Boyer's time having consisted almost exclusively of refunding operations, the 1938 loan brought in more capital for the improvement of the country's economic equipment than had any of its predecessors.

That the relief of unemployment by the promotion of productive enterprises is Haiti's most pressing problem was tragically demonstrated in the autumn of 1937, when the world was shocked to learn of the wholesale slaughter of Haitian migratory laborers in the Dominican Republic.[36]   However subject to criticism the conditions of labor on American sugar plantations in Cuba and Santo Domingo might be, they still represented opportunity unknown at home to the hard-pressed peasants of overcrowded Haiti.[37]   These emigrants, never welcome except to their employers, since they depressed wages and took jobs that might otherwise have gone to natives, became the objects of increasing hostility as sugar prices began to decline in 1928, curtailing operations and giving an added advantage to cheaper labor in the struggle to find employment. Finally, in 1937, the Cuban dictator, Fulgencio Batista, decreed the expulsion of these poor souls, thousands of whom were returned to Haiti.   His Dominican counterpart, Rafael Trujillo, faced with a similar situation, avoided the trouble and

[34] *Ibid.*, pp. 3, 84-87.
[35] *Ibid.*, pp. 4, 76-78, 87-89. The work was to be on projects of a productive nature such as "feeder" roads, shipping facilities, irrigation and drainage systems, and agricultural development. The engineering corporation's monthly accounts for materials and services are to be paid with five-year promissory notes at 5 per cent, which the Export-Import Bank has agreed to purchase at face value.
[36] New York *Herald-Tribune*, Nov. 10, 1937. There were some sixty thousand Haitians in the Dominican Republic. Estimates of the number killed vary from five to twenty thousand.
[37] The number of seasonal emigrants to Cuba increased from ten thousand in 1922-1923 to twenty-three thousand in 1925-1926, about one third remaining abroad each year (*Report of the Financial Adviser-Receiver General, 1925-1926*, pp. 96, 119).

expense of deportation by launching a pogrom calculated to make the survivors glad enough to remove themselves.

Dominican censorship smothered the story for a month, and even after that, Dominican diplomacy denied that anything more serious than a local incident had occurred. However, Trujillo, whose megalomania is sufficiently well established to give credence to the story that he describes Hitler as a disciple, was prepared to argue that, if the reports were true, such action would be justified for the preservation of Dominican Aryanism. That idea is only slightly less fantastic than it sounds. The "white" republic (one part white, one part black, five parts mulatto) possesses two thirds of the area, but only one third of the population of Hispaniola and fears that infiltration from the overcrowded black republic may eventually engulf it in a "rising tide of color." Failing in its efforts to induce white immigration, it must at least repel the black hordes. However, it is also pertinent to note that a Dominican presidential election was impending, and that, although Trujillo would surely count in his henchman, it might provide an occasion for revolt, considering the discontent bred of hard times. What better way could be found to divert Dominican ire from the shortcomings of the administration than to direct it toward the despised aliens whose low standard of living enabled them to take employment away from native sons? This tactic, unfortunately not unknown in the history of the United States, could be employed with impunity since the Garde d'Haiti, a domestic police force of twenty-five hundred, could not cope offensively with the larger and more fully equipped Dominican army. Moreover, while American states would intervene to prevent a war, they could not act in time to frustrate the plan.

The Haitian government did the best it could in requesting the joint intervention of the United States, Cuba, and Mexico. Eventually Trujillo agreed to pay $750,000 damages, $250,000 down and the balance in instalments which might or might not be forthcoming as the universal indignation subsided. Meanwhile the Haitian authorities pondered what to do with tens of thousands of refugees. The obvious solution was to provide such opportunity at home through economic development as to make it unnecessary for them to seek employment abroad, but the solution of that problem was not so obvious. They had gone to work on American plantations, but American plantations were not wanted in Haiti. Progress along any other line would be painfully slow, no matter how much more satisfactory in the end.

Twenty years before the Dominican atrocities would have resulted in a landing of United States marines as guardians of order and civilization, but unhappy experience had altered the American attitude toward Caribbean disorders. Gone was the Wilsonian idea that, once the weeds of tyranny and revolution had been cleared away, native democracy would spring up *ex proprio vigore*. Gone also was the illusion of the Harding era that only a little social and economic cultivation was required to accomplish that result. It was realized that democratic stability could be achieved in the Caribbean only after long evolution outlasting the century, and, consequently, while dictatorship of the Trujillo type might tax the patience of the most indulgent neighbor, that in the style of Sténio Vincent was regarded as the best that could be hoped for. Any threat to peace in America continued to be a matter of concern to the State Department, but the United States no longer claimed an exclusive "international police power."

The new Caribbean policy had been foreshadowed in Franklin D. Roosevelt's statement in 1928 that "single-handed interventions by us in the internal affairs of other nations must end; with the co-operation of others we shall have more order in this hemisphere and less dislike."[38] Five years later the "good neighbor policy" announced in his inaugural address was translated into action in the Pan American Conference at Montevideo. There, on December 6, 1933, Secretary Cordell Hull signed a treaty declaring that "no state has the right to intervene

[38] Franklin D. Roosevelt, "Our Foreign Policy: A Democratic View," *Foreign Affairs*, VI (1928), 585.

in the internal or external affairs of another."[39] That this policy, although differing from the interventionism of Theodore Roosevelt with its assumption of special prerogative by reason of pre-eminent virtues, did not mean absolute nonintervention was indicated by a presidential address delivered on the twenty-eighth of the same month, in which Franklin D. Roosevelt said:

The maintenance of constitutional government in other nations is not a sacred obligation devolving upon the United States alone. The maintenance of law and orderly processes of government in this hemisphere is the concern of each individual nation within its own borders first of all.

It is only if and when the failure of orderly processes affects the other nations of the continent that it becomes their concern; and the point to stress is that in such an event it becomes the joint concern of a whole continent in which we are all neighbors.[40]

"International police power" had been assumed originally for the protection of purely national interests, a function that could not well be shared. The concept was not to be abandoned, but henceforth it was to be made international in practice as well as in name. The association of Cuba and Mexico with the United States in dealing with the Haitian-Dominican trouble of 1937 was in keeping with the new policy.

The change in attitude toward Caribbean problems was designed to bring about an appeasement in inter-American relations, and implied no departure from traditional policy regarding an extension of European political influence in that region. The canal still constituted a vital interest which the United States would defend without deference to anyone. In the absence of any serious European threat, the United States was glad to abandon a quixotic role as champion of democracy and constitutional government and to share with other American states the responsibility for the maintenance of neighborly order. However, if any European power were to seek a too

[39] Ratified June 29, 1934. *Treaty Series No. 881.* This referred to political intervention and did not prejudice the accepted right of states under international law to interpose to protect lives and property endangered by conditions of anarchy.

[40] New York *Times,* Dec. 29, 1933.

intimate relationship with any Caribbean state so misguided as to prefer King Stork to King Log, it would quickly discover that the pristine Monroe Doctrine still expressed the sentiments of the American people and that the American government would be ready to adopt whatever measures necessity seemed to dictate for the maintenance of the security of the Antillean passages.

That the restored government of Haiti fully appreciates this situation and the identity of Haitian and American strategic interests is indicated by the fact that it has accepted American naval use of the harbor of Gonaives (without ceding its sovereignty there) and by its proposal of a formal mutual assistance pact between the United States and the three Antillean republics.[41] In these developments it may appear that friends and allies are better won by favor than by force.

[41] *La République d'Haiti dans la politique inter-américaine*, pp. 25-29.

BIBLIOGRAPHY OF WORKS CITED

MANUSCRIPTS

STATE DEPARTMENT ARCHIVES

Instructions, Haiti (4 vols.); France, XXI; Great Britain, XXVIII.
Despatches, Haiti (47 vols.); Dominican Republic, II; France, VIII, XCVI, CIV.
Notes from Foreign Legations, Haiti (6 vols.); Dominican Republic, I.
Notes to the Haitian Legation (2 vols.).
Instructions, Special Missions, I-III.
Despatches, Special Agents, II, IX, XIII, XV, XVIII, XIX.
Consular letters, Cape Haytien, I-XVII; Port-au-Prince, I-IV; Santo Domingo, V.
Domestic Letters.
Miscellaneous Letters.

NAVY DEPARTMENT ARCHIVES

Cipher Messages, Sent and Received, 1888-1891.
Reports of Squadron Commanders, North Atlantic, 1888-1891.

LIBRARY OF CONGRESS

Department of the Interior, Letters Sent and Received Relating to the Slave Trade.
Haytian Bureau of Emigration, Official Correspondence.
Benjamin F. Tracy Papers.

PUBLIC RECORD OFFICE, LONDON

Foreign Office, 23/1-77 (Dominican Republic); 35/1-73, 107-127 (Haiti).

DUKE UNIVERSITY LIBRARY

David D. Porter. Journal of a Mission to Santo Domingo, 1846.

OFFICIAL AND SEMI-OFFICIAL PUBLICATIONS

Great Britain
    Department of Overseas Trade. *Reports on Economic Conditions in the Dominican Republic and in the Republic of Hayti, 1923-1936.* London, 1924-1936.
Republic of Haiti
    Redpath, James. *A Guide to Hayti.* Boston, 1861.
    Léger, Jacques Nicolas. *Recueil des traités et conventions de la République d'Haiti.* Port-au-Prince, 1891.
    Exposé général de la situation de la République d'Haiti. Port-au-Prince, 1890-

L'affaire de la consolidation. Port-au-Prince, 1906.
Rapport de M. Louis Borno. Port-au-Prince, 1918.
Documents diplomatiques, affaires diverses. Port-au-Prince, 1921.
Geology of the Republic of Haiti. Port-au-Prince, 1924.
Report on Irrigation Possibilities in the Republic of Haiti. Port-au-Prince, 1927.
Report of the Financial Adviser-General Receiver, 1923-1933. Washington, 1925; New York, 1926; Port-au-Prince, 1927-1933.
Rapport annuel du représentant fiscal, 1933-1938. Port-au-Prince, 1934-1938.
United States of America
American State Papers, Foreign Relations (1789-1828). 6 vols. Washington, 1832-1859.
　　Commerce and Navigation (1789-1823). 2 vols. Washington, 1832-1834.
Papers Relating to the Foreign Relations of the United States (1861-　　). Washington, 1862-
Report on the Commercial Relations of the United States (1856-　　). Washington, 1856-
State Department, *Annual Report of the American High Commissioner at Port-au-Prince, 1923-1929.* Washington, 1924-1930.
　　Report of the Delegates of the United States of America to the Sixth International Conference of American States. Washington, 1928.
　　Report of the President's Commission for the Study and Review of Conditions in the Republic of Haiti, 1930. (Latin-American Series, No. 2.) Washington, 1930.
　　Report of the United States Commission on Education in Haiti, 1930. (Latin-American Series, No. 5.) Washington, 1931.
　　Haitianization Agreement, 1931. (Executive Agreement Series, No. 22.) Washington, 1931.
　　Haitianization Agreement, 1933. (Executive Agreement Series, No. 46.) Washington, 1933.
　　Rights and Duties of States: Convention between the United States of America and Other American Republics, 1933. (Treaty Series, No. 881.) Washington, 1935.
Department of Commerce, *Statistical Abstract of the United States, 1907-1933.* Washington, 1907-1933.
　　Haiti: An Economic Survey. (Trade Information Bulletin No. 264.) Washington, 1924.
　　American Direct Investments in Foreign Countries. (Trade Information Bulletin No. 731.) Washington, 1930.
Navy Department, *Annual Report of the Secretary of the Navy, 1865, 1919, 1920.*
　　American Naval Policy as Outlined in Messages of the Presidents of the United States, 1790-1924. Washington, 1924.
　　Hydrographic Office Charts, No. 1487 and No. 3500.
War Department, *Rules of Land Warfare, 1914.* Washington, 1917.
　　Military Government. Fort Leavenworth, 1920.

Bureau of Insular Affairs, *Report of the Haitian Customs Receivership, 1916-1922.* Washington, 1919-1922.

The Congress of the United States
Annals of Congress, 1789-1824. 42 vols. Washington, 1834-1856.
Register of Debates in Congress, 1824-1837. 142 vols. Washington, 1825-1837.
Congressional Globe, 1833-1873. 46 vols. Washington, 1834-1873.
Congressional Record, 1874-   . Washington, 1874-
House Document No. 36, 27th Congress, 3d Session.
Senate Executive Document No. 113, 32d Congress, 1st Session.
Senate Executive Document No. 25, 34th Congress, 3d Session.
Senate Executive Document No. 37, 36th Congress, 2d Session.
Senate Executive Document No. 17, 41st Congress, 3d Session.
Senate Executive Document No. 64, 49th Congress, 2d Session.
Senate Executive Document No. 69, 50th Congress, 2d Session.
Hearings before a Select Committee on Haiti and Santo Domingo. 2 vols. Washington, 1921.
Senate Report No. 234, 41st Congress, 2d Session.
Senate Report No. 425, 43d Congress, 1st Session.
Senate Report No. 794, 67th Congress, 2d Session.

Clark, Joshua Reuben. *Memorandum on the Monroe Doctrine.* Washington, 1930.

Hasse, A. R. *Index to the United States Documents Relating to Foreign Affairs, 1828-1861.* 3 vols. Washington, 1914-1921.

Manning, W. R. *Diplomatic Correspondence of the United States: Inter-American Affairs, 1831-1860.* Vol. VI. Washington, 1935.

Moore, John Bassett. *A Digest of International Law.* 8 vols. Washington, 1906.

Richardson, James D. *A Compilation of the Messages and Papers of the Presidents, 1789-1919.* 20 vols. Washington, 1897-1919.

Commonwealth of Virginia
Henning, William Waller. *The Statutes at Large, 1619-1792.* 13 vols. New York and Philadelphia, 1823.

Shepherd, Samuel. *The Statutes at Large of Virginia, 1792-1806.* 3 vols. Richmond, 1835.

COLLECTED WRITINGS AND MEMOIRS

Adams, Charles F. *The Works of John Adams.* 10 vols. Boston, 1850-1856.
Memoirs of John Quincy Adams. 12 vols. Philadelphia, 1875-1876.

Baker, George E. *The Works of William H. Seward.* 5 vols. Boston, 1884.

Beale, Howard K. *The Diary of Edward Bates, 1859-1866.* Washington, 1933.

Donnan, Elizabeth. "Papers of James A. Bayard, 1796-1815," *American Historical Association Reports,* 1913, II.

Douglass, Frederick. *The Life and Times of Frederick Douglass.* London, 1882.

Firmin, Antenor. *Diplomates et diplomatie.* Cap Haitien, 1899.

Ford, Paul L. *The Writings of Thomas Jefferson.* 10 vols. New York, 1895-1899.

Hamilton, John C. *The Works of Alexander Hamilton.* 7 vols. New York, 1850-1851.

Hamilton, S. M. *The Writings of James Monroe.* 7 vols. New York, 1899-1903.

King, Charles R. *The Life and Correspondence of Rufus King.* 6 vols. New York, 1894-1900.

Langston, John Mercer. *From the Virginia Plantation to the National Capitol.* Hartford, 1894.

Lipscomb, A. A., and A. E. Bergh. *The Writings of Thomas Jefferson.* 20 vols. Washington, 1903-1904.

Menos, Solon. *L'affaire Lüders.* Port-au-Prince, 1898.

Moore, John Bassett. *The Works of James Buchanan.* 12 vols. Philadelphia, 1908-1911.

Morse, J. T. *The Diary of Gideon Welles.* 3 vols. Boston, 1911.

Porter, David D. "Secret Missions to San Domingo," *North American Review,* CXXVIII (1879), 616-630.

Sherman, John. *Recollections of Forty Years.* 2 vols. Chicago, 1895.

Sparks, Jared. *The Writings of George Washington.* 12 vols. Boston, 1834-1837.

Sumner, Charles. *The Works of Charles Sumner.* 15 vols. Boston, 1870-1883.

Turner, F. J. "Correspondence of the French Ministers to the United States, 1791-1797," *American Historical Association Reports,* 1903, II.

CONTEMPORARY PUBLICATIONS

AMERICAN AND ENGLISH

Balch, Emily Greene. *Occupied Haiti.* New York, 1927.

Beman, L. T. *Selected Articles on Intervention in Latin America.* New York, 1928.

Bird, Mark Baker. *The Black Man, or Haytien Independence.* New York, 1869.

Buell, Raymond Leslie. *The United States and Latin America.* New York: Foreign Policy Association, 1928.

The American Occupation of Haiti. New York: Foreign Policy Association, 1929.

Bonsal Stephen. *The American Mediterranean.* New York, 1912.

Borchard, Edwin M. "Commercial and Financial Interests of the United States in the Caribbean," *Proceedings of the American Academy of Political Science,* VII (1917), 383-391.

Brown, Jonathan. *The History and Present Condition of St. Domingo.* Philadelphia, 1837.

Chapman, Charles E. "The Development of the Intervention in Haiti," *Hispanic American Historical Review,* VII (1927), 299-319.

Colquhoun, Archibald R. "The Future of the Negro," *North American Review,* CLXXVI (1903), 657-674.

Greater America. New York, 1904.

Craige, John H. *Black Bagdad.* New York, 1933.

Cannibal Cousins. New York, 1934.

Crichfield, George W. *American Supremacy.* 2 vols. New York, 1908.

Davis, H. P. "Notes on Haiti and Santo Domingo," *Pan American Magazine,* March, 1919.

"Haiti and the Good Neighbor Policy," *Literary Digest,* April 28, 1934.

Dewey, Loring D. *Correspondence Relative to the Emigration to Hayti of the Free People of Colour.* New York, 1824.

Douglas, Paul H. "The American Occupation of Haiti," *Political Science Quarterly,* XLII (1927), 228-258, 368-396.

Douglass, Frederick. "Haiti and the United States," *North American Review,* CLIII (1891), 337-345, 450-459.

Lecture on Haiti. Chicago, 1893.

Eliot, George F. *The Ramparts We Watch.* New York, 1938.

Fletcher, Henry P. "Quo Vadis, Haiti?" *Foreign Affairs,* VIII (1930), 533-548.

Forbes & Tuckerman. *Papers Relating to the Colonization Experiment at A'Vache.* New York, 1865.

Foreign Bondholders Protective Council. *Annual Report, 1935-1936.* New York, 1936-1937.

Foreign Policy Association. *The Seizure of Haiti by the United States.* New York, 1922.

Froude, James Anthony. *The English in the West Indies.* New York, 1888.

Gruening, E. H. "The Conquest of Haiti and Santo Domingo," *Current History,* XV (1922), 885-896.

Haring, C. H. "South America and Our Policy in the Caribbean," *Annals of the American Academy of Political and Social Science,* CXXXII (July, 1927), 146-152.

Harris, J. Dennis. *A Summer on the Borders of the Caribbean Sea.* New York, 1860.

Hazard, Samuel. *San Domingo, Past and Present.* New York, 1873.

Herring, Hubert. "Haitian Troubles Continue," *Current History,* XLII (1935), 78-79.

Herskovitz, Melville J. *Life in a Haitian Valley.* New York, 1937.

Hill, Robert T. *Cuba and Porto Rico.* London, 1898.

Holly, James Theodore. *A Vindication of the Capacity of the Negro Race.* New Haven, 1857.

Howland, Charles P. *Survey of American Foreign Relations, 1929.* New Haven: Council on Foreign Relations, 1929.

Hugo, Victor. *The Slave King.* Philadelphia, 1833.

Hunt, Benjamin S. *Remarks on Hayti as a Place of Settlement for Afric-Americans.* Philadelphia, 1860.

Inman, Samuel Guy. *Through Santo Domingo and Haiti.* New York, 1920.

Johnson, James Weldon. "Self-determining Haiti," *The Nation,* Aug. 25-Sept. 25, 1920.

Johnston, Sir Harry. *The Negro in the New World.* London, 1910.

Kelsey, Carl. "The American Intervention in Haiti and the Dominican Republic," *Annals of the American Academy of Political and Social Science,* C (March, 1922).

Kuser, J. Dryden. *Haiti: Its Dawn of Progress after Years in a Night of Revolution.* Boston, 1921.

Lippmann, Walter. "Second Thoughts on Havana," *Foreign Affairs*, VI (1928), 541-554.

Loederer, Richard A. *Voodoo Fire in Haiti.* New York, 1935.

MacCorkle, W. A. *The Monroe Doctrine in Its Relation to the Republic of Haiti.* New York, 1915.

Mackenzie, Charles. *Notes on Hayti.* 2 vols. London, 1830.

Mahan, Alfred Thayer. *The Interest of America in Sea Power.* Boston, 1898.

Massachusetts Sabbath School Union. *A Brief History of the Island of Hayti.* Boston, 1831.

Mills, Ogden. "Our Foreign Policy: A Republican View," *Foreign Affairs*, VI (1928), 555-572.

Milspaugh, Arthur C. "Our Haitian Problem," *Foreign Affairs*, VII (1929), 556-570.

"Haiti under American Control," *Current History*, XXXI (1930), 919-926.

Niles, Blair. *Black Haiti.* New York, 1926.

Ober, Frederick. *In the Wake of Columbus.* Boston, 1893.

Our West Indian Neighbors. New York, 1904.

Prichard, Hesketh. *Where Black Rules White.* Westminster, 1900.

Roosevelt, Franklin D. "Our Foreign Policy: A Democratic View," *Foreign Affairs*, VI (1928), 573-586.

St. John, Sir Spencer. *Hayti, or the Black Republic.* London, 1884.

Schoenrich, Otto. "The Present American Intervention in Santo Domingo and Haiti," *Journal of International Relations*, XI (1920), 45-62.

Seabrook, William. *The Magic Island.* New York, 1929.

Streit, Clarence. "Haiti: Intervention in Operation," *Foreign Affairs*, VI (1928), 615-632.

Thompson, Waddy. *Remarks on the Proposition to Recognize the Republic of Hayti.* Washington, 1839.

Thorpe, George C. "American Achievements in Santo Domingo, Haiti, and the Virgin Islands," *Journal of International Relations*, XI (1920), 63-86.

Vandercook, John W. *Black Majesty.* New York, 1928.

Villard, Oswald G. "The Rights of Small Nations in America," *Annals of the American Academy of Political and Social Science*, LXXII (July, 1917), 165-171.

"Our Relations with Haiti and San Domingo," *Proceedings of the Academy of Political Science*, VIII (1917), 412-417.

Wells, Philip Patterson. "Hayti and San Domingo, 1802-1906," *The History of Nations* (ed. Henry Cabot Lodge), XXII, 491-504. Philadelphia, 1907.

Wilson, Huntington. "The Relation of Government to Foreign Investment," *Annals of the American Academy of Political and Social Science*, LXVIII (Nov., 1916), 298-311.

HAITIAN

Ardouin, Beaubrun. *La géographie de l'île d'Haiti.* Port-au-Prince, 1856.

Bellegarde, Dantès. *Pour une Haiti heureuse.* 2 vols. Port-au-Prince, 1929.

L'occupation américaine d'Haiti. Port-au-Prince, 1929.

Un haitien parle. Port-au-Prince, 1934.

Bonneau, Alexandre. *Haiti: ses progrès, son avenir.* Paris, 1862.

Charmant, Alcius. *Haiti, vivra-t-elle? Étude sur le préjugé des races: race noire, race jaune, race blanche, et sur la doctrine de Monroe.* Havre, 1905.

Delorme, Demesvar. *La misère au sein des richesses.* Paris, 1873.

Edouard, Emmanuel. *Essai sur la politique intérieure d'Haiti.* Paris, 1890.

Firmin, Antenor. *M. Roosevelt, président des États-Unis, et la République d'Haiti.* New York, 1905.

Justin, Joseph. *Étude sur les institutions haitiennes.* 2 vols. Paris, 1894-1895.
Les réformes nécessaires. Port-au-Prince, 1915.

Laventure, Leonidas. *Haiti: le danger de la patrie.* Port-au-Prince, 1893.

Le Rouge, Gabriel. *Ou vivre libres et respectés ou mourir lamentablement décimées par la guerre civile.* Port-au-Prince, 1916.

Magloire, Auguste. *L'erreur révolutionnaire et notre état social.* Port-au-Prince, 1909.

Marcelin, Frederic. *Choses haitiennes.* Paris, 1896.
Une évolution nécessaire. Paris, 1898.
L'haleine du centenaire. Paris, 1901.
Le passé. Paris, 1902.

Marcelin, L. J. *Haiti: ses guerres civiles.* Paris, 1892.

Moreau de Saint Méry, L. E. *Description de la partie française de St. Domingue.* 2 vols. Philadelphia, 1798.

Paret, Timothée. *Dans la mêlée.* Paris, 1932.

Paul, Edmond. *Questions politico-économiques.* 3 vols. Paris, 1861-1863.
Les causes de nos malheurs. Kingston, 1889.

Pierre-Louis, Damase. *Les mensonges de notre démocratie.* Paris, 1933.

Price, Hannibal. *The Haytian Question.* New York, 1891.

Price-Mars, Jean. *La vocation de l'élite.* Port-au-Prince, 1919.

Rosemond, Jules. *La crise morale et civique.* Port-au-Prince, 1915.

Saint-Justé, Tribonien. *La mort de l'illustre M. Antenor Firmin.* St. Thomas, 1912.

PERIODICALS NOT OTHERWISE CITED

African Repository, X (1834).
Current History.
Democratic Review (1853).
Literary Digest.
New York *Herald-Tribune.*
New York *Sun.*
New York *Times.*
Niles' Register, XXV (1824).
Philadelphia *Press.*
Public Opinion.

SECONDARY WORKS

Adams, Henry. *History of the United States.* 9 vols. New York, 1891-1898.

Alexander, Archibald. *History of Colonization on the Western Coast of Africa.* Philadelphia, 1846.

Baker, Ray Stannard, *Woodrow Wilson: Life and Letters.* Vol. IV. New York, 1931.

Bemis, Samuel Flagg. "Payment of the French Loans to the United States, 1777-1795," *Current History*, XXIII (1926), 824-831.
A Diplomatic History of the United States. New York, 1936.
Beveridge, Albert J. *Abraham Lincoln, 1809-1858*. 2 vols. Boston, 1928.
Birkhimer, William E. *Military Government and Martial Law*. Kansas City, 1914.
Caldwell, R. B. *The López Expeditions to Cuba*. Princeton, 1915.
Christie, Emerson Brewer. "Haiti's Contribution to Literature," *Pan American Magazine*, XLIV (1931), 216-226.
Cromwell, John W. *The Negro in American History*. Washington, 1914.
Davis, H. P. *Black Democracy*. New York, 1928.
Dennis, A. L. P. *Adventures in American Diplomacy*. New York, 1928.
Dorsainvil, J. C. *Manuel d'histoire d'Haiti*. Port-au-Prince, 1925.
Du Bois, W. E. Burghardt. *Black Reconstruction*. New York, 1935.
Dunn, Robert V.'. *American Foreign Investments*. New York, 1926.
Garrison, Wendell Phillips, and F. J. Garrison. *William Lloyd Garrison, 1805-1879*. 4 vols. Boston, 1894.
Gipson, Lawrence Henry. *The British Empire before the American Revolution*. 3 vols. Caldwell, Idaho, 1936.
Hill, Howard C. *Roosevelt and the Caribbean*. Chicago, 1927.
Hurd, John Codman. *The Law of Freedom and Bondage in the United States*. Vol. II. Boston, 1862.
James, J. A. "Louisiana as a Factor in American Diplomacy, 1795-1800," *Mississippi Valley Historical Review*, I (1914), 44-56.
"French Opinion as a Factor in Preventing War between France and the United States, 1795-1800," *American Historical Review*, XXX (1924), 44-55.
Jenkins, William Sumner. *Pro-slavery Thought in the Old South*. Chapel Hill, 1935.
Jessup, Philip C. *Elihu Root*. 2 vols. New York, 1938.
Jones, Chester Lloyd. *Caribbean Backgrounds and Prospects*. New York, 1931.
The Caribbean since 1900. New York, 1936.
Knight, Melvin M. *The Americans in Santo Domingo*. New York, 1928.
Kreiger, Herbert M. "The Aborigines of the Ancient Island of Hispaniola," *Annual Report of the Smithsonian Institution* (1929), pp. 473-506.
Laughlin, J. Laurence, and H. Parker Willis. *Reciprocity*. New York, 1903.
Lechaud, Thomas H. "Lettres du Général Leclerc," *Revue d'histoire et de géographie d'Haiti*, No. 27 (Oct., 1937), 28-32.
Léger, Abel Nicolas. *Histoire diplomatique d'Haiti*. Port-au-Prince, 1930.
Léger, Jacques Nicholas. *La politique extérieure d'Haiti*. Paris, 1886.
Haiti: Her History and Her Detractors. New York, 1907.
Lespinasse, Pierre-Eugène de. *Gens d'autre-fois*. Paris, 1926.
Levasseur, Emile. *Histoire du commerce de la France*. Paris, 1912.
Logan, Rayford W. "Education in Haiti," *Journal of Negro History*, XV (1930), 401-460.
Lokke, Carl Ludwig. "Jefferson and the Leclerc Expedition," *American Historical Review*, XXXIII (1928), 322-328.

Madiou, Thomas, *Histoire d'Haiti.* New Edition. 3 vols. Port-au-Prince, 1922.

Mehlinger, Louis R. "The Attitude of the Free Negro toward African Colonization," *Journal of Negro History,* I (1916), 276-301.

Metcalf, Clyde H. *A History of the United States Marine Corps.* New York, 1939.

Michel, Antoine. *Salomon jeune et l'affaire Louis Tanis.* Port-au-Prince, 1913.

Avènement du Général Fabre Nicolas Geffrard à la présidence d'Haiti. Port-au-Prince, 1932.

La XIVe législature. 4 vols. Port-au-Prince, 1932-1933.

L'emprunt de trois millions de piastres. Port-au-Prince, 1934.

Millspaugh, Arthur C. *Haiti under American Control, 1915-1930.* Boston: World Peace Foundation, 1931.

Munro, Dana G. *The United States and the Caribbean Area.* Boston: World Peace Foundation, 1934.

Nearing, Scott, and Joseph Freeman. *Dollar Diplomacy.* New York, 1925.

Nevins, Allan. *Hamilton Fish: The Inner History of the Grant Administration.* New York, 1937.

Nichols, Roy F. "Navassa: A Forgotten Acquisition," *American Historical Review,* XXXVIII (1933), 505-510.

Perkins, Dexter. *The Monroe Doctrine, 1826-1867.* Baltimore, 1933.

Pitman, Frank W. *The Development of the British West Indies, 1700-1763.* New Haven, 1917.

Pratt, Julius W. *Expansionists of 1898.* Baltimore, 1936.

Price-Mars, Jean. *Une étape de l'évolution haitienne.* Port-au-Prince, 1930.

"L'unité politique de l'île d'Haiti," *Revue d'histoire et de géographie d'Haiti,* No. 27 (Oct., 1937), 1-27.

"La diplomatie haitienne et l'independance dominicaine, 1858-1867," *Revue d'histoire et de géographie d'Haiti,* No. 32 (Jan., 1939).

Ragatz, Lowell Joseph. *The Fall of the Planter Class in the British Caribbean, 1763-1833.* New York, 1928.

The West Indian Approach to the Study of American Colonial History. London, 1935.

Rippy, J. Fred. *Latin America in World Politics.* New York, 1928.

"The Initiation of the Customs Receivership in the Dominican Republic," *Hispanic American Historical Review,* XVII (1937), 419-457.

Stanwood, Edward. *History of the Presidency.* Revised Edition. 2 vols. Boston, 1928.

Stoddard, T. Lothrop. *The French Revolution in San Domingo.* Boston, 1914.

Tansill, Charles C. *The Purchase of the Danish West Indies.* Baltimore, 1932.

The United States and Santo Domingo, 1798-1873. Baltimore, 1938.

Thomas, David Y. *One Hundred Years of the Monroe Doctrine.* New York, 1923.

Treudley, Mary. *The United States and Santo Domingo, 1789-1866.* Worcester, 1916.

Tuckerman, Charles K. "President Lincoln and Colonization," *Magazine of American History*, XVI (1887), 329-332.

Tyler, Alice Felt. *The Foreign Policy of James G. Blaine*. Minneapolis, 1927.

Vagts, Alfred. *Deutschland und die Vereinigten Staaten in der Weltpolitik, 1890-1906*. New York, 1935.

Washington, Booker T. *Frederick Douglass*. Philadelphia, 1907.

Weinberg, Albert K. *Manifest Destiny*. Baltimore, 1935.

Welles, Sumner. *Naboth's Vineyard: The Dominican Republic, 1844-1924*. 2 vols. New York, 1928.

Wertenbaker, T. J. *The Planters of Colonial Virginia*. Princeton, 1922.

Williams, Benjamin H. *Economic Foreign Policy of the United States*. New York, 1929.

Winkler, Max. *Investments of United States Capital in Latin America*. Boston, 1928.

Wriston, H. M. *Executive Agents in American Foreign Relations*. Baltimore, 1929.

INDEX